TABLE OF CONTENTS

UNDERSTANDING THE MUSIC BUSINESS

Dick Weissman

Prentice Hall

Boston   Columbus   Indianapolis
New York   San Francisco   Upper Saddle River
Amsterdam   Cape Town   Dubai   London
Madrid   Milan   Munich   Paris   Montréal   Toronto
Delhi   Mexico City   São Paulo   Sydney
Hong Kong   Seoul   Singapore   Taipei   Tokyo

Editor in Chief: Sarah Touborg
Executive Editor: Richard Carlin
Editorial Assistant: Tricia Murphy
Director of Marketing: Brandy Dawson
Senior Administrative Assistant:
Suzanne Jalaiel
Senior Marketing Manager: Kate Mitchell
Assistant Managing Editor: Melissa Feimer
Project Manager: Jean Lapidus
Composition/Full-Service Management:
Macmillan Publishing Solutions
Project Manager: Lindsay Burt
Senior Operations Supervisor:
Brian Mackey

Manager of Central Design: Jayne Conte
Cover Design: Axell Designs
**Manager, Cover Visual Research &
Permissions:** Karen Sanatar
Manager, Rights & Permissions: Zina Arabia
Image Permission Coordinator: Nancy Seise
Cover Photo: Grunn Guitars Shop in
Nashville, Tennessee
Source: Chad Ehlers/Stock Connection
Printer/Binder: Edwards Brothers
Cover Printer: Demand Production Center

Credits and acknowledgments borrowed from other sources and reproduced, with permission, in this textbook appear on appropriate page within text.

Many of the designations by manufacturers and seller to distinguish their products are claimed as trademarks. Where those designations appear in this book, and the publisher was aware of a trademark claim, the designations have been printed in initial caps or all caps.

Library of Congress Cataloging-in-Publication Data
Weissman, Dick.
   Understanding the music business / Dick Weissman.
      p. cm.
   Includes bibliographical references and index.
   ISBN 978-0-13-242313-7 (alk. paper)
1.   Music trade—Vocational guidance.   I. Title.
   ML3795.W434 2010
   780.23—dc22
                                    2009031260

Prentice Hall
is an imprint of

ISBN 10: 0-13-242313-8
ISBN 13: 978-0-132-42313-7

ACKNOWLEDGMENTS

I have spent quite a few years working in and studying about the music business. Over the years, I have benefited from the wisdom of a number of friends and associates. Frank Jermance has been a valued colleague and friend during my twelve years of teaching at the University of Colorado at Denver. I've shared many adventures with Marv Mattis, a former vice president of BMI. The late Tommy Noonan was probably the most informative and amusing lecturer that I have ever encountered. I can always count on some good exchanges at the meetings of the Music & Entertainment Industry Educators Association (MEIEA).

A number of colleagues who worked on various sections of this book are acknowledged elsewhere, but Ron Sobel has always been a valuable source of information and encouragement as I've watched him go through the various incarnations of his multi-faceted career. Terry Currier epitomizes everything good about the Portland music scene. He's always got an encouraging word, a helpful contact, and useful information at his fingertips. Professor Storm Gloor always has some news about digital formats or other new wrinkles in the industry. Professor (and performer) Deborah Holland and I share many of the same attitudes about the industry and teaching. Professor Tanya Butler brought to light many aspects of the Memphis music scene, and Tom May and I have shared information and gigs ever since we both moved to the Portland area. The late Don Johnson taught me most of what I know about the music merchandising aspect of the industry. Richard Carlin has been a great editor, putting up with my various lapses, notably my incurable need to deliver typos. He has nurtured this book through its first meanderings into a form that we both hope will be useful for those who wish to know more about the music business.

Finally, it is too easy to forget that this should be the MUSIC business rather than the BUSINESS of music. I have been fortunate enough to see and hear many great musicians, some of whom became my friends. So I'd like to acknowledge Jean-Pierre Rampal, John Coltrane, Barry Galbraith, the Reverend Gary Davis, and countless folk and jazz musicians that made me want to be a musician in the first place. Fellow musicians Dan Fox and Harry Tuft are good friends, and I'm always soliciting their opinions about music and many other things.

Over the years I've watched Susan Planalp pursuing a career as a visual artist, and have come to understand that musicians who complain about their economic situation ought to be grateful that they aren't painters, dancers, or actors.

In every town there are musicians and people working in the industry who have a real sense of community, and who dedicate a substantial part of their energies to helping other musicians. This book is my own modest attempt to do the same.

Dick Weissman

INTRODUCTION

Virtually every guide to the practices of the music industry covers the same material in a similar way. The general notion that governs these books is that the road to success is clear. First, the artist must develop a business team consisting of a manager and an entertainment lawyer. The artist must seek a record deal, preferably with a well-financed major label. This is supposed to be done by recording a CD "demo," which is then "shopped" to record companies by the lawyer or the manager. After some expression of interest on the part of record company A&R (Artist and Repertoire) executives, the artist's lawyer and the record company enter into a protracted negotiation; eventually, a deal is made. Guided by the personal manager, the artist enters into a booking agreement with a booking agent or agency, which obtains better and better gigs for the artist. The album comes out, the artist tours, money begins to roll in, and, through the lawyer or manager, a business manager enters the picture, who puts the artist's affairs on a business basis, dealing with matters such as taxes and investments.

From 1960 until 2000 or so, this wasn't an unreasonable scenario. But as the Internet became a huge factor in American life, and many young people became accustomed to obtaining their music through illegal file sharing, the system began to break down. CD sales started to tank, record companies were bought out or went out of business, record stores and even large record chains went bankrupt, and young people seemed to gravitate to other forms of entertainment, notably video games.

Fast forward to today and the industry as it currently exists. What were once six robust multinational record labels are down to four. The prophets of doom whine that not only is the CD dead, but the album is similarly on its death bed, because so many of the *legal* purchasers of digital music prefer to pick one or two songs out of an entire album. Not to mention those who still illegally download music despite the best efforts of the recording industry.

But just as the road to industry success or longevity never did necessarily lead through the artist's business team, today's industry is an increasingly complex beast. Managers are taking over some of the promotional functions of the industry that formerly were the domain of the labels. Some artists are, in essence, handling their own careers by merchandising themselves through the Internet, whether on their MySpace pages, their fan clubs, or via free legal downloads. Music publishing income goes up every year, while record sales trend down. New avenues for revenue for musicians have materialized through the ever-increasing demand for music used in movies, television, ringtones, ringbacks, and video games.

ABOUT THE AUTHOR

Photo by TS Ogsbury

Dick Weissman has been active in almost every facet of the music business. He was a member of the prominent folk-pop group The Journeymen, a record producer, solo recording artist, a studio musician with dozens of credits, and he has written numerous recorded songs and instrumental pieces. Dick has composed two feature film scores, and has written the music and songs for several theatrical works and conventions. He has written 18 published books on music and the music industry, and numerous instruction books for guitar, banjo and songwriting.

Dick was an Associate Professor in Music Industry program at the University of Colorado at Denver, and after moving to Oregon in 2002 he became an Adjunct Professor at Portland Community College. He is a member of the Executive Board of the Portland local of the musicians' union, and books and promotes concerts for the Portland Folk Music Society. He continues his career as an active performing and recording musician.

PART ONE

The Music Business and Its Components

CHAPTER 1

The Record Industry: A History and General Introduction

The history of the record industry can be told through the evolution of new technologies (recording formats), the growth of the record business (record labels), or through changing musical styles. Each tells us something about how the overall music business has grown and changed from the late nineteenth through the early twenty-first centuries. The interplay between these three trends created the music business as we know it today.

A BRIEF HISTORY OF RECORDING

Early Years: 1870–1950

The record industry owes its origins to the experiments of several French scientists. In the nineteenth century, the French inventor Charles Cros designed, but did not actually build, a device that could record sound. It wasn't until 1877 that the American inventor Thomas Edison developed an early version of the **phonograph**. Edison's original vision of the machine anticipated that it would be used as a sort of Dictaphone or recording machine. Edison's machines recorded on wax **cylinders**, resembling solid mailing tubes. Soon, prerecorded cylinders were being manufactured to be played back on Edison's phonographs.

Of course, Edison was not alone in these early experiments, and many others tried to improve on his invention. Notably, Chicester Bell, a cousin of Alexander Graham Bell, came up with a better way of recording onto the wax cylinders. For several years, Bell and Edison battled in courts over who owned the rights to this technology. Edison stubbornly refused to pay Bell, and launched his own Edison label to market his cylinders. Bell's patent eventually formed the basis for the second major recording company, the Columbia Phonograph Co.

3

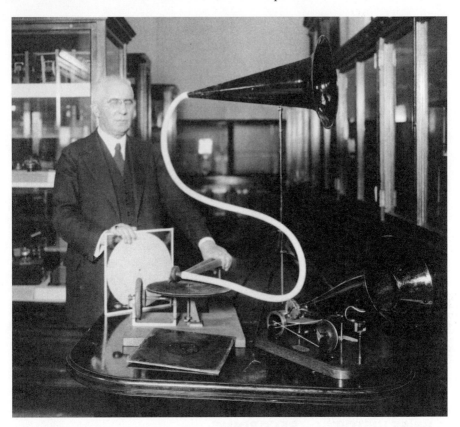

Emile Berliner holding an early flat disc record and standing next to a model of his first phonograph. National Photo Company Collection (Library of Congress).

A major advance in recording technology was made by a German-born engineer named Emile Berliner, who experimented in the 1880s with a disc-based phonograph, which eventually would replace the cylinder-based machines of the turn of the century. In 1891, Berliner formed a company to market his new flat **discs**, which eventually became the Victor Talking Machine Company, the third of the original recording companies.

After the disc format took over from cylinders around the first decade of the twentieth century, Victor and Columbia shared the rights to the "lateral cut" method of producing discs. Lateral cut discs featured grooves in which the needle moved from side to side to reproduce the sound. Edison opted for his own "hill and dale" technology, in which the needle moved up and down on a layered (and thicker) disc. No other labels could compete until around 1920, when the original patents were beginning to expire. A proliferation of smaller labels blossomed in the 1920s through the early 1930s, when a combination of free music (offered by radio) and the Great Depression led to a collapse of the recording industry. Edison ended his record business in the late 1920s, and Victor was absorbed by the radio maker RCA. Columbia struggled on through various owners, eventually falling into the hands of the CBS radio broadcasting company in 1948. One new label, Decca Records, emerged as a major player in the later 1930s, thanks to signing singing star Bing Crosby.

The standard recording disc of this era was played back at 78 **revolutions per minute** (or **rpm**). The heavy discs were not terribly durable, and early sound recording technologies—relying on "acoustic" recordings made through large horns—were noisy at best. The introduction of electric microphones in the mid-1920s helped somewhat, but records were still easily broken and would wear out from repeated playback. When radio was introduced in the early 1920s, it offered superior sound quality and limitless hours of music, plus the only cost was for the radio itself, so that an initial investment could yield years of entertainment. Phonograph records could not compete.

After World War II, a new recording format led to a rebirth of the record industry. Columbia pioneered a **long playing (LP)** disc that played back at 33⅓ rpm, offering both more playing time and better fidelity than the earlier 78s. RCA Victor responded with a 45 rpm "single" that was more economical to produce than earlier 78s. New materials were used to make these discs that were less prone to breaking than earlier 78s. The LP became the preferred medium for adult listeners, who tended to want to enjoy longer works, such as Broadway musicals or classical symphonies. The 45 single was pitched at the youth market, and would soon become the medium for a new musical style, rock and roll.

The Rise of the Independents

During the first fifty or so years of the recording industry, the business was dominated first by Edison and then by Columbia and Victor, which held the

Major Recording Formats, c. 1880–Today

Format	First Producer	Period of Popularity
Cylinder	Edison	c. 1890–1910
78 rpm Discs	Berliner (Victor)	c. 1910–1950
Long playing (LP) records (33⅓ rpm)	Columbia	c. 1950–1990
Singles (45 rpm)	Victor	c. 1950–1990
Cassette Tapes	Phillips	c. 1970–1985
Compact disks	Phillips/Sony	c. 1985–ongoing
mp3	Protocol for file compression developed by an international committee of electronics producers	c. 1995–ongoing

Victor 78 rpm record label from the late 1920s. Courtesy BenCar Archives.

crucial patents for making phonograph discs. Smaller labels began to develop in the mid-1920s when the patent stranglehold was broken. Smaller labels often catered to special markets, such as country or blues music. Many of these labels eventually were absorbed into one of the bigger outfits, so that by the end of the 1930s Victor, Decca, and Columbia were the major players in the market.

From the 1930s through the early 1950s, American popular music primarily came from Broadway and Hollywood, and the **major labels** focused primarily on these most popular forms. There were smaller audiences for country music and blues, but these musical genres sold to specialized audiences. Jazz sometimes crossed over into popular music, especially when the band had a singer as a featured soloist. Many of the popular music stars of the 1940s and 1950s, including Frank Sinatra, Peggy Lee, and Jo Stafford, got their start singing with big bands, and went on to become hit recording artists. The genre of popular music before rock was introduced became known as **middle of the road (MOR)** music. This term has come to mean easy listening music designed to appeal to a broad segment of the audience for music.

The growth of a West Coast-based music industry to feed motion picture production led many prominent songwriters to settle in Hollywood, including Johnny Mercer, along with many talented musicians. Mercer would partner with several others to form a new label, Capitol Records, in 1942, to tap into this growing talent pool.

However, the postwar years would see new musical styles arise that the major labels were slow to recognize. This gave an opening to independent producers from all around the country to get into the music business. In the early 1940s, rhythm and blues artists such as Louis Jordan had begun to cross over, to sell to audiences that represented different racial and economic groups. By the mid-1950s, rock and roll had begun to infiltrate America's musical landscape, and the era of middle of the road popular music began to be replaced by rock recordings. Because many of the A&R (artist and repertoire) executives at the major labels were middle-aged and had come out of either a jazz or pop background, they had little interest or enthusiasm for rock and roll. This led to the almost meteoric rise of **independent record labels**.

Independent Labels of the 1940s and 1950s

Label	Founding Year	Home Base	Some Major Artists
ABC Records	1955	Hollywood	The Impressions, Three Dog Night
Atlantic Records	1947	New York City	Ruth Brown and Ray Charles
Chess Records	1947	Chicago	Muddy Waters and Chuck Berry
Duke and Peacock Records	1952	New Orleans	Bobby Blue Bland
King Records	1944	Cincinnati, OH	James Brown
Mercury Records	1945	Chicago	Patti Page
MGM Records	1946	Hollywood	Connie Francis, Hank Williams
Motown Records	1959	Detroit	The Supremes, Smoky Robinson & the Miracles
Stax Records	1957	Memphis, TN	Sam & Dave, Otis Redding
Sun Records	1952	Memphis, TN	Johnny Cash, Elvis Presley
United Artist Records	1952	Hollywood	Sound track albums, Little Anthony & the Imperials
Warner Brothers Records	1958	Hollywood	Peter, Paul & Mary

Note: Some of these artists, such as Fats Domino, who recorded for the Imperial label, were nominally on other labels that the above labels bought.

The independent labels operated in a very different way from the major labels. At the major labels, decisions were often made by committee, with sales, promotion, and A&R staff all listening to prospective artists before agreeing to sign them. The independent labels were run on shoestring budgets and made decisions often based on gut feeling rather than on a disciplined approach to the bottom line. They signed artists quickly, based on their immediate reactions to the artist's work. Independent labels promoted their records in a freewheeling style that often included bribing disc jockeys or radio station program directors with cash or expensive gifts (see Chapter 2). The changing nature of the music business was best represented by the success of Sun Records, from Memphis, Tennessee. Operating out of a closet-sized studio with a tiny budget, Sun was able to successfully launch the 1950s' biggest-selling artist, Elvis Presley, without any major label support. Elvis was so successful in his first years of recording that Sun was able to sell his contract to industry leader RCA Victor for $30,000, a stunning sum in those days, when independent labels have sold for sums in the hundreds of millions.

In the 1950s, the major labels often didn't understand the new music that young people liked, and had no notion of how traditional song structures fit into the new idiom of rock and roll. But by the mid-1960s, the major labels had all joined the rock and roll parade. New and younger personnel moved the companies into the world of contemporary pop music, the artist roster of the major labels changed, and European record companies became worldwide competitors for the American majors. The European influence—particularly from Great Britain—was greatest in the mid-1960s when the Beatles and other **British Invasion** groups conquered the pop charts. By then, Capitol Records was owned by the British company EMI (Electrical Musical Industries), which subsequently acquired Liberty, United Artists, and Virgin labels, among many others. Similarly, German-based electronic maker Siemens and Dutch-based Philips combined their label holdings in 1962, creating Polygram Records, which in turn bought Mercury, MGM, and Decca, and then acquired Island Records as well.

American-based companies followed suit in merging into larger conglomerates. Warner Brothers bought Frank Sinatra's label Reprise and, more important, it acquired Atlantic in 1967, Elektra in 1970, and Asylum (David Geffen's label) in 1972. Columbia Records grew in related entertainment businesses, acquiring Fender Guitars, Steinway Pianos, and the New York Yankees baseball team.

The story since then has been one of continuing consolidation of the recording industry. In 1986, the German publishing company Bertelsmann bought RCA, and a year later Sony purchased Columbia Records; Sony and BMG would enter into a joint operating agreement for their labels in 2004. The Japanese company Matsushita bought MCA, then sold it to Canadian liquor company Seagram, which was in turn bought by the French engineering and sewage company Vivendi. Suddenly, Warner Brothers was the only

American-owned label. Today Vivendi's record division is named Universal, and besides owning Decca, ABC, and MCA, they also own rap record labels Interscope and Def Jam. Universal is now the largest record company in the world. In 2008 Sony announced that it was buying BMG's music holdings (including RCA), and ended the joint operating agreement under which the two companies had been operating. Warner Brothers and EMI are owned by private investors.

HOW MAJOR AND INDEPENDENT LABELS ARE ORGANIZED: BUSINESS AND CREATIVE FUNCTIONS

Major labels have branches in the critical American music markets—Los Angeles, Nashville (for labels that market in country music), and New York. There are several other important music industry towns, notably Atlanta for hip-hop recordings and Miami for companies that are active in the burgeoning Latin music markets. Nevertheless, the full staffs are based in one of the three major music centers. All of the labels have people active in the creative and business areas, as well as people who essentially function as liaisons between these groups.

The business area includes:

- *Chief executive officers*
- *Business affairs people* *to make licensing deals for records issued with foreign affiliates, or for issuing the recordings of foreign affiliates in the United States*
- *Accounting staff* *who pay royalties*
- *Legal personnel* *to handle contractual matters*
- *Sales and promotion people* (Note: many of the labels have sales and promotion people working in different regions of the country to get records into stores and to get them played by radio stations)
- *Product managers* *to coordinate release schedules and to ensure that recordings are released on time*

On the creative side of the ledger are:

- *The A&R staff* *to scout talent, and to interact with artists, helping to choose producers for a particular project, and keeping an eye on whether the recordings are being made in a timely fashion and within the budget allocated for the project. Some A&R staff people also function as record producers, for example, David Foster at Warner Music, who has been producing records for years.*
- *The art department* *to design and execute album covers, or to oversee freelance artists who are hired to work on the project*
- *The publicity department* *to write press releases, biographies of artists, and attempt to obtain media coverage of artists*
- *Liaisons to film and television* *who seek to place artists' work into film, television, or video games, both as a form of exposure for the artist and as a source of income for the record company and the artist*

Independent labels do not have the financial resources to maintain large staffs. The functions described here may be greatly reduced or farmed out to freelancers.

All of the major labels maintain music publishing operations. They do not actually print sheet music but, instead, simply collect royalties from the copyrights. Universal Music Publishing is the largest publisher; they bought BMG's publishing company before BMG Records merged with Sony. EMI's publishing wing is the second largest in the world, and many people regard that division of the company as its most viable asset, because the record company has not experienced great success for a number of years. Warner Brothers Music Publishing is the third largest music publisher in the world. Recently, Warner Brothers sold the music *print* portion of their publishing operation to Alfred Music. (See Chapter 6 for an extensive analysis of music publishing.) The music publishing area of the music business has become increasingly lucrative. This is because of the widespread use of copyright music in films, television, video games, and for ringtones and ringbacks.

Although the sizes of major and independent record labels are very different, they perform similar functions. They both sign acts, produce or select the producers of an artist's music, promote artists in a number of ways, and attempt to get records into the stores and on digital distribution platforms. There is a belief that independent record labels are therefore more artist-oriented and creative than the major labels. Many also believe that the indies, as they are often called, are more honest than major labels when it comes to paying royalties.

Why Publishing Rights Are So Important

Why is it so important that an artist own the publishing rights to their songs? In a nutshell, publishers get paid 9.1 cents per song for the sales of records, and half of this money goes to the songwriter, which is 4.55 cents. If the artist is able to retain rights to her own publishing, then the full 9.1 cents goes to the artist. If there are twelve songs on a record, the difference is 54.6 cents per CD. This assumes that the artist is the author of all his songs. If the artist only wrote two songs on the album, then the difference will be 9.10 cents if the artist owns the publishing rights.

In addition to the royalties paid on the sales of records, if the artist owns the publishing, then she or he will retain all of the performance rights, that is, the money paid for performances on radio or television. The value of those rights is less predictable, because the songwriter and publisher are paid according to airplay, which may or may not directly reflect the sales of the recording. The bottom line is that these rights can be worth hundreds of thousands of dollars. (For more on publishing rights, see Chapter 6.)

However, the situation is far too complex for such simple generalizations. There are many different sorts of independent labels, including:

- An artist-owned label that exists only to produce and sell the recordings of the owner, who is also the artist.
- An artist-owned label that is designed to record friends of the artist. One example of this sort of company is Amy Ray's Daemon records. (Ray is one of the members of The Indigo Girls.)
- A niche market label that is only interested in selling music of a particular genre, such as jazz, bluegrass, black gospel music, or punk music.
- A label that is nominally independent but is set up with strong financing and the intention of becoming a major label at a future time.
- A label owned by a company that is not primarily in the record business; Hallmark Cards, Toyota/Scion Cars, and Cracker Barrel Old Country Stores are examples.

Ani DiFranco's Righteous Babe Records is a prime example of a successful artist-run company, and a few of Ms. DiFranco's recordings have gone gold, the RIAA designation for recordings that have sold over five hundred thousand copies. There is a rich history of such enterprises. One of the most famous artist-run companies is Dischord Records, owned and operated by the long-time Washington, DC, punk band Fugazi.

Some of the **genre-specific labels** have gone on to achieve success far beyond their original plan. Rounder Records, for example, started as a folk-driven company that recorded blues, bluegrass, and folk music. They struck gold with George Thorogood but achieved their greatest success with Alison Krauss, who has had several platinum-selling albums (sales of over one million copies.) The most recent of these is her duet album with Robert Plant, the lead singer of Led Zeppelin.

Few if any independent labels can compete on even terms with the majors, in terms of financing and ultimate goals. In fact, TVT Records, one of the strongest of the independents, went bankrupt in 2008.

This chapter has outlined the differences in scope and scale between the majors and the independents, but what about their business practices? Readers may be dismayed to learn that there are some severe drawbacks to signing a deal with an indie label. Because these labels tend to have less money to operate with, the artist may find that there isn't enough money to finance the recording in a way that will realize his or her vision. From a contractual standpoint, the artist may have to contend with two other problems. In the current market, it is usually possible for artists recording with a major label to retain the publishing rights to their own songs, which is not always possible with smaller labels. The other potential problem is that if the indie label is distributed by a major label, then the royalty paid to the artist may be a lower percentage, because the indie label has to pay part of its income to the distributor. This table indicates the pros and cons of independent and major label deals.

Pros and Cons of Working with Major vs. Independent Labels

Positive Factors

Indie Label	Major Label
• Closer relationship with the artist • Artist may have more artistic control over production of album as well as over the album cover and liner notes • Less competition from other artists on the label • Because the number of albums released is not huge, there is more chance of getting a new album out relatively quickly • Easier to access the label • Contracts are relatively simple • May be more capable of promoting niche artists who experience reasonable, but not mass market, sales	• Better financial resources • Better distribution of recordings, including possible international distribution • Artist more apt to keep music publishing rights • Possible tour support • Usually doesn't try to force artists to give up their music publishing rights • Offer more publicity services to artist • May hire independent promoters in addition to their own staff promotional team • Possibility of a larger advance on signing the contract

Negative Factors

Indie Label	Major Label
• Label will often try to get music publishing rights • Royalty percentages may be lower than major label, because the company has to farm out distribution • Lack of financing may prevent a well-planned promotional campaign • Company may have poor distribution, or even lack national or international distribution • Some independent labels also want to manage the artist, creating possible conflicts of interest • Tour support is unlikely	• Artist may get lost in the shuffle as record company personnel change or as other acts on the label become hot • It may prove difficult to contact the decision makers at a major label • A&R people may not understand the musical direction of the artist • An artist's album may be buried in a release schedule that includes some obvious major hit recordings. Under these circumstances, the new artist is unlikely to receive much promotion. Because the release schedule is prepared months in advance, a new product may have trouble entering the schedule • The recording contract will be extremely lengthy and detailed

As of this writing, there are four major labels. They sell approximately 80 percent of the albums sold in the United States. The remaining 20 percent of sales go to the hundreds of independent labels. In addition to these categories, there are literally thousands of artists or bands who own their own labels for the sole purpose of recording and marketing their own records. There are numerous examples of artists who are dissatisfied with the performance of their record labels, both the majors and the independents.

Major Label versus Independents: Carlos Coy and the Decembrists

Carlos Coy established a career in Houston as a rapper, using the name South Park Mexican. In 1994, he established his own label and decided to market his recordings at swap meets, reasoning that there was a real market for Mexican-American rappers but relatively little product available. Coy sold the recordings himself, and when demand grew, he hired others to go to more swap markets, paying them a percentage of his receipts. The major labels became interested in Coy when they realized that he was selling many thousands of records, utilizing this unique system of distribution.

Carlos Coy, aka South Park Mexican. Photo courtesy BenCar Archives.

In 2000 he was paid a substantial amount of money by Universal for the right to distribute his albums, but unfortunately they were not able to expand the demand for his work with his next two albums.

Without knowing specifically went wrong with the Universal deal, we can hypothesize that a major label like Universal was probably not set up to market Coy's CDs profitably. It is difficult to imagine Universal establishing a presence at swap meets patronized by Mexican Americans in various parts of the United States. For one thing, what other product would they sell to these consumers? This would clearly not be a cost-effective way for Universal to utilize its sales and promotional efforts.

The Portland alternative-rock-folkish band The Decembrists recently moved from Olympia's Kill Rock Stars label to Capitol. In various interviews, the band has claimed to see little or no difference between their previous label and Capitol in the level of artistic control that they are granted over their recordings. Capitol has recently released their second album; they are playing larger venues and getting more publicity than they previously did. However, Colin McEvoy, the leader of the band, is recording solo material on the Kill Rock Stars label.

One difference between the workings of major and independent labels is that if a band such as The Decembrists sells, say, one hundred thousand records for Capitol, that album will be considered a failure. By contrast, for a small label such as their previous one, that level of sales would be considered excellent. The difference depends on the budget for recording the album, the money spent to promote it, and the difference in the staff and real estate overhead that it takes to maintain each of the labels.

Catalog Product

Because major labels have been in business for many years, they also have acquired the catalogs of many other companies. They make a considerable amount of income by reissuing old recordings, or simply creating compilations of material in their catalogs. Generally, no new recording is required in the reissue products, and **catalog product** in general has usually recouped any expenses in the initial recording costs.

Albums such as Michael Jackson's *Thriller*, various Beatles albums, or Pink Floyd's *Dark Side of the Moon* still sell thousands of copies a week, despite the fact that these albums have been available for decades.

Because independent labels are relatively young and usually have not acquired other record companies, they lack an in-depth catalog that can be reissued.

Related Businesses

Earlier in this chapter, I mentioned that major labels used to own numerous other businesses that related to music and entertainment but that most of these businesses were sold off years ago. A current example of these types of businesses is the in-house advertising agency Arcade Creative Group, which is owned by Sony Music. This business started in April 2008, and currently numbers among its clients Ralph Lauren, J. C. Penney, and the Coca-Cola Company Fanta beverage account. Because many commercials utilize current recordings, this would appear to be a natural tie-in.

Terms to Know

A&R staff *9*

British Invasion *8*

Cylinder *3*

Catalog product *14*

Genre-specific labels *11*

Independent record label *7*

Long playing record (LP) *5*

Major label *6*

Middle of the road (MOR) *6*

Phonograph *3*

Revolutions per minute (rpm) *5*

For Class Discussion

1. Discuss the changes that technology has brought to the physical production of recorded music.
2. Do you know anyone who has ever recorded a CD? Describe their experience.
3. Do you know anyone who has ever been under contract to a record label? Describe their experience.
4. Given a choice, if you were an artist or a manager, would you sign with a major label or an independent one?
5. Why is it so important for the artist not to give up publishing rights to a record label?
6. Why do independent labels generally seem to be the ones to introduce new genres of music, such as rock and roll or hip-hop?
7. Could someone start an independent label today that would grow into a major label in the future? Why or why not?
8. What does the story of Carlos Coy reveal about the difficulties that a major label has in promoting independent music to specific markets?

CHAPTER **2**

Record Distribution and Promotion

This chapter will cover the basics of record distribution for both the major labels and independents. It will address new developments, including digital distribution and how that has impacted traditional sales. Once records are in the stores or posted online, the music has to be promoted to be successful. We will look at how recordings have been traditionally promoted and at new ways of getting music before the listening public.

RECORD DISTRIBUTION

The chain of record distribution is fairly straightforward. The labels sell product to distributors, and the distributors in turn sell the CDs to record stores and other outlets such as one stops and rack jobbers (see later in this chapter). At its most basic level, the distribution system can be reduced to this simple flow chart:

Record label → record distributor → retail record store

The major labels own their own distribution networks. Major labels must distribute large quantities of records in order to justify the large overhead of their operations. Their distribution operations are geared toward dealing with selling large quantities of hit albums by established artists. The major labels distribute not only their own product but also recordings owned by some independent labels. The major label house distribution systems are geared to selling to the largest retailers, which are in the position to order the most product. Smaller stores may not do enough business to qualify for the special terms offered by these distributors.

By contrast, "independent" distributors sell a variety of smaller labels. Each label individually doesn't sell enough product or have a large enough catalog to justify the costs of distribution, but together there's enough business to keep the independent going. The independent distributor often offers other services, such as warehousing and shipping, and may also offer, for additional fees, marketing and other support that the small labels cannot afford or lack the expertise to do on their own. Independent record distributors can deal with the "mom and pop" and the independent music stores that seldom carry pop releases but specialize in alternative forms of music. An independent distributor has lower overhead, and may carry hundreds of labels, so that they may be happy to sell, say, three copies of one album, fourteen of another, and one copy of a third album to a single store.

Over the years, some independent distributors have been purchased by the major labels. Some majors have also created their own "independent" distribution operations. Although owned by a major, these independents still carry a variety of product from other labels, and operate as separate businesses. The major label may also channel some of its more specialized artists through its house independent distribution system, rather than its own, larger operation, especially when a particular artist or album is closer to the definition of alternative music than the label's more typical product.

Another link in the chain of record distribution is the so-called **one stop**. A one stop is a distributor that carries all record company product, even major label releases. Small record stores in relatively isolated areas prefer to deal with one stops, because they can order all of their product from a single source, rather than having to deal with a half-dozen different record distributors. One stops have to mark up the prices of major label releases, so the mom and pop store will pay slightly more for, say, a Warner Music album ordered from a one stop than one obtained from Warner's own distribution wing.

Another channel of record distribution is the **rack jobber**. A rack jobber stocks records in stores such as Wal-Mart or Target. Essentially, they are operating the record departments of these stores, stocking appropriate product, and replacing albums that are sold or returned. In some instances, the rack jobber actually owns or leases the record department in a particular drug store or supermarket. They may pay rent or a percentage of profits to the store owner. Rack jobbers usually make their decisions as to what to stock by following the charts of successful records in *Billboard*, the best known of the music trade papers.

Over the years, many independent distributors have gone out of business. When this happens, it can also cause the associated labels major financial problems. Let's say that a small record company has pressed ten thousand copies of a CD, and a particular large independent distributor has bought five thousand of them. Now imagine that the distributor has sold three thousand of these albums at the time that they declared bankruptcy. Independent distributors often delay paying the record companies as long as possible, because the record stores delay paying *them*, creating cash flow problems. If this distributor has paid the record company for five hundred records, that means that there are twenty-five hundred records that have been sold by retailers without the proceeds going to the record company,

Record display racks in a department store, c. 1975. Photo: Laimute Druskis, courtesy Z. Legacy, Corporate Digital Archive.

plus the remaining two thousand on hand at the distributor. Odd as it may sound, on bankruptcy the distributor does not generally return the two thousand unsold records to the record company. Usually the assets of the distributor are frozen, and their inventory is sold off at distress prices. The money goes to a long line of creditors, and most likely the small record company is way down on the list, and receives pennies on the dollar, if that.

The impact on a small label can be devastating. A friend of mine named Allen Shaw has a folk music label called Folk Era. His then distributor, Bayside, went out of business. Bayside had a very large percentage of the label's releases in its warehouse, which was frozen by the bankruptcy. Rather than return this inventory, the distributor offered to sell Folk Era *back* its own records for $1.25 per album. Bayside's reasoning was that, because their assets were frozen, Folk Era would get no income at all from these hundreds of records. By buying them back, Folk Era would be able to at least realize *some* income from the records by reselling them. Folk Era declined the offer, and wrote off the lost inventory.

Exclusives

From time to time, a single store chain will make a deal with an artist or label to be the exclusive distributor of a new CD. The Eagles's 2007 CD *Long Road Out of Eden* was available only at Wal-Mart. The move was troubling to the band's longtime fans, who pointed out that it was smaller, independent

Types of Record Distributors, and the Outlets that They Service

Major label distributors: EMI (Capitol), Warner, BMG-Sony, Universal. Distribute major label product to record stores

Independent but major label–owned distributors: Red (Sony), ADA (Warner Music), Caroline (EMI), Fontana (Universal). Service record stores

Independent distributors: Koch, Navarre, Alliance. Service record stores

One stops: Most major cities. Service small record shops

Rack jobbers: Pickwick. Service department stores, discount stores, and big box stores

Innovative distribution: Service art galleries, book stores, gift shops, greeting card stores, groceries, tourist shops, truck stops

Combined physical product and digital distribution of artist-owned labels: CD Baby collects $4 from the sale of CDs, and lets the artist set the retail price. They also farm out digital distribution to numerous outlets, and take a small percentage before paying to the artist.

Digital distributors: See below.

stores who supported the group during its long climb from Southern California country-rockers to mainstream hit-makers. The group was also able to produce the recording on their own, without dealing with a major label, and kept a larger portion of the profits from each sale. Similarly, the current Guns N' Roses album is being sold exclusively by Best Buy.

Of course, arrangements like this greatly simplify the distribution process, because there is basically only one channel of distribution. Another occasional distribution ploy is to give a particular chain an exclusive on a record for a certain period of time, before the album goes into general distribution. Naturally, both of these techniques are extremely irritating to retailers, who get requests for albums that they cannot order.

Wholesale and Retail Prices

Todd Lathrop, writing in the revised edition of *This Business of Music: Marketing and Promotion,* points out that there is more than one pricing level between labels and distributors. He places the price paid by the distributor as being between 35 and 50 percent of the **suggested retail list price (SRLP)**. Lathrop cites an example of one distributor who pays $7 for CDs, then sells them to the stores for $10. Furthering complicating the issue is that most retailers discount CDs by 10–20 percent off the suggested retail price. In addition, chain operations such as Best Buy heavily discount CDs in order to draw store traffic; once in the store, these customers might purchase big ticket items such as large-screen TVs or refrigerators. Another frequently adopted ploy is for a retail store to run specials on a few current and very desirable CDs. Once again, the rationale is to draw store traffic from customers who will then buy additional product.

Used CDs

Many retail stores are now accepting used CDs as trade-ins, and then reselling them at a large discount. Used CDs are a great profit center for stores, because the store often buys them at a very low price. The profit margin is considerably higher than for new product, often as high as 75 to 80 percent of the price of the CD. CDs are relatively indestructible, so many older consumers who are not necessarily concerned with buying the latest albums, or comfortable with the MP3 format, are happy to seek out used copies.

Review copies are often resold by music critics or even by radio stations. Promotional copies are generally marked "for promotional purposes only, not for resale." Some retail stores will not purchase promo records, as they are called, but others don't seem to mind. The record companies generally ignore this phenomenon, even though technically they are opposed to it.

It would be interesting to know exactly how much is earned annually through the sales of used recordings. Because record companies make no profits on used records, there is no compelling reason for them to gather this information. It might, however, be useful for the labels to collect this information and use it as an indicator of what catalog product might constitute viable reissues. Artists also make nothing on sales of used CDs.

Cut-Outs

Cut-outs are out-of-print albums that are resold at very low prices. A few companies specialize in cut-outs, which can be a lucrative business. There are no royalties paid to artists, music publishers, or songwriters on cut-outs, and this is specified in artists' contracts. Selling cut-outs and used albums can be a tricky business, because sometimes there is no demand for these obsolete albums, even at a low price.

Returns

Most record companies allow stores to return 100 percent of their unsold albums. Some companies will charge the stores a small percentage on albums that are returned long after they were originally purchased by the store.

Artist Sales

Many artists sell their albums at their performances. If the artist sells his own album, the profit margin far exceeds what the artist could get in royalties from a label. It is normal for artists to sell their CDs for $15 at performances. Many of the smaller record companies sell their artists' records at a greatly reduced price, typically $5–$7. This leaves a profit of between $8 and $10. Because the larger labels are intent on supporting existing brick-and-mortar record stores or their own distribution apparatus, they do not really encourage artists (and may actually forbid them) from selling their own CDs. The problem for the major label is that if artists sell their product at performances, then the local record store will lose the sales that may result from consumer interest that follows a successful concert.

DIGITAL DISTRIBUTION

Digital distribution has been both a major step forward in making a wide variety of music available to listeners and also somewhat of a troubling development for the music business. Digital files can be freely "shared" and various attempts to protect them from copying have yet to prove successful. Meanwhile, services such as **Napster**, Grokster, and countless others have emerged, which enable users to share their files without paying any fee. The music business claims this has resulted in a catastrophic loss of income to the labels and their artists, although others point out that free music available through radio and other media in the past has helped the industry sell more product by exposing more listeners to the artists.

Various subscription-based services such as eMusic and Rhapsody developed in the 1990s to allow listeners to freely listen and download music, as long as they paid a monthly fee. These services were slow to get off

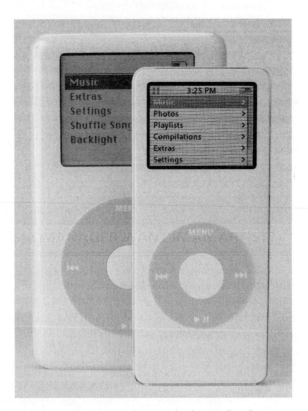

Apple iPod and iPod Nano. Courtesy Dorling Kindersley Media Library.

the ground, because they had trouble reaching agreements with the major labels. Consumers also balked at the idea of paying a fee each month, and they were particularly distressed when they lost access to all of their music if they let their subscriptions lapse.

Apple's **iTunes** represented a major breakthrough in the distribution of pop music on the Web. Apple introduced the **iPod** in 1991 and, by pioneering a simple model ($.99 per download), attracted the participation of all the major labels and most major performers, Apple was able to offer a simple-to-use service. Along with the company's innovative iTunes software and iPod players, Apple came to dominate the digital music market. As of summer 2008, iTunes claimed to be selling more product than Wal-Mart, the largest retail outlet for CDs. The major labels complained about the fixed pricing— they wanted to be able to charge more for hit records—but the Apple model was so appealing to users that the company was able to dictate its terms. Apple tried to get the labels to reduce the retail price of downloads, but they resisted doing so. Apple eventually convinced many of the major labels to abandon copy-protecting their files, although iTunes downloads could only be played on Apple players. This exclusivity has created considerable anger on the part of the Internet-using community, which believes that there are already far too many restrictions on the availability and duplication of music. Currently iTunes and the record companies are abandoning the notion of having a single retail price. The new method will set a higher price for the most desirable digital downloads, and a lower price for older catalog product.

But iTunes and the iPod are not simply a distribution format; they represent a new lifestyle for their owners. iPods can be used to create playlists, and fanatical fans of artists have created blogs that provide extensive details about specific songs and why the artist has written them. In his book *Net, Blogs and Rock 'n' Roll*, David Jennings points out that compiling a **playlist** allows the iPod owner to "project his own identity," and when these playlists are shared with others, social networks are developed or expanded. This is a revolutionary way of looking at the distribution and sales of music, because the impetus is for the most part coming from individual taste patterns, rather than being driven by corporate advertising.

The iPod has also changed the buying habits of the American public in another way. Rather than purchasing an entire album, the consumer can cherry-pick, buying only the songs that they like. Record companies are upset by this, because from a profit standpoint it is better to sell an album than a single tune. Artists don't care for it either, because they often envision the album as a complete entity, rather than a collection of twelve or fourteen songs. Consumers argue that they should not have to buy anything other than what they enjoy listening to.

Another aspect of the iPod is that the consumer can store hundreds of tunes on a single, portable device that is far more convenient than an old-fashioned stereo set. The portability factor is not entirely new; after all,

In Rainbows: The Digital Future?

Some labels and artists have taken to releasing songs or entire albums exclusively in digital format. Sometimes this is done in advance of a CD release to build buzz for the record among hardcore fans. In other cases, the digital release replaces fully a "real" album. A recent example of a successful digital release was Radiohead's seventh album, *In Rainbows*. In autumn 2007, Radiohead amazed the industry by initially making their latest "CD" a digital-only release, suggesting that their fans pay what they thought was a reasonable price for the download. The tracks had no copy-protection. Within a month, the band reported that 1.2 million people had downloaded the album, paying an average voluntary price of $8.00 per download (in the United States). In early 2008, the band then released a boxed set version of the release, with both CD and vinyl (LP) versions of the album and other bonus materials. Despite the material already being available online, the album debuted at #1 on the pop charts. Although Radiohead's experience was somewhat unique, it does point the way to a future in which established artists can break their ties with the major labels (Radiohead had previously recorded for EMI) and take their recordings directly to their fans.

Walkman devices have been around since 1979. MP3 files are clearly more convenient than cassettes, and more reliable for the user. They can also play video files, and can interface with Apple's iPhone.

The success of iTunes inspired others to try to enter the digital music market. The online bookseller Amazon.com and the search engine Yahoo are among the latest players in the online digital distribution world. As of summer 2008, **MySpace** had worked out a deal with all of the major labels to digitally distribute their product on the Internet. Because MySpace experiences enormous traffic, this could be a very significant development, if it proves to be successful.

RECORD PROMOTION

There are many ways to promote records. The type of promotion depends on what the label is attempting to accomplish. Normally, a label will want to promote a record to radio stations in order to get them to play the record. If the artist has made a video, the label will similarly want to promote the album to MTV or local or syndicated TV outlets that play videos. Other promotions involve getting the record played in retail outlets or favorably displayed there. Consumer advertising in print, radio, or television represents a further, if expensive, way to capture the interest of the consumer.

When a new recording comes out, the record company or the independent distributor prepare a **one sheet**, a one-page flyer that usually has a reproduction of the album cover, together with information about the album and the artist. The one sheet also includes a listing of the songs and a few brief reviews.

It is also the job of the company to take the recording to radio stations in an effort to get it airplay. Larger stations or members of chains such as Clear Channel usually employ music directors to select records for airplay, based on their popularity. Stations with freer music formats—for example, some satellite or college stations—may still allow the individual DJ to pick records to play. The company has to convince these people that its new recording can be a hit or will be popular with listeners to get them to add it to their playlists. As an incentive, the stations may be offered station IDs, in which the artist tells the name of the group and, in effect, endorses the station, with the station's catch-phrase, such as "WOLP is the hippest station in Shady Grove, Iowa." If the label is really pushing a particular record, they may buy advertising time on the station. When artists appear in a city, the record company will try to bring them to the important local radio stations in order to stimulate airplay. They may also arrange appearances at one or more major local record stores. Usually this involves the group doing a short performance at the record store, followed by signing copies of the new CD. This gives the artist's fans a chance to talk to the artist, and to get to know the music. These events are known in the industry as **in stores**.

Labels may give away thousands of copies of new CDs to music critics and record stores. Many record stores display huge posters of the artists, usually blow-ups of album covers. Sometimes merchandise, such as T-shirts and baseball caps, is given away to record stores or radio stations and they, in turn, give them to callers at radio stations or to retail purchasers of the album. Years ago, Atlantic gave away tiny model zeppelins to radio stations in order to promote Led Zeppelin at radio stations. I remember seeing these attractive and artistic toys at several radio stations.

Contests are another promotional ploy used to promote records. In order to promote a country band called Santa Fe, their label gave away free weekend trips to Santa Fe to meet the band. Local stations could hold contests for their listeners to win a trip, building listenership. This sort of promotion is attractive to radio people, because listeners like it, and it doesn't cost the radio station anything. A common and less expensive move is to give away tickets to the band's show.

Tour support is another means of obtaining exposure for bands. The tour support may be partial or complete. For example, a band may have an opportunity to open for a better-known band that seems almost certain to have large audiences at their shows. The concert promoter views the opening act as being relatively insignificant; consequently, they are offered almost no money to open the show. The record company may make up the difference by providing tour support, so that the new act can get more exposure. Obviously, the record company must view the two acts as being compatible, or the exposure will be worthless. For example, it wouldn't be wise to have a bluegrass band open for a rap artist. Part of the job of the personal manager is to attempt to convince the record company to invest money in tour support. As CD sales have continued to decline, tour support has become less and less common. Examples of how record companies have promoted artists include sending teen artist Tiffany on a tour where she played in shopping malls and having folk-pop artist Jewel play in West Coast coffee houses.

Another form of record company promotion is to get an act to play for industry people, especially radio people, at industry **showcases** that are not open to the public. Showcases give the label the opportunity to highlight new, promising artists for large groups of industry people, from influential writers to DJs to station managers and programmers. Showcases can be an effective way to build insider "buzz" for a new band, and also give the attendees a sense of belonging to an exclusive club of first-time listeners. Lavish spreads of food and drink make these events very attractive.

Many of the labels now utilize so-called **street teams** to promote records to consumers. These street teams post flyers and posters all over a city or neighborhood, creating excitement or buzz around the new group. They also may give away records to key people, such as mobile DJs, encouraging them to showcase the discs. Street teams are often young part-time employees of the record companies. They are paid little or no money, but they generally are willing to devote

Five Shots at a Hit Record

One of the brightest and most energetic people I ever encountered in the music industry was the late Tommy Noonan. Tommy was the national promotion director for Columbia Records during the late 1960s. At that time, Clive Davis, a young lawyer who had worked in the business affairs department of the company, had become Columbia's CEO. Mitch Miller, the previous head of A&R, regarded rock music as a temporary fad. Miller was an excellent, classically trained oboe player, with a predilection for jazz and middle of the road popular music. By contrast, Davis recognized the growing power of rock and roll and that Columbia was missing out on a highly lucrative teen market. Clive commissioned Tommy to find a long-haired rock band in San Francisco, in order to compete with Jefferson Airplane and some of the other Bay area groups. Tommy found Moby Grape, and Columbia signed the band.

The band recorded their first album, and both Clive and Tommy agreed that, although the album worked just fine, there was no hit single on it. Tommy then devised an unlikely scheme. He suggested to Clive that the company release five singles simultaneously, taking ads in trade papers stating that the album was so wonderful, that the label was letting the public decide which of the band's many dynamic songs would turn out to be their "hit." Tommy's intent was to create so much attention to the album by radio stations and industry people that the album would succeed whether or not the strategy literally produced a hit single for the band. The five singles came out with the ads, and one of the singles ended up making a respectable impact on the pop charts, although it did not become a giant hit. The album sold over five hundred thousand copies, so the ultimate objective was achieved.

This story shows how a creative promotion person, with the resources of a major label behind him, can make a tremendous difference to the promotion and ultimate success of a recording project.

their energies to record promotion because they want to pursue careers in the industry, or because they themselves want to become artists. Dance records are heavily promoted to mobile and club DJs in the hope that they will create a demand for these records by playing them at dances or dance clubs.

End Caps, Listening Stations, and Special Store Deals

End caps are places in the bins of record stores designed to call attention to particular new releases. Their name comes from their location at the end of a display case. Sometimes shelves are placed above the main case to enable the face out display of individual CDs, rather than the "stacking" that occurs in the main display case. This allows specific new or special releases to be highlighted. **Listening stations** are areas in the store where the consumer can listen to new releases on headphones. Record companies pay thousands of dollars to have their albums placed on listening stations at chain stores such as Borders. Once again, smaller labels are at a disadvantage, because they cannot afford these expenditures.

Sometimes the labels will promote records by offering special price reductions. For example, a label might give away one new album for every ten purchases by a store. Because this puts more money into the store's coffers, they have an incentive to encourage customers to purchase this particular album. Another variation on this approach is to simply offer a lower introductory price on an album by a new artist. This may draw more consumer interest. When a record salesperson has a relationship with store managers or sales personnel, they may give away extra copies of an album to store employees in the hope that they will enjoy the album and be more apt to play it in the store. Store record play is a great way to alert consumers to new recordings, especially if the new album is not getting as much radio play as the label would like.

Some artists have released records that are sold for a time only at specific record stores. For example, Starbucks sold a recent Bob Dylan release in their stores exclusively for several months before the album became available to other stores. There are also instances in which labels release bonus recordings or DVDs as part of a package that is sold only at specific stores. These releases may be available only at the stores of one of the independent record organizations, or at Target or Wal-Mart. When this happens, it often irritates competing stores, which feel that they are losing out on the considerable sales that often greet new releases by an important artist.

Niche record stores, stores that specialize in a specific musical genre, function as consumer taste makers for musical consumers whose music of choice does not get much radio play. Once in a famous record store in San Antonio that specializes in Tejano music, I observed a DJ consulting the owner about the quality of a few new releases. Clearly the DJ had a great deal of respect for the store's owner, and her knowledge of what was saleable in this particular musical genre. Asking her advice was only common sense, because it undoubtedly reflected the taste of her customers.

Specialized Latino record store in Little Havana, Miami, Florida. Photo: Eugene Gordon, courtesy Z. Legacy, Corporate Digital Archive.

Online Promotion

With the creation of the World Wide Web, any artist or band could promote themselves through posting a Web page. The trick was to drive traffic to— that is, get people to look at—the Web page. This usually is accomplished by posting new content on a regular basis, including band news, previews of songs, fan **chat boards** (where fans can discuss their favorite songs or other related issues), photographs, and other materials. As a band or artist became more popular, these official pages were often joined by "unofficial" ones posted by fans themselves. Sometimes, a band or artist will have a page hosted by their record label.

With the increasing popularity of social network sites such as MySpace and Facebook, musicians have entered a new era of interactive promotion. MySpace has been such a successful venue for hosting new music that it has started a separate MySpace Music division. Until recently, this was a place where bands and artists could post a limited number of their songs for fans to hear, along with other materials. So-called **viral marketing** is used as a means of spreading the word about these pages; building lists of "friends" has become increasingly important, because it is this core group of fans who will help spread the word when the musician wants to announce a new record or tour. MySpace Music has recently announced a new initiative to become a digital download source for music, following the model of iTunes.

PAYOLA AND OTHER ILLEGAL PROMOTIONS

Because the market for records is so competitive, record company promotional people will do anything they can to get records on the radio. This has created a fine line between what is legal in promoting records and what is not allowed. Basically, any quid pro quo or "pay for play" deal is illegal if the station does not announce the arrangement to its listeners. It is perfectly legal to take radio station people out to lunch or dinner, give them free tickets to artists' shows or Christmas gifts. It is also legal for record companies to buy time on radio, as long as the station announces to the public that the time has been purchased by the record company.

Payola is the term used when record companies resort to illegal tactics to get records played. The history of payola is an old one, dating to the turn of the twentieth century, when music publishers placed "spies" in the audience to request songs or to enthusiastically applaud when artists performed the songs the publishers hoped to promote. Sometimes a popular performer was paid to sing a particular song on stage or given a "piece" of the music publishing by being listed as one of the song's "composers" when in fact the performer had no hand in its writing.

On radio, the practice goes back to the early days of rock and roll, in the mid-1950s. At that time, DJs did their own programming, and certain DJs, including Alan Freed and Bill Randall, were considered to be so influential that regular play on their programs virtually guaranteed that a song would become a hit. When the independent labels realized this, they began to offer all sorts of incentives to DJs. These perks included cash payments, trips, gifts, and

Alan Freed was a disc jockey who had a show in Cleveland in 1951. His program, "Moondog Matinee," was among the first to feature black artists on a show aimed at a white teenage audience. Freed is said to have coined the term "rock 'n' roll" for the new musical style that combined country and R&B influences. His popularity was so great that Freed was hired by WINS in New York in 1954, where he developed a tremendous following in the early rock era of the mid-1950s and also had a TV show. In addition to a highly rated radio show, he also presented numerous concerts at New York theaters, drawing thousands of teenagers to cheer on their musical heroes.

Freed used his popularity and power as a way to extract payments from record companies in return for his endorsement of a new record. He was aggressive and blatant in his promotional efforts. In addition to accepting money from record companies, he also was credited as the author for songs that he had absolutely no hand in writing. He was the first person prosecuted by the **FCC (Federal Communications Commission)** for accepting payola, and he was indicted, and fined $300 in 1962. His career never recovered from this scandal.

fraudulent songwriting credits. DJs were also involved in the ownership of record companies, record pressing plants, and music publishing companies.

Over the last sixty years, the U.S. Congress has periodically examined the use of payola, occasionally making scapegoats of specific DJs, notably Freed, or slapping the hands of others, such as Dick Clark. Radio stations responded by taking the programming role away from DJs and placing it in the hands of music directors or station managers. This did not, however, eliminate the problem; it simply meant that there were fewer people involved in the decision-making process.

Payola in the 1980s: The Notorious Network

As a result of the payola scandals of the 1950s and 1960s, the labels decided to hire "independent" promoters to work with radio stations to get music on the air. In this way, label staff would not be tempted to use any illegal techniques to press the stations for airtime. Instead, these independents would be an arm's length away from the labels; how they used their influence to get the records played was up to them.

Unfortunately, this change led to further abuses in the system. Frederic Dannen's book *Hitmen* tells the story of a group of independent record promoters known as The Network who began to subcontract work for the major labels during the 1980s. The labels paid these independent promoters fees to promote records. The people involved in The Network developed close relationships with radio station music directors, and were able to virtually guarantee airplay to the labels. They simply billed the labels for their services, without listing the way that they spent the money. In other words, they were paying off the appropriate people, sometimes with money, sometimes with gifts of various sorts, legal or illegal. Because the record companies were not directly involved in this process, they were essentially absolved of guilt.

The most extreme example of the power of The Network cited in *Hitmen* involved the band Pink Floyd. They were scheduled to do four sold-out concerts at the Hollywood Bowl in 1980, but despite this obvious consumer interest, Columbia Records, their label at the time, was unable to convince the four leading Los Angeles rock radio stations to play their albums. At the last minute, Columbia, which had resisted employing The Network in order to receive what appeared to be automatic radio play, relented. They hired the independent promoters, who managed to get three of the four stations to play Pink Floyd. They followed this up with a note to the label saying that they could have gotten the fourth radio station as well, but decided not do so in order to teach the label a lesson! The promoters never presented the label with any specific expenses or evidence of what they had done in order to "convince" the stations to play the band's albums.

Ultimately, several of the key members of The Network were prosecuted, but although these prosecutions had mixed success, the power of The Network itself was rendered ineffective. The Network, in turn, was replaced by some independent radio promoters who billed the labels in much the same way that an advertising agency would do.

Eliot Spitzer and Payola

In 2006, when Eliot Spitzer was the Attorney General for the state of New York, he investigated all of the major labels, charging that they had made prohibited cash payments in order to receive radio play for their recordings. Ultimately, the labels paid $25 million into a state fund, which then used the money to establish grant programs in music. Among the practices that Spitzer claimed to uncover were cash paid to stations in the guise of consumer radio contests, and the use of independent music promoters in the style of The Network. Jeff Leeds's May 12, 2006, story in the *New York Times* mentioned that other perks uncovered included hotel accommodations, free tickets to sports events, and radio station Web site maintenance, as well as paying consultants to make fake request calls to radio stations. Leeds reported:

> In one e-mail message released by Mr. Spitzer's office, a Universal executive asked an outside company to place "curiosity calls," inquiring about a new Ludacris single, to dozens of stations. "Calls should be 75 percent female, 25 percent male 18–24 years old," the e-mail said.

As a result of Spitzer's work, the FCC looked into the way that radio stations apportioned the airplay of recordings. The FCC reached a more lenient settlement with the record companies. This agreement called for radio stations to offer airplay for local artists in various radio markets. In this case, the issue was not especially payola but the responsibility of radio stations to serve their local communities. It is not clear exactly which stations will play local artists, and at what hour of the day these recordings will be played.

A similar tack was taken by Local 99, the Portland, Oregon, local of the American Federation of Musicians. Local 99 challenged the licenses of three Portland radio stations for not playing the music of local artists. The challenge for two of the stations was rejected outright, and the third license was not suspended, but the station received a letter of admonishment for inadequate recordkeeping. (Radio stations must record everything that they play in a log that is available to any member of the public that requests the right to inspect it.)

Manipulating Airplay Charts

Billboard and *Radio and Records* are two music industry trade papers that publish charts of records that receive airplay. Over the years there have been various radio **tip sheets** that include information about songs added to playlists, or songs on their way up or down on the pop charts. These are highly influential for radio station programmers, so record company promotion departments and independent promoters have targeted them for manipulation. They attempt to persuade these publications to report a recording as being added to playlists or moving up on local charts. At times the promotion people may focus on key stations in a particular market, knowing that if the record is added in that market, it will provide ammunition for promotion people in other cities to pressure the stations in their market to add the record.

Record companies often offer bonuses to their promotional staff, or to independent promoters, based on various plateaus of airplay. For example, getting a record added on a key station might result in the promotion person receiving one level of a cash bonus, getting it added on a number of stations might escalate that payment, and reaching a high chart position at the station might lead to yet another escalation of cash. There is nothing illegal about the creation of such incentives, providing, of course, that the promoter has done nothing illegal in order to get these results.

Incidentally, there are songs that are extremely popular on radio that consumers do not necessarily buy. These are referred to as **turntable hits**. Certain artists—for example, Sammy Davis Jr. and Lena Horne—seem to be popular with DJs but less so with record buyers. The Kingston Trio recording of "Where Have All the Flowers Gone?" was a turntable hit, but supposedly sold only about 150,000 records. It was an important record for Capitol Records and the Kingston Trio, because it was the first new release since Dave Guard, the original leader of the group, had been replaced by John Stewart. The label and the group's management were intent on reassuring the public that the group's sound was unchanged. Although a DJ can create a turntable hit, ultimately the public determines what music will sell.

Can Payola Be Prevented?

It is probably impossible to prevent the practice of payola entirely. However, careful regulation by state and federal authorities can limit the extent of its influence. This might involve the FCC insisting that stations observe their responsibilities to do community-based programming, examination of the relationship between airplay and actual record sales, and even cooperation with the Internal Revenue Service (IRS) on reported income.

The power of radio has diminished since the halcyon days of the 1980s. In addition, there are other outlets, notably XM and Sirius Satellite Radio, which merged their operations in late 2008. Because satellite radio is so involved in niche programming, the ability of a label to buy cost-effective airplay is necessarily far less than it is on other radio stations. The problem with satellite radio is the relatively high subscription fees that the consumer must pay in order to access the programs. Because each of these outlets has dozens of channels devoted to various specialized musical genres, they represent a new opportunity for record companies. Internet radio and various syndicated radio programs such as *A Prairie Home Companion, River City Folk, Mountain Stage,* and *E Town* represent a new opportunity for promoting records, and they allow acts to be heard performing live on radio. Cable television also has numerous channels of radio, representing still more opportunities for the promotion of records.

Terms to Know

Chat board *26*
Cut-out *19*
End caps *25*
Federal
  Communications
  Commission
  (FCC) *27*
iPod *21*
In stores *23*

iTunes *21*
Listening station *25*
MySpace *22*
Napster *20*
One sheet *22*
One stop *16*
Payola *27*
Playlists *21*
Rack jobber *16*

Showcases *24*
Street teams *24*
Suggested retail list
  price (SRLP) *18*
Tip sheets *29*
Turntable hit *30*
Viral marketing *26*

For Class Discussion

1. Do you currently buy music online or do you go to CD stores?
2. When you go to a retail record store, what captures your attention?
3. What sort of record store or Internet sales outlet do you enjoy?
4. How much of a factor is price when you buy a new album?
5. How could we find out what the actual sales of specific used albums are?
6. Can you think of an unusual record promotion that captured your attention?
7. Does repeated radio airplay lead you to buy a recording, or does it turn you off?
8. How do you get introduced to new music, and what makes you purchase it?
9. Can you think of an example of a turntable hit?

CHAPTER 3

Record Deals

HOW ARTISTS GET RECORD DEALS

According to most books about the music industry, the typical path to a record deal comes through an act hiring an entertainment business lawyer or a personal manager to contact the label. These books tell the reader that it is a waste of time for artists to try to contact labels directly. It is true that some labels will return unsolicited packages to the sender; however, a careful reading of the music trade paper *The Music Connection* tells a somewhat different story. *Music Connection* interviews record producers, label personnel, entertainment business attorneys, and music publishers. When asked if they accept unsolicited tapes, the record company replies fall into three categories. They are:

1. No
2. Yes
3. No, but if you really want to get a demo to me, you can figure out how to find me.

A surprising number of the replies fall into the last two categories. The third response is a bit confusing, but probably indicates that they can be approached through a secretary, through friends, by inviting them to a live performance, or through some other industry connection. Some of the people who do listen to unsolicited tapes will probably surprise the reader. One of the most recent "yes" replies came from Randy Jackson, the bass player, producer, and *American Idol* judge. Many other methods have been used by enterprising artists and new ones are evolving every day.

Music publishers and performing rights organizations are particularly rich sources of record company contacts. Music publishers are always looking to find songwriters who are also artists. Obviously, it is a great advantage to them to sign writers and place them with record labels. Many of the larger

Creative Sources for Record Deals

- Music publishers
- ASCAP, BMI, or SESAC representatives
- Record company sales and promotional people working in regional music centers
- Booking agents
- Family contacts who have some business or social connection with record company employees
- Record producers
- Recording engineers
- Web sites where the artist has posted material, including MySpace, YouTube, or the artist's own site
- Music videos
- Unsolicited tapes
- Live performances
- Meeting record people at music business conferences, such as SXSW
- Industry showcases
- Meeting record company people in social situations, whether planned or by accident
- Music industry services, such as Taxi
- Opening a show for an act that the label came to see, but they actually liked your band
- Through people who are friends of record company people
- Radio station music directors or DJs
- Social relationships with children of record company employees
- Chance meetings
- Recommendations by club owners or concert promoters
- Listings in music industry guides or annual publications
- Performing a song in a film, television show, or in a commercial
- Contests
- Recommendations by other artists already signed to the label

publishers have reasonably sophisticated recording studios that they use to make demos of songs. Some of these studios are sufficiently well-equipped to produce excellent albums. Publishers also have many contacts with record producers and may be willing to finance a well-produced demo in exchange for picking up the publishing rights to your songs.

Performing rights organizations are constantly in contact with music publishers and record companies, and can serve the function of opening doors for the songwriter-artist. They receive no specific financial gain for providing this service, but it is to their advantage to sign promising writers to their performing rights organization.

The influence of regional record sales, promotion people, or radio station personnel depend on the label's opinion of their ability to spot talent. This will vary according to the relationship between these people and a particular

Lyle Lovett

The late Merlin Littlefield was an executive at ASCAP in Nashville for some years. One day a young man named Lyle Lovett walked into his office. Lyle had a unique look, including a brushed-up hair style, which was rather unusual for Nashville during the mid-1980s. Lyle had tried to get record and publishing deals but had no luck in his quest. Rather than being put off by Lyle's appearance, Merlin found himself drawn to this intriguing artist. It turned out that both Lyle and Merlin were Texans, and that further cemented their relationship.

Merlin made a few calls, but initially everyone that he spoke to thought that Lovett was "too weird for Nashville." In the meantime he continued to encourage Lyle by telling him that he thought he was an exceptional songwriter. As a result of his efforts, Lyle signed a music publishing agreement with what was then MCA (now Universal), and this in turn led to a record deal and Lyle's long-term success as a writer and recording artist. Today, no one would question Lovett's writing or performing abilities, as evidenced by the longevity of his career. However, he needed to be introduced to the Nashville power brokers in a way that they could understand. Without Littlefield's assistance, this might have taken a long time to happen, or Lovett might have become discouraged and given up his dreams. Furthermore, many people in Littlefield's position would have given up after some industry movers and shakers rejected Lovett.

record label. It is difficult for the artist to know whether the label will respect the judgment of these people, or consider them to be a nuisance. In some cases, record company employees are reluctant to assist local groups because they are afraid that if the powers that be at the label don't like an artist, it may reflect badly on them.

Family and social connections are, of course, unpredictable. However, if you live in one of the music industry centers, it is definitely an option that is worth exploring. You may have a cousin or an in-law who has a connection in the industry. This is not a card that can be played with great frequency. If someone in your family has connections in the music industry and they present a demo of your band that is poorly received, they may be jeopardizing their own standing in the business.

This brings up an interesting point with regard to record deals. Many of the most successful acts have been repeatedly rejected by record companies. The Beatles, for example, were supposedly turned down twice by every label in England, and one label representative even told their manager that they were one of the worst groups that he had ever heard. No matter who is handling your band's business, whether it is a personal manager, a lawyer, or a friend, they should be in it for the long haul, and not become discouraged at record company rejections. If one or two negative comments deters your business representative from pursuing other record companies, then you may have hired the wrong person to represent you. By contrast, repeated rejections, with some of the same artistic objections to a group, such as "the lead singer sings out of tune," "they can't write coherent songs," or "their style has no individual identity," should lead the representative to have a serious conversation with the band in order to explore whether these comments are accurate.

There might be any number of reasons why a record company rejects a band, and some of these factors have little to do with the band itself. Here is a list of some sample objections:

- The songs aren't focused
- The band doesn't play well together
- I don't hear any hits (this is probably the ultimate cliché in record company rejections)
- We already have too many (fill in the blanks, for example boy bands, rap groups, female bluegrass lead singers)

There may be other reasons that the record company does not reveal:

- I (the A&R person) am about to quit to go to another label
- We have signed too many bands this year already
- We are cutting our artist roster
- I don't like or understand this style of music

There also may be other unpredictable factors involved, such as the fact that the person listening to the demo may be distracted by something going on at the company or by another personal situation.

Industry showcases may be set up by the artist or the artist's manager. The key question is whether the showcase will attract record label people who have the power to sign artists. In order to achieve this result, the artist must create some sort of industry buzz that brings label people out, or the artist must be associated with a personal manager or a record producer who has a reputation of finding and developing outstanding acts. If enough industry people attend the showcase, it may stimulate the interest of a label that would not otherwise be open. If the artist does a great show, it may even create a bidding war between two or more companies.

Playing at conferences or other industry events is a different sort of showcase. **SXSW (South by Southwest)**, an annual event in Austin, is a week-long scene of showcases, exhibits, and music industry panels. If an act is fortunate enough to be selected for a showcase in Austin, they will be competing with over one thousand other bands, and may find relatively few people in the audience. Quite possibly, none of the audience will be industry people, and the audience will consist of music fans and other musicians. Nevertheless, it is possible for a band to break through this seemingly unproductive wall if a performance is good enough to cause audience members to spread the word to other conference attendees. SXSW has become such an important industry event that some bands come down to Austin to play in the street, hoping that a label representative or a music publisher will hear them! This is a very, very long-shot approach, but nothing is cast in stone in the music industry.

Niche music organizations, such as the IBMA (International Bluegrass Music Association) and the North American Folk Music and Dance Alliance offer annual meetings replete with conference showcases. Because these

The White Stripes Take Off

Although the early SXSW festivals were credited with helping to launch the careers of many bands, most performers today feel the festival works best for those bands who already have a record deal who are looking to expand their base or make new connections in the business. This can be as simple as booking gigs to finding a Japanese distributor for the band's recordings.

Still, there are those legendary shows that have become part of the festival's lore. The White Stripes were not totally unknown when they appeared at the festival in 2001, having already released three albums. Through their booking agent, Dan Kaplan, they were able to land a prime spot on Saturday night at the festival. They had just completed recording their album *White Blood Cells,* and the buzz from the festival helped make the record a break-out independent hit. Among those in the audience was the British critic Steve Chick, an influential writer for *NME* (*New Musical Express*). He loved the band's performance, and spread the word to England. From being a moderately successful regional band, the Stripes became the "saviors" of rock and roll.

conferences are attended by smaller independent record labels, a particularly spectacular conference showcase may lead to a record deal with one of these outlets. However, this level of music conference is more apt to result in a band getting gigs than in a record deal.

The younger label reps spend quite a bit of time on the Internet, and for them MySpace and YouTube constitute important sources of talent. Some industry people prefer to make their first contacts with acts on the Net, because in a matter of minutes they can determine whether an act interests them. By contrast, going out to clubs or to industry showcases requires spending an entire evening eating dinner out, driving to wherever the act is showcasing, parking, and so forth.

There are also online services that help artists find recording deals. Taxi is a subscription service available to artists or songwriters. The artist pays a start-up fee, and then may submit material to the Taxi staff for evaluation. There are additional fees for each song submitted. In return, the Taxi professional staff submits a written critique of the work. They may then submit the work on behalf of the artist to record companies, music publishers, or music supervisors. (Music supervisors, sometimes referred to as the "new A&R," for their role in placing songs in film and on television, supervise the use of songs in these media.)

The Taxi reviewers have a background in A&R or music publishing. Whether they are the appropriate people to hear your particular music is difficult to know. In my opinion, Taxi best serves people who live in relatively remote markets and have no access to industry professionals. People who do have such access need to make their own decisions as to whether Taxi can connect them with enough contacts that they don't already have to justify the expense.

Scaling the Heights on MySpace

The power of MySpace is illustrated by hundreds of bands who have gained loyal followings—some bigger, some smaller—without having a traditional music industry contract. Jeff Howe reported in an article "The Hit Factory" in *Wired* magazine (November 2005) about a hardcore punk band originally from Dayton, Ohio, called Hawthorne Heights. The band knew that their music was popular among a group of dedicated listeners but wasn't currently topping the charts—or even generating moderate interest among mainstream labels. After signing with the small independent Victory Records, the group decided to market themselves through establishing a MySpace profile. By spending several hours a day on the site, and cultivating their "friends," they had landed twenty thousand fans by the time the album was released in 2004. This number grew tenfold to two hundred thousand quickly, as band members responded personally to every new fan. Their debut album sold over five hundred thousand copies, and they were the headliners on 2004's Warped Tour, a leading showcase for punk rockers.

Howe summarized how MySpace was revolutionizing the music business:

> [MySpace] artists have discovered what could be the first serious business model for music in the post-Napster era. The old way of doing things, which counted on a few blockbusters to finance dozens of expensive failures, is yielding little besides a decline in major label revenue. By contrast, "MySpace bands," as the site's publicist refers to them, keep production and promotion costs as low as possible. They give away their best two or three songs as downloads or streams and use social networking and email blasts to reach an audience hungry for new music. Converts become zealots, more than making up for any lost CD revenue through sales of concert tickets, T-shirts, messenger bags, hoodies, posters, and bumper stickers. With little fanfare, these groups are creating a new middle class of popular music: acts that can make a full-time living selling only a modest number of discs, on the order of 50,000 to 500,000 per release.

There are numerous contests that take place on a regional and local basis that provide the winners with prizes such as a record release, free recording time, a music publishing deal, or cash. Entering these contests is a bit like playing the lottery, and the large contests get thousands of entries. They can also be lucrative events for the sponsors, because there are generally fees charged to enter. I suggest that if you enter a contest, whether it is a songwriting event or one for recording artists—*despite* the rhetoric used by these contests that the quality of the recording is of no importance—try to make a good-quality recording, insofar as you can do so without breaking the bank. Imagine having to listen to dozens or even hundreds of badly recorded demos, and I think you will understand why this is necessary.

One other path to recording deals exists for singer-songwriters or record producers. There are a number of instances where artists got record deals because they had written hit songs for other people. Because the industry pays close attention to hit songs, this gave the artists credibility with record company people. Naturally the songwriter or producer had to establish his credentials as an artist, as well as a writer or producer. A few examples of people who entered the record world this way include Jesse Harris, John Denver, and Missy Elliott.

TV PLACEMENTS AND COMMERCIALS

A relatively new source of record deals or promoting albums is the placement of an artist's songs on TV commercials or network shows. It is sometimes possible for the act to negotiate a screen credit that leads the viewer to the artist's Web site. If the show is a top-rated one, this will definitely get the attention of record labels. The same device is used to promote artists who already have existing record deals. In some instances, as I will discuss later, the act takes a reduced fee or no fee at all in exchange for the screen credit.

RECORDING CONTRACTS

When a record company decides to sign an artist, the first step is usually to draw up a **deal memo**. A deal memo is a short list of the major points that will be present in the contract. It will include such matters as the term (length) of the agreement, the **advance** (an amount of money paid up front that is recouped later from royalties) and royalty percentages, and recording budget offered to the artist.

When the actual contract is presented, most first-time artists will go into shock. It is not unusual for recording contracts to have over a hundred pages of densely packed prose, covering all present and future possibilities in the industry. Clearly, there are few if any artists who have either the expertise or patience to wade through such a document. This is when an entertainment industry lawyer enters the picture. Artists who live in small towns or remote areas of the country are well advised to use a lawyer who is a specialist in the entertainment industry to negotiate on their behalf. The best entertainment lawyers are usually found in the major music industry towns. Entertainment lawyers simply have more experience in negotiating these agreements and often know the people with whom they are negotiating.

Fees for entertainment lawyers range from $300 to $600 an hour, or they may be hired for a percentage of the deal. Some entertainment lawyers also take on the responsibility of shopping record deals, although this is becoming less common as the major labels have cut down on the number of artists that they are willing to sign.

If an artist agrees to pay a lawyer a percentage of the deal, the artist should be careful that the percentage only includes income earned from records, not money earned from live performances or other sources, such as merchandising deals. The artist and manager also should take care that the lawyer doesn't focus on the initial advance to the exclusion of the percentages set forth as royalties. To put this in another way, the lawyer may prefer to land a large advance, rather than ongoing royalties, because it will result in his obtaining an immediate return, whereas royalty percentages are only meaningful down the road after one or more albums have been released. The artist is planning on a long-term career, but the lawyer knows that the majority of artists, unfortunately, are not successful.

It should be obvious that an artist should never hire a lawyer recommended by a record company, because this can result in a conflict of interest for the lawyer.

Contents of Record Company Contracts

LENGTH OF AGREEMENT   The first thing mentioned in the contract will be the length of the agreement. This used to be expressed in terms of the number of years, but current practice focuses on the number of albums that the artist will deliver over the course of the agreement. Under the previous system, a band might record, for example, two albums in a period of five years, and then would have completed its obligations to the record company. If the agreement specifies that the band *must* deliver five albums, then this same artist would clearly remain under contract to the company after five years, until they had delivered the appropriate number of albums. Note that, in California, personal service agreements are capped at seven years. The artist and their representative should pay attention as to where the contract is executed, because the state of Idaho, for example, has no entertainment law, and no such restrictions on the term of personal service contracts.

OPTIONS   The length of the contract will be expressed in terms of **options**. Although the word "options" implies mutual choice, in this case the options are entirely on the side of the record company. At a time specified before the end of the first year, the record company must exercise its option to continue recording the artist. This option must be exercised in written form to the artist's business representative.

GUARANTEES DELINEATED IN THE CONTRACT   The artist guarantees that he or she is not under contract to any other record company. The record company guarantees to record the artist during a specified period. The artist also may attempt to get the record company to guarantee that the recording will be released. This is to protect against the company recording the artist but not releasing the product. By contrast, a guaranteed release is not a guarantee of promotion. The company might put out a very limited number of records, or sell them only in one part of the country. I have known several artists whose records were indeed released, directly into cut-out bins, where they could be bought for pennies. A talented singer-songwriter named Peter McCabe had an album out for a label in Denver that had a distribution agreement with a major. A mutual friend told me about this "just released" album, which I bought about two days later out of a cut-out bin in New Orleans for $.59.

DELIVERY REQUIREMENTS   The contract sets forth that the artist will deliver a master tape to the company. It may also specify that the company must find the finished product to be "commercially viable." This is tricky territory, indeed, for one person's notion of what is "commercial" may vary wildly from that of another listener. The company can—and often does—use this clause as a way of canceling the contract. If the original person who signed the artist has left for another job, or has been fired, no one else at the company may be familiar with or supportive of the artist. If that person left because of a disagreement with management, the new A&R staff will be less likely to want to continue supporting his or her artists. Possibly the current staff would never have signed the artist in the first place. Under such circumstances, it is not so much that the new album is regarded as being noncommercial, but that the band is identified with a former employee.

Another variation on this theme occurs when an act known for a particular style of music decides to move in another musical direction. The label may see promoting the new musical style as an impossible task, because clearly the band's original fan base will not support the new album. Neil Young's *Trans* and Joni Mitchell's *Mingus* albums represented the artists moving in directions that the labels felt would not be acceptable to the fans, who had other musical expectations of these artists.

PUBLICITY   This part of the contract specifies that the artist allows the record company to use her photograph in press releases and in any advertising.

Transcending Fans' Expectations

When Neil Young released his *Trans* album in 1983, his fans were baffled. Following decades of heartfelt material sung in Young's expressive, reedy voice, here was an album where a Vocoder—an electronic device designed to distort a singer's natural voice—was used to rob Young's singing of any of its distinguishing factors. Song titles like "We R in Control" and "Computer Cowboy" sounded like rejects from a Kraftwerk album. And Young's trademark grungy, hard-rock accompaniment was replaced by anonymous sounding synthesizers and drum machines. The album was rejected by Young's long-time label, Reprise, and led him to sign with a new label, Geffen.

Young's willingness to try on various styles was most evident in the 1980s when he veered from acoustic country, country rock, grunge, electric blues, and social-protest. Although it allowed Young to stretch his artistic muscles—sometimes with successful and sometimes with less than meaningful results—it left his fans gasping for breath as each new album unveiled a new style. Geffen gave up trying to support the artist after just four years, and he returned to Reprise with a blues-rock CD, *This Note's For You*, in 1988. Clearly unrepentant, Young has continued to follow his own muse into the twenty-first century. However, it is a rare artist who has the luxury—or the clout—to defy the industry in this way.

OWNERSHIP OF MASTERS AND RERECORDING LIMITATIONS Unless it is otherwise specified in the contract, the record company owns the physical **master** recording, and can reissue it, delete it from the catalog, or do whatever it wishes with it. Artists at a more advanced stage of their careers seek to either obtain ownership of the master, or be allowed to buy it back from the record company in a set period of time after the contract expires or the recording is deleted from the company's catalog.

Most contracts state that a song cannot be rerecorded by the artist. That limitation may be structured as a period of time after the original recording was made, or after the expiration of the contract.

"INDIVIDUALLY AND SEVERALLY" It is quite common for members of a group to leave the group, or for the group to break up. In order to protect their investment in a group, record companies specify that in addition to the group being under contract to the record company, each member of the group is also under contract to it. The language that is often used in contracts states that each group member is **"individually and severally"** a party to the contract. This clause is a result of a dispute between a 1950s doo-wop group The Platters and their record company (Mercury) when Tony Williams, the lead singer of the group, left the group to go out on his own. Mercury sued to keep him under contract but lost the suit because the contract did not specify that he was under contract as an individual artist in addition to his obligations as a member of The Platters.

Usually all that the record company wants is a right of first refusal. In other words, if a group breaks up, they want to have the right to record the various members as soloists or in new groups, but they reserve the right not to do so if they feel that the new group has no commercial potential.

RECORDING RESTRICTIONS ON LABEL ARTISTS Most labels will demand that artists not perform in a lead role on other recordings. If the artist appears as a back-up singer or instrumentalist, the company will usually require that it be asked for written permission, and that a credit on the album read "Jane Jones appears through the courtesy of Conglomerate Records." The company may also ask that no photographs, or at least no photographs of the artist alone, appear on other artists' albums.

Under certain circumstances, such as movie soundtrack albums, or projects where artist A sings on artist B's album and then artist B returns the favor, the label may allow its artist to appear as a soloist on another label's album.

KEY MAN CLAUSES I have already outlined several situations where a label employee signs an artist and then moves on to a new position, leaving the artist with no advocate. The solution to this dilemma resides in the **key man clause**.

The key man clause specifies that if the person who signed the artist to the label leaves the company, the artist has the right to abrogate the contract and leave. This clause may also appear in personal management and other contracts. Although the label may resist agreeing to such a provision, it is one worth fighting for. It is a necessary protection that recognizes the transitory nature of the entertainment business. The key man clause can also be invoked if the person at the label retires or dies.

UNIONS   Major label deals specify that every member of an act must be a member of either AFM (the American Federation of Musicians), if they are instrumentalists, or AFTRA (the American Federation of Television and Radio Artists), if they are singers. All of the major labels and many smaller labels are signatories to the agreements of these unions, and must agree that their artists are union members.

ADVANCES AND UNION PAYMENTS   The major labels all agree to pay union wages to their artists, and to contribute to the unions' health and welfare and pension funds. Many of the major labels now follow the custom of paying for a union session for each song that a band records. (This is $370, including pension and health and welfare under the AFM agreements.) The union in turn waives its provisions that a recording session is three hours long, and that overtime must be paid after three hours. That agreement still applies to any studio musicians that the band hires in addition to their normal personnel. (Details about the union agreement are covered in Chapter 5.)

Advances are any monies paid to the artists above the union wages, and not included in the making of the record, such as studio fees, production fees, instrumental rentals, and so on. In periods when the record business was in better economic shape, large advances were not an unusual phenomenon. Today, large advances are only given to proven artists, or to new artists whose talents are so obvious that they have provoked a bidding war between the labels. There are two types of advances. In one, the artist is simply given money as a **signing bonus**; the other is an advance against royalties, and is charged against the artist's royalty account.

ROYALTIES   Royalties are paid after the costs of making the recording are earned back. This is referred to as **recoupment**. Some record companies compute royalties based on the **wholesale** price of records (the price that a record store is charged for the record), whereas others use the suggested **retail** price (the suggested price for consumers to pay for a record). The standard calculation is that a 10 percent of retail royalty is roughly equivalent to a 20 percent of wholesale one. There is some disagreement among the authorities regarding the current typical royalty rate. According to the tenth edition of *This Business of Music* (2008), the typical record royalty rate is 9 to 12 percent of the suggested retail selling price. The sixth edition of Donald S. Passman's *All You Need To Know About The Music Business* (2006) claims that royalties for new artists are 13 to 16 percent of the *wholesale* selling price (6 to 8 percent of retail), mid-level artists receive 15 to 17 percent of wholesale (7.5 to 8.5 percent of retail), and superstars get 18 to 20 percent of the wholesale price (9 to 10 percent of retail.) The fifth edition of Jeffrey and Todd Brabec's *Music Money And Success* (2008) states that royalties for new artists range from 10 percent of retail at the low end to a high end of 12 percent. All of these writers are actively involved in the music industry, and it's not clear why their numbers vary so much. In any case, this gives the reader a general approximation of where record royalties sit in today's music marketplace.

Many recording contracts contain **royalty escalation clauses**. These rises in the royalty rate occur either on the renewal period of the contact (annually) or they are based on the artist's album's sales. These escalation clauses are highly negotiable, but may be based on sales figures of 250,000, 500,000, a million units, or more. These possible increases are part of the contract because the record company recognizes that it is making considerably more money at the higher sales rates, and they anticipate that a happy artist will remain with the company beyond the term of the contract. They will also likely recommend the label to their peers, and even call the company's attention to other artists that they feel might be a good match for them.

Different Types of Contracts

For many years, contracts were relatively cut and dried. The artist was signed to an album or a singles deal. If one or more of the singles was successful, an album contract followed. As the record business expanded, other types of agreements came into play. For example, during the 1960s labels started to sign artists to **development deals**. Essentially, the company offered financial support to the artist, usually one who was young and unproven, in return for which the artist would be under contract to the company when it deemed the artist was ready to record. Kate Bush, the British art-pop-rock artist, was signed to such a deal with EMI when she was only sixteen years old. In the next section, I will discuss a number of the deals that are currently being made by record companies.

ONE-OFF DEALS   Some small labels allow an artist to make a single album and then leave the label. The label may have a very specific project in mind, may not believe in tying artists up in lengthy agreements, or they may really want to work with a particular artist, but the artist is reluctant to make a long-term commitment. It is highly unlikely that anyone making a major investment in an artist is going to accept a one-off deal.

When Sub Pop Records in Seattle recorded the band Soundgarden, the band was signed to a one-off deal. The record took off, and the band was then signed by Epic. Sub Pop then realized that they had basically jump-started the career of the band, only to have the real income harvested by Epic, a subsidiary of Columbia Records. When Sub Pop signed Nirvana, the deal was a more typical contract. Geffen Records was desperate to sign Nirvana, and they paid Sub Pop a production royalty on future recordings for the rights to record the band. Supposedly, the first royalty received by Sub Pop under this deal amounted to more than a million dollars, an immense fortune for a small and struggling label.

UPSTREAM DEALS   Sometimes independent labels make deals with major labels that are called "P&D," or **promotion and distribution deals**. Under these deals, the smaller label gives the major a percentage of its receipts, and in turn the major label promotes, distributes, and even manufactures the product. A current modification of this deal is an **upstream deal**, where the major label has an option to take over the artist's contract. In return, the independent will receive a production royalty for having discovered and signed the artist. An artist who doesn't wish to be signed to a major label should beware of upstream deals. Other artists may regard an upstream deal as a form of validation, knowing that being on a larger label will provide more promotion, exposure, and, hopefully, more sales.

360 DEALS   One of the newer wrinkles in record deals is the so-called **360 deal**. In these deals the record company makes a strong financial commitment to the artist, in return for which the artist gives part or all of its income from recording, publishing, merchandising, and touring. EMI has a deal like this with the band Korn and the British pop star Robbie Williams. In 2008, to the surprise of many observers, the tour promotion company Live Nation announced multimillion dollar deals of this nature with Madonna and hip-hop artist Jay-Z. Warner Music has even signed opera star Katherine Jenkins to a 360 deal. The deal, according to *Billboard* magazine, includes sponsorships and merchandise. Given the poor sales of most classical recordings, these areas may provide a stronger revenue stream for the label than the record sales will achieve.

Three hundred sixty deals date back to independent labels such as Motown, where the record company owned the music publishing of the artists, produced and managed the act in-house, and also had choreographers on staff to teach an act dance steps. The current deals can include virtually every aspect of an artist's career, and they spill over into music merchandising rights, which weren't much of a factor during in the 1960s.

An artist in the early stages of a music career will not be offered anything like the reported $120 million that Madonna is getting for her 360 deal. It is up to the artist and manager to determine whether an additional small infusion of cash is worth giving away rights for a long period of time. If the artist is a good songwriter, even a percentage of the publishing rights could be worth millions of dollars over time. From an artist's point of view, one advantage of a 360 deal is that under the terms of a superstar 360 deal, the investment that the company must make in the artist virtually guarantees extensive promotion and commitment from the label. As record companies search for new sources of revenue, and industry enterprises such as ticketing and concert promotion companies do the same, 360 deals will undoubtedly be structured in new ways.

Live Nation

Live Nation is the premiere producer of concerts and also owns a number of venues. Before 2008, it was not in the record producing business, but it made sense for the company to expand into this area, so that it could enjoy a percentage of an artist's entire revenue flow: records, concerts, and merchandise.

What is the advantage to an artist like Madonna to signing with Live Nation? In her case, the company guarantees her a large infusion of cash over a long period of time (ten years, in her case). Essentially, Live Nation is betting that she will retain her popularity over at least the next decade, so that a share of her merchandising rights, for example, will continue to be of value nine years down the road. Because Live Nation is not a traditional record company, Madonna is likely to have more freedom in producing her records, although this is probably not much of a factor with a proven artist with a long track record of successful albums. In any case, her income from recording is probably far smaller than it once was; she no longer tops the charts, and the record industry in general has seen declining sales of all artists. So it makes sense to focus on live performing and merchandising as areas for growth.

Always anxious to exploit new business models and build on her recording income, Madonna is shown on a satellite feed as Apple chief Steve Jobs announces that her music will be available for the first time on iTunes, in 2005. Photo: © Krista Kennell/Zuma/Corbis, all rights reserved.

There was another advantage to Jay-Z to sign with Live Nation. Live Nation controls several major concert arenas, which can hold large crowds and thus guarantee good income to artists. However, concert promoters are notoriously wary about presenting hip-hop shows in arenas, because the insurance for these shows is appreciably higher than, for example, country and western shows. Because of this deal, Live Nation will be motivated to present more shows with Jay-Z than they probably would have done otherwise.

Live Nation's deals with other groups vary depending on what the company and the artists hope to achieve. Their deal with superstar band U2, for example, does not include records. The band was able to negotiate part of their fee to be paid in Live Nation stock, allowing them to reap some of the benefit of the company's ongoing success.

PARTNERSHIPS   A few small independent labels establish a partnership with the artist. Each party contributes half of the costs of making the recording and manufacturing the CD. They also share fifty-fifty in any profits.

A partnership works best for artists who are in a niche market. Usually, these acts will have a fairly good idea of how many albums they will be able to sell. Taking the risk of financing half of the album clearly results in their earning a much higher royalty rate then they will get under any other deal. Furthermore, because the expenses of making the recording are quite clear, the many deductions that the reader will soon see constitute a part of the "normal" recording contract do not come into play.

WHY FEW ARTISTS EARN ROYALTIES FROM RECORDS

In order for an artist to earn royalties from the sale of albums, the company must first recoup the cost of making these records. It would seem to be a fairly easy computation to make, and one wonders why many artists claim to never earn a cent—or to be in debt to—their labels. However, these horror stories are real, and they are based on the fact that many more expenses than you might first believe can go into making a record.

In order to make computations simple, let's assume a royalty of 10 percent of the retail selling price of an album, and set that price at $20. The artist therefore will be earning $2 in royalties for each album sold based on retail price. Let's assume that the album sells five hundred thousand copies, so theoretically the artist will have earned a million dollars from the project. This table shows the various deductions that may be taken from these royalties.

Expense	Total Cost	Total Royalty
		$1,000,000
Recording album: studio time, preproduction, lodging and food allowance, same for actual production, including packaging costs, CD copies, use of outside musicians, trip to Los Angeles to record the album	$250,000	$750,000
Two videos: $100,000 for each, half charged to artist	$200,000	$650,000
90 percent of sales provision: Many label contracts specify that the artist will be paid on only 90 percent of total sales. This dates from the breakage fee from the days of 78 rpm records when many fragile records were broken before they could reach the market.	$100,000	$550,000

Expense	Total Cost	Total Royalty
Foreign sales reductions: one hundred thousand copies of the album were sold in Europe and the contract specifies that these are paid at 75 percent of the normal rate.	$75,000	$475,000
Record club royalties and any other special sales: The contract stipulates a 50 percent royalty rate for these sales; fifty thousand albums at a 50 percent rate.	$50,000	$425,000
Producer advance: $50,000: Artist royalty now $355,000. However, because the producer's royalties must be paid from the first copy of the record sold, after the record has recouped, and five hundred thousand copies were sold, the producer's 3 percent royalty earned him $150,000.	$150,000	$275,000
Independent Promotion: At the insistence of the artist's manager, the company hired independent promoters. It cost $100,000, half charged to the artist.	$50,000	$225,000
Reserves: The label reserves a certain amount (in this case, 25 percent) of the royalties against possible future returns. This amount is held for a period defined by the contract.	$250,000	($25,000)

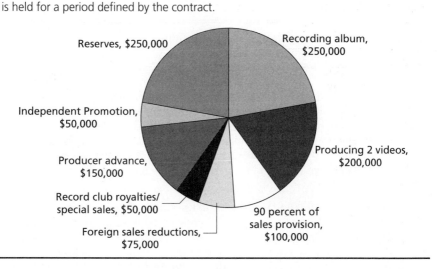

The bottom line: The artist gets no payment, and in fact owes the company $25,000.

Understanding how recording royalties are calculated underscores the importance of songwriting income—that is, publishing—to the success of any artist, and why it is so important that performers write their own material. (See Chapter 6 for a complete discussion of publishing income.)

Cross-Collateralization

What does it mean for the artist to be in debt to the record company? What it means is that when the next album gets recorded, an additional amount (the remaining unearned royalty on the first album) must be earned *before* the artist gets any royalties for the new album. This is known as **cross-collateralization**. Hopefully some of the royalties from the reserves will be released to the artist, assuming that some of those 125,000 albums are sold. If, however, there are more returns than the reserve, there will be an additional charge to recoup the already credited royalties! Once the same process is repeated for the second album—complete with all of the deductions along with a new reserve for its sales—the artist's debt may actually grow rather than shrink.

It should now be apparent why most recording artists never earn any significant royalties from their record deal. Those that are fortunate enough to retain their music publishing rights (assuming that they write songs, which is not always the case) at least will earn money for their songwriting work. However, remember that if the record label owns the artist's music publishing rights, they may also cross-collateralize monies that would normally be paid to the artist as a songwriter. That money will also be charged against the costs of making the album.

Semisonic Semisuccessful

Despite high hopes, few bands make a cent from recording, whereas the major labels are shielded from much loss by the many "deductions" they can take against royalties. Jake Slichter, in his book *So You Want To be A Rock and Roll Star: How I Machine Gunned A Roomful of Record Executives*, describes how his band Semisonic had a million-selling single, but made no money because their initial album bombed, and because their videos and independent promotion charges were high. Slichter describes how the terms of his first deal were laid out by executives from Elektra Records in a hot and noisy bar. Confused by the details, he vaguely realized that it would take enormous sales to cover all the costs; nonetheless, the excitement of having a major label express interest in his band led him to ignore his doubts:

> I listened to all this and was unable to keep all the Byzantine details of the agreements clear in my mind. I understood the basic principle— that the record company gets to charge all of its costs . . . and that it would require sales of a huge number of records before our recoupable debt could be cleared. . . . But the tingling excitement of discussing our pending deal with Elektra Records while sipping merlot in Minneapolis's fashionably bohemian Loring Bar . . . didn't facilitate sober assessment of our future . . .

ARTIST-OWNED LABELS

Because the cost of CD manufacturing has come way down, quite a few artists have started their own record labels. Some of these artists simply want to have some product to sell at their gigs. Others are more concerned with controlling the creative and business aspects of their recordings. Some of these artists have been able to build quite successful operations. John Prine's Oh Boy label has had some good-selling albums. Many observers cite Ani DiFranco as the poster child for the do-it-yourself ideology. Ani's Righteous Babe Records operates out of her hometown of Buffalo, New York. In addition to enjoying sales of over half a million copies on some of her albums, she also puts out albums by other artists. Women's music artist Holly Near operated Redwood Records during the 1980s. In addition to her own recordings, Near also issued recordings by other women's music artists and by artists who shared her radical political beliefs.

Early in their career, the Denver alternative rock band Big Head Todd & the Monsters employed several people on staff running their label. Partly because they were enjoying excellent sales in Denver, they then were able to get a major label deal with Irving Azoff's label Giant. They had one success-ful gold-selling album, and after the next few albums did not do as well, they returned to putting out their own records. Another Colorado label, the Boulder-based SCI, is a partnership between the band The String Cheese Incident and their managers. Their management team then signed another band, Yonder Mountain String Band, to the label. SCI functioned somewhat like a cooperative, sharing the ownership of several other businesses, includ-ing a travel agency for touring artists.

The problem with artist-run labels is that artists are generally quite busy with their own careers, and so they really need to have some assistance in the business area to make it all work efficiently. This can be the artist's manager, or, as is the case with DiFranco's label, a staff of a half a dozen or more people.

FINANCING YOUR OWN RECORD

A number of artists who don't have enough money to make an album have come up with creative ways of financing their production. One model is to sell advance subscriptions for the album. Utilizing the artist's fan base, the artist sells copies of the album in advance, much as magazine subscriptions are sold. The Canadian group Stringband made an album more than thirty years ago called *Thanks to the Following*. They were able to finance a quality production in a Toronto studio and in gratitude they listed the names of all of the subscribers on the back of the long-playing record (in very small type, of course). Recently, topical singer Anne Feeney did something simi-lar, and so did alternative rock artist Jill Sobule. I suspect that there are many local markets where artists have implemented their own version of this model.

Another way of raising money is to get it from family or friends. However, the artist must be very careful to explain to the funding sources that there is an excellent chance that they will see no return on their money. Otherwise, there are liable to be some very unpleasant repercussions to what were formerly close relationships.

Artists who have some reputation and credibility can sell shares in a forthcoming record. This requires a stockholder offering, and if it is a public offering, there are numerous hurdles to jump over in the form of federal regulations.

On countless occasions friends or even brief acquaintances of a group offer to "lend the band $10,000," or some amount of money because "you need to have an album." When these offers come in a club where alcohol is readily available, and when the person making the offer hardly knows the band, they are wisely dismissed as "whiskey talk." More serious offers should be examined carefully, remembering that if the act gives away percentages of the profits on their album, this giveaway will come on top of the commissions going to artists or managers.

Another way of getting a record deal is through the labels that colleges with music business programs operate. Schools such as the University of Miami, the University of Colorado at Denver, and Drexel University all have record labels. Each of these labels has its own rules, and sometimes at least one member of a band must be a student at the college. Working with one of these labels is a bit like signing with a young, inexperienced, and hungry manager. You get lots of energy, but not much experience. To find out more about opportunities of this sort, check out the Web site of the Music & Entertainment Industry Education Association (MEIEA) or MEISA, its student affiliate.

The band The Fray is a current hit act. They started their career in their hometown of Denver, when two of them were students at the University of Colorado at Denver. Their first recordings were done for the school's CAM Records label. The band has now achieved superstar status on Epic Records, with a major internet presence, many songs on television shows, and a platinum album. The Fray's second album was released in February 2009.

Distribution

Naturally, obtaining distribution is a necessity if an artist wants the album to be sold in record stores. This is a bit easier when distributing works digitally, because it isn't necessary to ship a physical product to the consumer. Many artists ship digital downloads from their Web site, using services such as PayPal to accept credit cards. It is also possible to sell CDs in this way, but they must be shipped to the consumer. This is an additional expense.

Diane Sward Rapaport's *How to Make & Sell Your Own Recording* is an excellent introduction to its subject. However, the last edition was written in 1999, and therefore includes comparatively little information about the

Internet and the digital age. It does cover such matters as developing a fan list, how to create album graphics, how to sell recordings at performances, and how to find a distributor or to sell albums on consignment at record stores.

The problem with consigning records is that the artist then has to devote considerable energy to collecting money. This involves phone calls, trips to the store, finding what day the person who writes the checks comes in to work, and so forth. As far as picking up distribution, unless the artist has something of a following, a distributor isn't apt to be interested. Large

Omaha Labels Make Good!

Omaha, Nebraska, not generally regarded as a music business hotspot, is home to two interesting independent record labels. Mannheim Steamroller is essentially the brainchild of a single person, engineer-producer-musician Chip Davis. Davis is a classically trained bassoon player, who toured with the Norman Luboff Choir. Later, he got a job writing jingles for an advertising agency in Omaha. Davis created a character named C. W. McCall, who delivered bread for the Old Home Bread Company. The role of C. W. McCall was played by Bill Fries, a copywriter. The commercials led to a successful recording career in country music for Fries. Davis wrote and produced the hit records "Convoy" and "Wolf Creek Pass" for him.

Meanwhile, Davis composed music, combining the use of such older musical instruments as harpsichord and recorder with synthesizers. He was unable to get a record deal for this music, so he released the recordings on his own American Gramaphone label. He named his "group" Mannheim Steamroller. His music combined eighteenth-century classical music influences with rock and roll. He marketed his first album, Fresh Aire, primarily to audio dealers, rather than record shops. Because of the high quality of the recording, it made an ideal "demo" record for high-end stereo equipment. Potential buyers were so impressed that they began to ask where they could get it. In 1984 he began to record Christmas music, and since that time, his holiday records have sold over twenty million records, and he has also toured successfully during the holiday season. Davis's story, operating his own record company and coming up with an off-the-wall idea that captured the imagination of millions of listeners, is an indication that it isn't only the major labels that experience big league success.

As if to show that lightning can indeed strike twice, two young Omaha rock enthusiasts named Mike Mogis and Robb Nansel established their own record label in 1993. Saddle Creek Records is named after a street in Omaha, and it was designed to capitalize on a number of Omaha artists, notably Conor Oberst (also known as Bright Eyes). A number of the label's artists have been friends since their school days, and the label has now expanded to include some artists who are not from Omaha. Oberst himself started a label called Team Love in 2004. His recordings have charted, and he can sell out large venues in major cities. Oberst left Saddle Creek in 2008, and he now records for Merge. In 2007, Saddle Creek opened a music venue in downtown Omaha.

independent distributors carry thousands of records on hundreds of labels, and they really can't be bothered to sell product unless it turns over on a fairly regular basis. If you attempt to get an independent distributor, you should check to see whether they distribute outside your immediate area. If they don't do this, you may do as well or better handling your own sales.

Here are some important points to consider before starting an artist-run record label:

- Is there sufficient financing to make a quality recording?
- Can the artist produce an album within reasonable budget restrictions?
- Is there evidence that there will be some demand for the product?
- Can the record get airplay?
- Is someone other then the artist handling the business so that when the artist is on tour the record company still functions?
- Is the artist well-organized enough to meet the demands of a business, undertaking a release schedule, writing new material, touring when the album comes out, and developing a fan base?
- Is the artist prepared to go on the road to promote the album?
- Is a mechanism in place to copyright the songs, produce album graphics, get a bar code, and send review copies to newspapers and magazines?
- Is the artist a self-starter, with enough motivation to start the project and finish it within a reasonable amount of time?

Niche Marketing

There are a number of ways to market records that are directed toward specific interest groups. Putamayo Records started out as a world music label that was an offshoot of a store that imported clothing. Initially, the records were simply sold in the store. As the record label became increasingly successful, the owner sold his clothing business in order to concentrate on the label. It is now a successful full-time business and the records are sold not only in record stores but also in health food markets and other clothing stores.

Certain recordings, such as albums that involve the sounds of the great outdoors, can be sold in tourist shops in national parks, and in the towns where tourists come to enjoy scenery. There are some artists who have specifically written music that is intended to be marketed at places such as the Grand Canyon. This music is intended as a musical depiction of a locale, and can be an attractive souvenir for visitors. Similarly, albums can be designed around historical themes, such as a famous battle or the history of a particular area. This sort of album can do very well in the place that the music describes, and it is not generally necessary or wise to market it on a national level. Songs about a particular sport, such as skiing, can be sold at ski shops or ski lodges.

Specialty retailers can be ideal outlets for records. Children's records are often sold in toy stores or stores that sell educational materials. Some bookstores and art galleries sell recordings, particularly if the artist is known in a particular area, or plays at art gallery openings. Christian music can be marketed through Christian bookstores, as well as at churches.

Starbucks became such an important outlet for music that the company even started its own record label, and has enjoyed mass-market sales with well-known artists such as Bob Dylan and Ray Charles. In 1999, Starbucks purchased the Hear Music label, which had previously produced CD collections for the retailer. Hear eventually signed individual artists, such as Paul McCartney, who would appeal to the Starbucks demographic. Recently, Starbucks has trimmed its staff and efforts in this area, but similar retailers such as the Whole Foods supermarket chain have begun to carry albums. The older demographic that fans of these artists present is not a problem for a coffee chain whose items customarily sell for $3 or more.

In gospel music, bluegrass, folk, and polka music, among other styles, audiences expect the artist to sell albums at performances. It is up to the artist to make a strong connection with the audience that will inspire them to purchase albums during or immediately after the end of the show. This can be accomplished by the artist performing selections from their newest album, and also by mentioning that the album is available at a table outside the performance space.

Niche marketing can be practiced by the individual artist, by a record label, or by a company that seeks to match its customer base with the entertainment consumer.

PIRACY, BOOTLEGGING, AND FILE SHARING

The record business has faced several severe crises over the last ten years. **Piracy** is the illegal duplication of recordings. Pirates copy recordings either by illegally accessing master tapes or by copying directly from commercially available CDs. In many parts of the world, notably China, it is possible to buy current pirated copies of CDs at a fraction of their normal price.

The U.S. and Chinese governments have been involved for years in an odd dance. This scenario begins with the U.S. government threatening the Chinese with restrictions on trade if the Chinese do not police intellectual property rights. The Chinese then close down one or more CD manufacturing plants that are illegally duplicating copyrighted product without permission. Life then returns to normal, and illegal duplication continues, until the American government protests again. The problem is that the illegal duplication of CDs is a relatively small piece of the trade that takes place between the two countries. Moreover, the Chinese government owns millions of dollars in American treasury notes and bonds. Neither country wants to destroy or limit the commercial relationship between the two nations.

For the time being, illegal duplication continues, not only in China, but virtually all over the world. In several African countries, major labels have closed down operations, because piracy was so widespread that legitimate sales were nearly nonexistent.

Bootlegging takes place when someone or some company illegally obtains access to recordings that were never commercially released, or have been allowed to go out of print. The bootlegger then issues the album as a new release, often in a plain white package. It is illegal to sell bootlegs over the counter, because the bootleggers do not legally have the right to manufacture these albums.

Bootlegging started during the 1950s. The long-playing record had just entered the marketplace, and the large record companies often sat on incredible treasures. This was particularly true of jazz recordings. The companies decided that there wasn't enough of a market for jazz to reissue it. Some dedicated jazz fans began issuing bootleg copies of these recordings. One label even trumpeted its piracy by calling itself Jolly Roger Records. Peculiarly enough, some of these bootlegs were pressed by the RCA Victor label, the very label that was the source of the original recordings. Eventually, the major labels took action against the bootleggers. They also began to legally reissue some of these recordings.

For whatever reason, Bob Dylan's sessions with The Band made during Dylan's recuperation from his motorcycle accident in 1966–1967 were among the most popular bootlegs. Many of the songs, written or cowritten by Dylan, were intended as demos designed to get other artists to record them. Clinton Heylin's book *Bootleg* offers many details of how the bootleggers operated, and how they were able to make a profit peddling their musical wares.

File sharing is the illegal duplication of recordings on the Internet by consumers. File sharing programs such as Napster, among many others, have gone in and out of business as the record companies have threatened to prosecute them for giving away music on the Internet. The Recording Industry Association of America (RIAA) has prosecuted both the Internet service providers such as Grokster, and the consumers who ripped these MP3s off the Web. The subject of the Internet and its effects on record sales and the music industry is discussed extensively in Chapter 10.

Terms to Know

For Class Discussion

1. What does an A&R person mean when he says that he doesn't accept unsolicited material but you can figure out how to reach him?
2. What would you do to score a record deal?
3. What is an industry showcase?
4. Are there any regional music conferences in the area where you live or attend school?
5. Are there any entertainment lawyers, record producers, independent record distributors, or record companies of any significance in your hometown or the city where you attend school?
6. Why are some formerly successful record stars quite poor in their middle or old age?
7. Would you sign or avoid a 360 deal? Why?
8. Omaha seems an unlikely location for two successful record companies. Can you point to any other relatively isolated area that has enjoyed similar success?
9. Have you ever bought a bootleg record? Why did you buy it?

CHAPTER 4

Intermediaries: Booking Agents, Personal Managers, and Business Managers

It's one thing to be a talented performer or singer/songwriter; it's another thing to know how to build a career. In this chapter, we look at a group of intermediaries—the professionals who represent talent—who can help to make a great performer a major star. These include booking agents, personal managers, and business managers. Each plays a unique role that changes over the course of an artist's career. They are generally the source of employment, image making, record deals, and endorsements. Good intermediaries can nurture talent and help new artists avoid bad decisions that can haunt them for years to come.

BOOKING AGENTS

Booking agencies, quite simply, function as employment agencies. They deal with anyone seeking to hire entertainers, and offer the talent to customers such as concert promoters, night club owners, college concert presenters, or anyone seeking to hire musicians. Booking agents can operate on a local, regional, or national level. They often can access work that is seldom available to the individual musician. One example is regional or national conventions. Every regional population center has events that draw people from neighboring cities. It may be a regional meeting of auto dealers, a medical gathering, a national convention of restaurant owners, or something similar. Many cities have built large convention centers and hotels in an attempt to gain this business.

Conventions book a variety of entertainers for their events. There may be music with meals, music for dancing, or musical shows. I refer to this sort of gig as "invisible work." It is invisible in the sense that it is not open to the public, and the entertainer is rarely advertised, although if a corporation

Working the Convention Circuit: The Dixie Chicks

Before they were major Nashville stars, the Dixie Chicks were a hard-working Texas-based quartet who made a good part of their living by playing local conventions. They made the most of their Texas roots by dressing in cowgirl costumes, emphasizing the Western Swing part of their repertoire. This was a real crowd pleaser for Texas-based corporations, who hired the Chicks to play at many national and regional conferences, mostly in their home state.

Although the work was lucrative, as time went on the band members realized they'd have to choose between regular business gigs and building their careers. The business jobs did little for their overall reputation, and limited the type of material they could play to what would be acceptable to their largely conservative audiences. Eventually, they decided it was more important to pursue a full career than to continue working conventions. The original lead vocalist, who had shaped the band's cowgirl image, left to be replaced by a more pop-oriented lead singer, Natalie Maines. The convention work ended, but the group landed a recording contract with Monument (a division of Sony), and went on to become a major country act, also crossing over into the pop charts.

flies a major act to a resort for a convention, there will be publicity within the company.

Conventions are often organized by people who do not live in the town where the event is taking place. It is natural for them to turn to booking agents in order to find talent. The corporate person involved in the convention will call the agent, describe what sort of music they want, and the two parties will agree on an act and on some level of compensation. The agent is paid a commission by the artist in exchange for procuring the job. It is the agent's responsibility to collect the money from the client and to pay the act.

Agents and Exclusivity

The size of booking agencies varies from a single person to organizations like the William Morris Agency with its worldwide staff. No major agency will represent an act unless the act signs an **exclusive agreement** with it. The agreement will specify that the agent must be paid a **commission** on any work that the artist obtains, whether or not the agent has literally procured the work for the artist.

It is possible for the artist to limit the scope of the contract in various ways. For example, the artist may have an ambition to write novels. Unless the booking agency has a very large and complex structure, there is no reason to believe that it will be particularly skilled at obtaining a book deal for the artist. Similarly, an artist who has dreams of becoming an actor might be signed with, for example, a regional booking agency in Minneapolis. The artist might want to retain his right to negotiate films deals for himself, or simply farm it out to a Hollywood agent. There are two goals in these examples. One is to withhold rights to aspects of a career that the artist feels the agent does not have expertise in negotiating. The second is to avoid a possible situation in which the artist is paying double commissions because an additional agent needs to be hired and paid separately.

One of the key questions in dealing with an agent is his demand for exclusivity. If you are working in a small town, signing an exclusive agreement means that you cannot work with other agents. Your initial agent may be well connected locally but lack the ability to market you beyond the local or regional area. If you are planning to expand your career to other areas of the country, signing with this agent can be a fatal mistake.

If a major agency wishes to sign you, it is important to come to an agreement about what sort of work you wish to obtain and to have some assurance that the agent can deliver that work. An artist should look carefully at the agency's artist roster, and determine whether the acts on the roster are musically relevant to the artist's musical style, and whether the agent with whom the artist is dealing has a basic understanding of where the act wishes to play. It is also a smart idea to talk with the other acts on the agency's roster and ask if the agency is doing a good job for them.

SELF-BOOKING

For an act working in a local market, there may be no compelling reason to use the services of a booking agent. However, if the artists wants to book themselves, then they have to develop good promotional materials, make dozens of phone calls, and follow these up with more calls, and handle pricing and contractual negotiations. Over the years, I have only met a handful of musicians who are good at handling all of these tasks. Even musicians with business talent usually have to eventually turn over the reins to a booking agent.

During the early stages of a band's career, many groups divide up these tasks among the band members: One person might handle the booking, one might be responsible for transportation, one might handle developing a graphic portfolio, and so on. Should you be in this position, I highly recommend Jeri Goldstein's book, *How to Be Your Own Booking Agent: The Musician & Performing Artist's Guide To Successful Touring*, second revised edition. Goldstein is a former booking agent, with considerable experience. Frankly, after you see all of the details that a booking agent handles, you may well decide that the band is better off farming out these details to a qualified agent.

Typical tasks performed by an agent include:

- Making dozens of calls and follow-up calls
- Making sure contracts are received, well in advance of the actual date
- Collecting substantial deposits on jobs, especially if the agent has never previously done business with a promoter or a club manager
- Making sure that the act's publicity is well written, attractive, and current

- Dealing with the college market, where a student may control what artists perform, and the person holding that position changes from year to year
- Buying tickets for the band, making sure that transportation is as cheap as possible, and providing the artist with clear and specific information about where they are going
- Double-checking all aspects of the contract, such as the name of the building, the time and date of the performance, the length of the show, the sound system, and so on
- Making sure there is a provision for accommodations in the contract that specifies whether the act gets single rooms or that a particular hotel or motel chain be used
- Carefully examining any restrictions in the contract that have to do with limitations on the geographic area where the band can appear on the same tour
- In the case of clubs, is there a provision that allows the owner to book the act again? If so, is there something in writing that provides for increased income for future bookings?
- Does the contract specify a time for equipment load-in, and a time for a sound check, well in advance of the show?
- Is there a provision for selling band merchandise? Will the band have to find someone to man the merchandise table, or will the promoter provide someone? Does the contract state that the promoter or hall receives a percentage of any merchandise sales?
- Is there clear and specific information about payment, for example, 50 percent on signing the contract, 50 percent in cash or certified check on completion of the engagement? If there is a percentage on top of the guaranteed payment, does it clearly define what constitutes legitimate deductible promoter expenses, such as advertising, the number of free tickets to the press, and hall rental?

Advantages of Using an Agent	Advantages of Doing It Yourself
Agent has many contacts that the artist could not access on her own	Artist pays no commission
Agent will probably get the maximum amount of money possible for the job	Artist makes all the decisions on her own without feeling any pressure to take jobs she does not wish to play
Agent will make calls and keep careful records, as well as doing many follow-up calls	Artist can pick and choose the type of venues that she prefers
Will deal with all contractual matters	Handles own travel arrangements and accommodations, (which could also be considered as a disadvantage.)
An agent may offer an act to a buyer when another act under contract to his agency is too expensive for a particular client, or is simply unavailable to do a gig	

Disadvantages of Using an Agent	Disadvantages of Doing It Yourself
10 to 20 percent of your gross income goes to the agent if he operates under a union franchise, sometimes much more if it's a nonunion gig	Necessity for relentless record-keeping
	Must make numerous follow-up calls
	Must keep track of and negotiate all contracts
May not understand your musical preferences, could pair you with an act that you do not like	Must try to establish whether the buyer is honest or financially stable
May develop routing for the artist that leaves him exhausted because of continual travel	
Not really equipped to deal with small-budget situations like house concerts	
May demand exclusivity	

THE COLLEGE MARKET AND BLOCK BOOKING

The college market offers many opportunities for beginning as well as better-established acts. College audiences seek the latest music, and are open to experimenting with new sounds. Colleges often have excellent performance spaces, which are designed for listening—unlike clubs, which can be noisy and more oriented toward drinking and socializing. Colleges often have reasonable entertainment budgets, and usually meet their obligations with a minimum amount of fuss—again, in contrast to some clubs that can be slow to pay, or may disappear over night without a trace. For all these reasons, agents often target the college market for their acts.

The most efficient way to reach the college market is through national or regional talent conferences. There are a number of these conferences sponsored by the college activities group **NACA (National Association for Campus Activities)**. Other events are sponsored by local or regional arts councils, such as Arts Northwest, or other organizations, such as the North American Folk Music and Dance Alliance and the International Bluegrass Music Association (IBMA). These conferences have brief showcases, in which acts do a short show for an audience of buyers from colleges, arts councils, or community arts organizations. Artists usually have to pay a fee to submit their CDs, electronic press kits, and MP3s or videos.

Some organizations or music festivals require that all submissions be made through a company called **Sonic Bids**. Sonic Bids submits an artist's recordings, videos, and promos electronically to the buyers' organizers. The artist must join Sonic Bids and pay a membership fee, plus an additional fee for each gig applied for. Sonic Bids sends out lists of festivals and gigs to all of its members on a regular basis. If the artist were to submit an application for each gig, these fees would mount up. Another down side of the process is that sometimes the event has only reserved a few spots for Sonic Bids members. By contrast, some events only consider artists who have submitted electronically through Sonic Bids. If used judiciously, membership can be advantageous to the artist.

The organizations jury the submissions and select the acts that get to showcase at the conferences. There are also exhibit tables where the showcased or nonshowcased acts or booking agents have their CDs or videos and playback equipment, along with brochures about the artist. If the artist is doing a showcase without the services of an agent, the artist will need to staff the exhibit table over a relatively long period of time, keep a positive attitude as the traffic at the table ebbs and flows, and to identify the buyers who are simply "tire kickers," who are simply developing a catalog of acts without seriously intending to book you. In addition, the artist must keep careful and accurate records of any conversations with the talent buyers, so that follow-up calls or e-mails can be sent later. The artist or the agent must also be prepared to give away dozens of CDs and press packages, knowing full well that many of these items are probably not going to result in gigs.

When an act does well at one of these showcases, typically a group of presenters from a particular region get together and try to book the act for a series of dates in their region. This is known as **block booking**. The client will attempt to get a reduced price for the act, using the argument that they are offering, say, five or six consecutive days of work, with limited travel. Depending on the distances involved, the demand for the act, and whether accommodations are part of the package, this can be a reasonable argument, and one that is equally advantageous for the presenter and the artist. It can also simplify the process of finding the gig and negotiating a price with six different buyers, because in effect the purchaser of the talent is coming directly to you or to your agent. It is important not to reduce the price too much or the artist will be obtaining a series of jobs, but not ones that prove profitable.

Some Problems with Agents

There are a number of possible problems that can arise when dealing with agents. One of the biggest issues occurs when a tour is set up. Because the agent gets commissions based on the gross earnings of the artist (usually 10 to 15 percent), the more bookings arranged, the higher the fees earned. The agent doesn't have to worry about *how* the artist will keep the schedule, necessarily. This may include booking impossible itineraries such as placing the artist in Portland, Maine, on one night, and Portland, Oregon, the next. This leads to unnecessary travel expenses for the artist, but even worse it means that the artist is exhausted after a lengthy flight. Later in this chapter, I discuss personal managers. It is the job of the manager to lean on the agent in order to avoid unnecessary expenditures of energy or money.

Another kind of problem can occur when an artist is signed to a major booking agency. Large booking agencies represent dozens and even hundreds of acts, and it is vitally important that the artist works with a particular agent who understands what the artist does, and knows how to sell that musical style to talent buyers. It is easy for a particular band to get lost in a massive talent roster, especially if their agent leaves to go to work for another agency.

Artie Traum: Making It on Your Own

Artie Traum was an example of a musician who carved out a career through his versatility, writing instructional materials, performing, writing songs and instrumental pieces, and producing records. His career exemplifies both the pluses and minuses of working on your own.

Artie Traum. Photo by Dion Ogust. Courtesy Happy Traum.

Artie Traum's first record, *Bear*, was a major label release, for MGM Records in 1967. In 1969 Capitol signed Artie and his brother Happy. They did two albums for Capitol with "generous budgets," and the label "gave our first album a big push. We didn't sell enough albums so Capitol dropped us after our second one. But they put us [on] the map, even if it was a small corner of the map."

From Capitol, Artie put together an album for what was then a small independent label called Rounder. It was a sampler of musicians from Woodstock, New York, where Artie lives. The budget for this album, called *Mud Acres*, was around $500, and he believes that it sold twenty thousand copies in a few years. A follow-up double album was not promoted, and didn't sell. This left Artie with some bitterness toward small labels and their promotional muscle. His next CDs for another independent label, Shanachie, were smooth jazz instrumental albums, and one reached the top of the smooth jazz charts for radio play.

Beginning in the 1990s, Artie made his own records, and hired independent radio promotion people to try to get airplay. He received excellent reviews but didn't see them resulting in a spike in sales. He also tried several companies that claimed to drive traffic to Web sites without much in the way of results. He also utilized other companies such as Pump Audio and corporate music venues to get in-store play at discount stores and even gas stations. He did not employ an agent but would have been happy to find a good one in order to free himself from the many tasks of booking himself.

Note: As this book was entering the editing process in July 2008, Artie Traum passed away in Woodstock, New York. At the time of his death he was working on a memoir, describing his experiences in New York and Woodstock

DOUBLE CONTRACTS

I have known several local or regional agencies who utilize a quaint system known as **double contracts**. One contract is between the agent and the talent buyer, and the other between the agent and the talent. Here is how this works:

> The agent calls up the leader of a rock quartet and says, "What would it cost me to have your group play at a college fraternity

party next week for two hours?" The leader thinks for a minute, and says $500. The agent then turns around and sells the act for $1,000 to the buyer. The band assumes the agent is taking a commission but doesn't dream that it is 50 percent of the gross. This, of course, is far more than any member of the group is making.

During my years in Denver, I was a member of a band represented by an agent who had a union franchise that limited her commission to 20 percent. This agent filed the same contract with the union as the one that we received. However, she signed a different contract with the buyer, stipulating a fee twice as high as the one in our contract. In this way, she could collect the 20 percent fee on the initial contract and then pocket the extra dollars from the fee charged to the presenter.

We discovered that this was going on when we did a convention gig for an out-of-town buyer. At the end of the evening, the client asked the leader of the band if he could give him the 50 percent balance that remained to be paid to the agent. Because the client lived in Iowa, and we were in Denver, it saved him the trouble of having to mail the check to the agent. When the band leader opened the envelope with the check, he discovered that the 50 percent of the money covered by the check was the total amount of money that our five-piece band was going to be paid for the gig!

It is possible for a band to file charges with the union in such a situation, but this may result in two unsatisfactory outcomes:

1. The band will never work for that agent again.
2. The client probably will not willingly testify that this occurred. The buyer wanted a band, and he expected to pay x dollars for the band. The last thing the client wishes is to get involved in is a dispute between the agent and the band in a union-mediated hearing.

BAND FRANCHISES

Another source of work for local, but not usually touring, musicians is the model used by the famous New York orchestra The Lester Lanin Band. The demand for Lanin's band was so great that he had a half-dozen or more bands that could perform on the same night. They all used the same musical arrangements, and their music stands all said "Lester Lanin Orchestra." This orchestra was wildly popular at debutante parties, weddings, and bar mitzvahs; in short, the so-called casual gigs that exist in many large cities. Lanin himself would make an appearance at one or two of the most lucrative gigs, or the ones that he knew would reliably hire his band repeatedly. Of course when he himself showed up, the price for the band escalated. I have known bands of this sort to operate in Denver, Los Angeles, and Phoenix, all based on Lester's model.

On New Year's Eve, there might be more than a dozen bands coming out of the same office, playing for revelers. A music office is a sort of booking agency that is run under the name of a particular bandleader. The bandleader provides whatever musical services a client wishes. These events are typically birthday parties, bar mitzvahs, dances, debutante parties, or any social occasion where the client wants live music. A music office can provide groups that play in various styles: rock trios, country bands, big bands, and so on. There is actually a corps of musicians in these towns whose primary income comes from one of these offices. Generally, these gigs pay reasonably well, somewhat above the union minimums. The band leader acts as the booking agent, and has a huge list of musicians who can cover anything that a client might wish, from a Hawaiian band to a hot R&B combo. The band itself generally plays music that has "something for everybody": an old standard, a country tune, a few rock standards, some light jazz. The concept is that at a party where there are people with a wide spread in ages, or at a corporate event, everyone will find something that they enjoy and recognize. These bands usually include a male and/or female vocalist as well.

"Too Loud, Too Bad"

My friend Alan Remington was a symphonic bassoon player who moved from Texas to Los Angeles. He gradually broke into the film business as a composer. Some of his film contacts asked him to provide music for their social events. Gradually he became so involved in creating groups to play for film people that he stopped writing film music, and became a sort of West Coast Lester Lanin. One day a corporate client called with a request for a rock trio to play at a party that many of the company's young employees would be attending. Alan selected a trio that he knew, and they arrived at the job on time, raring to go. All of the young people were smiling and dancing up a storm, when the leader of the group noticed that the head of the company was frantically gesturing him to turn down the volume. Sporting a big grin, the guitarist stepped up to the microphone, hit a power chord, and exclaimed "too loud, too bad."

The next day the client called Alan, complaining about the group's volume. Alan invited his client to lunch, explaining that it was his job to provide what his clients asked for. In this case because the demand was for rock and roll dance music, he felt that the guitarist wasn't out of line. Before the lunch, Alan had only worked a couple of jobs for this company. After the client realized that it really was Alan's intention to provide music based on what the client wanted, they became good friends, and Alan continued to provide music for him for many years.

The point of this story is that when musicians are hired to fill a specific need, they need to tailor their show towards that end. Corporate events are not places where a musician can play original, esoteric love songs, or twenty-minute saxophone solos.

PERSONAL MANAGERS

Personal managers have much more responsibility than booking agents because a manager's work covers almost every imaginable aspect of an artist's career. One of the difficulties in finding a motivated and competent personal manager is that management contracts say virtually nothing specific about how the manager will represent the artist's career. Phrases such as "will exercise his best efforts," are clearly so vague as to be both incomprehensible and worthless. In *Managing Artists in Pop Music,* Mitch Weiss and Perri Gaffney point out that in order to manage a Broadway show, the manager must apprentice for three years with an experienced show manager, take seminars on all sorts of business matters, including advertising, payroll, embezzlement, and taxes, and must also pass both an extensive written and oral examination. Although a number of personal managers have begun their careers by working for more experienced managers or as booking agents, there are really no formal legal or business criteria that qualify someone to be a personal manager in the entertainment industry. This makes an artist's choice of a manager not only one of the most critical decisions in his career but also one of the most difficult ones. Very few artists have the business background or general understanding of the entertainment industry to make an intelligent choice in selecting a manager.

A manager's work begins in earnest when the act procures a record deal. The manager must spend large amounts of time cultivating various personnel at the record company, getting to know everyone from the president of the company to the sales and promotion people, the A&R staff, and others. The manager must be the artist's cheerleader at the company, stimulating enthusiasm for the artist's work, telling the company about successful gigs, positive reviews, and airplay.

Here are some of the functions of a personal manager:

- Rides herd over the booking agent in order to make sure that the artist is being booked at an appropriate price, in venues that will lead to career-enhancing situations.
- Attempts to find a record deal for the act, with or without the help of an entertainment industry attorney.
- If the artist writes songs, the manager will seek a music publishing deal or assist the artist in setting up his own music publishing company.
- Assists the artist in finding a road manager, lighting technicians, publicists, choreographers, hair stylists, sound engineers, or any other personnel needed by the artist.
- When the artist begins to earn reasonable amounts of money, recommends a business manager to the artist or assists the artist in finding one.
- Coordinates every aspect of the artist's work. The manager is the one who makes sure that the band gets to play the venues where the band is getting airplay. When the band plays a major gig and there are no

CDs or posters in the local record stores, it is the manager who raises this issue with the record company.

- Seeks new opportunities for artists. For example, maybe the bass player of the band is a talented composer. The manager begins to seed television and film people with demos of the bass player's work, without even necessarily telling that bass player that this is going on. This is to shield the musician from possible disappointment. If all goes well, this musician may end up with a lucrative film or TV score.
- Pairs the artist with other acts that the manager represents, when this is appropriate.
- Offers personal advice and counsel or even mediates in disputes between group members.
- Works with the booking agent, sharing contacts that may assist the agent in finding work for the band. For example, the manager may know the person who books a show on a TV network and assist the agent by introducing him to that person

The Economics of Personal Management

Managers receive commissions from an act's earnings that range from as low as 10 percent to as high as 50 percent. Typically, managers get 15 to 20 percent of an act's earnings. However, this number can be extremely misleading. It may be based on the act's gross earnings, or certain expenses may be deducted before the commissions begin. For example, if a band has a $250,000 recording fund to make an album, and the album costs $200,000 to make, if the manager deducts his commission from the larger amount, the act will be left with no advance, while the manager walks away with $50,000. It makes much more economic sense for the manager's commission to be based on the remaining $50,000.

Naturally, there is some **conflict of interest** between a manager who is seeking to make the maximum amount of money and an act that has a large amount of overhead, including paying a road manager, buying expensive airline tickets, and other expenses. The act needs to consult an entertainment industry lawyer, and not one that is also representing the manager. That would constitute a clear conflict of interest.

WHEN DOES AN ACT NEED A MANAGER?

In the early stages of an artist's career, it is probably unwise and unnecessary to hire a personal manager. There simply isn't enough money to pay one, and the artist probably has a very limited notion of what qualities to look for in a good manager.

At the point where an act becomes serious about obtaining a record deal, it is virtually obligatory for the act to be represented by a manager. In fact, many labels will think twice before signing an act without a manager, because they want to see a consummate professional moving the act's career forward.

There are several alternatives to paying a manager's commissions when a band is in the early phases of its career. One possibility is for the manager to work without commissions for a set period of time. Another option is to simply defer commissions, with the band understanding that down the line the debt will be due. Occasionally acts that have been in the business for a long time have even hired managers on a salary basis.

Finding a Manager

First of all, it is worthwhile to look at some things that almost invariably lead to disastrous managerial agreements. The beginning act should *never* hire:

- Family members to manage your career
- People whom you have emotional entanglements with: the bass player's girl friend, the piano player's father, and so on
- A manager simply because they are willing to invest money in the band
- Managers who live in isolated parts of the country, unless they have the financial wherewithal and the time to spend to regularly visit the major music business centers to pursue whatever deals or meetings are necessary
- Managers who won't give you a list of references (current acts that they are managing). If someone used to manage a band, they may have been fired for doing a poor job. When possible, try to talk to acts that the manager currently manages, or managed in the recent past. If the manager will not allow you to talk to these "references," that in itself is a red flag
- Manager-Svengalis, who are more interested in molding the band according to their vision of what it should do, as opposed to the vision of the people in the band
- Managers who don't share most (or at least some) of the same musical and career-building goals. It is a mistake to hire someone who is only concerned with making money, if the band has other goals

For bands that are already enjoying some degree of success or notoriety, it is possible to create a contract that addresses specific career plateaus. For example, if a band made $100,000 last year, and under its new manager grosses $110,000 after commissions are paid, the band will be making *less* money than they did before they had a manager. The act will want the contract to state that the manager will only receive commissions after the act grosses a specific amount of money. Another way to handle this problem is to have the contract provide extremely low commissions until the act reaches a particular earnings plateau. If the band makes $100,000, commissions are 5 percent; at $150,000, the fee goes up to 10 percent; at $200,000, the fee goes to 15 percent.

In the case of some superstar groups, the commission might go in the other direction. If the band grosses $2,000,000, commission is 20 percent, but on amounts over that the commission goes *down* to 15 percent. The logic here is that it isn't much more work for the manager to raise the band's income above the $2,000,000 mark.

As with any negotiations, it's a question of how much the manager wants to represent a band, and how much the band is set on using that particular individual to represent them.

Music Publicists

If an act is popular enough, a music publicist may be added to handle all of its public relations (PR). A publicist is the spokesperson for an act, and is responsible for placing stories about the act on radio, television, newspapers, periodicals, or net sources. Publicists are usually hired either on retainer, with a monthly fee, or by the hour. Liz Rosenberg has handled publicity for Madonna for many years, with occasional breaks when the star is not performing. When a publicist works for a superstar, not only do they procure publicity for an act, but they also act as a spokesperson on personal issues that the superstar does not choose to discuss with the media. To put it another way, they can be utilized for damage control, if the star does something that is going to hurt her fan base.

Publicists can work for companies that hire a staff of people, or they can have their own independent company.

Independent Record Promoters

Independent record promoters are hired by artists, their managers or record companies to procure airplay for recording artists. They are usually hired on a project basis, with monthly fees. Some promoters work regionally, and some work nationally. It is extremely difficult to get national airplay without the use of a record promoter.

WHAT DOES A MANAGER WANT IN AN ARTIST?

Looking at the process from the other perspective, a manger wants an act that:

- Is willing to go on the road and to tour relentlessly to establish a fan base
- Shares musical and economic goals, and genuinely like one another (unfortunately anyone who has ever been on the road with a band knows how quickly a band that seemed to get along can develop serious and nasty personal antagonisms)
- Is conscientious about their rehearsal schedule, and has enough self-discipline to continue to write songs and meet a recording schedule
- Is cooperative with radio and record people, and presents enough of a positive self-image to get these people to help them

- Understands the manager's role enough not to resent having to pay commissions
- Plans to stay together for a long enough period of time to justify the manager's investment of time and energy
- Understands that musicians' romantic commitments or emotional problems may interfere with a career
- Has the potential to grow beyond its current fan base and develop its artistry as well as its commerciality

Power of Attorney (POA)

When someone signs a **POA (power of attorney)**, it means that they are giving another person the legal authority to sign contracts for them. Because artists often are involved in lengthy tours, it is not unreasonable for a manager to request this right. However, it is critical that the artist limit the extent of this power, because there have been instances where that power has been abused, and managers have signed over artists' funds for their own use. With the current prevalence of computers, cell phones, and fax machines, a manager should only have to use a power of attorney in rare instances. One such example might be a situation in which an agent requires an immediate answer about whether an act will accept a specific date, and the act is traveling on an airplane or out of cell phone range.

The American Federation of Musicians (AFM) does not regulate or franchise personal mangers in the way that they deal with booking agents. Therefore, the artist cannot expect to get any protection from the union when dealing with personal managers.

Sunset, Breaking Contracts, and Manager-Artist Disputes

Sunset is the expression that is used to indicate the end of a managerial contract. The contract may be expressed in terms of the number of years or the number of cycles of albums that the artist is releasing. Typically, these contracts last from three to five years, and in California it is illegal for personal services contracts to last for more the seven years. Most states do not have laws governing the length of personal service contracts.

On expiration of a management contract, many issues often surface. The manager in particular may want to:

- Continue receiving a commission on existing recordings
- Be compensated for any greatest hits recordings that are packaged in later years and include recordings made when the manager represented the band
- Be paid commissions on any songs written by band members while the manager was on board
- Receive full commission on any gigs that were booked while the manager was working with the band. Sometimes these circumstances are

arguable, such as a gig that was being negotiated at the time the contract expired
• Continue to enjoy commissions on other band revenue sources, such as commercials, endorsements, or merchandise deals that were in place while the manager represented the group

By contrast, the band will want to restrict the manager's share of future income as much as possible. This is sometimes done by the manager getting a full commission for a certain amount of time after the contract ends, and having the commission become lower each year until it expires. If the manager was getting a 20 percent commission, that percentage might go down to 10 percent in a year, and then expire the next year.

The worst part of this process from the artist's point of view is that the artist will often be in the process of signing with a new manager, and that manager, of course, will also want a percentage of earnings. It is important that the artist try to avoid paying full commissions to two managers at the same time for the same work. There are certain notorious cases, notably with the doo-wop group The Platters, who allegedly were paying so many different people commissions they literally earned nothing on their gigs. Obviously the band had not received any useful advice from an entertainment attorney. This probably occurred because the band either couldn't afford an attorney, or used one who was also working for one of the band's managers. This is a breach of professional ethics, but it does still occasionally happen.

A different sort of sunset occurs when an act decides that it is in their best interests to get out of an existing contract. When this happens, unless the artist can prove fraud, theft, or some other misappropriation of the artist's funds, the artist must threaten to sue, or actually do so, to get out of the contract. The manager will wish to be additionally compensated for the term of the agreement that the artist is trying to abrogate.

When a band sues to get out of the contract, there are usually bad feelings between the act and their former manager and lawyers for both sides will have lengthy arguments about the terms of the contract's dissolution. Naturally, both parties must pay the lawyers while these arguments are being resolved. This is an unattractive prospect for both sides.

In Dr. Stephen Marcone's *Managing Your Band, Artist Management: The Ultimate Responsibility*, he examines several highly contentious disagreements between bands and their managers. They include family situations in which a parent was managing an artist, and the artist decided to leave the nest; family members extorting money from an act; and charges that a company was mismanaging an artist. One reason that most people in the industry suggest that acts not allow family members to manage them is some family relationships, especially marriages, may lead to a divorce. If the spouse of an act is serving in a management role, the divorce can become exceedingly complicated, and the resulting publicity can be very ugly for both sides.

In California, it is illegal for a manager to obtain work for an act. The state requires that a licensed booking agent obtain such work. When bands start out they are generally desperate to get any gigs that they can. Often a manager will bend the rules to try to get the act some work. There are a number of instances in which this has come back to bite the manager, when the act later successfully sued to get out of a contract, using the argument that their manager was illegally booking them.

Classical music functions in a different way. Several large firms, notably Columbia Artist Management (CAMI) in New York, book and manage classical artists. Various agencies sponsor community concerts, booking artists in relatively small and distant cities. An arts organization in one of these cities commits to hiring several relatively lesser-known artists in a series of concerts. These gigs provide a sort of training ground for young classical musicians, putting some money in their pockets, and enabling them to develop performing skills. It also provides music for little-served communities. Currently these concerts include music in other genres as well. There are also some agents who work with organizations that book touring programs in the schools.

A Classic Artist-Manager Dispute

One of the best publicized and messiest artist-manager divorces was the one between Bruce Springsteen and Mike Appel, his original manager. Appel was a huge Springsteen supporter and fan at a time when Bruce was performing primarily in small clubs in New Jersey. Eventually, Appel signed on as Springsteen's manager. Supposedly the contract was signed on the hood of a pickup truck in an unlit parking lot. It provided that Appel would not only manage Springsteen but also that he would produce his records and publish his songs.

In 1972, Appel arranged for Springsteen to record for Columbia Records. There was a large amount of industry buzz about Springsteen, but his first two albums sold modestly, supposedly less than fifty thousand copies each. Springsteen began to wonder why his record sales weren't better when he was getting excellent publicity, and his performances were selling out all over the country. He met a journalist named Jon Landau who was a writer for *Rolling Stone*, and they spent quite a bit of time together trying to figure out why Bruce wasn't doing better. Bruce decided that Landau would be a better producer than Appel. However, to Bruce's surprise, he discovered that his label, Columbia Records, had no choice in the matter, because their contract was with Appel, not with Springsteen. Eventually Appel and Landau "coproduced" Bruce's next album, *Born To Run*, which launched Springsteen's career as a recording superstar. After much bad blood and lawyers' meetings, Springsteen paid Appel a handsome sum to get out of his contract. A few years later he also bought back the publishing rights to his songs. Interestingly, Landau also became Springsteen's manager.

For those who wish to read both sides of the story, Dave Marsh's *Born To Run: The Bruce Springsteen Story* tells it from Bruce's side, and Mike Appel offers his version of the story in his coauthored *Down Thunder Road: The Making of Bruce Springsteen*, written with Marc Eliot.

PITFALLS TO AVOID

Managers Investing in a Band

Some acts will sign with a manager because that person has agreed to invest in their career. However, the fact that a person has the ability to invest in a group does not prove that the money will be invested wisely, or that the putative manager knows anything about the entertainment business. When a competent manager does choose to invest their own funds in a band, they will probably ask for a higher percentage of commissions. If the band becomes successful, that could ultimately be very costly to the act.

Double Dipping

Sometimes a manager may offer to start a music publishing company for their band. In some cases, they tell the band that they will split the income from the publishing company with the artists. If there are four band members this means that the manager will get 50 percent of the income from music publishing, and each of the band members will get 12.5 percent of that income. When the manager is **double dipping**, he will then turn around and take his usual commission from the artists' songwriting income in addition to the publishing money.

When the Manager Creates the Band

Over the years, a number of bands have been created by personal managers, rather than by the musicians themselves. Groups such as the Archies, the Village People, or 'N Sync have names that were created and trademarked by the band's manager rather than by the group itself. In such instances, the manager chooses the members through auditions. Under those circumstances, the manager can make deals for the use of the band's name without permission of the members of the band. If the band breaks up, or if they wish to renegotiate their deal with their manager, the manager can replace the original group with another band without the permission of the original members. He can also avoid paying them for the use of the name. Under such circumstances, the original members of the band essentially have no rights.

Advantages of Having a Personal Manager

When an artist has a good personal manager, they can then turn to the creative aspects of making music, resting secure that their business interests are being capably handled. Some managers have come up with some amazingly successful ploys for their clients. Albert Grossman's careful grooming of Bob Dylan's career, first introducing him as a songwriter and then as a performer, is a classic example of good personal management. A quality manager spends countless hours building an artist's career and image, and trying to take her career to the next level.

"Hey Landlord"

Albert Grossman began his career running a nightclub in Chicago, Illinois, in the late 1950s. He noticed that folk music acts were drawing large crowds, and so he began to book and manage local singers. Moving to New York by the early 1960s, Grossman formed a folk trio—Peter, Paul, and Mary— that he molded into a successful act. He also heard about a young singer songwriter who had just come to town named Bob Dylan, who was attracting a lot of buzz. Grossman signed Bob Dylan soon after the legendary Columbia Records producer and talent scout John Hammond had signed Dylan to Columbia. Grossman understood that Dylan's vocal style and presentation was a little rough for the folk-pop audience. He decided to promote Dylan as a songwriter first, having Peter, Paul and Mary cover Dylan's songs. When the trio had two huge

A young Bob Dylan, 1963. Dylan's image as a scruffy folksinger was carefully built by his manager, Albert Grossman. Photo: Don Hunstein, courtesy Lebrecht Music & Arts Photo Library.

hits with "Blowing in the Wind," and "Don't Think Twice, It's Alright," this provided the credibility that Grossman needed to promote Dylan to a wide audience.

Grossman and Dylan initially were very close. Dylan respected Grossman's financial savvy and understanding of how to build a musician's career. Grossman started a music publishing company with Warner Brothers Music for Dylan's songs, convincing the singer that he would make a higher profit off his songwriting in this way. The unconfirmed but widely circulated story is that Dylan didn't know that Grossman owned part of that company, and was receiving publishing income while also collecting his commission on Dylan's songwriting royalties. When Dylan discovered this, he angrily fired Grossman; some fans believe his song "Hey Landlord" is a wry comment on Grossman's double-dipping.

Expanding Role of the Manager and Managerial Expenses

As record sales have declined, record companies have been cutting their staffs, and some of their promotional efforts. Some managers operate as sole practitioners, but others operate as a group, working under the same roof. The Firm, a management company based in Los Angeles, has actually expanded its operation to include record promotion duties. When such a situation occurs, the company's clients can probably anticipate that their commission burdens will become heavier. Often these management groups in turn split up, as some of the managers decide to form their own company. When this occurs, the managers who leave usually take key clients with them.

In the course of representing an artist, a manager will undertake a variety of tasks that involve spending money. For example, a New York manager may take a trip to California to negotiate a record deal for a client. That is a legitimate business expense, which will be charged back to the artist. Other matters, such as whether the manager flies first class or coach, are not necessarily in the interest of the artist. There should be some mechanism in the management agreement where the manager can charge minor expenses, say, under $500, to his client, without having to provide detailed justification of these expenses. Larger expenses should require the approval of the artist. As management firms expand their roles into areas formerly covered by record companies, it is important that the artist not provide her manager with a blank check to cover such expenditures.

Lately, some management firms have even started record labels to represent their artists. This can be seen as either an ideal marriage or a situation rife with possible conflicts of interest. Irvin Azoff's Front Line Management is a large consortium that includes a number of other important personal managers under the Front Line umbrella.

Conflicts of Interest between Artists and Managers

Over the years, a number of record companies have also endeavored to manage artists. Motown Records was one of the most famous examples of this approach and the recently failed British record and management company Sanctuary is a more contemporary example.

When an artist's management and record company are under the same ownership, the logical question for artists to ask is how well will her management company represent them in negotiating with the record company? What incentive does the manager have to improve the financial terms of the recording agreement, when it is the record company that is paying the price for these improvements? Remember that it is also the record company that is paying the manager. Any artist confronted with a joint recording and management agreement should have an unbiased attorney carefully examine the contract.

As major record labels move to the recent 360 deals, management is one of the areas that they may attempt to include in the record company contract. The potential problems are obvious: if the artist and record company have a dispute, whose side will the manager take?

FINDING A MANAGER

For the artist who doesn't live in a music business center, finding an appropriate manager is likely to prove difficult. There are two organizations of personal managers, the Conference of Personal Managers and the Music Managers Forum. Most of the people who belong to these organizations are well established and unlikely to listen seriously to unsolicited material. The invaluable music periodical the *Music Connection* publishes lists of personal managers quarterly, but most of them are based in Los Angeles. Another directory is the annual publication *Musician's Atlas.*

This brings up the question of whether it is necessary to sign with an experienced manager. An experienced manager may provide good guidance for an artist, but by contrast an old hand at management may not have the drive and hunger to succeed that is part of being a good artist's representative. A younger manager may be hungrier and more motivated to promote an artist. It's a difficult dilemma, because younger managers are basically learning while they are earning. Skilled professionals don't need to do that, but they may not be as apt to devise creative ways of promoting an unknown artist. It comes down to who the artist trusts, and who has a combination of a winning personality, good energy, and enough of a business background to successfully represent the artist.

If the artist elects to go with a company that employs multiple managers, the artist may want to insert a key man clause (see Chapter 1). It is not unusual for managers to take some clients with them if they move to another office. However, if there is no provision in the management contract for this to occur, and if the manager leaves a firm under bad terms with the other partners, they may resist giving up their rights to the group.

BUSINESS MANAGERS

When an act is successful and expects to enjoy a relatively stable income base, the group will have to make many business decisions. Personal managers don't deal with such details as taxes, placing a band on salaries, or making investments in retirement funds or businesses that will generate more income for the group. Under these circumstances, many artists hire yet another team member, a **business manager**. A business manager should be a certified public accountant (CPA). Most states license CPAs, and require that the applicant have a college degree in accounting and pass a qualifying examination. Most business managers want a fee of 5 percent of the artist's gross income for these services. The term *business manager* has never been formalized in a legal sense. Consequently, business managers can set up shop without meeting any professional qualifications, just as personal managers can do. It seems obvious that no artist would hire a financial representative who had no background in business, but there are undoubtedly some salesmen who could sell golf balls to tennis players.

As is always the case, artists should be wary of hiring a business manager who has close ties to their personal manager. As we have seen, personal management agreements do not tend to be long-term relationships. Once again, it is best not to hire family members to do your business.

After warning the artist against these involvements, it is also realistic to assume that in the early part of a career, it is normal for people to assume roles without necessarily having formal credentials for the tasks that they are undertaking. *Someone* has to collect the band's fees, buy gas for the van, pay hotel bills when you go out of town, and so forth. When a band is barely surviving, they are not going to be able to afford a business manager. These arrangements must be temporary and these tasks handed over to qualified professionals as soon as possible.

Business Manager–Artist Interactions

A business manager should provide these services for artists:

- *Tax advice.* Most artists have only a dim idea of what constitutes deductible expenses, and most bands find it difficult to keep specific and legible records for an accountant. The business manager needs to set up record-keeping with one of the band members—or with the act's road manager, if they have one—in order to make sure that the band is claiming every legal tax exemption possible. Examples of appropriate receipts include business lunches, travel expenses, equipment purchases, accommodations, and airline tickets.
- *Establishing income allowances and savings.* Assuming that the band is bringing in relatively regular income, the business manager, working with the band, should figure out weekly salaries for the band that take into account food, housing, transportation costs, income withheld for taxes, etc. The business manager should also begin to involve the band in some sort of stable investment opportunities, including setting up tax-deferred retirement savings accounts. There should be a clear understanding on the part of the artists as to what areas they wish to invest in and how much risk they are able to tolerate.
- *Records of income and expenses.* The artists should receive statements on a monthly or quarterly basis that delineate income and expenditures. In many cases, it is advisable that the manager explain to the band how to read such statements.
- *Manage record and music publishing royalties.* The business manager should make sure that all royalties are paid in full and in a timely manner for both recordings and music publishing (income from songwriting). If necessary, the business manager should handle any auditing of record companies or publishers to account for these payments.
- *If the band tours internationally, deal with international tax laws.* Many countries withhold taxes when a band appears in their country, but the band may be able to reclaim some of this income by filing foreign tax returns.

Just as with personal managers, business managers may occasionally need power of attorney to act for the artist. In these cases, the artist needs to be careful to place limitations on the contracts or agreements that the business manager has a right to sign in the name of the band. The band also should have the right to **audit** (or independently check the financial records of)

A Penny Deferred, A Dollar Lost

My friend Eric Weissberg had a tremendous hit record in the early 1970s with "Dueling Banjos," the theme song from the *Deliverance* movie. He consulted an accountant to help invest his money. During the 1970s, there were a number of people in the entertainment world who were investing in various businesses that were designed as tax shelters, such as cattle ranches. The investments were supposed to lose money initially, but bring in income in later years, when it was assumed that these artists would be earning less money. The initial losses could be written off against the entertainers' income, lowering their overall tax bill. And when the income finally began coming in, the gains would be taxed at a lower overall rate, because the entertainers' total income would be lower, placing them in a lower tax bracket.

Of course, the Internal Revenue Service (IRS) has the authority to determine what constitutes a legal tax shelter and what is not legal. In this particular case, it took the IRS some years to reach the decision that this particular tax shelter was not legal. When the IRS reaches such a decision, not only must the taxpayer pay the amount deferred, but she or he must also pay interest charges, which can be as high as 25 percent. The accountant elected to fight the charges, a proceeding that dragged on for several years. During this time, the accountant died and the IRS ruled that the unfortunate musician had to not only pay taxes, but also the extremely high interest charges on the time that had elapsed between the tax deferral claim and the closing of the case. The moral of this story is that a musician needs to be extremely careful when a business manager comes up with an intriguing tax deferral scheme.

the business manager if they feel that he or she is not taking proper care of their money. The business manager's office should be accessible to all band members. Finally, the business manager should have some sort of insurance that protects clients against the mishandling of the artist's income. In Don Passman's *All You Need to Know about the Music Business,* he points out that it is a good idea for this insurance to cover both accounting services and investment advice.

Terms to Know

For Class Discussion

1. When should an artist look for a booking agent?
2. Do you believe that artists can handle their own business without using an agent?
3. How important is the convention business in the town where you live or go to school?
4. Is it reasonable that states do not regulate personal managers?
5. What are reasonable expectations that an artist should have about a personal manager's performance?
6. Why should an artist be wary of giving anyone a power of attorney?
7. Do you know anyone who has or used to have a personal manager? What was their experience in working with a manager? How do these experiences compare with what is described in this book?
8. How would you prepare yourself for a career as a personal manager?
9. When does an artist or a band need the services of a business manager?

CHAPTER 5

Talent Unions

Historically, unions have existed in order to equalize the power relationships that render individual workers relatively helpless when dealing with large corporate employers. Unions serve their members interests by negotiating for better working conditions, hours and pay, and health benefits, among other issues. In this chapter we'll trace the history of unions that specifically represent "talent" (performing artists, songwriters, etc.) and how their role has evolved and changed to today.

BACKGROUND OF THE UNION MOVEMENT IN THE UNITED STATES

Originally, unions were formed in the skilled and semi-skilled trades, representing such groups as carpenters and electricians.. Collectively these unions consolidated in a national group called the **American Federation of Labor (AFL)** in 1886. The **Congress of Industrial Organizations (CIO)** was formed in 1935, primarily to represent unskilled workers working in large factories. Twenty years later, the two combined as the AFL-CIO. The role of the AFL-CIO is to support its member unions through organizational help and to back political candidates who would support pro-union legislation. The larger individual unions, for example, the UAW (United Automobile Workers) were able to obtain agreements across an entire industry.

THE AMERICAN FEDERATION OF MUSICIANS (AFM)

The first organization formed to protect the rights of performing musicians was the **American Federation of Musicians (AFM)**, founded in 1896 as a part of the AFL. The AFM grew out of so-called Mutual Aid Societies that musicians had begun to form in the mid-nineteenth century to provide payment to musicians or their families in cases of extended illness or death. Within a decade, it grew from three thousand to forty-five thousand members with 424 locals in the United States and Canada. In 1904–1905, the union set minimum wages for touring musicians with Broadway shows, operettas, and grand operas, a first for professional musicians.

The coming of phonographs, radio, and sound film in the period from the turn of the century to the late 1920s led to the loss of many jobs for "live" musicians. The AFM sought to protect these jobs, while recognizing

The Petrillo Years

James Petrillo was president of the AFM from 1940 to 1958. He believed that records and jukeboxes were destroying employment opportunities for musicians. Records eliminated the need for radio to utilize live musicians, and juke boxes provided music in venues that—in Petrillo's judgment—ought to be utilizing live musicians.

Originally, the record companies had tried to restrict radio's use of their material, fearing that people would stop buying discs if they could hear the same music "for free" on the radio. For this reason, until the 1940s, many radio stations employed live musicians and even orchestras. By then, however, the

Former president Harry S. Truman (at the piano) plays with James Petrillo, president of the AFM, at their 1954 convention. Copyright Unknown, courtesy of Harry S. Truman Library.

record companies had begun to see radio as a means of selling records, and it had been clearly established that legally they could not limit radio play of their releases. Fearing the loss of union work, Petrillo initiated a strike against the record companies. The strike lasted for eighteen months, beginning in 1942. No recordings could be made by union musicians during this period. Petrillo wanted to create a performance royalty for musicians whenever a record was played anywhere. This would have been somewhat similar to what songwriters and music publishers receive through the performing rights organizations. Eventually, the strike was settled, without the creation of such a fund.

A later and shorter strike in 1947 resulted in an interesting compromise between the union and the record companies. A fund was created that paid for live music in such public facilities as nursing homes and schools. The fund was called the Music Performance Trust Fund (MPTF), and a royalty from the sale of records funded it. MPTF survives today under the name of the Music Performance Fund.

these new technologies. In 1928, it set a minimum wage scale for musicians playing for phonograph recordings and early sound films. In the 1940s, union leader James Petrillo gained notoriety for his fights with radio and the recording industry, leading to two strikes that crippled both industries.

Disability and pension funds for musicians were established by the union in the 1950s. Recent issues have included compensation for performing musicians and fighting musical piracy and illegal digital copying.

Today, the American Federation of Musicians is concerned with the following issues:

MINIMUM WAGES FOR SPECIFIC JOBS, OR CATEGORIES OF JOBS

- *Working conditions.* For example, a trumpet player simply cannot play a horn for three consecutive hours without some rest period.
- *Unusual demands of the job.* For example, it requires a high level of skill to be able play multiple instruments, such as clarinet, sax, and flute. Consequently, the union requires increased payments when the player is expected to play multiple instruments on the same job.
- *Bonuses or repayments, known as residuals.* Instrumentalists receive additional compensation for their performances on union recording sessions, through the **Special Payments Fund**. The Special Payments Fund pays bonuses to union musicians, based on the number of union recording sessions that they have played on, and the total sale of records. The bonuses don't depend on the sale of the particular records that a musician played on but on the sales of all recordings by companies that are signatory to the union agreements. A similar fund exists for musicians who play on film scores, but their bonuses are based on the gross receipts of the particular film that the musician played on.
- **Residuals** are repayments that musicians who play on commercials receive when commercials continue to play for more than thirteen weeks.
- *Music Performance Fund.* This fund, a joint effort between the AFM and the recording industry, funded by the latter group, pays musicians to perform live music in schools, nursing homes, senior centers, and other venues. No religious or political activity must take place during the performance, and it must be free and open to the public. This fund is supported by contributions from record companies, based on record sales.
- *Guaranteed contracts.* This program guarantees union musicians are paid when the job is covered by a union contract but the employer refuses to pay the musicians. There is an extended discussion of contract guarantees later in this chapter.
- **Pensions.** Musicians who work under national contracts, such as recording agreements, or musicians in a few of the larger locals who work gigs such as Broadway shows, enjoy contributions to their pension plan. Usually the employer pays about 10 percent or more of scale

wages into the pension plan. Musicians can take the pension at age fifty-five, although, as with Social Security, taking the pension earlier reduces the amount of money that a musician receives. Most symphony orchestras also have a pension plan for their musicians. In order to be eligible to actually receive a pension, a member must have accumulated at least ten years of full credits. Full credits are earned when the musician makes a minimum annual amount of $3,000 in wages that are covered by the pension plan. If the musician makes less, he can earn credits in one-quarter increments. In other words, earning $750 results in a one-quarter pension credit.

- *Disability Payments.* Musicians can also receive disability payments through the pension plan. A wonderful banjo player named Bobby Thompson was one of the busiest studio musicians in Nashville during the late 1960s and the 1970s. One day he came to a session and found that he couldn't move the fingers of his right hand. Bobby was diagnosed with multiple sclerosis. Fortunately, he had accumulated a considerable amount of money in the pension plan, even though at the time he was only in his forties. Bobby was never able to play professionally again. He told me that if it hadn't been for his union pension, he would have been a "bag person." Bobby died in 2007, but by that time he had been receiving pension benefits for over twenty years.

The AFM Today

Although the AFM has lost membership over the last three decades, dropping from a high of three hundred thousand members to ninety thousand today, it still is very powerful, particularly in two areas:

1. Symphony, Big Band, and Broadway orchestras, where there are a large number of musicians employed
2. Recording situations employing freelance (session) musicians

The union works best when it represents a relatively large number of musicians who are negotiating with a single entity. Symphony orchestras fit this model; there may be up to forty to over one hundred musicians in an orchestra, and they all work for a single "boss," the symphony's board of directors or management. Because even the smallest symphony orchestras employ forty or fifty musicians, it is more advantageous for these players to negotiate as a unit, than to try to negotiate their wages individually. The union negotiates a minimum wage for all of the orchestra members; the principal players, such as the first flutist, negotiate their own wage above these minimums. The basic wages in the major symphonies, like Boston, Chicago, Cleveland, Los Angeles, and New York, are currently above $100,000 a year. These orchestras use a complement of 105 players, occasionally augmenting this group for special works or pops concerts. Of course, the wages in smaller cities are much lower; indeed, in really small towns no one can make a full-time living playing in the symphony.

In the 1930s, big band jazz combos followed a similar structure; musicians worked for a bandleader, such as Duke Ellington or Benny Goodman, and unions helped them negotiate their wages and working conditions. When a musician went out on the road, the bandleader had to pay union wages, and other contractual conditions prevailed. For example, the bandleader could not fire anyone at will, but had to give two weeks notice. Broadway orchestras also follow a similar structure, and they too benefit from union regulation. However, since the 1950s, a new "model" for bands has developed, particularly in rock, country, and R&B styles. These are smaller combos that lack a designated "leader." Since many of these rock and country groups are self-contained, they function more as cooperatives than groups that have a leader and side musician. Often the money is split evenly between the various group members.

The union still has a hold on big-time recording gigs. A small corps of musicians in Los Angeles, Nashville, and New York utilize union contracts to do recording dates in these cities, and sometimes elsewhere. Including pension and health benefits, the wage for a three-hour union recording session is about $400. When these musicians play on commercials (often referred to as jingles) the musicians earn $110 an hour, an additional holding fee before the commercial goes on the air, residual payments every thirteen weeks that a commercial gets played, and pension and health benefits. Hollywood film musicians earn similar wages to the payments made to musicians who play on recordings. There are certain differences between the contracts for the different media. For example, there are different minimums for films, depending on the budget of the film, and slightly lower minimum wages for larger orchestras. Musicians who play two instruments in a film earn an additional 50 percent, but on recordings that increment is only 20 percent. There are also variable scales for recordings, based on the budget of the recording.

From the 1960s into the 1980s, there were a small but substantial number of musicians making a handsome living in the studios. They were known as **session musicians** because they worked primarily in the studios, not on the road (see Chapter 14). As more rock and rap bands began to function as self-contained units, the amount of recording work available for studio musicians began to dry up. The extensive use of synthesizers, samplers, and drum machines also had a negative impact on the wages of studio musicians.

Although there are still a certain number of Hollywood film scores that utilize large orchestras of studio musicians, the lower budget films have tended to use scores played with a small orchestra augmented by electronic synthesizers and drum machines. In addition, some producers have used orchestras in places like Hungary and Czechoslovakia, finding that it is cheaper to fly the composer there and to use an orchestra that works for much lower wages. Another problem has been the use of non-union orchestras, especially in Seattle and Salt Lake City, to record film scores. The Seattle Symphony is not a union orchestra, so it is not necessary for a producer to pay their musicians the union minimum wages or benefits.

The Chicano Star Movement

San Antonio is an important center for the recording of the Mexican-American musical style known as *norteño* or *tejano* music. For years, small record labels and some larger ones have done a thriving business in the Southwest with Spanish-language music. This music was never recorded under union contracts, and the payment to these musicians was pitifully small. Some of these musicians, notably Flaco Jimenez, are world-class artists with credits on famous recordings by such people as Ry Cooder and Paul Simon.

During the late 1990s, the AFM tried to organize the San Antonio recording industry. They referred to this effort as the Chicano Star Movement. As the Chicano music market grew, a number of the Latino labels were owned by the major labels, like Sony. Sony operated under union agreements for its own recordings but refused to honor them when the smaller labels that they owned made recordings. The major labels took the position that their smaller subsidiaries were being operated independently from the mother companies, so they were not covered by union agreements.

The union began to enlist well-known Latin talents, such as the actor Edward Olmos, to lobby on behalf of the musicians. They succeeded in getting some publicity and they began to circulate petitions that were then delivered to the heads of the labels. A few labels began to comply with the union agreements, but Sony and some of the others resisted. The union then turned to the tactic of using political pressure. Some of the Hispanic representatives in the U.S. Congress became involved, and they threatened to hold public hearings on the issue. All of the labels then agreed to negotiate union contracts. Today there is a special wage scale that reflects the more modest but not inconsiderable budgets of these recordings. The scale reflects these lower figures, but gives the musicians set wages and pension benefits.

Unfortunately for the AFM, these agreements were reached at about the same time as the 9/11 crisis occurred. Consequently, the union received very little publicity for this important victory.

The AFM used to control the night club scene. However, several lawsuits have resulted in restrictions on the AFM's ability to negotiate on behalf of a band with a club. Today, the union can set minimum wages, but the musicians are considered independent contractors. It is the band leader who negotiates with the club, not the union. Because of this, the union pretty much lost control over gigs in clubs.

In some towns, notably Las Vegas and Reno, the union had negotiated contracts with the casinos, requiring them to hire relatively large orchestras and pay good wages. However, by the 1980s, the casinos felt that these rules were onerous, because it was expensive to maintain large orchestras and most performers no longer required the kind of lavish accompaniment that once was part of a typical Vegas stage show. The AFM called a strike against the Las Vegas casinos in 1989 over this issue. The union saw jobs disappearing, and wanted to establish set contracts with large orchestras at casinos. The casinos turned to taped music and, to this day, maybe of the casinos use either taped music or a combination of taped music and a small live combo. The strike lasted seven months, and the union was defeated. When the union lost its ability to negotiate with clubs, the musicians who worked these gigs felt that there was no longer any point to being in the union. The membership of the Las Vegas local plunged from 2,200 in 1979 to 1,110 in 1989 and 850 today.

This paralleled the loss of members in the entire AFM. Between losing control of the night clubs and the changes in musical styles that resulted in small combos rather than big bands becoming the prevalent musical style, the union membership fell from its high in the 1970s of three hundred thousand to about ninety thousand members today.

Contract Guarantees

If a band leader or the agent files a contract with the local musician's union, they will guarantee to pay the artists if the client defaults. All of the musicians listed in the contract must be members of the AFM for the guaranteed contract clause to operate. The union has minimum wage agreements, set by each of the 250 locals of the union in the United States and Canada.

Usually traveling artists are paid more than these minimum payments. If the client defaults, the union will immediately pay the artist the minimums and then go to court on behalf of the artist to collect the rest of the money. If they are successful in this endeavor, they then pay the act the balance due. To take advantage of the union contract guarantee clause, you must file a contract, and all the musicians must be members of the musician's union.

This is particularly useful to a touring act. Imagine yourself driving to Fargo, North Dakota, in the winter, and finding out that the person who signed your contract no longer books music for the club. You are tired, broke, and extremely cold! By calling the union's 1-800-ROAD-GIG number, you can talk to a live human being, and get enough money so the band can at least get a motel room.

I was once in a band that played in a Broadway musical being performed in Denver. The producers of the show claimed that the owners of the theater should pay us, and of course the theater owners said exactly the opposite. Each of the seven musicians involved were paid $1,100 by the Denver local, representing rehearsals and a number of performances. I have no idea whether the union ever recovered the money from the producers or theater owners.

Another way that the union deals with booking agents is that if the agency fails to get any work for the act within a specified period of time, the artist has a right to invalidate the agreement. This prevents an agent from stringing the act along without getting it any work. The union allows agents to collect commissions of 20 percent on one-night gigs and 15 percent on gigs that run for two days, although many of the more powerful acts pay agents a smaller percentage in commissions.

Special Groups within the Union

The AFM has specialized subgroups of musicians who have organized within the AFM framework. **International Conference of Symphony Orchestra Members (ICSOM)** and **Regional Orchestra Players Association (ROPA)** represent the classical musicians, whereas the **Recording Musicians Association (RMA)** deals with the work of studio musicians.

AFTRA AND SAG

Performers who work in television, radio, or film have two more unions that they must join. The **American Federation of Television and Radio Artists (AFTRA)** governs work on videotape or live television shows, while the **Screen Actors Guild (SAG)** deals with work on film. In addition to pension benefits, members who earn a certain amount of annual income under union contracts (most recently $5,000 a year), receive free health insurance. Membership in SAG or AFTRA requires the payment of a large initiation fee, one that varies according to the region where the member has joined. Dues are based on the member's earnings. Although the American Federation of Musicians has about 250 locals spread throughout the United States and Canada, AFTRA and SAG have regional offices. The Denver office, for example, services the entire Rocky Mountain region. (The AFM seems to be gradually moving toward the AFTRA model of developing a regional presence, rather than a local one. Its 250 locals represent a reduction from 600 about twenty years ago, and the future will probably see even more consolidation.)

Because most singers and actors do both kinds of work, they are obligated to join both of these unions. Voiceover talent for films and commercials is also covered by these groups. There is, however, a discount available for whichever union the singer joins second.

Contracts for commercials, like the AFM contracts, pay residuals every thirteen weeks. The payments are much more complicated than the ones that go to musicians, because unlike AFM contracts, they are based on a number of factors. These variables include the time of day that the commercial is broadcast and whether the commercial is broadcast locally, regionally, or nationally. The union minimums for singers are somewhat higher than they are for musicians, but the key difference is in the residuals, which can be enormous. For a national campaign that is saturated on the airwaves, a singer can earn as much as $100,000 from a jingle for a single product. There are also provisions for paying background singers bonuses at various sales plateaus of recordings, starting with a bonus when five hundred thousand copies are sold.

There have been several attempts to fold AFTRA and SAG into a single union in the last ten years. So far, these attempts have not succeeded.

Which Comes First: The Contract or the Union Card?

Several years ago, I was at the SAG office in New York City. A young man came in and told the union representative that he needed to get a SAG card in order to work in a film. The actor claimed that the director of the film had told him to go to the union and get a card, and then he would cast him. Unfortunately, for this actor, SAG rules state that the director must write a letter promising employment before the card can be given.

The young man became very upset when this rule was explained to him. It seemed obvious to me, as an onlooker, that the director was trying to get rid of the actor by making the union the "bad guy," rather than rejecting him outright. This sort of union rule is a result of the unfortunate fact that there are far more actors than there are plays or films for these actors. A similar rule is used by ASC, the cinematographers' union, where at any given moment, the bulk of their members are unemployed.

In disbelief, the actor asked if he could see a supervisor. He became virtually reduced to tears when he found out that the young woman who was telling him what he didn't want to know was the supervisor of that particular department.

OTHER TALENT UNIONS

Actor's Equity, the American Guild of Variety Artists (AGVA), and the American Guild of Musical Artists (AGMA) are other talent unions that cover performers. Actor's Equity deals with actors, AGVA handles jugglers and comedians, and AGMA deals with singers, dancers, and musicians who are involved in classical music. Each union has its own rules and admission requirements. Other talent unions represent stagehands, cinematographers, and broadcasters.

When one of these unions goes on strike, members of the other talent unions often honor the picket line and also refuse to work for the company that is on strike. Individual union members sometimes take a similar position. In late 2008, Neil Young cancelled a concert in Los Angeles because the stage hands union (IATSE) was on strike against the facility where the concert was scheduled.

The AFM publishes a monthly magazine, *The International Musician*, which contains articles of interest to members. It is a valuable resource for classical musicians, because it lists vacancies in symphony orchestras and the procedures for applying for these jobs.

THE OUTLOOK FOR ENTERTAINMENT UNIONS

During the past forty years, a number of roadblocks have obstructed the ability of unions to function efficiently. The Taft-Hartley Act, passed by the U.S. Congress in 1947, limited the power of unions to boycott employers and

The Pros and Cons of Talent Unions

Pros	Cons
Contract guarantees	Initiation fees and annual dues, as well as work dues
Residual payments	
Minimum wage scales	Restrictions about working with non-union musicians
Bonuses for union recordings	
Pension funds	Certain musicians must join, rather than choose to join on their own
High wage scales for recording work	
Health insurance contributions or paid health insurance	Rules governing rehearsals and performances may be burdensome for artistic projects that musicians enjoy, but which have very little financial support
Discounted legal services	
Job referrals	
Job protection, for example, a conductor of a symphony cannot fire a member without undertaking a mediation process	
Rehearsal facilities for members	
Assistance in obtaining work visas to play in foreign countries	
Special services-some locals of the AFM have recording studios, which they rent to members at low cost	

Note: All of the benefits listed may not apply in a particular local. For example some of the smaller AFM locals necessarily provide limited benefits. Some locals of the AFM have recording studios that rent time to members at discount prices.

led to legislation in a number of states that specifies that no one can be compelled to join a union. These states are known as **right-to-work states**. Many of the movie studios do nonunion productions in these states, which enables them to pay lower wages and to avoid making pension and health contributions. On the recording scene, the prevalence of home recording studios and artists who own their own labels have negatively affected the union's influence in the recording industry. At the same time, the AFM has almost entirely lost control of the night club business, as already discussed.

For a person who plans a permanent career as a full-time professional musician or singer, joining the union is a fairly obvious and inevitable step. For younger musicians whose long-term career goals are uncertain or part-time musicians who have another profession, the benefits of union membership are less clear.

The musician's union has attempted to reach younger members through an extensive Web site, and by beginning to develop a presence at music industry conferences. (Some of the union locals have Web sites and send e-mails to members about job opportunities.) The national union has also worked with other talent unions to lobby for legislation that is beneficial

Protecting Local Musicians

In 2006 the Portland, Oregon, local of the AFM challenged the licenses of three local radio stations, on the grounds that the stations were not fulfilling their community obligations by doing local programming, or playing the recordings of local musicians. Radio station owners must agree to present a certain amount of local programming in order to receive a license from the **Federal Communications Commission (FCC)**. However, many stations confine these community obligations to late-night programming.

The FCC held hearings on this issue. Two stations were found to be following the rules, but one station received a letter of admonition for not keeping appropriate records of what recordings they were playing. The campaign received nationwide publicity, and helped the Portland local in establishing a contemporary identity on the Portland music scene.

to musicians. For example, the AFM and AFTRA are both trying to establish a performance right for performers, so that they can be compensated for radio play in the same way that songwriters and music publishers currently receive such income.

Talent unions work most efficiently when they service large groups of employees, such as symphony or recording musicians. These musicians can then fight for contracts that establish good working conditions, job protection, and reasonable wages. In recent years, the unions have tried to adjust to the changing musical world, where musicians are less likely to work in a larger ensemble. They have focused on developing a bit more flexibility, setting recording wages for example, based on the budgets of these records, rather than on using a "one size fits all" model. Although the AFM franchises booking agents, an increasing number of unions have organized referral services that help musicians find work.

Terms to Know

American Federation of Labor (AFL) *79*
American Federation of Musicians (AFM) *79*
AFTRA *86*
Congress of Industrial Organizations (CIO) *79*
Federal Communications Commission (FCC) *89*

International Conference of Symphony Orchestra Members (ICSOM) *86*
Pensions *81*
Regional Orchestra Players Association (ROPA) *86*
Residuals *81*
Right-to-work states *88*

Recording Musicians Association (RMA) *86*
Screen Actors Guild (SAG) *86*
Session musician *83*
Special Payments Fund *81*

For Class Discussion

1. Why do you think that AFM membership has declined so steeply?
2. How could the unions do a better job of representing local musicians?
3. What sort of job protections can talent unions offer to a self-contained rock or country band?
4. If you were to organize a modern musician's union, how would you do it differently from the AFM?
5. Do you know any professional musicians who are or have been members of a talent union? How do they describe their experiences with the union?
6. Why do you think that the AFM has trouble organizing young musicians?
7. What is a guaranteed contract clause?
8. Do you think that the union movement has a future in the United States?
9. Are there any talent unions in the town where you live, or where you go to school?

CHAPTER 6

Copyright and
Performance Rights

COPYRIGHT

Copyright exists to protect the interests of songwriters and music publishers. Historically, copyright in the United States goes back to the U.S. Copyright Law of 1790. In terms of the music industry, the Copyright Law of 1909 governed copyright in the United States for sixty-seven years. The 1909 act provided for copyrights to be protected for twenty-eight years, with a provision for a renewal that brought an additional twenty-eight years of protection, doubling the longevity of the copyright to fifty-six years. When the Copyright Law of 1976 was passed by the U.S. Congress, that protection was extended to the life of the last surviving author plus an additional fifty years. In practical terms this meant that if a twenty-two-year-old song writer collaborates with a fifty-five-year-old songwriter, their song will be copyrighted for fifty years after the death of the last author. In this case, the chances are that the twenty-two-year-old will be around long after the death of his coauthor, so the children and even grandchildren of both writers will continue to collect income from the songs that they composed. In 1998, copyright protection was extended for an additional twenty years, so the term of copyright is now the life of the last surviving author plus seventy years.

Copyright is something of an abstract concept, in the sense that copyright exists immediately after the moment of the creation of a song. In other words, if the reader writes a song on June 2, 2009, she owns the copyright to the song written on that day. In spite of this, the songwriter needs to formally register the song in order to entirely validate that copyright. First of all, if the songwriter can write out the music, he produces a "lead sheet," of the song. A lead sheet contains the melody, chords, and lyrics of the song. On the lead sheet the author then writes: "'Grey Day Dance,' words and music by Edgar Stanton © 2009." If there is a publisher, and if the author belongs to

---

"Happy Birthday to You": The Gift That Keeps on Giving

In 1893, schoolteacher/sisters Mildred and Patty Hill composed a song titled "Good Morning to All." The sisters taught kindergarten and published the song in a collection for young children that year with the Chicago publisher, Charles F. Summy. By around 1910, the song had gained a new verse, beginning "Happy birthday to you . . . " using the Hills sisters' melody. A performance in Irving Berlin's 1934 Broadway musical, *As Thousands Cheer*, provoked a lawsuit from a third Hill sister, Jessica. She won, and in 1935 Summy copyrighted "Happy Birthday" with the new lyrics. In 1990, Warner Chappell Music, one of the world's largest music publishers, purchased Summy for $25 million, specifically to gain the rights to the song, which was then estimated to earn an annual income of at least $1 million in royalty payments (different sources quote up to $5 million as its annual income). Warners claims that, under the 1998 copyright law, the song will remain protected until 2030.

The hazy nature of copyright has led many to question Warners' position. The Hills' original song and melody were probably based on earlier nineteenth-century songs that had similar titles. Nonetheless, most performers continue to pay fees to Warners for its use. For this reason, major restaurant chains have substituted their own birthday songs for this more familiar anthem.

---

one of the performing rights organizations, Mr. Stanton then adds the phrase: "Stanton Music, BMI."

To officially copyright the song, the songwriter sends it to the Copyright Office at the Library of Congress, along with a fee of $45. There are two ways that a song can be registered. In lead sheet form, the writer uses **copyright form PA (Performing Arts Works)**. If the songwriter doesn't feel comfortable with music notation, he can make a tape of the song, and send it to the same place. In this case the songwriter uses **form SR (Sound Recording)**. Because $45 is a fairly steep fee, if the writer is prolific and writes numerous songs a week, many songwriters copyright a group of songs together, using form SR. If Edward Stanton were to write a series of songs called *Springtime Songbook*, the fee would be $45 for the entire collection of songs. If you follow this practice, it is a good idea to announce the songs on the CD, so that if any dispute arises, the particular song in question can be easily located. Should any of the songs in the collection actually get recorded, it is a good idea to copyright them individually.

Reasons for Copyrighting a Song

If a song is copyrighted and another artist records the song without compensating the author, the author is entitled to sue for damages. This is known as **copyright infringement**. For example, if an artist decided to record the song "Blowin' In the Wind," one of Bob Dylan's famous songs, the artist would have to obtain a license from the publisher of the song. There are two categories of infringement that determine what amount the writer may seek to recover. *Nonwillful infringements* can result in awards of $750 to $30,000 for registered songs. A more serious category is *willful infringement.* In the latter instance, the court may award as much as $150,000 in damages to the aggrieved party. In the nonwillful category, the infringement is regarded as accidental, in a willful case, the violation was deliberate. The court also can award attorney's fees to the songwriter whose songs have been ripped off. There are a handful of copyright experts who deal with infringement cases. They appear in the courtroom with elaborate charts comparing melodies and lyrics in an attempt to prove their clients' cases.

Virtually every successful songwriter has faced some sort of infringement suit at some point in her or his career. Generally, publishing contracts

That's Not Alright, Mama!

One of the strangest cases of royalty disputes was the controversy between blues singer Arthur "Big Boy" Crudup, and Hill & Range Music. Crudup wrote a song called "That's All Right Mama," which became one of Elvis Presley's major hits. The song was originally published by Lester Melrose, who had produced Crudup's own recordings.

Some years later, Crudup hired Dick Waterman, a blues enthusiast and scholar, as a booking agent. As Waterman tells the story in his book, *Between Midnight and Day: The Last Unpublished Blues Archive,* he discovered that Crudup had been getting virtually no income from the song. Hill & Range had acquired the song, so Waterman attempted to get the appropriate royalties from them. A

Arthur "Big Boy" Crudup, c. 1970s. Courtesy Delmark Records.

verbal agreement was reached that Crudup would receive a one-time check for $60,000 accounting for his back royalties. Crudup drove up from Virginia only to have the company's president refuse to sign the check. His lawyer passed along the message that the company had concluded that any resulting litigation would be less expensive than signing the check.

Crudup went home, and died a year later. Shortly afterwards, Hill & Range was in the process of being sold to publishing giant Chappell Music. Chappell's attorneys discovered the dispute between Crudup's estate and Hill & Range. Chappell insisted that the dispute be settled before they purchased the company. Instead of a single payment, Crudup's estate received an immediate check for $248,000. As of 2003, the estate had received over $3 million dollars in royalties.

The moral of this story is that no one should underestimate the value of a copyright, or the importance of copyright to a song.

specify that the writer must do original work, and if they have plagiarized an existing song, the publisher is released from any financial responsibility for the consequences. Many music publishers and record companies now return all unsolicited material, because of the number of frivolous lawsuits that they have had to defend. By refusing even to open the package, the publisher asserts that it was totally unaware of the song and couldn't have possibly copied it. Often there is indeed some similarity between two songs, but not necessarily something substantial enough for the courts to act. A song title alone is not considered an infringement of a copyright.

INFRINGEMENT

In addition to proving substantial similarity between your work and the one that you feel has infringed your copyright, you must prove that the other writer had access to your work before creating their own song. This proof requires that you go beyond what anthropologists like to call **independent invention**. In songwriting, independent invention occurs when you are sitting in Vermont writing a song about the turning of the leaves, and at roughly the same time someone in Australia has come up with the same melody, and many of the same words. If you are unable to prove that the Australian songwriter heard your work, you will not win a copyright suit.

There are certain genres of music where many melodies are roughly similar, such as three-chord blues or country songs. In order to prove infringement, you will have to show that the infringing song shares more with your original than a generic tune that sounds like many prior blues or country songs. In such cases, you may be more apt to focus on an unusual set of lyrics to substantiate your claims of originality. For example, I doubt that an infringer could get away with plagiarizing the lyrics to the song "I'm Going To Hire A Wino To Decorate My Home."

A Cincinnati producer-writer named Shad O'Shea once sent a lyric to one of the many shady music publishers that advertise in popular magazines, offering to get songs recorded. These shady operators are known in the industry as "song sharks." O'Shea submitted a lyric that contained the phrase, "ooh baby, ooh," repeated over and over again. He got the requisite form letter from the shark applauding his talent, and requesting a fee in order to set this creative lyric to music! Songwriters should never pay to get their songs recorded. No legitimate music publisher will make such a request.

PERFORMANCE RIGHTS ORGANIZATIONS: ASCAP, BMI, AND SESAC

The story of **performance rights** in America begins with composer Victor Herbert in 1909. He was having dinner and realized that an orchestra was playing several of his compositions. Herbert felt that it was unjust that the restaurant owner was using his music to promote the establishment, but that he received no financial reward for this service. Together with composer Rudolf

Department of Folklore & Mythology

I have heard hundreds of musicians state that it is legal to copy up to four bars of music. There is absolutely nothing in the copyright law that justifies copying *any* portion of a musical work. The law uses the phrase "substantial similarity," and obviously this very phrase is grounds for lengthy and bitter arguments between songwriters who think that they have been ripped off.

The other bit of wishful thinking that is quite common among musicians is the notion that it really isn't necessary to copyright songs formally; you should just send them to yourself via registered mail. This quaint notion is based on the idea that the date on the postmark will prove that you wrote the song before whoever it is that you claim has infringed your copyright. The problems with this approach are that you will not be entitled to statutory damages, even if the court were to accept your claim of prior authorship, and even worse, the courts do not recognize this as a legitimate way to protect your music. Oddly, this method, which for some reason is known as a **poor man's or Oklahoma copyright**, is apparently accepted by the courts in England.

Friml and several others, Herbert formed the **American Society of Composers, Authors and Publishers (ASCAP)** to address this situation.

ASCAP levies fees on night clubs and other entertainment venues. This enables these establishments to perform anything in the ASCAP catalog. Although ASCAP was born before radio existed, it also became the vehicle for publishers and songwriters to receive royalties from music played on radio, and later television.

The fees charged to venues vary according to their size. Radio station fees are a small percentage of the gross earnings of the stations. In 1940, ASCAP attempted to raise their radio station fees, and the radio stations revolted. The stations did two things. First, they began to play many recordings of songs that were older than fifty-six years. The copyright to these songs had run out, and they had fallen into the **public domain**. (A song in the public domain does not require payment to the publisher or composer of the song.) The radio stations also took a more radical step. They organized their own performing rights organization, called **Broadcast Music Incorporated (BMI)**.

ASCAP was dominated by composers of show tunes and operettas and in those days the organization was snobbish about country and blues music. BMI immediately attempted to attract these writers, many of whom had never been admitted to ASCAP. When rock and roll began to become important during the mid-1950s, BMI songs dominated the charts. Almost all of the young writers joined BMI, and it was the work of these writers that came to dominate American popular music. Eventually, ASCAP realized that to compete in the performance rights arena, they would have to change their attitude. Today, both organizations welcome hundreds of writers in every conceivable genre of music.

Victor Herbert, c. 1914. Courtesy Prints and Photographs Div., Library of Congress.

SESAC (Society of European Stage Authors and Composers) was founded to deal with Latin-American and European music. Although it remains much smaller than the other performing rights groups, SESAC is now more competitive with the others than it has been at any time in its history. Both ASCAP and BMI are publicly owned, nonprofit organizations, and their activities are closely monitored by the courts to make sure that they are observing the various federal antitrust rules and regulations. SESAC is privately owned, and has a bit more flexibility in its operation. A few years ago, SESAC signed Neil Diamond and Bob Dylan, by giving them lucrative advances and presumably some guarantees. This was the first example of major league poaching by SESAC on songwriting superstars.

How Performing Organizations Operate

Many songwriters have little understanding of how the **performing rights organizations (PROs)** collect and distribute money to publishers and songwriters. The money collected from venues largely goes to pay administrative costs. Clearly, it would not be cost-effective for the performing rights organizations to monitor every song played in every small restaurant or bar in the

United States. Until recently, the same thing held true for the monies collected from concerts. Recently, the PROs began to pay some of the top-grossing acts that are also songwriters by getting a list of the large venues where they were playing and the songs that they were performing.

The PROs cover all network television programs, by having the producers submit log sheets of the music played on the show. This includes instrumental music as well as vocal music. Cable television credits are gathered in a similar way, and local television is also logged, although not as comprehensively. In the United States, songwriters do not receive royalties from movie theater showings, although in Europe they do receive money from this source. This is an oddity of the U.S. Copyright Act and one that is of great concern to songwriters and composers. As soon as the movies go on television, the PROs pay royalties to these very same people!

The biggest bone of contention between songwriters and the PROs is the way that the groups deal with radio airplay. The different societies use a combination of physical logs from radio stations, Broadcast Data System (BDS) information, watermarks, and charts from music trade papers. Depending upon who one talks to, the results are perfectly fair or wildly unacceptable. The bottom line is that when songs appear in major cities on important radio stations, the publishers and songwriters will certainly receive appropriate credits and royalties. The rewards are small for genre-specific writers whose works are better described as niche-market items. None of the societies pay much attention to community or public radio, outside national network programs. All of the societies claim that "it balances out in the end." If you have a local or regional hit, you may not receive any income, they argue, but in another year, when attention is being paid to a specific market, you may actually be overcompensated. This is an interesting argument, although I have never met anyone who has enjoyed one of these theoretical bonanzas.

Radio in many countries is government owned and operated, and every single song is carefully logged. Songwriters specializing in less popular genres therefore find themselves receiving performing rights checks from Canada, the United Kingdom, Japan, Germany, and so on. It would seem that contemporary computer technology ought to enable the PROs to log everything played on American radio, but at present this is not happening.

PROs and Income

Performing rights can be worth a tremendous amount of money. The key to the highest income streams is to have a crossover hit, a song that tops the pop charts, but also performs well on country, R&B, or hip-hop stations. Such songs can earn $250,000 and up for a single year's performance rights. Performing income is distributed separately to the songwriter and the publisher, so the writer is paid regardless of whatever their deal may be with their music publisher or record company. When the songwriter is also the publisher, he or she receives both royalty pots. If the songwriter is the

There's Gold in Them Thar Songs!

Gary White was a songwriter and musician who was a member of a 1960s band called Circus Maximus with Jerry Jeff Walker. In the late 1960s he wrote a song called "Long, Long Time." Linda Ronstadt recorded the song in 1970, and it became a **career record** for her. A career record is one that establishes the artist's identity, and which her fans will always identify with the artist. White's song appeared on five different recordings by Ronstadt. It was a hit single, it was on the album "featuring the hit single," it appeared on two live performance albums, and it was included on a *Greatest Hits* album. Every one of these recordings went platinum or multiplatinum, indicating sales of over a million copies.

The performing rights income over the years must be truly amazing, and of course there are also the sheet music rights. As icing on the cake, Alannah Myles covered the song in 1993, and Mindy McCready recorded a country version in 1997. Once again, the lesson is that no songwriter should sell the rights to a song.

co-publisher of the song, she or he gets the songwriter's share and half of the publisher's share.

When songs are logged on radio and television, the weighting formulas are complex. In radio, the money generated will depend on the time of day the song is played, and the size of the market that the station covers. The factors involved when a song is aired on television include the way the song or instrumental is used on the show (foreground, background, title song, and so on). Commercials are also logged, and receive a smaller amount of money per use. (See later in this chapter on for-hire agreements.)

Is There a Difference Between the PROs?

All three of the PROs will tell you that they offer things not delivered by their competitors. To a certain extent, this is true. ASCAP and BMI both have some really excellent educational programs, and SESAC has begun to expand its educational offerings. However, to take advantage of these programs, you have to live in one of the major music business centers. BMI, for example, offers an excellent workshop in writing for the musical theater, and ASCAP and BMI both offer workshop programs in writing music for film.

Both ASCAP and SESAC offer ways for songwriters and composers who are writing outside the confines of mainstream pop to generate some income. ASCAP's program is called ASCAP Plus. A writer lists all of the works that he composed during the last year, any recordings that he has made of his songs, any recordings of his songs made by other people, and all of the places that performed original music during the year. There is also a place to fill out any honors that he has achieved, such as awards from local or national songwriting associations, or any prizes received for his musical contributions. The forms are monitored by several reputable music critics, and the writer then receives awards based on the organization's assessment of their level of activity and accomplishment. All ASCAP writers are eligible, unless they have earned over $25,000 from ASCAP during the application year. SESAC has a program that pays a songwriter for songs that they are performing on gigs. The songwriter-performer must send the organization a list of songs played, and which venues they were performed at. BMI currently has no comparable programs like these.

ASCAP also gives annual awards for critical books about music, and BMI used to do this as well, but they are not currently doing so. All three groups offer ceremonial plaques for hit writers, and sponsor some showcases to introduce new songwriters to the industry.

Another difference between the three groups is that songwriters must pay $25 to join ASCAP, and have had a song published or recorded. BMI and SESAC do not charge membership fees, and do not require the writer to have a previously published or recorded song.

Other Reasons for Joining PROs

The staff of the PROs are not only involved with songwriters and music publishers, but interact constantly with record and film companies. If a writer is able to establish a relationship with one of these PRO staff members, they can open the door for possible record deals or introduce the writer to music supervisors and film or television producers. There are a number of examples of situations where these people have helped writers get by the gatekeepers at the major labels.

Establishing relationships with the PRO staff people is not easy, but it is not an insurmountable obstacle either. The PROs send representatives to the major music conferences, and they also conduct educational seminars in various parts of the country, sometimes for songwriting organizations. This offers a chance to meet with them face-to-face and impress them with your talents. Obviously, the writer must impress the PRO rep first, because when someone in the industry makes a submission or a recommendation to a decision maker, the person submitting the material is being judged as much as its creator. In other words, if the SESAC rep recommends you to other industry executives, and they find your work to be poor, that is also a reflection on the rep, who loses credibility as a judge of talent.

When visiting a major music industry center, songwriters should attempt to meet with one of the writer reps at the PROs. Although these people are busy, it is important for their own careers within the PRO to be able to find exciting new writers to promote. Should one of these reps succeed in opening doors for you, it is only common courtesy for you to join their organization rather than one of the competing groups.

PERFORMANCE RIGHTS FOR ARTISTS

In Europe, artists enjoy performing rights income even when they do not write songs. Currently, there is legislation in the U.S. Congress that would create similar compensation for artists for American airplay. Background musicians, vocalists, and record companies would also be compensated. Songwriters who are also recording artists would be compensated for both of these functions. Should this legislation pass, performing artists would also receive income from radio play in Europe. Because the United States does not offer such compensation at present, the European performing rights organizations do distribute income to artists when their songs are played on European radio stations.

PUBLISHING AND THE SONGWRITER

Songwriters' Organizations

Just as many artists have chosen to produce and own their own recordings, there are songwriters who have chosen to retain their publishing rights. For these writers, local, regional, or national songwriters' associations are a valuable resource. There are tens of thousands of wannabe songwriters in the United States. Most cities have local organizations where songwriters can network with one another. Lyricists can hook up with composers, and these groups often hold workshops featuring guest writers or publishers who critique songs and may even sign some writers. The majority of these groups are run by volunteers, so their effectiveness and even the scheduling of their meetings may vary.

The **Nashville Songwriters Association International (NSAI)** is the largest of these organizations, and also has local branches in some other cities. The NSAI numbers among its membership major songwriters and publishers, and has seminars and classes at its well-staffed Nashville headquarters.

MUSIC PUBLISHERS

It is important to grasp exactly what it is that publishers do, before a writer makes the decision to retain his own publishing rights. Here are some of the major responsibilities handled by music publishers:

- Register copyrights
- Make song demos
- Contact producers, recording artists, and managers to obtain recordings of songs
- Lease print rights to music print publishers
- May provide office space for writers, with piano and recording equipment
- May own a recording studio for song demos and even record productions
- Contact music supervisors to place songs in films and TV shows
- Attempt to exploit digital rights: ringtones, ringbacks, and so on
- Critique songs to songwriters
- Help songwriters find collaborators
- Pay a weekly or monthly "draw" to writers
- Make sure that songs are properly copyrighted
- Undertake audits to collect unpaid money

- Obtain foreign sub-publishing deals
- If the songwriter is also an artist, help writer to obtain a record deal
- Keep a careful record of all song pitches
- Continually develop and exploit industry contacts in film, television, and at record companies
- May own a record label

In return for these services the publisher receives 50 percent of all of the songwriter's income. The songwriter must make the decision as to whether these functions justify losing half of the gross income from songwriting and publishing. Obviously, songwriters must take a careful look at what sort of investment in time and energy they must make, when determining that they would rather publish on their own. The disadvantage of attempting to own one's own publishing is the amount of time, energy, and even investment that it takes to pursue all of these functions while writing songs on an ongoing basis.

The obvious benefit in retaining one's own publishing rights is keeping all the income. But there are some other advantages:

- All creative and business decisions controlled by songwriter. For example, the songwriter may not want her music used in certain product commercials because of personal beliefs.
- Songwriter may prefer to develop her own business contacts, dealing directly with producers and artists. This may result in an ongoing relationship in which a hit artist records many songs by the writer
- A publisher must divide its time between the various writers under contract to him. A writer may feel neglected in favor of someone who is the "flavor of the month."
- The songwriter can tailor demos to fit personal musical ideas, rather than dealing with publisher input

The songwriter needs to examine some key questions before abandoning the idea of working with a music publisher:

- Does the writer have the time to pursue industry contacts?
- Does the writer have the skills to keep clear and specific records of whom the songs were pitched to, how they responded, and so on?
- Is the writer willing to devote the necessary hours to follow-up calls, after making initial contacts?
- Does the writer live in a major music industry center?
- Does the writer have contacts with artists, producers, and managers?
- Is the writer a self-starter who does not need input on songs or demos?
- Does the writer have enough money to make reasonable demos, and to pitch songs on a regular basis?

Exclusive Deals

When a music publisher wants to represent a songwriter on an exclusive basis, the publisher offers a weekly salary, in exchange for owning the music publishing rights of anything that the songwriter writes. These deals are generally one-year deals with additional options on the part of the publisher. They may pay the writer anything from $100 to $500 a week, which is an advance against royalties. For writers who have a track record of having written successful songs, the weekly draw may be as high as $1,000 a week, or even more. The publisher will also generally finance demo recordings of the writer's songs, usually charging half of the costs against the writer's royalties.

These contracts are generally written with specific delivery terms built in. This means that the writer must deliver a certain number of what are termed *commercially acceptable* songs to the publisher. Failure to do so will end the agreement. Problems may arise when the songwriter and publisher disagree about the definition of what is commercially acceptable.

At the end of the year, the publisher decides whether to renew the contract. Some contracts have escalator clauses that require the publisher to increase the amount of the weekly draw in order to renew the agreement.

Copyright Termination

A songwriter can regain the publishing rights to his or her compositions from a music publisher at the end of thirty-five years from the date of the song's publication. If the songwriter is deceased, this termination can be undertaken by the writer's heirs. In the case of valuable copyrights, some songwriters have used this termination clause as a way of obtaining additional advances from a publisher in exchange for granting the publisher renewal rights to a song. This applies to songs written during or after 1978. Songs written earlier but still protected by the copyright act can also be recovered but not until five years following the original copyright date and renewal of fifty-six years.

Co-publishing

Songwriters who have some history of success with their songs often turn to **co-publishing** as an alternative to giving up all of their own publishing rights. In a co-publishing deal, the ownership of the publishing rights is shared, as shown in this table.

Writer & Publisher	Two Different Publishers
• The writer is an established artist with a track record of having written successful songs. • The writer has just secured a major record deal and trades half of her publishing rights for a substantial amount of cash.	• The songwriter often works with another writer and they are each under contract to different publishing companies. • Both songwriters operate their own music publishing companies and therefore split ownership of the publishing rights

In the case of contemporary hip-hop music and to a lesser extent in country music, it is not unusual for three or more songwriters to write a song together. They may each be under contract to different publishers, so that the publishing is owned by three different music publishers. There are also instances when an entire band chooses to share publishing rights, so that five different people may each receive 20 percent of the publishing rights to a song.

Some students have difficulty understanding the way that rights are split in co-publishing deals. Think of songwriting and publishing rights as a large pie. In a standard writer-publisher deal that is not a co-publishing agreement, half of the pie belongs to the writer, half to the publisher. In a co-publishing agreement, the writer retains his own writer's income, plus half of the publisher's rights, thus receiving 75 percent of the total pie, while the share of the publisher is reduced to 25 percent.

Administration Rights

Nowadays, publishing rights are often owned by two or more publishers, who split the rights. Often, this is because there are two or more songwriters, all under contract to different publishing companies. If a song is owned by two publishing companies, the company that decides whether or not the song can be used in a commercial is the one that controls the **administration rights**. If there is only one publisher, then they control these rights. If the songwriter owns half of the publishing, unless it is specified that both companies share in the administration rights, then one publisher controls the rights.

The reason that this can be an important aspect of the publishing deal is that the artist, for example, may not want her music used in commercials that promote the sale of alcohol. As long as the publisher and the songwriter maintain a good relationship, then the publisher will usually accede to the writer's wishes. If the songwriter moves to another publisher, then the original publisher may simply take the position that they will exploit the song in any way they wish to generate income.

Another type of administration deal comes into play with superstar songwriters. A major singer-songwriter may wish to retain all of the publishing income from his songs. Many artists write songs that are closely tied into their particular style of performing, and so their songs do not tend to be covered by other artists. Under these circumstances, the singer-songwriter may hire a law firm to file all of the necessary copyright forms, and to act as a sort of answering service, should requests come in to use the writer's material in movies or on television. The artist then retains the writer's and publisher's share of the song, and simply pays the administrator a percentage of the gross income, usually about 15 percent. Under such an agreement, the administrator basically offers secretarial and legal assistance, and does not seek to exploit copyrights. If the songwriter wishes to have the administrator try to obtain other recordings of his songs, then typically they receive an additional percentage if the song gets covered by another artist.

Foreign Rights and Sub-Publishing

As overseas travel has become commonplace and the world has moved more into the digital domain, the importance of making worldwide publishing deals has greatly increased. The very largest publishing companies, like the major record labels, have offices in various countries around the world. Medium-sized or smaller publishers farm these rights out in various ways.

This table indicates the advantages and disadvantages of having a single publisher who controls all foreign rights.

Advantages	Disadvantages
• One source for all payments • One party deals with all paperwork • Probably a large entity, consequently royalties are paid in a timely fashion	• Company may have less power in some countries than others • Very large companies sometimes don't promote energetically, because they have too many products to deal with

This table indicates the advantages and disadvantages of using a variety of foreign publishers.

Advantages	Disadvantages
• In each country or region, you can determine the most effective publisher • Possibility of garnering a number of different cash advances	• The American publisher must spend a great deal of time and energy monitoring the performance of a number of different publishers • Collecting royalties from six different foreign publishers can be a dreadful nuisance and payment may not be made in a timely manner

WHAT FOREIGN PUBLISHERS DO   Smaller U.S. publishers may seek out a foreign partner to handle overseas markets. When a piece of music is licensed to a foreign publisher for a specific territory, the foreign publisher is called a **sub-publisher.**

One function of foreign publishers is to provide translations of English lyrics into other languages. Although much of the international music business operates in the English language, France, in particular, reserves a percentage of airplay for songs sung in the French language. A good foreign publisher will have insight into which songs are most apt to work in translation, and they will also have easy access to lyricists who are capable of translating English language lyrics.

The foreign publisher will also assume some of the same functions as an American publisher does, such as trying to obtain new recordings of a song and dealing with synchronization rights and film and TV uses of songs. Foreign commercials and publicity for local artists who record the publisher's songs are among other responsibilities of the sub-publisher, as well as the collection of foreign royalties and the registration of works with local performing rights organizations.

Some of the foreign performing rights societies allow American publishers to directly collect foreign performing rights, which eliminates the necessity of commissions being deducted by both the American and the foreign PROs. The songwriter's share of the performing rights income, however, is paid by the foreign PRO directly to the American PRO that the writer belongs to.

Foreign sub-publishers sometimes receive 25 percent of the foreign performing rights fee, with the remainder going to the American publisher. According to the current edition of *This Business of Music*, the fees received by the foreign sub-publisher are proportional to the amount of work that the publisher undertakes. If all the foreign publisher does is to collect income, rather than seeking to exploit a song copyright, the fee will be limited to 10 to 15 percent of gross income but will rise up to 25 percent in other cases. When a local version of the song occurs, the percentage is more apt to escalate to 30 to 50 percent of receipts. This is because the foreign publisher has usually obtained that recording by shopping the song.

The lyricist who translates an American lyric into the local language will get 12.5 percent of the publisher's gross income for mechanical and synchronization licenses, and 25 percent of the writer's public performance income, and for local printed editions of the song.

The term of sub-publishing agreement is set forth in the agreement, often for three to five years. The deals may be renewed or abrogated. Many agreements are one-year deals with options on the part of the American publisher.

FOREIGN DEALS   Deals can be made for a single song, for entire catalogs owned by an American publisher, or for all of the works of a specific writer under contract to an American publisher. Usually the American publisher will seek an advance. The amount will vary, according to the notoriety of the writer involved and the foreign publisher's desire to represent the writer. The American publisher will need to pay attention to the fluctuation of the foreign currency rates in relation to the American dollar. The value of the British pound, for example, has varied from $1 to more than $2 over the last 20 years.

For example, today a 10,000-pound advance is worth almost twice as much in American dollars than it was in 1985.

Song Collaborations

Songwriters have been collaborating to produce hits since the birth of the modern music industry. It is typical in Broadway musicals or Tin Pan Alley pop songs to have one person writing the lyrics and another person writing the music. In the contemporary music market the breakdown may be less clear, with one person writing most, but not all of the music, and the lyrics being concocted in a similar manner. When two people are sitting in the same room playing guitars or guitar and keyboard, the writers may not even remember who wrote which parts of the melody or lyrics.

It is a good idea to have a collaboration agreement in place *before* the writing occurs. When two people work together on a regular basis, they usually do not count the words to a song to divvy up the percentages. The attitude that prevails is that I wrote more of this one, you wrote more of the last one, but we're working as a team. In Nashville, many writers cowrite with a half-dozen different writers over the course of a few months, so it becomes critical that each person understand who owns what percentage of the rights.

When the writers do not have a collaboration agreement in place, they may haggle over one person getting, say, 65 percent of the rights. Another collaboration occurs when a third writer is brought in simply to write a bridge. Is the song now split three ways, or does the new writer get a smaller share?

My favorite example of odd collaboration splits was the strategy adopted by my friend the late John Phillips, leader of The Mamas and The Papas and writer of numerous hit songs. John loved to stay up all night and write. If you simply kept him company and threw in an occasional suggestion, he would give you a small percentage of the writing credits.

Collaboration can be a great thing, but it doesn't work for everyone. Some people work faster than others, some like to work in the morning, some late at night, and some writers prefer to receive a finished lyric or melody before they even begin to work. If the two writers understand each other, any of these difficulties can be overcome. Some writers simply prefer to write on their own without input from anyone else.

Songpluggers

Some songwriters, especially in Nashville, hire **songpluggers**. These people are, in effect, sole practitioners, not affiliated with law or accounting firms. They generally are paid a fee and a percentage of the copyright, which varies according to the success of the recording. In other words, there are bonuses based on the sales of the recordings that the songpluggers obtain.

Songpluggers are sometimes hired by songwriters who are under contract to large publishing companies, and who may feel that their work is lost or poorly represented in a huge catalog. Nashville has become a prime center for songwriters, because there are still quite a few country artists who do not write their own songs. In the rock and hip-hop fields, the artist generally either writes her own material or co-writes with a producer. This makes it increasingly difficult for the new or unknown writer who is not an artist to get songs recorded.

Terms to Know

Administration
  rights *103*
American Society of
  Composers, Authors
  and Publishers
  (ASCAP) *95*
Broadcast Music
  International
  (BMI) *95*
Career record *98*
Copyright *91*
Copyright forms
  PA (Performing
  Arts Work) and
  SR (Sound
  Recording) *92*

Copyright
  infringement *92*
Copyright termination
  and renewal *102*
Co-publishing *102*
Independent
  invention *94*
Nashville Songwriters
  Association
  International
  (NSAI) *100*
Oklahoma (poor man's)
  copyright *95*
Performance
  rights *94*

Performing rights
  organizations
  (PROs) *96*
Public domain *95*
SESAC (Society of
  European Stage
  Authors and
  Composers) *96*
Songplugger *106*
Sub-publisher *104*

For Class Discussion

1. In your opinion, is the current length of copyright protection fair?
2. What two elements determine copyright infringement?
3. Why has music publishing adjusted better to new media technology than the record business has been able to do?
4. Why has almost all of the coverage of the negative effect of file sharing focused on record companies and artists, when it is the songwriters who are most profoundly affected?
5. What are the chances that an unknown songwriter would win a songwriting contest?
6. Do you know anyone who has had a song recorded? Who published the song, and did the writer receive any income from it?
7. What is the function of the Harry Fox office?
8. Why was BMI formed?
9. In addition to collecting money, how can a performing rights organization assist a songwriter?
10. Name as many possible sources of income for a successful song as you can think of.

CHAPTER 7

Music Publishing

W hen most people see the term *publishing*, they think of the printed word. Although printed music was indeed the key financial aspect of music publishing from the nineteenth century to the mid-twentieth century, this is no longer true today. In this chapter, we look at the various ways that songs generate income, the different media—from print to recordings to radio, film, and television—that feature music, and much more.

PUBLISHING RIGHTS

Music publishing entails a **bundle of rights**—literally, a group of specified rights—that go with it. These include:

- *Mechanicals.* Money obtained for songwriters and music publishers from the sale of recorded music
- *Performance rights.* Income derived from radio and television play as well as from works performed in shows
- *Print.* The income derived from the sale of printed music
- *Synchronization rights.* Income derived from the syncing of music to picture, as in television and movies
- *Grand rights.* Income derived from the use of music in theatrical works
- *New media.* Income derived from the use of songs in ringtones, ringbacks, video games, and platforms not yet in existence
- *Other rights.* Income derived from reprints of songs on greeting cards or in books or magazines, the use of music in music boxes or toys

MECHANICALS

The term **mechanicals** dates back to royalties that derived from the sale of piano rolls. Piano rolls mechanically recreated a performance of a piece of music, by being "played back" by a player piano. Similarly, phonographs are mechanical devices that recreate a musical performance. Today, the term refers to royalties paid to songwriters and music publishers from the sales of recordings. The copyright law enacted in 1909 remained in place until 1976. It provided for royalties of two cents a song to be paid to the publisher, who then split that income with the songwriter. If there were two songwriters, they would split a royalty of one cent, while the publisher retained a full penny. As the price of phonograph records went up, and as inflation came into play, there was a great outcry from songwriters and publishers that this royalty rate was archaic and unfair. After some years of congressional debate and inaction, a new and more generous copyright law was finally passed that went into effect in 1976. Not only were rates raised, but provisions were made for periodic adjustments of that rate. As of 2009, these royalties have risen to 9.1 cents per song, or 1.75 cents a minute, whichever figure is greater. This is particularly important for classical music and jazz composers, whose works often run as long as 20 minutes.

But it wasn't only the amount of the royalty that was raised. As I noted in the previous chapter, the copyright term had been for a period of twenty-eight years, with a possible renewal for an additional twenty-eight years, but was raised to the life of the last surviving author of the song, plus an additional fifty years. The Sonny Bono Copyright Act of 1998 extended that period to the life of the last surviving author plus seventy years. Sonny Bono was himself a hit artist and songwriter who was a member of the U.S. Congress from 1994 until his death in 1998. His wife Mary was re-elected in his place, and she was one of the sponsors of this law, named after Sonny as a memorial to his efforts in the world of copyright. Many music publishers do their actual licensing work through the Harry Fox office in New York City. They charge publishers 6.5 percent (the fee varies from year to year) and they complete all of the paper work for the publisher.

The reader should be aware that the publisher can control the first recording of a song, but that any further versions cannot be prevented. In other words if a singer-songwriter has written a song, and wishes to be sure that the first recording of the song that reaches the market is his own version, the publisher can prevent any other versions from being made until the singer-songwriter's version is released. Once that takes place, the publisher is compelled to license any further recordings of the song by other artists. This is referred to as a **compulsory license**. Because the literal compulsory licensed song must report royalties every month, publishers use a "negotiated license," which releases the record company from having to pay royalties every month.

In the fall of 2008, after much negotiation, the U.S. Copyright Royalty Board set the rates for digital downloads at 9.1 cents per song, the same fee used for royalties from the sale of a record. Ringtone royalties were set at 24 cents per tone.

Copyright Termination

A songwriter can regain the publishing rights to his or her compositions from a music publisher at the end of thirty-five years from the date of the song's publication. If the songwriter is deceased, this termination can be undertaken by the writer's heirs. In the case of valuable copyrights, some songwriters have used this termination clause as a way of obtaining additional advances from a publisher in exchange for granting the publisher renewal rights to a song. This applies to songs written during or after 1978. Songs written earlier but still protected by the copyright act can also be recovered, but not until five years following the original copyright date and renewal of fifty-six years.

Controlled Composition Clauses

When the Copyright Act of 1976 took effect in 1978, record companies became concerned that their royalty costs were going to increase on a fairly regular basis, because the act provided for a Copyright Tribunal to investigate these rates on a regular basis. In order to control these costs, the record companies came up with a device known as a **controlled composition clause**. This clause limits the royalties paid on the sale of records by lowering the rate paid for each song. Generally, record companies ask for a 75 percent rate of the existing fees. The current 9.1 cents fee per song then becomes 6.825 per song. The music publisher cannot be compelled to accept this rate, but by contrast the record company can elect not to record songs unless the publisher accepts this fee.

Record companies then developed the notion of limiting the total mechanical royalty paid on a particular album. This could be done in several ways:

1. The record company agrees to pay 9.1 cents per song to the publisher, but limits that royalty to a total of ten songs. If the artist records 12 songs, the royalty remains a total of 91 cents.
2. The record company records an artist who writes all of her own songs and the company also owns the publishing. The record company adopts method 1, limiting the royalties paid to ten songs, and also accepts a three-quarter rate for each of the ten songs: 6.825 cents per song. Therefore, the total mechanical royalty is 68.25 cents

Here is an even worse scenario. Let's suppose that the artist is also a songwriter but rarely records her own songs. On her new album, she has recorded ten songs, including two that she wrote herself. The record company adopts method 1 and limits the royalty to 6.825 cents, even though they don't own the publishing rights to ten of the songs on the album.

Unfortunately for the artist, she has recorded ten songs by famous songwriters, none of whose publishers have accepted the controlled composition clause. Therefore, the publishers have demanded a total royalty of 72.8 cents. This is 10.55 cents more than the record company is willing to pay. The artist is now subject to the following conditions:

- The 10.55 cents per album is now a further deduction from the artist's royalty
- Under this agreement, she gets no mechanical royalty income at all.

PRINTED MUSIC

In the early days of the music business, printed music constituted the most lucrative source of income for writers and publishers. In the early part of the twentieth century, hit songs could sell more than a million copies. At that time, sales of phonograph records were relatively small. In addition, the piano was the most popular instrument in the United States, and most of the people playing it learned new music by purchasing sheet music. Publishers hired piano players to demonstrate new music in five-and-dime stores. Printed music was also promoted by having a current star appear on the cover of the sheet music. Sometimes that performer was also cut in on the royalties for the tune. This custom continued many years later when Elvis was cut in on songwriters' royalties, even though he may never have written a single note of music.

"Maple Leaf Rag": The First Million-Selling Hit

Little did composer Scott Joplin know when he wrote a piece in honor of St. Louis's Maple Leaf Club—a hangout for barroom pianists and other musicians—that he would launch the ragtime piano craze. Published by a local music store owner named John Stark, "Maple Leaf Rag" quickly became a major national hit, selling over a million copies, and establishing Joplin as "King of Ragtime."

Unlike other publishers who often paid a flat fee for the rights to publish a piece, Stark actually agreed to pay Joplin a royalty. This was doubly unusual because Joplin was African American, and ragtime was a disreputable musical form associated with barrooms and bawdy houses. Stark probably felt that the music would sell locally to Joplin and his cronies, but wouldn't have much greater appeal. Imagine his surprise when sales took off, and suddenly he owed Joplin significant royalties.

The piece's success enabled Joplin and Stark to move to New York, then the center of music publishing. Joplin would go on to write countless classic rags, along with *Treemonisha,* a ragtime opera that was never successfully staged in his lifetime. Stark built his business on ragtime, signing other notable composers including James Scott and Joseph Lamb, but was never able to expand into the lucrative vaudeville song market. When ragtime's era ended in the late teens, so did Stark's publishing career.

The radio and the phonograph became increasingly popular as the century wore on, and the birth of rock and roll in the mid-1950s produced a generation of musicians who learned music by ear rather than by reading it. As rock emerged, the piano's popularity was replaced by the guitar. It is more difficult to read music for the guitar than for the piano, and there were many self-taught musicians who played by ear, rather than by taking formal lessons. When electronic keyboards became more common than pianos, many of the younger keyboard players also played more by ear than by reading music notation. Because so many musicians used their ears rather than their eyes, the market for written music became much smaller.

Print Royalties

One interesting aspect of print music is that some of the music that sells very well on records does not sell well in sheet music. Dance songs and hip-hop music, for example, often never go into print. This is partly because there is so much more emphasis on beats than on melody. By contrast, singer-songwriter music is much more apt to be issued in print.

Sheet music is not typically a huge item in today's music marketplace, although sometimes songs from plays and films, or songs meant for special occasions, such as weddings, may do well as print items. Typically, sheet music royalties pay 8 to 12 cents on music that usually sells for $2.95 to $3.95. **Folios** that are either collections by a particular artist, or a collection of popular songs by a number of artists, can earn 12.5 percent of the retail selling price of the work. If there are ten songs by ten different writers, then usually they split the royalties on a pro rata basis. Often a publisher will request a **most favored nation clause**. Under this provision, the publisher protects his interests and the interests of the songwriter by making a deal with the print publisher specifying that their share of the royalties will be no lower than that of any other publishers and writers in the folio. If the publisher agrees to pay Bob Dylan a royalty of 5 percent for use of one song, for example, then all others in the folio must be paid at the same rate. Royalties may also increase with sales, with the percentages escalating at various sales plateaus.

ARRANGERS AND ROYALTIES   Composers don't often make their own arrangements for publication. Songbooks may require simplified versions for beginning players, or specialized arrangements for various bands or ensembles. The people who make the musical arrangements for these folios, or who transcribe pieces from recordings, almost never receive royalties. Their fee is generally based on the length of the musical arrangement. When a song is in the public domain—for example, *The Star Spangled Banner*—the music arranger may be able to negotiate royalties for their specific arrangement of the piece. If anyone else uses that specific arrangement, the arranger will receive royalties for its printing or recording. As of 2009, anything written before 1923 is in the public domain. This includes many folksongs. Often we have no idea who composed a two-hundred-year-old folksong.

ROYALTIES IN CHRISTIAN MUSIC   An organization called **Christian Copyright Licensing International (CCLI)** licenses and collects royalties from churches that reprint Christian music. According to an article by Susan Butler in the February 2, 2008, issue of *Billboard,* during the last nineteen years churches have paid over $172 million to music publishers. Many churches were unaware of these obligations until CCLI contacted them. CCLI has gained access to over two hundred thousand Christian churches in twenty-four countries. The copyright law exempts churches from paying performance royalties, but any visual projection or printing of songs must compensate music publishers. CCLI represents music publishers for a small percentage fee, in the same way that the Harry Fox office functions. Half of the churches in the United States are currently licensed. CCLI charges rates ranging from $49 to $4,260 to churches, depending on the size of the church. They also license music online, and even provide a player that enables the user to change the key of the music.

Some churches have very strong music programs, and have begun to publish songs written by their own music directors or members.

PRINT PUBLISHERS

Gradually, the many music publishers who were involved in the music print business either were acquired by larger music print publishers or they went out of business. Today, there are a handful of music publishers that dominate this aspect of the industry. These are the leading print companies, and where they are headquartered:

- Hal Leonard, Milwaukee, Wisconsin. This is the largest music print publisher in the world. It has acquired many companies during the last ten years, and also distributes the works of many others. Hal Leonard publishes popular music of the day and much instructional material, also music for band and choirs. It also has a book division that publishes books about music and the music industry.
- Alfred Music, Van Nuys, California. They recently acquired the print division of Warner Chappell Music, which vaulted Alfred to the second largest of print publishers. They previously specialized in educational material, but acquisition of Warner Chappell brought Alfred into the pop music arena.
- Neil Kjos Music, San Diego, California. They are active in the educational market—music for school bands and choirs. Kjos also publishes other instructional material.
- Music Sales Corporation, New York, but owned by a British company. They publish many instructional folios for various instruments. Music Sales was among the first print publishers to actively pursue folk music during the folk music revival that began to flourish in the 1960s. Hal Leonard recently acquired the right to distribute all Music Sales publications.

Writing for Print Publishers: A Success Story

The standard agreement between the authors who write instructional material and the music print publishers provides that the writer gets a royalty that pays the author 10 percent of the retail selling price of the book. Usually there is some provision that pays the author less for quantity sales that are heavily discounted. The different companies pay royalties on a quarterly basis, every six months, or once a year.

Some instructional books have sold in the millions, such as the John Thompson piano series, or the Mel Bay guitar method. One of the most amazing success stories that I have heard came true for an electric bass method that Roger Filiberto wrote for Mel Bay Publications in 1963. The original book sold for $2.95 and was thirty-two pages long. It sold over a million and a quarter copies, some at the $2.95 price, later raised to $3.95. If you figure that the average royalty was 30 cents s book, the author received $375,000 for writing this brief book. The book has been revised and remains in print today.

- Mel Bay Publications, St. Louis, Missouri. The leader in guitar music, with many other publications for other instruments. They also operate a record label.
- Cherry Lane Music, New York. They are active in a variety of fields, and publish music by such varied composers as Quincy Jones, Tom Paxton, John Denver, and Will.i.am. Hal Leonard distributes music published by Cherry Lane.

Other print companies include Kendor Music, which specializes in high school and college band music; International Music Publishers, active in the area of classical music; and Carl Fischer, active in instructional music. Other specialty print publishers deal with specific musical genres, such as choral music, or music for specific instruments.

Guitar Music and Tablature

In the days when the piano dominated the American musical landscape and the world of printed music, the guitar was definitely an afterthought for music publishers. Gradually, publishers began to write the chord names over the written music, and that was followed by printing guitar chord diagrams. By the 1960s, it was obvious that a large number of rock and country artists either didn't have a keyboard in their bands or, when they did, it was subservient to the presence of two or three guitars. I have already pointed out that many guitar players often cannot read music notation.

During the folk music revival, Pete Seeger was a leader in introducing a music notation system known as **tablature**. Tablature is an instructional tool that replaces music notation with a system of numbers that indicate which string should be played, and at what fret the left hand should be fingering that string. By the 1970s, music publishers realized that although many guitar players were intimidated by music notation, they could comfortably follow the tablature. Even complex heavy metal solos were written entirely in tablature.

Although books of tablature didn't entirely revive the market for printed music, it certainly enabled the surviving print publishers to enjoy a new source of revenue.

Sound Sheets, Cassettes, and CDs

Music Sales Corporation pioneered the use of sound sheets to offer audio examples to accompany their instructional books. These flexible plastic records were bound into the books. The student could play the musical examples on their record players, while reading the tablature or notation in the instruction book. Sound sheets never caught on, because the quality of the recorded sound was poor and they were awkward to play on turntables because the sound sheets were so light. By the 1980s, print publishers began to bind cassettes into their instructional folios. This made for a cumbersome package, because of the way cassettes "stuck out" of the paper. Cassettes also had to be manually rewound each time the player wanted to hear a particular musical passage, a necessary step in learning. Cassettes also tended to jam or even break, which was a further annoyance to the consumer.

By around 2000, CDs totally dominated recorded sound. Publishers replaced the cassettes with CDs. When the jewel boxes were eliminated, CDs comfortably fit into music books, and today many of the existing music books contain CDs where the author of the book demonstrates the music for the student. CDs are relatively cheap to manufacture, and the discs themselves are relatively indestructible. Some instruction books even offer DVDs to show more fully exactly how to play an instrument.

The Future of Print Publishing

The demand for printed music will never return to the glory days of the 1920s. But as long as people play and listen to music, there will be a demand

Music Minus One

Music Minus One records were based on a simple idea: There are thousands of want-to-be musicians in the country who long to play with professional accompaniment. A jazz drummer named Irving Kratka recognized this need, and began issuing recordings that featured all of the parts except for a lead instrument. For example, Schubert's Trout Quintet could be ordered missing any one of the five instruments! Kratka hired studio musicians and radio orchestras to do the actual recordings. Although he began by issuing classical music exclusively, the company really took off when he added jazz favorites to the list. The print publishers loved it, because the aspiring musician had to read from the printed music score. The score was packaged with the recording.

for instructional material. Video provides a new forum for the interested learner, because the viewer can observe such matters as breathing technique on wind instruments, the correct way to hold an instrument, and how players can handle various challenges of genre or of creating sounds.

As is the case with recordings, the print publishers have vigorously fought against the free distribution of music on the Internet. This has certainly affected the sales of music folios, but according to the quarterly numbers shown in the various music trade publications, sheet music continues to experience single-digit growth from year to year. In the meantime, the National Music Publishers Association is attempting to shut down Web sites that post copyrighted music for the consumer to download without paying any royalties. Some of these sites offer music instruction and others simply print lyrics to songs without permission.

One of the tactics that the print publishers have taken is to design their books paying close attention to the genre of the music and the tastes of the fans of that genre. Nowadays music folios contain pictures of the artists who are popular in the style that the folio is designed to present. There may be poems or individual messages and photos from the artist-songwriter that are not available on their albums or in any other source. The music book then is really functioning as a sort of souvenir, almost like the program book at a large concert.

SYNCHRONIZATION RIGHTS

Synchronization rights entail the right to use music on film or television. The economics of synchronization rights operate entirely differently from the royalties from the sale of recordings or performance rights. Essentially, there is no standard deal for the use of synchronization rights. Here is a table with possible scenarios that might involve the use of a song or instrumental piece in a film, on television, or for a commercial.

Film Use	TV Use	Commercial
Title song	Theme, played every week	National network
Song performed during closing credits	Background music	Prime time
Instrumental theme, repeated numerous times during the film	Song used on a TV show	Regional commercial
One of 15 songs used in a film	Foreground music	Local commercial
Used on soundtrack album and DVD	Syndicated on cable in many countries	Used on both radio and TV

Let's take a look at each of these uses, and discuss the sort of fees that might be involved.

Film

Title songs and songs played over the closing credits of a film are the most lucrative for the songwriter and publisher. The fees vary based on whether the song is specifically written for the film or is an existing song that the producer and the director wish to use in the movie. According to Todd and Jeff Brabec, these fees can run anywhere from $30,000 to $500,000. Not only are there no set fees for these uses, but the publisher might deny the use of the song in a film. For example, a folksinger who considers herself a serious artist may not allow one of her songs to be used in a Kung Fu movie. In a different kind of problem, the publisher for a song such as Paul McCartney's "Yesterday" would undoubtedly ask for a lavish synchronization fee for that song to be used in a film.

Generally, all of the instrumental music in a film is written by the same composer. The music budget for a film is usually based upon the overall budget, and is set at about 3 percent of total costs. According to Donald Passman, the fees for film composers range from $50,000 to well over $1 million, with well-known composers receiving from $500,000 to $700,000. This excludes the costs of hiring musicians or recording the score, which are budgeted separately. The composer will not be paid additional money for a theme repeated in the film, but if this theme constitutes, for example, two cuts of the recording of the film score, then the songwriting royalties will be paid for two songs rather than for one. If the song is one of a number of songs in the film, the customary fee will be $15,000 to $25,000 per song, shared between the songwriter and the music publisher.

Until recently, it was virtually unknown for film composers to retain any share of the music publishing rights for their music, but recently some composers have at least been able to enjoy co-publishing. In movies, the composer is still able to make income from the performing rights if and when the song goes on television or on a soundtrack album. Currently, film composers are being asked to sign agreements that allow for use in new media, and on, for example, worldwide cable shows, without additional compensation.

When a young composer writes music for a film school project, often there is literally no money in the budget, but the composer is able to keep complete control of the publishing rights. It is also wise for the composer to have some sort of written agreement with the film's producer and director that provides for the composer sharing in the rights to the film if it goes into commercial distribution.

MUSIC SUPERVISORS   Often it is the music supervisor who chooses what music goes in a film, subject to the approval of the film's director.

Deborah Holland: Composing for Film

Deborah Holland is a singer-songwriter and composer, and also a professor in the Commercial Music Program at California State University, Los Angeles. She began her career as a singer and songwriter in the band Animal Logic, which also featured ex-Police drummer Stewart Copeland. She got a start in film when she took a number of songs that were "collecting dust on my shelf," and gave them to a music publisher-friend. One of them, "Sure Fire Lover," was placed on an NBC TV show and another made it into a movie. Deborah's original deal was that she received the writer's share of the royalty income and co-publishing rights.

Deborah Holland with her group, The Refugees. L to r: Wendy Waldman, Holland, and Cindy Bullens. Photo: Lance Craig, courtesy The Refugees.

Deborah has since composed songs on her own and also worked with collaborators. Working with another composer, she placed two songs on USA Films and Fox TV. This was a so-called **back end deal**, where there was no front money, but the worldwide syndication rights turned out to be quite lucrative. Deborah has also placed three songs in episodes of the soap opera *The Young and the Restless*. At one point Deborah even hired a manager just to place her song in films.

Some other songs have made their way into film and television, some through a film editor and another through Miles Copeland, who used to manage Animal Logic. She has also co-written songs with her ex-bandmate Stewart Copeland, who does film scoring work, and several of their songs have been used in movies.

Deborah is a fine singer, and has performed some of her compositions in films. In other cases, other people performed her songs. In one instance she over-dubbed all of the vocal parts for a film, but the song ended up on the cutting room floor. This sort of work is sometimes done on a speculative basis, and if the song is not used, the composer is not compensated for her time. On another occasion, Deborah wrote a song for a movie that was replaced by a Frank Sinatra song. She received a $5,000 **kill fee**, although her song wasn't used. Kill fees are often paid when a songwriter is commissioned to create a composition but then, for whatever reason, the piece isn't used. Under the terms of the deal, had the song been used, she would have been paid three times as much money.

Most of her work has not been done with music supervisors, because the films had relatively low budgets. In her experience, the performance income earned from work for even mediocre films can be significant. When they air on television, they often are shown all over the world. She has also found that when she writes songs with songwriters signed to major music publishers, sometimes their publisher refuses to license the song unless they receive a large synchronization fee. If the movie or TV producer is unwilling to pay the fee, this kills the deal.

The supervisor is the liaison between the director of the movie and the publisher or record company that control the rights to the songs. It is always the director who has the final say as to what goes into the movie, with a varying degree of input from the producer of the film.

DVD AND SOUNDTRACK RIGHTS   These days, the movie company is likely to fold DVD rights into the synchronization fee for the movie, or, failing that, pay a slightly higher fee that includes these rights. On a soundtrack album, the song will generate mechanical royalties, as in the case of a normal album.

TV

The theme song—or the instrumental theme that is played at the beginning of each episode of a TV show—has the greatest visibility and can earn a composer considerable money over the long run. Although the initial fee paid may be small, the composer can collect performance rights during the run of the show, the re-runs, and the cable syndication of the show. Many successful shows run for years all over the world. When this occurs, performing rights can be enormously lucrative. The synchronization fees paid for instrumental music for television are comparatively low. Composers do this work primarily for the payoff in the performance rights.

Using Existing Records and Songs in Film and TV   When the director wants to use the original performance of a song on a record in a film or television show, there are two rights that must be obtained: publishing (for the songwriter) and recording (for the record company). We have already covered the rights that come from the publishing and songwriting end of the picture. The other rights that need to be granted are those that come from the record company that issued the original recording. Once again, the fees vary greatly, and are based upon such issues as:

- Is the record still in print?
- Is the record closely identified with an artist, so that in effect the producer is using the record as an advertisement for the film?
- Is there any advantage to the artist or the record company to having the record in the film? For example, the song "Stand By Me," used in the film of the same name, revived the career Ben. E. King, who made the original recording. The song reached #1 on the Billboard charts for the second time in twenty-five years, and caused a new demand for King's services on the part of both record companies and the general audience.

New artists sometimes accept the use of their songs in films or on television for minute fees, or even no fees at all. Their thinking is that getting a credit in the film may jump-start their career. Also, if the film *does* become a success, they will receive lucrative performance fees from their PRO when the film goes on television. This ideology is known as holding out for money at the back end. The "back end" refers to the monies generated after the film has aired on television. The validity of this strategy is open to debate. It is difficult to predict whether a film is going to be a blockbuster or a bomb, although if the artist/songwriter's manager knows the budget of the film, then he will have some indication of whether this is a worthwhile chance to take.

Ron Sobel: Keeping "American Idol" Singing

Ron Sobel runs a multifaceted company called North Star Media. North Star publishes songs, owns a record label, buys existing music publishing catalogs, and licenses music on behalf of the *American Idol* television show.

Acting as a publisher, and sometimes as a placement agency, the company pitches songs from its catalog to the music supervisors who select songs for film and TV. North Star has to negotiate all aspects of the deal, such as the fee for the use of the song and the term of the license. These fees are highly negotiable and vary according to the way the song is used in the production,

Ron Sobel with his office staff at North Star Media. Courtesy Ron Sobel, o/b/o North Star Media.

how much of the song is used, and whether the use involves a new version or an existing recording. Unless Ron's writers control their own recordings, the right to use the recording must be negotiated separately with the record company. If the act is unknown, or little-known, the show may be unwilling to pay two separate fees for publishing and the recording. Because the record company receives no money from ASCAP or BMI for TV shows or reruns, the record company often requests more money than Ron's publishing operation does. Sometimes the publisher will sacrifice part of its fee to make it possible for the song to get this important exposure.

Ron shared this story, which indicates the complexity of negotiating this sort of deal in today's music world. North Star recently pitched an emerging-indie band's music to an extremely popular TV show. The show loved the band's music, and decided to place a song in a prominent place in an upcoming episode. North Star was able to negotiate a $12,000 fee, an excellent fee in today's difficult economy for a band that had attracted a good buzz but was not well known. However, in lieu of this fee, the show made a counteroffer to place a "music card" at the end of the show. The card is a prominently displayed visual credit, which shows the band's name, the title of the track, and gives the band's Web site address. This type of credit has resulted in immediate attention for a new band, including positive hits on Web sites, and assisted greatly in the sales of such contemporary acts as Death Cab for Cutie and The Fray.

Ron then asked the band: Would you take the $12,000, or sacrifice the fee for prime-time national exposure through the music card? This led to extensive discussions among band members, managers, publishers, and North Star. A good argument could be made for either choice, based on short-term income versus an investment in the group's future. Which option would you choose?

Commercials

Most commercials are written under **for-hire agreements**. These agreements specify that the writer is willing to sign away their rights to a song or instrumental work in exchange for some specified amount of money. In a for-hire agreement, the composer is essentially giving up any rights to a composition. It is very difficult to write a commercial without giving up these rights, so that the original composer may not even get performing rights credit for the work.

The largest share of the financial pie in commercials doesn't come from writing the music for them, but rather from singing on the commercial. The AFTRA codes about the use of commercials have many different categories, but all generate very large amounts of money for the vocalist. Therefore the composers of commercials often attempt to sing on them, with mixed results. For composers who simply write the commercials, the secret is to generate as many projects as possible. If they do not sing, they will at least want to be on the AFM contracts for playing an instrument, usually as the bandleader. This is because the leader gets double the income and double the residuals of the other musicians. Other fees can be generated if the composer also wrote the musical charts for various instruments.

When an existing song is used for a commercial by a national product, there is no set fee governing the rights. If a previously issued record is being used, there are two rights that the advertising agency must negotiate. The first negotiation is with the record company, which must determine what they will charge for the use of the record. They will usually split the rights with the artist on a fifty-fifty basis. If the record was recorded under a union contract, the advertising agency must also pay a new usage fee to the musicians and any backup singers involved.

The other negotiation is with the music publisher. Because the rates are not set by the copyright law, they are entirely negotiable. For a national product, these rates can climb into the stratosphere, to the tune of $500,000 and up. The sort of issues that will be involved in setting a fee will be the strength of the product, the way that the commercial is being used (local, regional, or national use), and the question of exclusivity. If we are doing a commercial for Budweiser beer, obviously we don't want the same song to be licensed for a competitor. The exclusivity may involve a competing product or any product at all. The more the agency wants to restrict the song from other commercial uses, the higher the fee is apt to be.

It is not unusual for the advertising agency to re-record the original record, in order to avoid having to pay any money to the record company. They may also wish to re-record because they are using the original melody, but making changes in the lyrics.

Many commercials, and film music as well, compel composers to sign "for hire" agreements. These agreements give the advertising agency, or the film producers, control of the publishing rights, and also how the songs will

"Revolution" in TV Commercials

In 1987, the Nike surprised Beatles' fans by producing a TV commercial featuring the original recording of John Lennon's 1968 anthem, "Revolution." Nike licensed the recording from Capitol-E.M.I., paying a reported fee of $250,000, and the publishing rights from Michael Jackson's SBK Music. Jackson had purchased the Beatles' catalog as an investment, following the advice of Paul McCartney who himself had become a major owner of publishing rights. McCartney was miffed that Jackson had outbid him for the Beatles' catalog.

The Beatles had always vowed to keep their music "pure" and not to allow its use for promoting any commercial products. Through their Apple Corps Ltd., the group sued, claiming that their original label, Capitol-E.M.I., did not have the right to license the recording without the permission of all four surviving Beatles. (Yoko Ono represented John Lennon at the time, as Lennon's widow.) Fans of the group felt betrayed, although Ono herself initially said she liked the idea of exposing a new generation of listeners to Lennon's music.

Nike continued to use the song in advertisements through early 1988, and eventually the Beatles settled a number of suits with Capitol—including this one—for undisclosed terms. Ironically, by the mid-1990s, the use of popular songs in commercials had become widely accepted, and major artists including the Beatles regularly licensed both original recordings and new versions of their hits for commercial use. Yoko Ono later licensed "Instant Karma" to Nike, and a Beatles' song, "Hello, Hello," has appeared most recently in national advertisements for the discount chain, Target.

be licensed in the future. Under these agreements the songwriter still will be paid songwriting royalties, but the company controls when and how the song will be licensed.

GRAND RIGHTS

The rights to music used in plays differ from all the other rights we have discussed. These are known as **grand rights**. Royalties are shared between the person who writes the music, the lyricist, and the author of the book, or script, of the play. These three parties generally share six percent of the gross receipts of the play. However, as is the case with most royalties, it can be a bit more complicated than that. The work may initially be optioned by a producer, who pays the three parties a fee to obtain an exclusive option to produce the play. The producer has one year to mount such a production. This fee is determined by the **Dramatists Guild**, the trade organization that covers theatrical productions. Because there are many instances where a producer may have difficulty raising the necessary funds in a year, further options are available for an additional year, and a third year, if necessary. These "advances," are recoupable from 50 percent of the royalties that the writers earn from the show.

Before a show comes to Broadway, it often plays in Philadelphia or Boston. The three writers receive weekly fees for up to twelve weeks of these performances. After that time, the creators get a 4.5 percent royalty, in further "tryout" towns or on Broadway. Once the costs of producing the play are recouped, the royalty goes to 6 percent.

The majority of shows do not end up succeeding. However, when a show does become a hit, the royalties can be enormous. First of all, there is the Broadway show. Six percent of the receipts in a large theater with tickets averaging $100 or more and with eight performances a week can be a bonanza. This is particularly true if the show runs for a number of years, such as *Rent*, which ran for twelve years. Additional revenues come in from the Broadway cast album, if the play is turned into a movie, and from the resulting film soundtrack album. But this is only the tip of the iceberg. There may be London productions, and there also often are road companies that tour in such cities as Denver, Portland, or Dallas. All of the road company productions bring in additional revenue for the creators of the show.

In addition, some years after the show is considered to be dead, a producer may mount a new Broadway version of the show, creating a whole new revenue stream. Other productions may be done by dinner theaters, high schools, or colleges. Several leading agents for dramatic rights, such as Samuel French, sublicense the rights for the latter groups, who pay fees based on the size of the theater, the length of the run, and the capacity of the house.

When a song has not been written expressly for a show, but someone wishes to use it for that purpose, they must make a deal with the music publisher who controls the copyright. The publisher and songwriter will either receive a weekly fee, or a royalty that is pro-rated together with other songs used in the production.

Off-Broadway shows or an instrumental piece that is used in a show that has no other music will receive weekly amounts of money, once again based on the size of the theater and the price of the tickets.

The reader should note that most music publishers do not deal with grand rights. Songwriters who customarily write for the theater may be able to retain their own publishing rights. There are also a handful of music publishers who specialize in grand rights. The writer of a play does not own the copyrights to the songs. For example, if Tony Bennett wants to record a song from a Broadway show, the lyricist and composer get all of the income from that recording.

Composing for the Theater

The great majority of musicals are cowritten by a lyricist and a composer. Stephen Sondheim is one of the few Broadway composers who typically writes both the words and the music, although even he began his career as a lyricist. Sometimes the lyricist also writes the script for the show, which means that she or he will be entitled to two-thirds of the royalties generated.

Writing songs for a musical is different than any other form of songwriting, in the sense that when a show is in the rehearsal stage, often new songs are introduced on a regular basis, and other songs may be taken out of the show, because in the opinion of the director they don't advance the action of the show. The lyricist and composer must be willing to write far more songs than will go into the final production. On a number of occasions, songs written for Broadway shows or for films that weren't used in the original production were used elsewhere. Some of them have even become hit songs.

Regional Theater and Grand Rights

Musicals are generally the most expensive theatrical productions. This is because, in addition to the actors, there are costs associated with the orchestra, as well as additional money that needs to be spent on choreography and dancers. Consequently, only the most ambitious regional theaters, such as the Mark Taper Theater in Los Angeles, or the Denver Center for the Performing Arts, produce musicals. A number of shows have come out of the DCPA, notably *Quilters,* which not only achieved success on Broadway but engendered road companies and other regional productions. College music departments also produce original musicals from time to time.

The prospective theatrical writer needs to take care not to sign option deals with producers who will simply tie up the work but not be able to raise sufficient funds to actually produce the show.

THE OUTLOOK FOR MUSIC PUBLISHING

Although the market for recorded product has diminished, music publishing has continued its steady growth. The two major American PROs are approaching annual revenue of two billion dollars, the print business grows from year to year, and some really exciting growth opportunities have emerged in new media outlets, such as ringtones and ringbacks.

All of the major labels own music publishing outlets, and in the case of EMI, their publishing company easily exceeds the income potential of their record division. Indeed, some of the publishers are really assuming the traditional roles formerly occupied by record companies. These roles include finding and developing artists, even to the point of helping artists to perform on the road. Primary Wave Music Publishing is even in the process of developing a cartoon series that is designed to promote the catalog of Hall and Oates.

Music publishers understand that the decline of CD sales means that they will receive less income from mechanicals and consequently they are seeking new streams of revenue from film, television, and digital media.

Because publishers and PROs will continue to be paid for the use of songs in film and the ever-growing medium of cable television, and because Internet and satellite radio will also bring in increased revenue, the outlook for the future of music publishing is bright.

Terms to Know

Back end deal *118*
Bundle of rights *108*
Christian Copyright
  Licensing
  International
  (CCLI) *113*
Compulsory
  license *109*

Controlled
  composition
  clause *110*
Dramatists Guild *122*
Folio *112*
For-hire
  agreement *121*
Grand rights *122*

Kill fee *118*
Mechanical *109*
Most favored nation
  clause *112*
Synchronization
  rights *116*
Tablature *114*

For Class Discussion

1. Name five rights in the bundle of rights.
2. Do you think the current term of copyright is fair and appropriate?
3. What are the arguments for and against controlled composition clauses?
4. When was the last time you bought a piece of printed music? Where did you get it?
5. Who publishes the instrumental music that you are currently using in lessons, band or choir?
6. Do you know anyone who has had a song used in TV or in film?
7. Name a song used in a recent commercial.
8. Is there a theater in your hometown that has had a play with new, original music? Who wrote the music?

■ ■ ■ ■ ■

CHAPTER 8

Regional Music Markets

This chapter will be devoted to a discussion of the music markets outside the major music industry cities. Some of these regions are defined by a specific musical style, such as Cajun music in Louisiana, while others are based on their geographic location. Denver, for example, is at least five hundred miles away from any other medium-sized city, and thus is the center for a large geographic region. We will begin by examining the ingredients that go into making a regional scene a success, and then trace some regional stories that illustrate how these ingredients interact in the real world.

THE RISE AND FALL OF REGIONAL SCENES

Over the years, certain cities have emerged as important regional music centers, including Atlanta, Memphis, Nashville, Philadelphia, San Francisco, and Seattle. Often a town develops a strong musical identity that captures the imagination of the entire country. Suddenly record companies sign many artists from that particular area, music publishers jump in and attempt to sign writers, and a music industry infrastructure develops. All too often this rise to prominence is a temporary one, and when the industry's attention turns elsewhere, the music scene suffers a quick decline.

Here are some of the ingredients that make up a viable regional music scene:

- Creators
  - Musical talent (Prince in Minneapolis; Nirvana in Seattle).
  - Musical style that is recognizable to the industry (grunge music in Seattle).

- Presence of a corps of musicians who have enough versatility to play on a variety of recordings (existence of a jazz and classical music scene that includes versatile instrumentalists).
- Inventive record producers and recording engineers, along with quality professional recording studios.
- Music superstars who support the local music community, and talk it up outside the community itself. Willie Nelson has played this role in Austin, as has Prince in Minneapolis.
- Performance Opportunities and Promotion
  - Performance spaces: clubs, coffeehouses, bars, colleges, and large concert venues.
  - Radio stations willing to play local artists. Some of these stations specialize in musical niches, such as Denver jazz station KUVO.
  - Syndicated radio shows that give regional talent national exposure. *Austin City Limits,* a PBS TV show, has been running for years, and some other examples are *A Prairie Home Companion* radio show in Minneapolis and Boulder's *E-Town* radio show. These shows often start out as important outlets for local musicians, but as they extend their audience, local musicians are somewhat less prominently featured.
  - Local television shows. Local news programs sometimes feature local musicians.
  - Record stores that feature local musicians in live performances. Some record stores, such as Music Millennium in Portland, Oregon, Twist and Shout in Denver, or Waterloo Records in Austin, are major networking centers, and major supporters of local music groups.
  - Music festivals or seminars such as Austin's South by Southwest (SXSW), which draw music industry people from music industry centers.
  - Media that specialize in covering music. Many of these regional music publications have a brief shelf life. Local alternative weeklies, such as *Creative Loafing* in Atlanta or the *Boston Phoenix,* usually provide extensive music coverage beyond what the daily newspapers offer.
- Music Business Infrastructure
  - Local music organizations: songwriters' organizations, talent unions, chapters of the **National Academy of Recording Arts and Sciences (NARAS)**, and so on. The songwriters' groups offer feedback and encouragement to local writers, and usually include some presentations from major market songwriters or music publishers. Some of the local talent unions offer networking opportunities, and the NARAS chapters offer not only networking opportunities for local performers, producers, studio musicians, songwriters, and record company personnel, but also offer seminars and workshops.
  - Personal managers, agents, and entertainment industry lawyers. These people may be attracted by the presence of talent or by the general lifestyle that an area offers.

- Local record labels that have some distribution outside their immediate location. Sub Pop Records in Seattle and Saddle Creek Records in Omaha are examples.
- Presence or development of music publishers. The presence of music publishers is often a result of major songwriting talent residing in a city, or the presence of producers who also write songs.
- Freelance writers and publicists with the ability to generate publicity outside the market itself. Sometimes the so-called buzz is generated by writers who *do not* live in the market. This occurred with the famous articles about the Seattle grunge scene in the British magazine *The New Musical Express.*
- Advertising agencies that produce regional or national commercials.
- Local Support
    - Some regional characteristic that makes artists desire to stay there or to move from their current location (climate, friendly atmosphere, cheap housing, etc.)
    - Support by local government, in terms of zoning, printed directories, or tax breaks for new businesses moving in (most applicable to the movie industry). Georgia and Texas have offered such support.
    - Support from a local college or university music program that also offers some music industry classes or even a degree program. Examples include the University of Miami and the University of Colorado at Denver.

It is not necessary for every one of these ingredients to be present to create a music scene, but the more elements there are, the longer the scene is likely to last. When the business components of the scene are not present, they will often materialize when lawyers, managers, and agents realize national interest is developing around a regional music.

A weekly newspaper that focuses on music, like the now-defunct, much-lamented *The Rocket* in Seattle, can really create a sense of musical community, as do clubs and record stores that become known for supporting the local music scene.

The function of local organizations, whether they are union locals or regional music organizations, is to provide musicians with the chance to network with each other. Artists meet producers, managers find artists, songwriters begin collaboration, and so forth. When these events occur, there is an infectious level of excitement that develops. Local governments can also play a role in building a vibrant music scene, as has occurred in Austin, Texas. In 1985, Texas created the Texas Music & Film Commission, and the city of Austin became very conscious of the viability of encouraging the local music scene as a stimulus to the city's economy. The city hired a liaison to the music community, who offered some immediate assistance by helping to change parking regulations that impinged on the ability of musicians to load their equipment into venues. Currently, Austin also has a **City Creatives' Industries Loan** program, which offers loans for music, film, and art projects.

Other areas have followed Texas' lead. Georgia offers tax incentives to musicians who record there, and Denver has a unique arts program, which will be discussed later in this chapter.

Creating the Buzz

When a regional music scene begins to flourish, music trade papers write feature articles about the scene. Record company A&R personnel appear and start to organize or attend talent showcases. Sometimes consumer magazines pick up the story and suddenly a city becomes "hot." Existing recording studios become better known and new ones appear. Clubs re-model and new clubs open. If the scene shows signs of lasting, as Atlanta has, music publishing companies and even performing rights organizations open offices. This is the upward cycle of the boom. A record is released, radio stations play the record, it sells locally, regionally, and even nationally. New recording studios open, existing studios expand, record companies come to

The Buzz that Failed: The Boss-Town Sound

In the 1960s, certain cities were well known as breeding grounds for rock bands, particularly San Francisco. With the success of Jefferson Airplane, the record companies went into a major bidding war to get other Bay Area acts under contract, including the Grateful Dead and Moby Grape. Major rock magazines wrote features on the "San Francisco scene," which further encouraged groups to form and led to a large immigration of young people to the region.

Although the San Francisco sound grew organically, some in the record industry felt that similar "sounds" could be easily marketed with the right mix of PR and groups. One was Alan Lorber, a producer, arranger, and composer who had signed a number of psychedelic rock groups to his management company. In 1968, he brought three of these groups—Orpheus, Ultimate Spinach, and the Beacon Street Union—to then major label MGM, proposing that they market their debut albums as a group. The groups happened to be from the greater Boston area, so Lorber announced he had discovered a new trend, the "Boss Town Sound," a play on the slang expression "boss" (meaning cool or groovy). MGM took out major media ads in publications like *Rolling Stone* and *Billboard* announcing the new "hip" sound.

Unfortunately for the acts involved, the underground press that was widely read by rock fans took offense at the label's attempt to "hype" a bunch of groups around what the press considered to be a manufactured movement. Rolling Stone accused MGM of creating "an extremely heavy promotion . . . and the question should really be whether or not there is anything beneath the hype." Most of the respected rock critics savaged the group's works, although it's hard to tell how much of this was related to the perceived hype rather than to the music itself.

With the antihype backlash, the Boss Town sound quickly faded as both a marketing and stylistic phenomenon.

town to scout additional talent, articles appear in national music trade papers, musicians and bands move to town, and local managers and entertainment attorneys surface or even move to town.

In the downward cycle, record companies stop signing regional artists and turn their attention elsewhere. Sales of local acts diminish, and the interest in the scene's musical style begins to evaporate. Musicians stop moving to the town, or even leave, recording studios close, record company personnel are no longer to be found, and the boom begins somewhere else.

NASHVILLE, TENNESSEE: COUNTRY MUSIC U.S.A.

When we think of country music, we think of Nashville, Tennessee, the hometown of the popular **"Grand Ole Opry"** radio show since the early 1920s. The city has become synonymous with the creating, performing, recording, and promotion of country music. But this was not always the case; in fact, before World War II, there wasn't a single permanent recording studio in Nashville, and only one recording session was held there, in a local hotel. So how did Nashville become "Country Music U.S.A."?

Radio played a key role, although it took several decades for Nashville to win out over several other strong contenders as home to country music. In fact, the first national radio show to gain popularity broadcasting country performers was Chicago's WLS' National Barn Dance, originally sponsored by Sears, Roebuck. George D. Hay—the announcer who would win fame running Nashville's "Grand Ole Opry"—began his career working at WLS, and was in fact hired by Nashville's WSM to create a show patterned on the hit Chicago program. The Opry had humble beginnings in 1925, but as the 1920s ended, the show became more sophisticated, and began to feature acts who had experience performing in vaudeville and other venues, including banjo playing star Uncle Dave Macon. Still, the Opry was just one of literally hundreds of imitators of the successful Chicago National Barn Dance.

Some important changes occurred in the 1930s that caused the Opry's stature to grow. Although the National Barn Dance began to book more popular-sounding acts, Hay at the Opry stuck to the tried-and-true country music and comedy that made the show successful. The Opry developed a booking agency for its acts so that there was a financial incentive to becoming a member of the cast. Musicians could tour local venues during the week and be back in Nashville in time for the weekly Saturday-night broadcast. The Opry also hired backup musicians to form a "house band" to accompany its singing stars, giving talented musicians a regular source of income. Finally, NBC's national network picked up one hour of the Opry for broadcast, which made the show available from coast to coast.

Still, there were no recording studios in Nashville. It was only after World War II that the first independent studios and labels began to crop up in town. Among the first was one run by local entrepreneur Jim Bulleit, who started Bullet Records—however, Bulleit was interested in R&B, not country music, at least initially. At about the same time—the early 1950s—Owen Bradley established a recording studio in a Quonset hut (a temporary building left over from World War II) that he erected in his backyard; Bradley would become a leading producer and A&R man for Decca Records in the 1950s and 1960s, working with Patsy Cline. RCA opened its first recording studio, eventually promoting studio guitarist Chet Atkins to be its head of A&R. It was New York RCA executive Steve Sholes who recruited a reluctant Chet, who saw himself as a guitarist rather than a record producer. The studios needed musicians to play on their sessions, and drew on the local talent pool from the Opry and elsewhere to fill these slots.

With major hitmakers like Eddy Arnold and Hank Williams on the scene in the mid- to late 1940s, suddenly music publishers realized there was money to be made in country music. Roy Acuff—who had major hits himself in the later 1930s and early 1940s with his "Wabash Cannon Ball" and "Great Speckled Bird"—partnered with pop songwriter Fred Rose to form the first Nashville-based publisher, Acuff-Rose. The publisher hired songwriters for their house staff to supply the new record studios and hit artists. Fred Rose signed Hank Williams (Sr.) as a writer, and worked very closely with Hank, even editing many of his songs.

Hill & Range Music, headed by music publisher Julius Aberbach, became a leader in country publishing. BMI—which was formed by radio stations to counter the powerful ASCAP monopoly (see Chapter 6)—took a strong interest in country music and opened lavish headquarters in Nashville in the 1950s; ASCAP and SESAC would follow.

Both Atkins and Bradley pioneered what came to be known as "The Nashville Sound" in the 1950s. Turning their backs on traditional country sounds—including twangy banjos, raspy fiddles, and songs that focused on "the good old days"—they introduced a more modern, pop style, featuring vocal choruses and lounge-style instrumentation, including smooth piano and flowing strings. By the 1960s, country music represented a popular alternative to the teen-oriented rock and roll that in many ways was dominating radio and record sales.

By the early 1960s, the country music industry solidified its position in Nashville as a major power broker. The **Country Music Foundation (CMF)** was formed to promote country music on radio and in the media; eventually the CMF built The Country Music Hall of Fame, which has grown into a major tourist attraction and sponsors an annual awards ceremony. Although country has enjoyed periods of boom and bust ever since, in Nashville it remains the primary industry, and its leaders continue to wield influence locally and nationally. Label leader Mike Curb, for example, has endowed a major Music Business program at Nashville's Belmont University, which has become a center for training new generations of Nashville executives. Another major music industry and audio engineering program is housed at Middle Tennessee in Mursfreesboro, about an hour's drive from Nashville.

Nashville is a unique music market. It has survived as a major music center while concentrating on country and Christian music. It's not that there aren't amazing musicians in Nashville, or that other musical styles aren't represented in the town, it's simply that country music dwarfs all other musical styles in this market. None of the other regional music centers that concentrated on a single musical style have been able to stay major factors on the national scene. Nashville has been doing exactly that for close to sixty years.

LITTLE LABELS THAT COULD: THE MEMPHIS STORY

Although Memphis has not achieved the long-term success of its sister Tennessee city, it has won a special place in the history of R&B and rock and roll through the visionary work of several recording pioneers: Sam Phillips and his Sun Studios in the 1950s; Jim Stewart and Estelle Axton with **Stax Records** in the 1960s; and Willie Mitchell with Hi Records in the 1970s. Each created a special "sound" that changed American popular music in profound ways.

Recording engineer Sam Phillips founded his Memphis Recording Studio just after World War II as a small studio to do custom recording and provide amplification for local events. In the early 1950s, Philips initially was most interested in the music of black Memphis, and recorded many local performers including Howlin' Wolf, licensing his work to larger labels, including Chess Records out of Chicago. Memphis had already established an identity as a regional blues center, with artists migrating to Memphis from the Mississippi Delta. After a while, he began issuing the records on his own label, which he named Sun, but soon he realized that he would never make a financial killing from marketing black music to white audiences. Phillips, in his own words, was "looking for a white boy who could sing the blues." He finally found him in the form of Elvis Presley, and from 1953 until November 1954 he enjoyed a number of hit records. In November 1954, he sold Elvis' contract to RCA Victor Records, but he continued to have success with his other artists, especially Carl Perkins, Jerry Lee Lewis, and Johnny Cash.

Phillips's contribution to the Memphis scene was that he created a label that achieved national success and notoriety. At his recording studio he developed a corps of studio musicians who played on the records as well as a group of recording engineers, songwriters, and record producers. He was willing to nurture his artists over a period of time, until they discovered a hit-making "sound." Elvis first showed up at Sun to pay to make a recording for his mother of a popular song; he then began dropping in at the Sun offices, hoping to attract Philips's attention. Philips was uninterested in recording Elvis as a pop singer but instead suggested he work with guitarist Scotty Moore and bass player Bill Black, two musicians who had previously recorded for Sun in a Country &Western band. After barnshedding for a while, the trio returned, but still could not produce a satisfactory recording.

It was only when Elvis began "goofing around" at the end of a session that they hit on their characteristic rockabilly style with the song "That's Alright, Mama." Philips was canny enough to keep the tape machine running, and within days they had a regional—and soon national—hit.

Similarly, Carl Perkins recorded a few country-style records before—influenced by Elvis' success—he wrote "Blue Suede Shoes." Johnny Cash went from singing his own minimalist country music to teen-pop ballads (influenced by Sun house producer Jack Clements). Cash was never happy with his later Sun recordings, despite their popularity, and in 1958 left the label. Other Sun artists—including Perkins, Lewis, and Roy Orbison—also moved on to better opportunities as they presented themselves—and also left Memphis to seek bigger audiences. Many of the artists were able to get higher royalty rates from other record companies. Philips struggled on but eventually sold Sun in 1969. The music scene in Memphis did not die, however, but experienced a revival that eventually eclipsed its early success when Stax Records was born.

After some brief forays into the record business, Jim Stewart and his sister Estelle Axton started Stax in 1960. They experienced some success with a Memphis DJ named Rufus Thomas, and later the company became wildly successful through the work of Otis Redding and Sam and Dave. Stax also developed a terrific rhythm section, Booker T & the MGs, who themselves became a hit recording act. House songwriters like Dave Porter and Isaac Hayes and Steve Cropper (lead guitarist for Booker T.) produced hit material for the label's acts. Stax had a unique significance in the Memphis community because it was successful in selling black music to white Americans, and because Booker T & the MGs, was an integrated group, with a black organist leading a group composed of a white guitarist and bass player and a black drummer. Stax had its own recording studio, as well as a corps of engineers, producers, and studio musicians. It was very much like what had happened at Sun Records, but the record business had become much more lucrative in the 1960s then it had been in the 1950s. Stax's studios attracted the interest of Jerry Wexler of the larger New York label, Atlantic Records, who offered them national distribution and sent some of their own artists—including Wilson Pickett—to Memphis to record there.

A series of tragedies and bad business decisions ultimately led to the demise of Stax. In 1967, Otis Redding was killed in a plane crash. Soon afterward, Stax lost its distribution deal with Atlantic Records. Atlantic was sold to Warner Brothers, and kept the original Stax masters, leaving the smaller label with no product. Jim Stewart sold the company to Gulf and Western, and his sister left the label. However, in 1970, Stewart bought the label back, together with the company's new vice president Al Bell. Booker T & the MG's disbanded, and although Isaac Hayes's theme from the movie *Shaft* was a big hit, and other artists such as the Staples Singers enjoyed some success, it wasn't enough to sustain the company. In 1972, Stax signed a distribution deal with CBS Records, but when CBS president Clive Davis left in

1973, Stax again lost national distribution. With its distribution in chaos, and disco taking over America's pop charts, some unwise bank loans brought Jim Stewart to the brink of ruin. In December, 1975, Stax declared bankruptcy and all of its assets were sold for a little over a million dollars.

In addition to the Stax Records scene, Al Green and his producer Willie Mitchell experienced considerable success at Hi Records. Although Hi had been around since the 1960s recording both country and R&B music, it experienced its greatest success in the 1970s with a series of hits by soulful singer Al Green, which Mitchell produced. Another major force in Memphis was producer-songwriter Chips Moman, who also was active during the late 1960s–mid-1970s, producing a number of major artists at his American Group productions at his own studio, including Elvis, Merilee Rush, and Sandy Posey. Moman also cowrote some very successful songs with Memphis songwriter-musician Dan Penn. However, by the end of the 1970s, Moman's run had ended, and Al Green had became a minister and left secular music. Although Green has made periodic comebacks, he has never recaptured mass popularity.

What Happened to Memphis?

Memphis's story is not an unusual one for a regional scene; its rise was powered by a group of small record labels, run by visionary founders, who were able to recognize and nurture local talent. Their success in turn inspired other musicians, music publishers, PR people, and a music business infrastructure to grow in the region. However, when the artists either died or left town seeking greater opportunity, the labels were unable to compete with larger national labels who had coopted their original innovations. As the local labels themselves aged, they became less innovative. Label heads themselves retired or died and were not replaced by a new generation of entrepreneurs. Just as quickly as it arose, the business infrastructure collapsed because there was no longer any talent to feed it. Memphis was unusual as it was able to generate not one but three independent labels that offered unique sounds to the listening public. But its eventual demise was not unpredictable either.

Memphis Today

Today, Memphis is living off its musical past to some degree. Memphis is currently promoting its musical history with the rebirth of the Beale Street district, and the annual W. C. Handy Music Awards. The old Stax studios have been rebuilt as a museum, and the original Sun studios are a popular tourist attraction. However, these are artifacts of the past, rather than the creations of a thriving contemporary music community.

Memphis has a local chapter of NARAS and it offers periodic panels and workshops in an attempt to educate the music community and assist in reviving the local music scene. The city government has created the

Memphis and Shelby County Music Commission to support and promote local music. A private offshoot of the commission called the Memphis Music Foundation is attempting to raise money in order to build a Musician's Resource Center in the South Main District. The University of Memphis has a thriving Music Industry program, which trains students in music business and music technology.

Memphis is still the home of Ardent, a major recording studio, but the scene has never come close to regaining its early notoriety. Although the local hip-hop group Three 6 Mafia received an Academy Award in 2002 for their song "It's Hard Out Here For A Pimp," it is obvious that that Atlanta has a much stronger hip-hop scene than the one found in Memphis.

"Rhythm is Gonna Get You": The Miami Sound Machine

Miami, Florida, became a major music center in the 1970s thanks to its ethnic and social diversity. The local black and gay club communities were a hotbed for the development of disco music, whereas Miami's historic role as a gateway for Hispanics to America—particularly Cuban émigrés—led it to be a purveyor of a slicker dance sound in the 1980s that married disco with Latino rhythms and was embodied by singer Gloria Estefan and her pro-ducer-musician husband, Emilio.

In the mid-1970s, Miami emerged as a center of the new Disco craze, thanks to a thriving club scene that attracted local black, Cuban, and gay patrons. One of the most successful bands to emerge from this scene was KC and the Sunshine Band, led by Henry Wayne "KC" Casey. Casey and fellow band-founder Richard Finch met in 1972 when they were both employed by a local Miami label. They began writing songs together, forming KC and the Sunshine Band in 1973, but went hitless until they broke through with the disco anthem, "Shake Shake Shake (Shake Your Booty)" in 1977; their "Boogie Shoes" was featured in the disco film classic, *Saturday Night Fever* (1978). After scoring a few more hits, the group suffered from the general backlash among critics and listeners to disco, and disbanded.

The **Miami Sound Machine** was in many ways a natural outgrowth of disco, with its heavy emphasis on dance music, but it brought much more to the table. Originally formed in the early 1970s as the Miami Latin Boys, an instrumental group that grew out of the Cuban-Caribbean dance music craze in the city, the group recorded instrumental albums first, and then with the addition of group leader Emilio Estefan's wife Gloria, they began to record Spanish-language ballads and dance songs in the later 1970s. Gradually, they added English language material to their repertoire, finally breaking through with "Rhythm is Gonna Get You" in 1986, which combined a sprightly melody with Latin-influenced percussion over a steady Disco beat and Gloria's appealing vocals. Many more hits followed through the early 1990s, as Estefan alternated her up-beat dance personality with a more divalike approach to emotional ballads, for example, in 1989's "Don't Want to Lose You Now." The strong influence of disco on Estefan and her music was acknowledged in 1994 with her album, *Hold Me, Kiss Me, Thrill Me,* featuring remakes of 1970s disco hits.

Today, many of the major labels have branch offices in Miami, which has become the headquarters of the Latin American music industry. There is quite a bit of cross-fertilization between Spanish-language music recorded in Miami and other music that is imported from Central and South America. Because it plays this unique role in American life, and because of its proximity to Latin America, Miami's scene will probably retain and even expand its role as a regional and international music center. The rapidly increasing Spanish-speaking population of the United States will also contribute to this effect.

RAP-A-LOT: ATLANTA

Atlanta has become a major center in the growth of hip-hop music. In the late 1980s and early 1990s, producers Kenneth "Babyface" Edmonds and Antonio (L.A.) Reid operated La Face Records there as a joint venture with Arista Records. They produced a number of hit records with Toni Braxton, OutKast, and TLC, before breaking up their partnership in 2000. Unlike the situation in Minneapolis, where the scene greatly diminished when producers Jimmy Jam and Terry Lewis moved to LA, other producers have filled the void. Jermaine Dupri, Mr. Bangladesh, L'il Jon, the Organized Noize production team, and DJ Tromp are among these successful Atlanta hip-hop producers. Among the major successful rappers from the region are Ludacris—who began his career as an Atlanta radio personality—and T.I.

Many of the producers and rappers are also songwriters, and Atlanta has become such a powerful scene that ASCAP has opened a regional office here. Atlanta's challenge is to sustain its growth as a music community if and when hip-hop diminishes in importance as a musical style. Atlanta is a cosmopolitan town with a large black population. The chances are that Atlanta's music community will be able to maintain its identity by purveying whatever black music styles are popular in the future. Because the infrastructure of producers, recording studios, and performing rights organizations is there, Atlanta has positioned itself to remain an important regional music center, at the very least.

ALTERNATIVE SCENES

Denver, Colorado, and Portland, Oregon, represent entirely different ways for a musical scene to evolve. Although they lack massive superstars, for a number of reasons they have been able to survive and develop without achieving mass popularity.

Denver

Denver and nearby Boulder, Colorado, in the 1970s, had a scene that appeared to be on the verge of "happening." The folk-rock vocal harmony group

Firefall lived in the Boulder area and so did singer-songwriter Dan Fogelberg. Producer James Guercio moved to Colorado from New York and, with the band Chicago, opened a studio in the mountains in nearby Nederland, Colorado, called Caribou Ranch, where some world-class acts such as Elton John and the Beach Boys recorded. Hit engineer-producer Bill Szymzyck (the Eagles, the J. Geils Band) started the Tumbleweed record label in Colorado in the early 1970s. John Denver was heavily identified with Colorado, writing many songs about the area and starting a record label, Windsong, in his hometown of Aspen, which recorded some local musicians.

Yet the Denver scene never really produced a distinctive style that caught the nation's ears. In some ways, the lack of a scene in Denver is very illustrative of the problems of regional music. From time to time, artists have been entranced by the Rocky Mountains. Rock stars Joe Walsh and Steven Stills lived in the mountains above Boulder for a while. Caribou was a major player, but didn't really influence the music of the area because it was in an isolated location and its owners never reached out to local performers. A few important artists recorded in the area but didn't stay. And John Denver, the one superstar who could have illuminated the whole Colorado music scene, valued his privacy. He did not appear to be concerned about building a local music community.

During the 1990s, it looked as though the greater Denver-Boulder-Nederland region would again pioneer a new sound. It was home to a number of bands active in the jam band movement, especially the String Cheese Incident and Yonder Mountain String Band. Together with their managers, these acts owned a record company and a variety of music business-related companies. The bands did quite well, but didn't make the spectacular national impact that would have ignited a regional music scene. Several local bands, notably Big Head Todd & The Monsters—which scored a gold album with their major label debut, 1993's *Sister Sweetly*—and The Samples have toured extensively through the United States. Both bands currently record on their own labels. Dressy Bessy is an independent rock band that tours nationally and records for New York-based Transformer Records.

Of all these Denver bands, only The Fray has broken through in a big way on a national level. The two founding members of the band—Isaac Slade (vocals, piano) and Joe King (guitar, vocals)—were nurtured by the pop music and recording program at the University of Colorado at Denver. After graduation, they remained in Colorado and began jamming together in 2002, enlisting help from Slade's younger brother, Caleb, and two other musicians who had previously played with Slade. Two self-produced EPs gained support on local radio and the Denver-based alternative newspaper *Westword* named them "best new band" of 2004. Their local notoriety, an enormous number of hits on their Web site, and Los Angeles management led to a record deal with major label Epic Records. The group scored a top ten hit with their first single, but they really broke through with "How to Save A Life," which was used to promote the big hit TV show, "Grey's Anatomy."

Isaac Slade and Joe King of the popular rock group, The Fray, return to the University of Colorado, Denver, to talk to current music students. Photo: Courtesy Cynthia Barringer, University of Colorado, Denver.

The result was a worldwide top ten hit in 2006. Their debut album of the same name went double-platinum and was subsequently named the best-selling digital album to that date. The Fray's success shows how a local band can leverage regional success into major pop status. Touring through 2007 and 2008, they have recently released a second album. Some of the songs have already been slated for TV shows, including a promo for the show *Lost,* and the album has made its way onto the Billboard charts. Of course, as is always the case, it is the public who will determine whether The Fray can sustain a long-term career.

The Denver band Meese released their first CD on the Atlantic label in June, 2009. It is too soon to say whether their career will be as successful as The Fray's has been.

Portland

Portland generally has been seen in the music world as the stepchild of Seattle. Portland is smaller, a bit less picturesque, and the pace of life is not as

The Denver Acoustic Music Scene

Although Denver never materialized as a major music market, the
acoustic music scene in Denver is
extremely strong. The first acoustic
music store in Denver was the
Denver Folklore Center, which
opened in 1962. It evolved into a
series of storefronts that included a
concert hall, a record store, a music
school, and an instrument shop. It
served as a kind of community
resource center and teaching facility

The interior of the Denver Folklore Center.
Photo: Harry Tuft.

for the town, nurturing several generations of folk performers. However, after an
unsuccessful move, the store closed in 1978. This was a serious blow to the acoustic
music community. Not willing to let the Center's legacy die, Harry Tuft, its founder,
and a group of other acoustic music lovers, formed a nonprofit organization
devoted to the promotion of acoustic music. The **Swallow Hill Music Association**
started its life renting space at a community center to give lessons on banjo, fiddle,
guitar, and mandolin, and to present occasional concerts at a local church.

From these humble beginnings in 1979, Swallow Hill developed a major
presence in the Denver community. It greatly expanded its teaching offerings, giving lessons in many more musical styles and on more instruments than the
Folklore Center ever did. It also has three different performance venues. Two the-
atres hold about 100 and 250 people, respectively, and a smaller coffeehouse venue
is used to present local or beginning performers.

Swallow Hill has benefited from one of Denver's unique government program called the **Scientific & Cultural Facilities District (SCFD)**. This is a tax,
adopted by five of the six counties in the Denver metropolitan area. The tax is a
small portion of the state sales tax, and it is used to fund the zoo, the art museum,
and nonprofit organizations like Swallow Hill. Organizations that have large
budgets are automatically funded in two tiers of funding, and smaller or beginning groups must apply for specific grant programs. Swallow Hill has upgraded
its presence from Tier 3 to Tier 2, and so it now receives automatic funding. Its
other sources of income are the music school, the concerts, other grants and dona-
tions by members and friends.

Because of the growth of Swallow Hill, Denver has now positioned itself as
one of the major acoustic music communities in North America. It is an interesting
model of how a musical genre can promote itself in a specific region.

intense as the lifestyle of its northern neighbor. Historically, Portland has not
had a major impact on the northwestern regional music scene, let alone the
national picture. After the demise of the Seattle grunge scene, however,
Portland began to experience considerable population growth, and many
musicians began to flock to the area, finding it a viable place to live.

The music scene is quite diverse. There is a well-established acoustic music scene with about a half dozen venues that feature acoustic music on a regular basis. Tom May, who lives across the river in Washington, has a syndicated radio show called *River City Folk,* which features acoustic music performers. There are several jazz clubs and a jazz radio station. A number of jazz musicians with national reputations live in town, including vocalist Nancy King, pianist-singer-songwriter Dave Frishberg, and Glen Moore, the bass player for the chamber jazz band Oregon.

Portland is also known for a thriving alternative rock scene. The alt-rock bands The Ginns, The Dandy Warhols, and The Decembrists have become national favorites, and there are an amazing number of independent record stores, notably Music Millennium. Terry Currier, who owns Millennium, also is a partner in BDC, an independent record distributor. Along with another Portland-based distributor, Allegro, Millenium distributes product on a national basis, which gives local musicians an opportunity to have their records available outside of Portland. Pink Martini is an independent band that incorporates elements of world music and lounge style. They have sold hundreds of thousands of records on their own label in Europe, and subsequently have become popular not only in Portland but throughout the United States.

World music is popular in Portland. There is an African drum community, largely a result of Obbo Addy, a fine African drummer, moving to town. This community currently supports two African drum shops. A massive blues festival in September draws hundreds of thousands of people to performances in the Portland waterfront park. Other annual music festivals feature jazz, acoustic, music and bluegrass. A number of local music organizations, including the Portland Songwriters Association, the Cascade Blues Society, and the Portland Folk Music Society serve interested musicians and music fans.

It would appear that Portland has been able to maintain a regional identity through the diversity of its music. It is doubtful that it will ever experience the sort of national fixation that greeted the grunge music scene, but it may continue to be a fine place for musicians to live and work.

The Mayor's Ball

From 1985 to 1992, Bud Clark was the mayor of Portland. Clark was a local businessman who had little prior political experience. Clark had a populist, free-wheeling style, and his wife played in the Oregon Symphony. For three years Clark sponsored the Mayor's Ball, an amazing event where local blues, rock, metal, pop, gospel, folk, and jazz players played all night long. Each year the event benefited a different charity.

The Mayor's Ball enabled musicians of all sorts to come together and listen to each other's music. It also galvanized local interest in the music community. When Clark left office, the new mayor had no interest in carrying on the tradition, but longtime Portland residents still remember the event with great enthusiasm.

In 2010, KZME, a new FM radio station that is designed to feature local music and independent touring acts, will debut in Portland. The station's goal is to play all local music, together with occasional touring acts who are playing in Portland. This will undoubtedly provide a positive influence on an already-active music scene.

The Lessons of Denver and Portland

The musicians and music critics who live in Denver and Portland often decry the fact that neither town has developed a national music scene. What these cities *have* gained in exchange for this is a wide-ranging music scene that includes a variety of musical styles. There are decent, if not world-class, recording studios, and a large group of competent musicians. Each town has a good live music scene and plenty of musical talent. Although there are a handful of entertainment lawyers and talent managers in both Portland and Denver, none of them are the sort of music industry movers and shakers who can transform the scene overnight. The infrastructure of music publishers, nationally connected booking agencies, or publicists also is not present. If the scenes haven't exploded, they also haven't imploded. In the meantime, the cost of living in both of these cities is appreciably lower then it is in such formerly large music markets as San Francisco and Seattle, and the life style that musicians enjoy in Portland and Denver is more laid back and less competitive.

SPECIALIZED SCENES

The United States is a diverse country and there are many communities that support locally vibrant music scenes. A good deal of ethnic music exists under the radar of the prevalent pop-rock scene. In Denver, for example, there is a very large Hispanic population, and there are clubs, record stores, and performance venues that cater to fans of this music.

Brooklyn has strong Arabic and West Indian communities, and some modestly successful labels that cater to these ethnic groups. New York is also the headquarters of salsa music, due to its large Puerto Rican population. The salsa music scene involves big bands, and many New York jazz musicians who are not Hispanic play in these bands. Similarly there are Vietnamese record labels in Los Angeles. Phoenix and Albuquerque are home to the two most important Native American music labels, and Albuquerque also has Spanish-language recording. Lafayette, Louisiana is Cajun country, and Cajun music is a significant regional music presence. San Antonio is very close to the Mexican border, and is a center for recording Tejano music, the fusion of the music of Northern Mexico and Southern Texas. Montreal has a thriving rock scene built around the artists in the group Broken Social Scene, who play on each other's recordings. The same sort of cooperative spirit governs Saddle Creek Records in Omaha.

Most of these regional or ethnic music scenes do not cross over into national success, although the Indian flute records of R. Carlos Nakai, on Canyon Records in Phoenix, Arizona, have achieved healthy national exposure and sales. (For more on specialized music, see Chapter 9.)

STUDIO DISPERSION AND REGIONAL SCENES

Over the past twenty years, studio equipment of professional or semiprofessional quality has become available at relatively reasonable prices. This has enabled musicians, engineers, and producers to develop their own studios in areas that have a relatively modest music industry. This has been particularly important for self-contained artists or bands, musicians who do not need studio musicians to perform on their recordings. A musician such as John Mellencamp can record in his own studio near his hometown of Bloomington, Indiana, using his touring band to provide the accompaniment that he needs.

A good deal of hip-hop music is producer-oriented music, so that producer-musicians such as The Neptunes and Teddy Riley are able to work out of their hometown of Virginia Beach without needing additional musical assistance. Synthesizers, samplers, and drum machines provide a large percentage of the sounds necessary for hip-hop.

CONCLUSION

It would be impossible to cover all of the regional music scenes in a single book, let alone a chapter of a book. In naming the factors that create a scene, I included such things as a distinct musical style, a business infrastructure, government support, recording facilities and the talent to operate them, a corps of musicians and live venues that can support them, and college music programs that are relevant to contemporary music, the music industry, and audio engineering.

A close study of the various scenes discussed indicates that many of them were tied to a specific musical style. When that style was in vogue, the scene flourished. When it became less popular, the musicians drifted away, the studios closed, and the business looked in another direction. Only Nashville is focused, although not limited to, a single musical style. Nashville has survived as a music center, because country has maintained its core audience, with occasional up and down swings. Moreover, country music has enough substyles—such as bluegrass, country swing, ballads, and cowboy music—that one of these styles is always in demand. The town has developed a musical mix that includes Country Music Television, the long-running *Grand Ole Opry* radio (and later a TV) show, which preceded the rise of Nashville as a major recording scene. There is also an extremely successful music publishing industry. None of the regional markets have been able to combine so many aspects of the music industry, although Miami, with its emphasis on Latino music, and Atlanta's position as a hip-hop music stronghold, could conceivably develop in a similar manner.

When it comes to New York and Los Angeles, both are large cities with massive populations. There is hardly a musical style that is not represented in these towns. When you combine this fact with the number of live music venues, the record companies headquartered in these towns, and the presence of the movie, television, and advertising industries, there is always going to be desirable work available for the best musicians.

Terms to Know

City Creatives'
  Industries Loan *128*
Country Music
  Foundation
  (CMF) *131*
Grand Ole Opry *130*

Miami Sound
  Machine *135*
National Academy
  of Recording Arts
  and Sciences
  (NARAS) *127*

Scientific & Cultural
  Facilities District
  (SCFD) *139*
Stax Records *132*
Swallow Hill Music
  Association *139*

For Class Discussion

1. What do you consider to be the critical elements involved in the creation of a regional music scene?
2. Which of these elements are present in the community that you currently live in?
3. Could a regional music scene be created in your hometown, assuming that none currently exists?
4. How would you go about doing this?
5. Are there specific bands or regional music styles that would lend themselves to development?
6. Where do you expect to live after graduating from college, and what is drawing you to that place?
7. Could the demise of any of the regional music scenes discussed have been prevented?
8. If you were given a generous gift of money, say $10 million, how would you go about creating a regional music scene?

CHAPTER 9

Specialized Musical Styles

This chapter is intended to be a brief introduction to the business aspects associated with various musical styles. In each style, the training of musicians and the way the music is marketed has its own variations. Entire books have been written about each of these styles, and the interested reader should refer to the appendix for information about some of these books.

CLASSICAL MUSIC

Most of this book has been devoted to the business of popular music. Popular music is definitely a for-profit business, although not everyone succeeds. Classical music has always been dependent upon philanthropy. Bach, Haydn, and Mozart were dependent on what we would refer to these days as government support. Symphonies are able to exist because private philanthropists contribute millions of dollars to build new facilities, maintain old ones, and support orchestral programs. Other income derives from fundraising drives or government grant programs. To put it very simply, classical music cannot pay for itself. The percentage of revenues that orchestras derive from ticket sales does not pay the bills.

Education

Although the training of pop music musicians or record company executives does not follow a single uniform pattern, classical musicians and the people in the classical music business generally have similar backgrounds. Classical musicians start to play at an early age. In the case of pianist and violinists, various authorities have said that to be a soloist, a musician must begin to play before the age of five. This is necessary in order for the musician to develop the muscular habits that are needed to perform at the highest levels. Other would-be instrumentalists get a bit of a pass. Brass players, for example need to begin before the age of twelve. The appropriate age for instrumentalists to begin relates to the particular set of muscles that the player needs to master a particular instrument.

The choice of a teacher is one of the major determinants of building a classical music career. The teacher will instill basic habits that an instrumentalist must employ. Violinists are taught how to hold a bow, pianists must learn proper positions of the hand and wrist, brass and woodwind players are taught how to control their breathing, and so forth. Because music education programs have suffered from cutbacks in funding in recent years, the choice of high school may be another factor in developing a music career. If a fourteen-year-old trumpet player has no high school band to perform in, it is going to be difficult to pass a college music school audition.

There are three different levels of college music education. The very highest level of college music training occurs at **conservatories**, institutions that offer nothing except music programs. At institutions such as Juilliard, the Eastman Conservatory, or the Curtis Institute of Music, the student takes music courses with only the lightest sprinkling of liberal arts classes. Most of the major recitalists or first-chair players in symphony orchestras come from these schools and a handful of other programs. The competition to be admitted into these programs is fierce and the student must pass a rigorous

Students performing in the Juilliard School Orchestra. Photo by Nan Melville, courtesy The Juilliard School.

audition in order to be accepted. Once the student is admitted, another level of competition occurs. Students strive to study with the teachers at the school that have the best reputations for training the highest-level players. In a sense, the students are auditioning the teachers, just as they were required to audition to enter the school.

Some college music students have already attended preparatory schools, such as the North Carolina School of the Arts, or summer music programs at Tanglewood in Massachusetts or Interlochen in Michigan. They may have already studied with the teachers that they will continue working with in colleges. Additionally, they may have taken classes at the extension departments of a major music conservatory, or if their parents have the financial resources, may have taken private lessons with these same teachers. A number of cities have high schools that specialize in the arts, including the fabled Music and Arts High School in New York City. Students who graduate from these schools already have achieved an advanced musical status before entering college.

The atmosphere at the top conservatories is more competitive than cooperative. Several books have cited all sorts of bizarre stories about Juilliard students locking other students out of practice rooms in order to get more practice time for themselves.

The second tier of students are those who either by choice or because they did not get admitted to a conservatory choose to go to a university that offers a Bachelor of Music degree. Three of the best-known schools of this sort are the University of Michigan, Indiana University, and the University of Southern California. Each of these schools have prestigious faculty members, many of whom continue to perform and tour as well as teach. Although the student in these programs also takes many hours of music classes, all three of these schools are universities, and the student must take more hours of liberal arts education than are required by conservatories.

The lowest rung of music students get a Bachelor's in music and take a large number of hours in liberal arts classes. Very few of these students end up performing in major orchestras or are able to enjoy successful careers as recitalists. Most become music teachers in elementary or secondary school settings.

Colleges offer Bachelor's degrees in other areas of music than music performance. Studies in theory and composition and music history tend to lead the student to graduate school and college teaching jobs, while music education majors usually aspire to teach music in the public school system. During the past twenty years, degrees in music therapy, music business, and audio engineering have emerged in more college music programs. Music therapists can work at hospitals or go into private practice, and music business and audio engineering programs have been discussed at some length (see Chapter 14).

ARTS ADMINISTRATION   Another music-related degree is offered in **arts administration**, or the management and operation of a nonprofit arts group.

This usually includes an internship with one of these organizations, like a symphony orchestra. Some students then go on to graduate school and later find employment as managers for symphony orchestras, arts council employees, or in other music-related nonprofit organizations. Oboe player Blair Tindall, in her entertaining book *Mozart in the Jungle: Sex, Drugs, and Classical Music,* cites ten orchestras that paid their chief executive officers over $300,000, and three who earned over $700,000, but these salaries are far from typical. Similar positions in less prestigious orchestras pay much less. Moreover, these salaries generally do not compare to the for-profit sector of the arts industry.

Working as an arts administrator requires a number of skills to meet the various challenges that non-profit organizations face. Most nonprofits are set up with a staff and a board. It is the board that makes policy and the staff that carries out that policy. Often the staff feels that it has more practical knowledge of the organization's problems than the board does, because board members are volunteers who typically spend far less time dealing with the organization's problems. Although the executive director of a nonprofit can attempt to influence policy decisions, doing so may lead to conflict and/or even being fired.

Another problem that can surface is that the board often includes people who are making generous financial contributions to the organization. They may want some degree of control over, for example, the musical repertoire of an ensemble or orchestra. This places the staff in the awkward position of mediating between the artistic director of the ensemble, who wants the freedom to develop programming without interference, and the board member, who thinks that she or he has earned a voice in programming by donating money.

In addition to working with the board of directors, an arts administrator is involved in fund-raising, the writing (or giving) of grants, and, in the case of larger organizations, hiring staff members. It is a rewarding job when the administrator believes in the organization, but it is a tremendous commitment of time and energy.

Solo Performance Careers

Instrumentalists Yo-Yo Ma and Itzhak Perlman are two performers who have reached the pinnacle in classical music careers. According to Blair Tindall, Perlman charges $65,000 for a night's work and Yo-Yo Ma commands $80,000. Tindall also tells about a friend of hers who accompanied Perlman on the piano a number of times in the middle part of his career. For these shows, Perlman was paid $33,000, and this accompanist claimed that he received only $1,000 for his work!

Some recitalists also pursue careers in conducting, much as pop artists may move into record production. This contrasts with a typical conductor who is generally a capable musician but not a world-class instrumentalist.

A college-age pianist working with his teacher to prepare for a recital. Photo: Laimute Druskis, courtesy Z. Legacy, Corporate Digital Archive.

Tindall cites one conductor of the New York Philharmonic who earned $2.3 million for 14 weeks of work. Conductors are the rock stars of the orchestra, and Tindall writes that in 2003 seven major orchestras paid their primary conductor over a $1 million a year, with two earning over $2 million.

Instrumentalists who succeed in becoming touring soloists and perform worldwide receive excellent compensation, because their fees approach those of medium-successful rock stars. One difference is that the classical soloists have no road managers, and their "bands" are either local orchestras or possibly a single accompanist. Like pop stars, the gigs are obtained through classical music managers and agents, who are usually one and the same. CAMI, Columbia Artists Management, is one of the major classical music management firms, with dozens of clients who range from young winners of international contests to well-established and distinguished musicians.

Symphony Orchestra Careers

The contemporary symphony orchestra was largely created by the **Ford Foundation**. Starting in 1966, Ford donated money to sixty-one orchestras. The resulting publicity and the improvement in the quality of symphony orchestras helped raise the number of symphony orchestras in the United States from 58 in 1965 to 225 in 1988. The Ford Foundation's goal was to create a nationwide network of symphonies that would pay musicians a fair wage for full-time work. Until the Ford Foundation began its support, many symphonic musicians had to work at another job to survive. As recently as 1964, the New York Philharmonic only paid musicians $10,000 a year, and the orchestra was not active fifty-two weeks a year.

Today's highest pay scale for symphony orchestra musicians begins at a $110,000 minimum wage at the Boston Symphony. The other major orchestras, Chicago, Cleveland, Philadelphia, and Los Angeles pay slightly less. San Francisco, Pittsburgh, and St. Louis are in the next tier. Orchestras in cities such as Portland, Omaha, and Denver are in the $40,000 minimum range. In smaller cities, the pay is as little as $10,000 a year or even less.

Principal players negotiate their own wages above the minimum. As of 2003, Tindall notes that the minimum wage for the New York Philharmonic was $103,000, but the wages of the principal players ranged from $216,000 to $255,000, and the concertmaster, who leads the violin section, was paid $366,000.

When the symphony hires players who are not regular members of the orchestra, they are paid a much lower wage, with set amounts of money paid for rehearsals and for performances. These players are often hired when the symphony does pop concerts, where the music may call for an electric guitarist, for example.

Career Paths

The typical symphonic player starts out with a small orchestra in a town such as Charlotte, North Carolina. As the player gets more performing experience, she continues to audition at better orchestras, with the objective of ultimately being a principal player in a major orchestra. Auditions are advertised in the *International Musician,* the journal of the American Federation of Musicians (AFM), each month.

AUDITIONS Symphony jobs are obtained through an audition process. The player sends a resume and/or a sample performance recording, and the personnel committee narrows down what may have been hundreds of applicants to a handful. The applicant pays her own fare to go to the audition, which is held in the city where the symphony is located. Blair Tindall had twenty-five unsuccessful auditions, which she estimates cost her $30,000 between flights, hotels, and some last-minute lessons. The more prestigious the orchestra, the more candidates will apply for the job.

The auditions are often held behind a screen, so as to eliminate any sort of positive or negative prejudice toward the applicant's race, gender, or appearance. This process is a result of allegations that symphonies discriminated against women and people of color during the audition process. Historically, there is evidence that there were biases against female musicians. It wasn't until 1952 that a woman became a principal player in a major orchestra, when the Boston Symphony hired flutist Doriot Anthony Dwyer. The New York Philharmonic didn't hire its first female member until 1966.

In New York, many Broadway shows still use orchestras, and classical musicians can apply for these positions. These jobs pay a minimum of more than $1,000 a week, plus extra money for playing multiple instruments, vacation pay and benefits, and the orchestra member can hire substitute players when other opportunities come up, without fear of losing the job. There are, however, several obstacles. First of all, many of the Broadway musicians are expected to double or triple, playing two or three instruments. A flute player may also be expected to play clarinet and saxophone. Classical musicians don't tend to develop these skills, because they are not required in a symphony orchestra, except in a few instances, such as the flute player being expected to also play piccolo, or the percussion players, who play a variety rhythm instruments. The other problem with Broadway shows is that it is totally impossible to predict whether they will run for twelve years, as the musical *Rent* did, or if they will close in a single night. Other employment is available when a Broadway show goes on the road. This is lucrative work, but if the tour lasts for a year, then the player may lose some hometown contacts. For ambitious classical music freelancers, that town is usually New York.

In Los Angeles, Nashville, and New York, there is a fairly consistent amount of recording for films, commercials, television, and records. When classical players are required, they are recruited either from the symphony, if scheduling permits, or from the large pool of freelance musicians who live in these towns.

Other work is available in New York and Los Angeles, playing in chamber music groups, orchestras that play for operas or ballets, or freelance work. A handful of opera companies, including the Metropolitan Opera in New York, even employ full-time orchestras. Freelancers play everything from parties to conventions, in the same way that pop music freelancers do. None of this work is very stable, except for the few opera orchestras. The symphony offers a regular paycheck, instrument insurance, and medical and dental benefits, and the major symphonies have excellent pension plans.

Another sort of symphony is a **community orchestra**. These are secondary classical orchestras, which are mostly comprised of amateur or semi-professional musicians. Usually the only musicians who get paid are first chair players, who are often professionals. The performance schedule consists of a few concerts, and the pay is pitifully low.

Many symphony players also teach, some of them at colleges or universities, and others give private lessons. It is the first chair players who are most apt to get college appointments. There are also some jobs available playing and teaching at summer music camps and festivals in places such as Aspen, Colorado, and Tanglewood, Massachusetts. Musicians with strong reputations are sought after for private lessons, and can earn considerable amounts of money teaching. In the largest cities, lesson fees can be $100 an hour.

Many classical musicians are enamored with chamber music, and throughout the country there are many chamber music groups, such as string quartets or woodwind groups. A handful of these groups work full time at colleges, balancing a performance schedule with teaching. This is a good solution for both parties. It provides a stable income for the performers, and excellent publicity for the colleges where they are in residence.

CONTESTS AND RECITALS There are two tried and true ways for a classical music performer to become better known. One is to enter an international piano or violin competition. Van Cliburn, the classical piano player, rose to fame by winning an international piano competition in Moscow during the height of the Cold War. The American media treated his victory as an almost military triumph, and he even appeared on the popular Ed Sullivan TV show.

Recitals almost invariably are done in New York, usually at a small hall. All of the expenses of a recital are paid for by the performer, including the hall rental, the payment to any accompanists, and any publicity expenses. The musician also often hires a recital manager who charges a fee and makes all of the arrangements for flowers, publicity, and reception food and drink. Tindall's 1991 recital cost her $8,000, and obviously it would cost considerably more in 2009. One of the primary goals of a recital is to get a rave review in the *New York Times*, which in the best-case scenario will lead to a management contract with a prestigious firm, which in turn can lead to a recording contract.

Classical Recordings

Classical music constitutes less than 3 percent of the record market in the United States. The major American symphonies all used to have recording contracts with major labels, but today none of them do. Part of the problem is that the classical music buyer generally wants to hear standard repertoire, and there are already many recorded versions of the classics. Because symphonies have so many members, paying union scale to over one hundred musicians is a large expense for an album that will have modest sales. The major labels would rather reissue older versions of the standard repertoire, recordings that do not represent any new expenditures.

Left without recording contracts, the symphonies have begun to produce their own recordings, and to make them available as digital downloads. It is too early to judge how successful this will prove to be. A budget-priced label called Naxos has been very successful in releasing a large number of classical music records mining both obscure and well-known repertoire. Naxos does not pay royalties to its artists and sells the albums for less than half the typical retail price. Some younger artists have used the label to

Classical Crossover Artists

The marketing people at the labels look for classical music that has what they call "crossover appeal." **Classical crossover artists** sell to both classical music fans and to general audiences. James Galway playing Irish songs on the flute is a crossover project, because it sells to classical music fans, to flute players, and to the general public looking for "pretty music." There are artists who cater exclusively to this audience, like the blind opera star Andrea Bocelli, who is generally dismissed by opera fans but is beloved by a broad, popular audience.

Some of the younger classical players, notably the Kronos Quartet, commission new music. Kronos did an album of Jimi Hendrix songs arranged for string quartet, and they have also recorded an album of African music. Their fans are a younger demographic, and they have undoubtedly opened up some ears to contemporary classical music. Yo-Yo Ma has also recorded a number of crossover projects, including his Silk Road project of Asian music, and his country music-oriented trio with fiddle virtuoso Mark O'Connor.

When Plácido Domingo, José Carreras, and Luciano Pavarotti toured together as The Three Tenors, they were extraordinarily successful. Originally performing together in the early 1990s at a charity event, the three realized they had hit on a golden idea, and subsequently recorded million-selling albums and embarked on a series of highly successful tours. Their performances tapped into a larger audience than the typical classical music or opera fan. Other "threesomes" were born in their wake in the hopes of repeating their success. Among some of these groups, cited by *Wikipedia*, are the Three Canadian Tenors, Three Tenors and a Soprano, the Three Sopranos, Three Mo' Tenors, Three Countertenors, the Three Chinese Tenors, the Three Cantors, and the rap group The Three Terrors.

increase their exposure and audience appeal, and some more established artists have used it to record repertoire that is too obscure for the major labels to touch.

Is There a Future for Classical Music in America?

Periodically, doomsayers announce that classical music is dead or dying. They cite budget deficits, a static or declining attendance, and ever-increasing costs for recitalists, conductors, and even the rank-and-file musicians. In many parts of the world, classical music is considered a cultural staple and there is no expectation that the symphony orchestra will break even, let alone make money.

Music schools continue to turn out thousands of graduates, and we have reached a point where there are no additional symphony orchestras appearing on the scene. In fact, a few symphony orchestras have even gone out of business. There will always be a demand for brilliant soloists and, realistically, other performers will end up teaching or doing freelance jobs. Conservatories need to adjust to the fact that the contemporary music market requires versatility. To put it another way, the average professionally competent trumpet player is never going to make a living by performing concertos for trumpet and orchestra.

It is possible that Internet and satellite radio can help to improve the market for classical music. Many of the classical radio stations have gone out of business and even some of the NPR stations are playing less music than they used to. Oddly enough, however, classical music sells more strongly through iTunes and other download sites than it does in the "physical" world of CDs. Orchestras have begun offering downloadable files of their performances to take advantage of this trend. Nonetheless, the truth is that the average American simply does not listen to much classical music.

The recession of 2008–2009 has had a very serious effect on symphony orchestras. Many of them have endowments that were invested in the stock market. They became dependent upon the income from these investments to meet their annual budgets. When the market became severely depressed, this income diminished. This has left many symphonies, as well as other non-profit organizations with diminished incomes.

JAZZ

Amazingly little has been written about the business of jazz. Herman Gray's book *Producing Jazz*, discusses the production of jazz recordings. He divides jazz record labels into three categories:

- Labels that do not specialize in jazz but produce occasional jazz recordings when they think an artist has commercial potential.
- Labels that really like the music, but are also trying to make money from these records.
- Labels that only produce music that they like, and never expect to make any money from these recordings.

As is the case with classical music, there are a great number of jazz reissues, often featuring legendary jazz musicians like Charlie Parker or Ella Fitzgerald. There is a market for these reissue packages, which are often produced as handsome box sets with extensive liner notes and pictures. Because the cost of recording these sets has long ago been paid, these packages represent a high profit margin when they sell in any quantity.

From time to time, major labels spend money promoting jazz, such as Sony's attempts to catapult Wynton Marsalis into stardom in the early 1980s. Typically, these efforts fail to realize the company's dreams of financial bonanzas. Consequently, the labels usually give up on these artists, as Columbia did with Marsalis. Certain artists, like Chick Corea and Herbie Hancock, seem to be able to float in and out of the jazz and rock worlds, maintaining the respect of their jazz audiences because of their abilities and reputation. From time to time they sell a large number of records through the use of electronic keyboards, drum machines, and current "in vogue" sounds.

But Is It Jazz?

It might surprise you to learn that the best-selling saxophonist on record—in any style, not just jazz—is Kenny G. Jazz musicians and critics almost universally dismiss Kenny G and the music that he plays, which is part of a movement that originated in the early 1970s known as **Smooth Jazz**. The idea was to take elements of easy listening, disco, and jazz instrumentation and meld them together to form a kind of background music for upscale consumers. Smooth jazz radio enjoyed great popularity in the 1970s and 1980s, and continues to draw listeners today.

   Kenny G has managed to both ride the smooth jazz wave and transcend it. The sales numbers of his CDs are truly staggering. At the height of his success, his 1992 album *Breathless* sold over fifteen million copies, true rock star territory. Although of late his sales have diminished—as all CD sales have declined—Kenny G remains among the most commercially successful musicians of all time.

   The labels that were noted for jazz recordings from the 1950s through the 1980s, such as Prestige, Riverside, Blue Note, and Fantasy, have all been purchased by other labels. The Concord label, in particular, has a tremendous catalog including Prestige, Riverside, and Fantasy Records albums. And the well-respected Blue Note Records was purchased by EMI.

   Although there are jazz musicians everywhere, New York is definitely the center of the jazz universe, with thousands of musicians who describe themselves as jazz players. In order to make a living, many of these players moonlight by playing in salsa bands or in the bands of popular soul artists, or by touring with singer-songwriters such as Paul Simon or Sting.

   Because jazz musicians often double on a number of instruments, they are well suited to playing in Broadway shows. Those jazz players who are good sight readers find their way into studio work, and play in bands on TV shows such as *Saturday Night Live*. In Hollywood, they can be found playing on film soundtracks. Other opportunities exist in giving private lessons, teaching at high school or college level, or teaching at music stores that offer lessons. A number of colleges have jazz orchestras, and more and more colleges are offering jazz performance majors. Jazz composers also get some support from grants. The National Endowment for the Arts offers some grants that are specifically devoted to jazz. Many rock musicians are fascinated by jazz, and very respectful of its comparative complexity. Rock jam bands are simplified versions of jazz bands, featuring long and extended jams that can be exciting, but lack the harmonic complexity of jazz.

   There are jazz clubs in most American cities of any size, and New York boasts a number of them, including the venerable Village Vanguard. Although the best-known jazz musicians can make a reasonable amount of money by playing at out-of-town clubs, many of the local musicians working in their hometown clubs earn a pittance. When big bands appear in clubs in New York and Los Angeles, it is basically a labor of love, because clubs are simply not large enough to pay a reasonable wage to fifteen or more musicians.

There are those who say, as others do with classical music, that jazz is dead. The continual emergence of young jazz talent from all over the world contradicts these beliefs. Jazz has indeed lost its place as a major attraction for young adults, but its international popularity has replaced this loss, to some extent. It is one of the ironies of life that the existing audience for jazz is primarily white, while many of the best musicians continue to be black.

CONTEMPORARY CHRISTIAN MUSIC

Crossover Christian music or **contemporary Christian music**, as it is often called, represents a broader range of music than many people realize. It includes:

- Music used in church as part of the worship ceremony
- Music used in church as evangelical music, designed to galvanize the audience
- Music sold in Christian record stores
- Music played on contemporary Christian radio stations
- Crossover Christian music, designed to convert nonbelievers with a less specific religious message
- Crossover Christian music designed to capture a market niche

Songs that are too rhythmic and do not specifically mention religious figures may be rejected by Christian radio stations, churches, and bookstores. A number of the more radical Christian artists have revolted against the standard formulas found in some contemporary Christian music, and feel resentful that their songs are, in effect, subject to censorship. These artists feel many of the popular Christian artists are not writing songs that reflect any sort of emotional struggle or evolution, but are essentially appealing to the converted.

Christian artists often play churches for offerings, and this phenomenon has its similarities to playing for the door, in the sense that the artist cannot count on receiving any particular amount of money. Famous artists Amy Grant and Michael Smith perform at large concert venues sponsored by church groups or radio stations.

Originally, the Christian labels were independently owned and their product was carried primarily by Christian bookstores, but today all of the leading Christian labels are owned by major labels, and can be found at the major discount chains, such as Best Buy, Target, and Wal-Mart. There are numerous smaller Christian labels, such as Seattle's Tooth and Nail, but the majors dominate. Word Entertainment is owned by Warner Music Group, Sparrow by EMI, and the Provident Group, including Brentwood and Reunion, are owned by Sony BMG. Christian retail outlets account for 36 percent of the sales of Christian/Gospel recordings, and normal retail channels sold 64 percent. The Gospel Music Association places the dollar volume of Christian music at over $700 million at the end of 2006.

The top-selling Christian album of 2006 was *Precious Memories,* recorded by country superstar Alan Jackson, which sold close to 1,300,000 copies, more than double the amount sold by the second place finisher, *Skyleaf.* Christian/ Gospel (gospel is the term generally used for black Christian music) was one of the few musical genres that enjoyed increased record sales in 2006, while most of the industry was mired in declining sales.

The same business issues surface in Christian music that artists cope with in popular music. For example, Tooth and Nail Records demands ownership of its artists' publishing, just as some independent labels do in the pop arena.

LATIN MUSIC

The Latin music market is not really a single market. The three leading Spanish-speaking groups in the United States are Mexicans, Cubans, and Puerto Ricans. The Mexican-American population is strongest in the southwest, where there are numerous Spanish-language radio stations. In the Mexican American group alone, different musical styles coexist. *Tejano* or *norteño* music is the music of the states that border Mexico. Other Mexican styles include older ballad styles, rock en *espanol,* mariachi music, and *banda,* a horn-based band and harp music from Vera Cruz. A great deal of *norteño* music is recorded in San Antonio, and for some years now many of the *tejano* songs are *narcocorridos,* songs that involve drugs. As discussed earlier, many of the same bands that are popular among Mexican-Americans are also popular in Mexico, and tour in both countries (see Chapter 8).

The Cuban American population is centered in Miami, and that city has become the headquarters for importing and exporting music to Central and South America. Cuba has always been a vital musical scene, and the many Cuban émigrés have heavily influenced the music scene in Miami. The Latin music scene in Miami focuses on the many dance clubs. Miami is also the headquarters for MTV Latino, MTV for Latin America. Sony International also has its headquarters in Miami, and there are many Latin TV studios located there as well (see Chapter 8).

Salsa matured as a musical style in New York with its fusion of Cuban and Puerto Rican musical styles and musicians. New York has a huge Puerto Rican population, as well as many salsa clubs and dances.

NARAS, the organization that created the Grammy TV show, also does an annual Latin Grammies show, and it has created a separate organization called **LARAS, the Latin Academy of Recording Arts & Sciences**. LARAS was founded in 1997, and has its own independent group of trustees. The organization is intended to serve music professionals in Spanish and Portuguese music, but unlike the Grammies, it admits international members. Both American and international releases are eligible for the annual awards.

A number of Mexican-American artists were or are stars within the Latin community. Don Tosta in Los Angeles and San Antonio *norteño* artist Flaco Jimenez were regionally popular Spanish-language artists. Selena was on her way to breaking through as the first Chicano superstar in the 1990s before she was murdered by a fan. The late Freddy Fender, the country music star, sometimes sang songs in English and Spanish. Latin salsa bands led by Tito Puente also succeeded in finding a successful musical niche that enabled them to survive. Several Latin artists have broken through to become stars in the United States, as well as the rest of the world. Gloria Estefan and the Miami Sound Machine achieved tremendous success in the 1980s (see Chapter 8), and today Colombian artist Shakira is an international superstar, singing in both English and Spanish.

Given the increasing population of Spanish-speaking people in the United States, the Latin music business will undoubtedly become an even stronger part of the music business there.

WORLD MUSIC

Other than Australian and British rock stars, and a few pop groups such as the Swedish singing stars Abba singing in English, very few groups from outside the United States have been able to achieve widespread popularity in the United States. Periodically, American record companies have tried to market foreign artists, even Japanese stars, to audiences in the United States. In most instances, these attempts have not proved successful.

Over the years, certain record labels have specialized in selling recordings of music from other cultures. Folkways Records, founded by Moses Asch in New York in 1948, was one of the first labels to offer music from other parts of the world. These records sold mostly to libraries and schools, and Asch never intended for them to reach the mass marketplace. These recordings were intended to be used by scholars and students, and were accompanied by extensive notes. Because most of the music was recorded in the field, the sound quality varied greatly.

Initially, Folkways had few competitors. Occasionally, other labels would issue some recordings made abroad, notably Alan Lomax's Columbia Records Library of World Music. This included eighteen long-playing records recorded all over the world in the 1950s. Lomax worked with folklorists in various countries on these albums, but again they were never intended to be mass market items.

There had been occasional pop music hits with songs from faraway places. The Weavers' recording of the South African song "Wimoweh" was a big hit record in 1952, and it enjoyed a rebirth in a mildly rock version by The Tokens retitled *The Lion Sleeps Tonight*. The South African singer Miriam Makeba achieved some chart success in the 1960s with novelties such as "Patta Patta."

Ethnomusicology, the study of **world music**, also helped to create an American audience for world music. Beginning in the late 1950s–early 1960s, schools such as the University of Washington, University of California at Los Angeles, and Wesleyan University had college music ensembles that play music from other cultures. They also brought in visiting professors from various musical cultures to teach students.

In 1967, Elektra Records' subsidiary Nonesuch Records produced a series of albums recorded in stereo in different parts of the world, including Java and Africa. These records were really the first world music records intended for the general listener, and there was less emphasis on scholarship and more attention paid to the sound quality and packaging than on the previous world music efforts.

At about the same time, The Beatles began incorporating world music sounds—most notably the sitar, which guitarist George Harrison learned from Indian master Ravi Shankar—into their music. Shankar's popularity was greatly boosted by appearances at the Woodstock Festival (1969) and the Concert for Bangla Desh (1971). Shankar was the first "crossover" star, although his music remained untouched by Western influences. It took the reggae explosion of the 1970s—with musicians such as Bob Marley and Peter Tosh—to bring the first world music style to the top of the pop charts. Reggae combined Western rock influences with native Jamaican rhythms, melodies, and lyrics. This would become the model for many other success-ful world music hybrids from the 1980s through today.

World Music and Copyright

Dealing with world music copyrights is often complex. Several platinum records have used uncredited samples, lifted from obscure ethnomusi-cological recordings, without payment to the performers or composers. Sometimes it is difficult to find the original copyright owners, even if a fair attempt is made. A song may have appeared on an obscure record, recorded by an ethnomusicologist who may not have stayed in touch with the artist whom the scholar recorded. Often years have elapsed between the original recording and its use by a later artist.

Another issue is the question of what part of the copyright of a tradi-tional song belongs to the artist who was recorded in the field and what part goes to the person who did the recording? There have been countless dis-putes about the rights to American folksongs, such as "Tom Dooley." This old murder ballad was collected by folklorist Frank Warner from a singer and banjoist named Frank Proffitt. The song became a big hit in a recording by the Kingston Trio in 1958. They assumed that it was a folksong, and copy-righted their version of it. Later Frank Warner sued, and his copyright was affirmed, but neither he nor Proffitt received retroactive royalties.

Labeling a Musical Niche

In the 1980s, world music became a category used to name recordings from foreign countries. Initially, the term was used to cover all of the music in the

The Strange Saga of "Wimoweh"

"Wimoweh" was originally composed in 1939 by a South African musician named Solomon Linda. Linda's group recorded the song for the South African division of Decca Records, and that record fell into the hands of folksong collector Alan Lomax. Lomax brought the song to the attention of Pete Seeger, who recorded it with his group The Weavers in 1952. Seeger thought that it was a South African folksong, and The Weavers copyrighted their arrangement of it. When Seeger found out that the song was a composed work, he sent Linda a check for what he thought would have been the composer's share of the song.

About ten years later, a pop vocal group The Tokens rerecorded the song, and their mildly rock version became a #1 hit in 1962. Their version was a rewrite of "Wimoweh," credited to their label owner George Weiss along with the well-known record producers Luigi Creatore and Hugo Peretti. The Weavers sued based on their copyright, and eventually a settlement was reached for a share of the royalties. More than thirty years later, the song was featured in the Disney production *The Lion King*, which was both a successful film and a hit musical on Broadway.

Over these decades, the only money that Linda ever received was the money that Pete Seeger sent him. Finally, a lawsuit against Disney by Linda's heirs (Solomon died in 1961) resulted in an undisclosed settlement and a continuing royalty interest in the song. Because of the many hit versions of the song and the extensive airplay that it received, the song's estimated value is $15 million.

world. Others limited the definition to "authentic" folk or ethnic music, in other words, noncommercially recorded music. However, in many record stores, it is used to highlight Afro-Pop or Celtic music, genres that are considered to have commercial potential.

The world music market was given a major boost in 1986, when Paul Simon's *Graceland* album was released. Simon recorded it with Ladysmith Black Mambazo and other South African artists. It received great critical acclaim and was also a great commercial success, reviving Simon's lagging career. Other Western pop stars, especially Peter Gabriel and David Byrne, also recorded projects using musicians from different parts of the world. Gabriel started a label, called Real World, which encouraged musical hybrids—musicians from different cultures playing together. American musicians Ry Cooder, Bob Brozman, Taj Mahal, Henry Kaiser, and David Lindley have each recorded with musicians from such places as Okinawa, India, Cuba, Madagascar, and Norway.

Putamayo Records was founded in 1993, initially to release anthologies of music from different cultures. Some of the recordings featured traditional musicians, but many others featured trance or dance music styles. Initially, Putamayo marketed their releases in clothing stores that featured imported clothing, coffee shops, and other non-traditional outlets. The series became so successful that many record stores started Putamayo sections. Consumers trusted the selections to be the best of a particular genre, thanks to the Putamayo name.

The most commercially successful world music album to date is the *Buena Vista Social Club* album released in 1997. Ry Cooder, the producer, recorded a number of older Cuban musicians, Wim Wender made a film about it, and the CD sold over seven million copies, five million of them outside the United States. Consequently, the record bins of well-stocked record stores are chock full of music from all over the world. Several magazines, including *Folk Roots* and *Song Lines*, both published in Britain, are largely devoted to world music. In the United States, *The Beat* and *Global Rhythms* are periodicals devoted to world music, and several other magazines cover world music as part of their overall music coverage.

A number of African and Indian musicians tour the United States with some regularity, and sell out concerts in major cities. World music seems to be more popular in Great Britain and France than it is in the United States. France is a world center for African music, particularly musicians from North Africa (which was originally colonized by the French).

HIP-HOP MUSIC

When **hip-hop music** first appeared in the United States in the late 1970s, it was tied into various cultural forms, including breakdancing, graffiti, and rap music. Rapping involved the use of rhymed verses, set to rhythmic beats performed on a powerful sound system using huge speakers. Some of the early Bronx DJs, including Cool Herc, were Jamaican, and sound systems were already in use on the streets of Kingston.

Not too surprisingly, the initial industry reaction to rap was that it was a temporary fad, which would soon disappear. Industry insiders assumed the same position that Mitch Miller had taken in the 1950s in his opinions about rock and roll. What has actually happened is something no one in the industry could have anticipated. Not only is hip-hop still around, more than twenty-five years later, but there are rappers all over the world, not only rapping in English but also in French, Spanish, German, and numerous other languages.

Hip-hop music was born in New York, and soon spread, especially to Los Angeles' Compton neighborhood. The rappers from the two cities developed dangerous rivalries, and along the way these rivalries turned violent. Since those 1980s days, rap has spread to Atlanta, Miami, New Orleans, and Houston. Atlanta has become an important music industry center, with producers, studios, artists and record company representatives drawing more and more artists there (see Chapter 8).

Hip-hop has brought an amazing amount of fame and fortune to a small number of producers-writers-engineers-beatmasters-artists. People such as Puff Diddy, Prince Paul, Jermaine Dupri, Kanye West, Russell Simmons, and Jay-Z are all multimillionaires, with their own label imprints financed by the major record labels, clothing lines, and a multitude of other remunerative enterprises. These producers have become megastars themselves, dominating the gossip pages and weekly magazines that peddle celebrity news.

The biggest problem hip-hop has encountered is that it has not been as lucrative for performers as it has for the multitalented producers. Part of the problem has been that insurance for hip-hop concerts is much more expensive to buy than, say, for an Eagles concert. Promoters are reluctant to add to their financial burdens and, because of the association of some of the music with crime and gangsters, they also fear that violence might erupt at a hip-hop stadium show. This means hiring extra security, another expense.

Another problem is that a large number of hip-hop performances are basically a rapper with a supporting cast of rappers, and someone making the beats, or playing tapes of beats. An entire show of beats, turntable scratching and lyrics without melodies does not necessarily make for a vastly entertaining evening. Singers such as Beyoncé have expanded rap to include more melodic ballads and slower numbers to give her performances more pace. She has also added elaborate costumes and dance numbers to her shows, again to offer more variety. In this way, major rap concerts now resemble typical pop shows put on by superstars such as Madonna or Britney Spears.

CHILDREN'S MUSIC

Children's music is unique, in the sense that it has to appeal to parents (who in the case of young children are the buyers,) and children, who are the listeners, or consumers. Some of the artists who perform for children do so exclusively; others perform for adults as well as children.

There are a number of tiers of children's music, each appealing to separate groups. Children's music can be divided into:

- Lullabies
- Music promoted through movies or television.
- Folk music, with a singalong emphasis
- "Friendly" rock and roll
- Music designed to help build children's self-esteem

Lullabies are found in virtually every culture and are universally used by mothers to soothe babies to sleep.

Disney has always been the major purveyor of what we might call movie-based kid's music. These days they have expanded their presence to creating preteen idols, such as Hannah Montana, whose performances are directed toward "tweeners" (preteen-aged girls). By cross-promoting the artists on records, movies, and television, Disney achieves the goal of using each medium to help build the other one. Personal appearances are the icing on the cake, helping to sell records and merchandise and to keep the fans excited. Disney owns several record labels, so that it has plenty of recorded outlets to choose from.

A number of **folk music** performers, beginning in the late 1940s–early 1950s with Pete Seeger and Woody Guthrie, wrote or performed children's songs, and Seeger has also created a number of children's stories built around songs. Guthrie's *Songs to Grow On* recording is considered a classic in the children's recording field. Cathy Fink and Marcy Marxer are two folk-oriented artists who also do quite a few performances for children.

Over the past few decades, Raffi has been the king of the folk-oriented kids' performers. He was originally a folk-rock artist whose career was not especially notable. Raffi's records and performances are designed to appeal to very young children, and he has been a major artist in this field for years. Raffi is Canadian, and CBC television airs a number of children's shows that have also been strong career aids to other artists. Another popular singer/songwriter in the folk-rock style is Tom Chapin, brother of Harry, who began his career singing for adults but achieved his greatest success as a children's artist.

"Kid-friendly rock" refers to rock-and-roll musicians who have done children's music that focuses on the rhythmic upbeat qualities of rock music. For example, the Music For Little People label issued a rock record for young children that featured Little Richard and other rock artists. Dan Zanes, who was originally in the successful rock band the Del Fuegos, now has a new identity and career as a children's artist. Sharon, Lois, and Bram specialized in creating songs that mimicked adult genres—including rock, reggae, Zydeco, and other styles—with lyrics suitable for children. This group also originated in Canada, and for years had a successful kids' show on the CBC.

A number of artists use music for kids as a sort of tool for moral teaching, designed to assist kids in building self-esteem. Peter Allsop is one of these artists, as are Suni Paz and the late Malvina Reynolds. Steve Seskin, who has written a number of hit country songs, has also written some songs designed to build self-esteem, especially a song entitled "Don't Laugh At Me." The song was cowritten with Allen Shamblin and they have turned it into a children's book.

Outlets for Children's Music

There are several unique performing outlets for children's music. Young Audiences is a national organization that has branches in most large cities. It sponsors performances in the public school system and employs numerous musicians in each city. The age group served by these performances varies. Performances at the high school level are generally songs or instrumental pieces accompanied by narratives that explain their significance. In some cities, Young Audiences cooperates with the Musician's Union, and receives partial funding from the Music Performance Fund, a fund drawn from the sales of records.

The Wiggles

The current superstars of children's music are The Wiggles, an Australian group that has sold over seventeen million DVDs and over four million CDs. The group originated among a quartet of childhood education majors at Australia's Macquarie University. Two of them had previously played in a local rock band, so it's not surprising that their music shows the influence of rock and pop music. They released their first album in 1991, which eventually went platinum thanks to their constant touring, first in Australia and then the United Kingdom and the United States. They sold out twelve nights at New York's Madison Square Garden when they brought their show there in 2003.

In addition to records, the Wiggles have an elaborate touring show, host a TV show, and have produced DVDs and films. They appeal to young children, and their costuming and the characters they depict are designed for their audience of preschoolers. When they tour, The Wiggles sell a large variety of merchandise. For the last several years, *Australian Business Weekly* has rated the group as the highest earning entertainers in the country. Their American record company is Koch, one of the strongest independent record labels, which also handles its own distribution.

The **Children's Music Network (CMN)** is a nonprofit organization of performers. It includes music broadcasters, educators, record producers, songwriters, and classroom teachers. Its regional chapters offer an opportunity to network with other music professionals who are active in the field.

Public libraries often sponsor shows for children. These performances are free, so the musician is paid a flat fee. Children's museums are another outlet for children's music.

The major labels have made forays into the children's market from time to time, but generally the market for this music isn't lucrative enough to maintain their interest.

It seems natural that tie-ins to movies and television will continue to be the most effective way of promoting children's music. Because children are now thoroughly immersed in computers and the Internet, YouTube and MySpace sites will certainly prove to be an effective promotional tool to reach them.

BLUEGRASS, FOLK, AND RELATED MUSIC

Bluegrass music has been a niche in the country music world for over sixty years. The success of Alison Krauss and Nickel Creek, along with the six million CDs sold of the soundtrack of *O Brother, Where Art Thou?* indicates that bluegrass is probably stronger now than ever. The International Bluegrass Music Association (IBMA) is the national organization that promotes bluegrass music (see Chapter 4).

Sugar Hill and Rounder Records are among the stronger record companies that specialize in bluegrass, although Rounder also produces recordings of many other musical genres. Lesser known artists often produce their own albums, and sell them at performances. One of the primary outlets for professional bluegrass musicians are the many bluegrass music festivals. They take place in all parts of the country, usually in the summer. Attendance often runs in the thousands. Other outlets include folk music societies and clubs. There are a number of music stores that specialize in bluegrass instruments and many of them also carry CDs. Music print publishers have a great deal of bluegrass instructional material available, often accompanied by CDs or DVDs.

Bluegrass has fans that prefer to hear traditional bluegrass music, but younger ones have splintered into so-called newgrass music, which reflects the influence of jazz and rock music as well as traditional bluegrass. Some of the more experimental instrumentalists of bluegrass, including Bela Fleck, Sam Bush, and Jerry Douglas, have moved into more improvisational music.

Nickel Creek and Alison Krauss perform a kind of crossover bluegrass. Traditional bluegrass features the "high lonesome sound," which some music fans find too nasal or abrasive and these younger musicians use a more mellow vocal sound.

The recent Robert Plant/Alison Krauss duet album united the former lead singer of Led Zeppelin with one of the younger bluegrass icons. The album was commercially very successful, and it also garnered numerous favorable reviews. No doubt some traditional bluegrass fans regarded this album as heresy.

Folk Music

The North American Folk Music and Dance Alliance plays the same sort of role in the folk music community that IBMA does with bluegrass. As is the case with bluegrass, a number of record labels issue folk music recordings. Smithsonian Folkways, Appleseed, Folk Era-Wind River, Red House, and Rounder are among the better-known labels.

There are a number of different genres of folk music:

- *Singer-songwriters.* Many of the singer-songwriters of the 1970s, including Joni Mitchell, Carly Simon, and James Taylor, had backgrounds in folk music. Over the course of time, they started writing their own songs, as a form of personal expression of the events taking place in their lives. Many of today's singer-songwriters have been more influenced by *other* singer-songwriters than by the icons of the folksong revival, such as Pete Seeger or Woody Guthrie.
- *Old-time music musicians.* People who perform old-time music, such as mountain music, which preceded bluegrass. Their models are the mountain string bands of the 1920s and 1930s, or, in some cases, The New Lost City Ramblers, urban revivalists of the late 1950s–1960s.

- *Singers of traditional folksongs.* There are still some performers who sing traditional songs and do not write their own material. Many of these artists deemphasize instrumental virtuosity, and sing some songs without accompaniment.
- *Protest singers.* Protest singers use folksongs, or their own new songs, as a means of expressing radical political ideas. Some of these contemporary artists, including Anne Feeney and Charley King, are as apt to be found singing on picket lines as in music venues.
- *New acoustic instrumentalists.* Musicians such as David Grisman, Bob Brozman, Tony Rice, and Darroll Anger play music that is a blend of folk styles, blues, bluegrass, world music, rock, and jazz.
- *Celtic and world music.* Celtic music is probably the most popular foreign-influenced folk music in the United States. They play the music of the British Isles, focusing on Irish, Welsh, and Scottish traditions.
- *Blues.* As is the case with bluegrass, there are acoustic and traditionally oriented blues musicians and musicians who play electric guitar in combos with drummers and electric bass players. Some musicians, including Buddy Guy, are capable of strong work in either of these styles.

The Folk Music Business

Folk musicians play in clubs, as do many of the other musicians we have discussed. Several other venues cater to the various genres of folk music:

- *Coffee houses.* These range from very small living room operations to sizeable venues. They specialize in nonalcoholic beverages and light foods. The smaller venues pay musicians through tip jars, but the larger ones usually have cover charges that either go entirely or largely to the musicians. Smaller rooms don't require sound systems, and the larger ones sometimes have their own systems, and sometimes require musicians to do their own sound reinforcement.
- *House concerts.* House concerts are a prime venue for folk performers (see Chapter 15).
- *Folk festivals.* As with bluegrass, there are many summer folk festivals, often held outdoors and featuring dozens of artists. The pay varies: some festivals provide only gas money, like the massive Seattle Folk Life Festival, some offer accommodations, and some pay performers. Generally, festivals are presented by nonprofit organizations. The Philadelphia Folk Festival and several of the Canadian Festivals, such as Winnipeg and Vancouver, have been in operation for several decades. Some festivals are more specialized, such as the Chicago Blues Festival and the waterfront Blues Festival in Portland, Oregon.
- *Folksong societies.* Many cities have nonprofit organizations that attempt to promote folk music by presenting it, usually on a monthly

basis. A few, such as the Swallow Hill Music Association in Denver, present shows on a more regular basis.

• *Mixed venues.* A number of venues do not limit themselves to one musical genre but present a mix of folk, jazz, blues, and rock shows.

OTHER MUSICAL GENRES

This brief survey does not begin to cover all of the musical genres and the ways that they create their own versions of music industry procedures. Polka music, the music of various ethnic groups, and the many genres of rock, such as heavy metal music or punk, each have their own approach to developing an audience base. Ethnic music exists under the radar of most music fans. For example, Mexican/American music is purveyed at clubs, dances, and taverns in a fashion that is invisible to most Anglo music fans.

Musicians in any of these fields face their own set of challenges, as do the entrepreneurs promoting their music.

Terms to Know

Arts administration *146*
Bluegrass music *163*
Children's music *161*
Children's Music Network (CMN) *163*
Classical crossover *152*

Community orchestra *150*
Conservatory *145*
Contemporary Christian music *155*
Ethnomusicology *157*
Folk music *162*
Ford Foundation *149*

Hip-hop music *160*
LARAS (Latin Academy of Recording Arts & Sciences) *156*
Smooth Jazz *154*
World music *157*

For Class Discussion

1. What musical genres are important in your hometown?
2. Have you ever attended a classical music concert?
3. Were you aware that top classical musicians earn superstar fees when performing?
4. Is there a symphony orchestra in your hometown?
5. Is there a future in the United States for classical music?
6. Is there a future in the United States for jazz?
7. Does your college have any jazz musicians on the faculty? What do they teach?
8. Are there any jazz clubs in the town where you are attending school?
9. In your opinion, what are appropriate subjects for Christian musicians to write about?
10. What music genres do your local radio stations play?

CHAPTER 10

The International
Music Markets

This chapter offers a brief introduction to music markets in areas of the world outside the United States. Several books have been written on the subject (see appendix), but it is time that all music business classes and students spend time looking at the differences and similarities in the way music is made and marketed in various parts of the world.

Until the British musical invasion of the 1960s, the U.S. music industry looked at other countries simply as places to sell American music. It also generally assumed that recordings from other parts of the world would not appeal to American listeners. However, once the Beatles hit the top of the U.S. charts, the floodgates opened, at least to other British artists. Wave after wave of British artists had hit records in the United States: Dave Clark Five, Gerry and the Pacemakers, Herman's Hermits, Petula Clark, Chad and Jeremy, Peter and Gordon, and many others. It seemed as though only Motown survived the assault of British music. A few American groups such as the Beau Brummels even sang like the British bands! The British also brought some other musical styles to the attention of American audiences. For example, George Harrison "promoted" his sitar teacher Ravi Shankar, who rose to stardom through his performance at the 1967 Monterey Pop Festival. Shankar had toured internationally and was well known to aficionados of Indian music, but Harrison made him a household name!

Suddenly, the country became aware that American music wasn't going to dominate world music forever. If we still had any doubts, by the mid-1970s reggae came to the United States, and Jimmy Cliff and Bob Marley became familiar figures to many Americans. Interest in world music exploded in the 1980s, with groups and performers from Africa, the Caribbean, and the Middle East attracting new audiences.

We have already seen how the original major American record labels, RCA, Columbia, and Decca, were all under foreign ownership by 1985. The money, which had always flowed from the rest of the world to the United States, began to move in the opposite direction. The United States remains the leading market for record sales, but Japan now sells more than half as much recorded product as the United States. As of 2006, the top ten markets, with their retail value in American dollars, are:

UNITED STATES	$11,501,000,000
JAPAN	$5,273,000,000
UNITED KINGDOM	$3,252,000,000
GERMANY	$2,091,000,000
FRANCE	$1,700,000,000
CANADA	$719,000,000
AUSTRALIA	$621,000,000
ITALY	$598,000,000
SPAIN	$497,000,000
MEXICO	$374,000,000

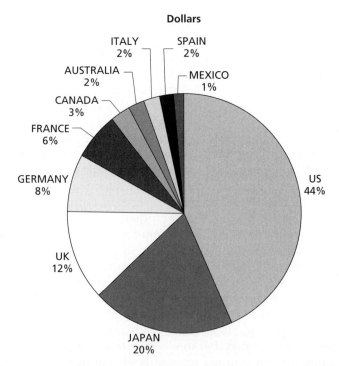

The total worldwide value of recorded sales was $31,813,000,000. As of the end of 2006, the United States market constituted just 36.1 percent of the sale of recorded music in the world. India and China did not make the list, and when one considers their population and the growth of their economies, if the piracy situation can be controlled, sales of recorded product should greatly escalate.

SIMILARITIES AND DIFFERENCES IN INTERNATIONAL MUSIC MARKETS

Because many of the same transnational record companies operate throughout most of the world, it is not any great surprise that the music industry has similar characteristics in many of these markets. There are record companies, music publishing companies, performing rights organizations, musical instrument and record stores, concert promoters, agents, personal managers, record producers, and recording engineers in each market. Live music is also a constant presence throughout the entire world. However, there are also profound differences in the way the music industry functions in different parts of the world. This chart shows some aspects of the music business that differ depending on the country.

Issue	Specifics
Role of government (see also legal)	• Government support of the arts vs. private philanthropy • Censorship of lyrics or musical styles • Restrictions on foreign ownership of local companies • Restrictions on performance of foreign repertory
Taxes	• Sales taxes • Customs duties
Unions	Extent of influence
Performing rights	Royalties to performers as well as songwriters and music publishers
Legal	• Copyright law • Antitrust Law
Radio & TV station ownership	• Public vs. private • Language restrictions
Touring	• Work visas • Technical problems • Censorship
Piracy	• Restrictions on digital copying • Enforcement of copyright laws

ROLE OF GOVERNMENT

Government support of the music industry can assume various roles. It can:

- Invest money in music business education
- Offer tax breaks for producers who come from outside the nation or immediate geographic region

- Give grants to musicians and music organizations to finance recording projects, videos, or tour support.
- Provide publicity to artists by giving them an honorary status
- Offer employment through government-owned radio or television stations
- Sponsor seminars or workshops that offer business assistance to musicians or music companies
- Impose import duties on imported recordings, making them more expensive to consumers, and consequently less attractive to retail stores

National support of music and musicians comes through government grant programs or from private philanthropy. In the United States, the latter role is the most significant. The entire budget for the National Endowment for the Arts (NEA) has hovered around $150 million. These dollars are split between music, the visual arts, dance, theater, and film. What America does provide, however, is tax deductions for individuals who donate to non-profit philanthropic organizations. This encourages individuals to support the arts.

European art support is much more generous. England even provides business education for musicians. According to Arthur Bernstein, in the book, *The Global Music Industry: Three Perspectives*, in Europe "the per capita spending on culture at the public level is, on average, far superior across Europe than in other regions of the world." Bernstein points out that the Arts Council in England projected that it would invest approximately $3 billion in arts initiatives in England. The Arts Council is funded through a combination of public funds and money from the national lottery. From 1994 to 2005, the lottery funds for music distributed nearly a billion dollars. The European Union (EU) provided $250 million for cultural programs from 2000 to 2006, and has budgeted $550 million for the years 2008 through 2013. Each country in the EU also has separate budgets for its own arts funding.

In general, government support for the arts in Asia is not comparable to what European countries provide. Australia provides government funding for the arts, and has programs that support musical groups touring in that country. Hong Kong supports the arts through government advertising in foreign countries that promotes performing arts groups. The South Korean government has a fund intended to encourage the development of local music, drama, and movies.

Another way in which governments help musicians is to encourage film companies to make movies in their country. For example, Canada offers government rebates for foreign companies that film there. Both Toronto and Vancouver have attracted millions of dollars in American film and television production due to a combination of these financial incentives. Australia has gone so far as to pay for Australian composers to fly to Hollywood to meet with American film producers in order to make contacts that they hope will lead to employment in film scoring.

Some state governments in the United States have offered considerable private support to the American film industry, when it chooses to work in their state. For example, Secretary of Commerce Bill Richardson has been the governor of New Mexico from 2002 through to the present. He established a 25 percent rebate to Hollywood film-makers and television producers on any money that they spent in his state. Consequently, from 2003 to 2008, more than 115 feature films and television series were made in New Mexico.

Censorship

Censorship varies according to the nature of a government and its fear of anything that might encourage people to turn against it. In Egypt, the government must approve pop songs that are played on the radio, and the same situation prevails in Cuba and in several African countries. Algeria has heavily censored rai music on the grounds of indecency. In Jamaica, several reggaeton dancehall artists have been fined for presenting "indecent" performances, and in France some rappers were prosecuted for denouncing French heroes in rap songs. Uganda, Cuba, and China are among the countries that tightly censor the lyrics of music that radio stations are permitted to play. The authorities in these countries fear that open expressions of antigovernment sentiment will be politically dangerous to the survival of their government.

In 1959, Brazilian musicians Gilberto Gil and Caetano Veloso, who had previously been arrested, were exiled. Ironically, years later Gil became the Brazilian Minister of Culture. Zimbabwean musician Thomas Mapfumo was forced into exile, when the government objected to his political protest music. Nigerian artist Fela Kuti was harassed by the Nigerian government, persecuted for his political and social beliefs, and his living compound was raided by the government. Algerian rai artist Matoob Lounes, who had been living in France, was murdered when he returned to Algeria in 1998. The Taliban banned musical instruments and music making of any kind during its reign in Afghanistan.

Musical Censorship in the United States   Although censorship in the United States is far less flagrant, the FCC bans the use of indecent words on radio or television and some radio stations have been fined for broadcasting songs with indecent lyrics. Wal-Mart has compelled some American artists to re-record their songs for the store on the grounds of indecency. They have also objected on other grounds. They refused to carry a Sheryl Crow CD that had a song that included a lyric about shopping for guns at Wal-Mart. At the same time they continued to sell her previous albums. Because the chain is currently the single largest seller of physical CDs, and they regard their customers as being conservative Middle Americans in terms of taste and values, Wal-Mart has had a big impact on what can be recorded.

During the 1950s, American folksinger Pete Seeger was blacklisted. He had been a founding member of The Weavers, a successful folk-pop group,

Victor Jara: *Plegaria a un Labrador* ("A Worker's Prayer")

Singer/songwriter Victor Jara led a life dedicated to championing the rights of Chile's oppressed rural population and its inner-city poor. Jara was raised on a farm, and came to Santiago, Chile's capital, when his mother and father split because of his father's heavy drinking. Jara attended college there, and was exposed to folk music through a small café operated by the singer Violetta Parra. Parra encouraged Jara to write his own songs, and he released his first album in 1966. Jara was a major supporter of social change in Chile, backing the socialist party led by Salvatore Allende, performing benefit concerts for the candidate. After several failed attempts, Allende gained the presidency of Chile in 1970, and it seemed that the reform movement would triumph.

Victor Jara entertains children in Chile, c. 1970s. Courtesy Fundacion Victor Jara.

However, forces were at work against Allende, both at home and abroad. Supported by the U.S. CIA, a successful coup was staged against Allende and he was murdered on September 11, 1973. Shortly thereafter, Jara was arrested and imprisoned. Five days later, masses of Allende supporters were taken to the Chile Stadium, where the military tortured, beat, and killed hundreds of them. Jara began singing a song in support of Allende's failed movement, and witnesses said his hands were broken (or amputated) before he, too, was gunned down. He died on September 15, 1973. His body was later retrieved from the mass grave at the stadium, which itself was renamed in his honor Victor Jara Stadium.

Jara pioneered the *neuvo cancion* movement, a style of song that combined folk melodies and themes with socially conscious lyrics. Among his songs that remain popular in Latin American countries today are *Plegaria a un Labrador* ("A Worker's Prayer") and *Te Recuerdo Amanda* ("I Remember You Amanda"). Performers as varied as Arlo Guthrie, the Clash, and U2 have written songs that name Jara as a leading voice of protest.

who had top chart hits in 1950 and 1951. The Weavers were listed as being communists in a publication called *Red Channels*. The group lost all of its lucrative live gigs and their Decca Records recording contract. Seeger was indicted in 1955 by the House Un-American Activities Committee (HUAC) for his refusal to answer questions about his political beliefs. This indictment greatly discouraged promoters from hiring Seeger, and he was reduced to occasional college concerts and teaching. At the same time, the U.S. government withdrew alleged communist-sympathizer singer-actor Paul Robeson's passport, which eliminated his ability to perform overseas. Another peculiar form of censorship victimized American musician, composer, and producer Ry Cooder. His production of the *Buena Vista Social Club* recording was a worldwide hit in 1997, but the United States government will not allow him to go back to record another album by Cuban musicians. It is currently illegal for Americans to travel to Cuba, although the Obama administration is beginning to relax these restrictions.

Nongovernmental censorship was exercised by American radio stations after the events of 9/11, when the Clear Channel radio chain sent a list of songs to its affiliates that they felt would not be acceptable to their stations' listeners. Clear Channel owns hundreds of stations, so this ban had a large impact on many artists. A less formal version of this phenomenon is to deny an artist radio play, because the station either disagrees with the artist's political statements or fears that their listeners or sponsors may be offended. Even hit artists such as Green Day and Neil Young have been censored in this way because they wrote, performed, and recorded songs criticizing George Bush and the war in Iraq.

Outside Ownership of Local Business

Many countries restrict foreign ownership of local businesses. Often the magic number is under 50 percent ownership, which means that control stays in the hands of local companies. In some countries, restrictions are more extreme. For example, in South Korea, foreign ownership of telecommunications companies cannot exceed 49 percent. In Thailand, foreign capital cannot own more than a 5 percent share in banks, and in Australia, foreign ownership of companies is limited to a 25 percent share.

Domestic versus International Repertoire

The extent to which domestic repertoire is played on the radio or sold in record shops is dependent on a number of factors. The government regulates the playing of foreign repertoire on the radio in Canada, France, and many other countries.

The Canadian government essentially established a Canadian record business by mandating that 35 percent of radio play must come from recordings that contain two of four Canadian components. These components are artist, producer, and on the songwriting end, composer and lyricist. This program is known as **CANCON**, or Canadian Content. Because so many major Canadian cities are close to the American border, there most likely would not be a Canadian music industry without the CANCON rules. These rules in turn led to the creation of a fund called **FACTOR (Foundation to Assist Canadian Artists on Record)**, because radio stations protested that they could not play Canadian music if there were no Canadian recordings to play. This grant fund provides musicians with loans that enable them to make recordings. If the recordings become successful, the musicians pay the loans back. Other Canadian government programs finance videos and foreign tours.

France's radio requirements are built around the idea that the government does not wish to have the English language dominate the airwaves. Their focus is on the French language, rather than where a recording was produced. The Canadian province of Quebec has a French-language component, and the percentage of Canadian content required on government radio is even higher than with CANCON in English.

Some other countries with minimum content requirement include Malaysia, which mandates that 60 percent of radio programming consist of local content, and Venezuela, which requires that 50 percent of FM radio programming be of local music between 7 and 10 P.M.

In many countries, multiple languages are spoken, and there may be a variety of ethnic groups as well. Sometimes these groups are in conflict with one another, like the Kurdish, Sunni, and Shiite groups in Iraq. In other countries, the difference is cultural, so that vocal styles and the instruments played by different ethnic groups vary greatly. Local pride and government policy are also factors in the use of domestic versus foreign repertoire. For example, in Europe the percentage of domestic repertoire in recordings sold in various countries varies from a low of 7 percent in Austria to a high of 94 percent in Turkey. France, Latvia, and Romania are other countries where this figure goes above 50 percent.

The factors include:

- Radio play mandated by the government
- Prevalence of local languages
- Indigenous musical styles that are resistant to foreign incursions
- Formats of recorded music. For example, in some developing countries, like India, cassettes are still the dominant format. This format is considered to be obsolete in the world's major music markets, and multinational labels have little interest in producing them.
- Availability of local repertoire. In many African countries there are few if any recording studios and no pressing plants. When there is no physical product available, except imports, clearly sales will be drastically affected.

Taxes

The sales of records in some countries are inhibited by three sorts of taxes: **import taxes**, **sales taxes**, and **value-added taxes**, which are taxes imposed in Canada and most European countries as a sort of national sales tax. These taxes vary considerably. In Uruguay sales tax is 23 percent of the value of the product, while in Ecuador it is 10 percent. The United States has no national sales tax, but most states enforce taxes that range from 4 to 11.5 percent. In some cases, cities impose a sales tax on top of the state tax. A few states do not have a sales tax.

UNIONS

The influence of musicians' unions varies country by country. I have already mentioned that the AFM, which represents the United States and Canada, has about ninety thousand members. FIM (Federation of International Musicians) is an international organization that represents members of seventy-two musicians' unions all over the world. The unions are strongest in Great Britain (32,500 members) and Germany (14,524). Countries such as Ireland, Iceland and Slovakia have less than one thousand members in their unions, whereas the Scandinavian countries each have between three and five thousand members. The Japanese union only dates back to 1983, and has six thousand members. This is a rather small number, when one considers that Japan is the second largest market for recordings in the world.

Performing Rights

Performing rights, as I briefly mentioned in the section on music publishing (see Chapter 7), are limited to songwriters in the United States. In Europe, they are also enjoyed by performing artists, who split the royalties with record companies and backup musicians and singers. In the United States, the only medium in which this occurs is in sales of digital files. As of this writing, record companies, performing rights organizations, unions, and other musicians' groups are agitating to create performing rights for performers as well as songwriters. Similarly, in Europe composers receive performing rights income when films are shown in theaters, but this is not the case in the United States. In England, writers and music publishers receive a 3 percent royalty of all ticket sales. The royalty goes to the British performing rights societies, which then distribute the money.

Each of the European countries has its own performing rights society. An international organization called **CISAC (the International Confederation of Societies of Authors and Composers)**, is a confederation of 217 societies from 114 countries. It deals not only with music but also with other creative works that can be copyrighted, including literature, audiovisual works, and graphic and visual arts. The organization has its headquarters in Paris, with regional offices in Budapest, Buenos Aires, and Singapore. The goal of this organization is to increase and protect the rights of creators.

African countries do little to enforce performing rights, because the presence of foreign repertoire is a negative drain on their national radio income. Denmark has dealt with this situation in a unique way, by upgrading the performance royalties for live music, which goes mostly to local musicians, and lowering the amount of performance income that is paid to artists from radio play.

Seventy-eight countries are signatory to the **Rome Convention**, which stipulates that performers as well as songwriters should receive income from performing rights. The United States has not signed this agreement, because it does not recognize performing rights for artists. A variety of music organizations are agitating to bring the United States into conformity with the Rome Convention.

The Australian music industry has some unique characteristics. The government does not allow agents that book a club to also be agents of the artists who play in the club. This is a common practice among local agents in the United States, who may get a retainer from the club, and earn commissions from artists that they are booking in the club at the same time. Australian entertainment business lawyers are paid by the hour, and do not receive a percentage of the artist's income. I am not aware of similar restrictions on agent double-dipping in any other country, nor have I ever heard of restrictions on lawyers receiving a percentage of their clients' income.

LEGAL CONCERNS

Anti-trust Law again?

Antitrust law is taken more seriously in Europe than it is in the United States. So far, the U.S. government has not objected to any of the various acquisitions and mergers of record and music publishing companies. However, in Europe, after the BMG-Sony joint operating agreement was originally approved, an independent record label appealed, which brought about a lengthy review of the merger. Ultimately, the merger was permitted, but the review was far more stringent than the American version had been. There is less concern about antitrust law in the rest of the world. In countries where the government controls the economy and restricts the ownership rights of foreign companies, or even expropriates them—like Venezuela— antitrust law is meaningless, because the government itself is the holder of a monopoly.

Copyright Law

Copyright law and the application of performing rights is becoming more uniform, with many nations subscribing to the various international music copyright conventions. Some developing countries have little interest in complying with these laws, because their own countries export very little music, and compliance with the rules would require the payment of substantial royalties to foreign songwriters and publishers.

Digital Issues

Although it is obvious that digital product will eventually dominate the market for recordings, in the United States this is far from being the case. In Asia, especially in Japan and Korea, this has already occurred. Europe is in a similar position to the United States in the sense that CD sales still dominate the market, but they continue to decline, while digital sales go up. Third World countries lag behind in digital sales, but they will undoubtedly catch up as computers and high-speed Internet connections become more widely available.

Small Label Licensing Deals

Small independent American labels can adopt a number of different strategies in order to get their product into the foreign marketplace. They can license their music to existing companies, form a joint venture that they share with the foreign company, or they can attempt to form a foreign subsidiary label. Each may have its problems. Licensed albums may not be promoted as aggressively as home-grown releases, because the profits are lower than with a wholly owned product. A joint venture means that the small label will be involved on a day-to-day basis, monitoring what is going on at the company, but it will not have total control because it doesn't enjoy full ownership rights. Starting a subsidiary label requires some financing, and a constant presence n the foreign market. This may not be feasible for a small label.

Some countries will not allow a foreign company to operate unless they have a local partner. Many deals for foreign rights are made at the annual European **MIDEM (Marche International du Disque et Edition Musicale)** music conference, where record companies and music publishers gather expressly for that purpose.

When an album is issued in a foreign country, sometimes local labels will request extra tracks that are only available in their territory. This is intended to make these albums unique and more attractive than the original releases, which are sometimes also available online or through local retailers.

IMMIGRATION

Many musicians have immigrated to foreign countries, not only to escape censorship but also to find better economic opportunities. In addition to the North African musicians who have relocated to France, other Africans have moved there in search of better economic and artistic opportunities. This includes access to recording studios and record companies and to managers and agents who may enable them to work in other countries. Kassav, the West India *zouk* band, is yet another foreign group that relocated to Paris. Some of these groups immigrate because they know that the presence of many other previous immigrants provides a built-in audience. Africans who come from French-speaking countries have a huge advantage

Jamaican songwriter Mikey Bennett gives a talk on songwriting at the Jamaican Songwriter's Bootcamp, held near Kingston, Jamaica. Photo by Dick Weissman.

in moving to France, because their songs are in the French language, and so they meet the nation's French-language quota. In England the strong Pakistani population has created the idiom of *bhangra* rock, which has integrated rap and rock music with Indian (Bollywood) film music.

A number of Cuban musicians have relocated to the United States in search of better-paying work, or because they felt inhibited by the restrictions that the Cuban government placed on them. Hugh Masakela, the South African trumpet player, went into exile in the United States and later in London to escape apartheid, the segregation of the races in colonial South Africa.

Other musicians immigrate for a variety of reasons. Rock guitar guru Jimi Hendrix, for example, was not particularly successful during his days in New York, until he moved to England and found a new identity in the Jimi Hendrix Experience. American folksinger Dean Reed became a superstar in Russia, because the communist government loved the idea that a communist American pop musician would move to Russia to pursue his musical career. Reed had experienced very little success in the United States. Many musicians have left European countries simply to avoid taxes. Their ranks include rock luminary Mick Jagger.

PIRACY IN EMERGING MARKETS

In the United States, we periodically read about raids on illegal CD factories, where copies of current recorded product are illegally duplicated. In other parts of the world, notably China, piracy is more the norm than the exception to the rule. Hundreds of thousands of CDs have been illegally duplicated.

According to the 2006 IFPI Piracy Report, the markets that have the most illegal CD duplication were Brazil, China, Greece, Indonesia, Italy, Mexico, and Russia. Note: this piracy does not refer to illegal Internet downloading, but to the illegal *duplication* of physical CDs. According to this report, China is the leading offender in the sense that it has the largest number of plants that are illegally duplicating CDs, with piracy representing 85 percent of the CD market:

Country	Percentage of Physical Piracy
Indonesia	88%
China	85%
Russia	67%
Mexico	65%
Greece	50%
Brazil	40%
Italy	26%

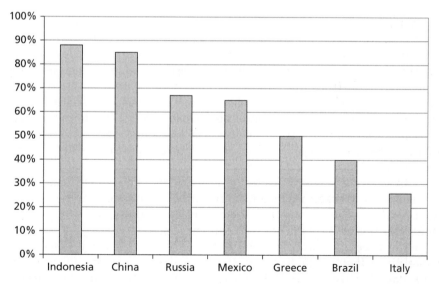

Percentage of Physical Piracy

This report doesn't minimize other examples of piracy. For example, a police raid in Lithuania on August 23, 2007, resulted in the confiscation of

210,000 pirated CDs. These particular albums were mostly of Polish and international repertoire. The point is that not all piracy is taking place in developing countries. It is an ongoing problem wherever shady entrepreneurs exist with the ability to duplicate and distribute the product.

The Chinese situation is especially serious, given the size of the country and the rapid expansion of its middle-class population. Popular U.S. CDs are copied and sold freely, with little or no enforcement by the Chinese government. China and the United States are bound at the hip these days, due to the tremendous amount of Chinese investment in the U.S. economy, and the large amount of Chinese goods imported into the United States. China exports relatively few CDs to the United States; rather, the flow of product goes the other way. In other words, the Chinese government has little to gain by eliminating the duplication of foreign recorded product. The ultimate resolution to this problem is the desire of China to be better integrated into world economic procedures and practices. It's anybody's guess as to if and when this can occur. It is difficult for the United States government to place strong pressure on the Chinese leadership to eradicate piracy because of the high level of Chinese investment in the American economy, especially its ownership of U.S. government securities.

TOURING

There are numerous challenges to touring abroad. Many governments demand that musicians from other countries have work visas or green cards, as they are called in the United States. It may take many months to have these arrangements approved, and in the meantime the projected tour may evaporate. If musicians try to enter a county without a work visa, the customs officers often will subject them to extensive questioning and not permit them to enter the country. For this reason, many musicians book foreign tours through agents, who are familiar with the necessary paperwork. Some artists who tour internationally on a regular basis may have a separate personal manager who only handles foreign work. This has to be arranged in such a way that the act isn't paying double management commissions. When it comes to international superstars, however, there is enough money around for everyone.

Even esoteric issues such as the differences in local electric supply can bedevil a tour. Amplifiers made to run on U.S. voltage will not work in European countries without modification. This small issue could greatly affect a band that depends on electric instruments.

Entrance into the United States to perform music has become much more difficult since the 9/11 disaster. Canadian musicians, for example, must pay $150 to enter the United States, and must provide a list of gigs that are confirmed with written contracts. This has greatly inhibited traffic across the border.

Roxette and the Role of Chance

Roxette was a Swedish duo in the 1980s that experienced considerable success in Europe. An American exchange student named Dean Cushman picked up their album *Look Sharp* in Sweden in 1988 and brought it back with him to his home town of Minneapolis. Capitol Records, the American affiliate of EMI, had decided against issuing Roxette's music in the United States. Cushman passed the album to a local radio station, which started, playing Roxette's music. As the record began to gain local interest, Capitol hastily issued the album. It became a multi-platinum seller, and Roxette had four #1 records in the United States. However, if that single American student hadn't brought the record back home with him, the chances are that it never would have been released in the United States.

This illustrates the idiosyncratic nature of becoming an international success in the music business. Each company must decide whether an act that is successful in its home country will be saleable abroad. In this case, Capitol obviously made the wrong decision.

Roxette went on to have a successful career in Europe, with on-again–off-again reunions that have lasted to the present day. Their success in the United States did not, however, continue beyond the early 1990s.

For African musicians, foreign tours are an absolute necessity, because there simply isn't enough money available in Africa to justify extensive touring within the continent itself.

CULTURAL MATTERS

Artists may be promoted differently in a foreign country than in their home territory. For example, Shakira is a major international superstar. However, her album covers tend to be much racier in the United States than they are in Latin countries, where that sort of bodily display may be an impediment to store display and sales. Oddly enough, United States television is much more prudish when it comes to displaying the body than most Latin markets!

In many instances, it is difficult to comprehend why certain artists do well in specific foreign markets. For example, American deep-voiced country singer Jim Reeves was a superstar in Norway. ABBA was an absolute super group all over Europe, but although they were successful in the United States, they did not reach anything resembling superstar status. Oddly, *Mamma Mia*, the Broadway show about ABBA, has been a gigantic hit in New York. The eccentric nature of this industry makes many of these events largely, if not entirely, unpredictable.

Terms to Know

Antitrust law *176*

CANCON (Canadian
Content) *173*

Censorship *171*

CISAC (the
International
Confederation of
Societies of Authors
and Composers) *175*

FACTOR (Foundation
to Assist Canadian
Artists on
Record) *173*

Import tax *174*

MIDEM (Marche
International du
Disque et Edition
Musicale) *177*

Rome Convention *175*

Sales tax *174*

Value-added tax *174*

For Classroom Discussion

1. What are the musical effects, if any, of foreign ownership of American record labels?
2. Should the U.S. government support the music industry? In what ways?
3. How can a government create a music scene where none currently exists, or where the music community has a small presence?
4. Are quotas that limit the airplay of foreign music a good thing? Why or why not?
5. Can you give any additional examples of musical censorship in the United States?
6. How big an impact can world music stars have on the American record market?
7. How can an American act promote itself in various parts of the world?
8. How can the Chinese government be convinced to eradicate CD piracy?
9. Is there any market for world music in your own community? Does this market correspond to the ethnic demographics of the community?

PART TWO

Careers, Entrepreneurship, and the Entertainment Business

CHAPTER 11

Music Business Education and Entrepreneurship

COLLEGE MUSIC PROGRAMS

For many years, college music programs focused on music performance, music education, music history, and music theory and composition. Students were expected to find careers as teachers or performers, but little attention was given to how they might find success in the music industry. However, as jobs for performing musicians shrank, schools began to realize the need to prepare students for careers that would combine their interest in music with "real-world" jobs. By the mid-1970s, several schools offered music business programs. The idea behind these programs was to give musicians accurate and useful information about the music industry so that some of these people could go on to work in the industry itself.

Gradually, music business programs became featured programs, as the number of students enrolling grew. A number of colleges began to offer music industry majors, handling their students in a variety of ways. Some were placed in business, mass communications, or other departments. However, most music business programs remained as part of the music departments, raising some interesting problems for the music business major. As music majors, they were still required to take the standard courses on music history and theory that all majors must take; yet these courses were becoming less relevant to the field.

For students who are unable or unwilling to take the required music classes, there are several alternatives. They can become straight business majors, and simply take the music industry classes as electives, or they can attend a community college, where the music requirements will be somewhat less rigid.

Academic Associations

As music business programs became an increasing presence in colleges, the **Music & Entertainment Industry Educators Association (MEIEA)**, an organization of music industry educators, was born. **MEISA (Music & Entertainment Industry Student Association)** is the student wing of MEIEA. It is a useful networking tool, and students meet peers with similar interests and skills. Some of these relationships will continue as the students work in the industry. The combined groups hold an annual conference where members discuss industry trends, curriculum issues, and meet with people working in the music industry. The faculty panels include a series of academic papers on various contemporary subjects, such as copyright issues, the digital market, and record distribution. The organization also publishes an annual journal that includes some of these papers, as well as additional articles and reviews.

At the same time, related programs developed in the music products field and in audio engineering. Often these programs were housed at the same institutions. The music products field deals with the manufacturing, wholesaling and retailing of musical instruments and sheet music. It quickly became supported by the **National Association of Music Merchandisers (NAMM)**. The educational wing of NAMM is known as the **NAMM Affiliated Music Business Institutions (NAMBI)**. Graduates of these programs became managers of music retail stores, employees of music wholesalers, or employees of musical instrument manufacturers, like Yamaha. Students were encouraged to attend the annual winter NAMM conference in Anaheim, California, as well as the summer conference, usually held in Nashville. NAMM gave scholarship support to a few of these students and grants to faculty members so that they could attend the NAMM shows. At the shows themselves, music stores and manufacturers actually interviewed students, and in some cases hired them. Students that weren't immediately looking for jobs were offered mock interviews, where they were coached on the sorts of things that companies were looking for in new employees. NAMM itself offers internships, which are required by most music product programs.

Audio engineering programs also experienced growth from the mid-1970s on. Many colleges built recording studios, and provided the students with hands-on experience in recording. Students who grew up with personal computers are often fascinated by technical gear, and the demand for college audio programs continues to be strong. Audio students also take internships, and the lucky ones eventually work in one of the major music markets. The **Audio Engineering Society (AES)** developed a satellite educational organization called **Society of Professional Audio-Recording Services (SPARS)**. SPARS members, like NAMBI members, often attend the AES annual meetings, which rotate between the East Coast and the West Coast.

Programs in the United Kingdom

I have encountered several music business programs in England that are more innovative than typical American programs. The Liverpool Institute of Performing Arts (LIPA) has tremendous music industry connections in England, because of its association with Paul McCartney, George Martin, and others. Some of their student internships have involved acting as a road manager on a tour that required the student to take a leave from school. Because their student base comes from all over the world, particularly various European countries, the school has a unique level of energy.

Westminster College in London offers programs in music performance that are especially relevant to contemporary music. For example, you can actually get a degree in rock and roll guitar. They also offer ensembles in reggae, for example, in which two instructors are employed. One teacher works at the college, covering grades and making sure that requirements are being met; the other instructor is a working professional musician who plays reggae music. He may have no academic credentials, or even a college degree. The practitioner teaches what he does every day as a working musician, and it is the task of the college professor to provide an academic context. This avoids the common pitfall of commercial music programs, in which an ensemble plays its one reggae tune, with the instructor doing a reasonable job of "faking it," without giving the students any real exposure to the style.

Two-Year and Certificate Programs

A number of community colleges offered two-year programs in music business or audio engineering, and some vocational schools also offered audio programs, notably Full Sail Institute in Florida. The music requirements, as well as general liberal arts requirements, at the vocational programs were much lighter than at the four-year schools.

WHAT STUDENTS SHOULD LOOK FOR IN A MUSIC BUSINESS PROGRAM

So far our discussions have centered on an educator's perspective about what ingredients make up a successful music industry program. Prospective students will necessarily have a somewhat different viewpoint. Here are some things that should govern a student's choice of program:

- *Are internships part of the program?* If the program does not include compulsory internships, the student should consider attending a school that does.
- *Does the school make the internship placement or is it the student's responsibility to find them?* Many students have no music industry contacts. If the school has a well-established program, they should have contacts at record companies, music publishing companies, music

organizations and recording studios. The student needs to know whether they will simply be given a list of names and numbers, or whether the faculty adviser will assist in setting up the internship.

- *What type of internships can students get?* Needless to say, working in Quincy Jones's office will be much more powerful on a résumé than interning at a home recording studio in Pueblo, Colorado.

- *Are there internships located in the geographic area that the student plans to live in after graduation?* This is particularly important if the student is going to school in an area far removed from the major business industry cities.

- *Are graduates of the program currently working in the music industry, and if so, in what capacity?* Often graduates of a program constitute a very useful network for current students. For example, if a graduate network exists in Los Angeles, the intern or new graduate can call someone who is already working in the industry there. That person can offer employment advice, thoughts about places to live, and general support during what is an exciting but stressful time. If the graduate has become established in the industry, she or he may be able to offer the student an internship, a job lead, or even a job. There is no substitute for practical advice, and it can be in the form of positive leads, or warnings to avoid companies that exploit interns.

- *How accessible are faculty members to their students?* Most faculty members post schedules on their office door. Prospective students should beware of professors who work two days a week, and have two or three hours a week listed as office hours. This is an indication that they are more interested in their outside careers than in teaching. After twelve years of full-time teaching, I would venture to say that some of the conversations that I had with students in my office were more valuable for them than our classroom meetings.

  Part-time faculty members often work in the industry and teach as a sideline. They do not generally keep full-time office hours and are seldom on campus when they are not teaching. There is nothing wrong with this, unless you sense that the faculty consists mostly of part-time teachers. They often lack the knowledge to advise students about college requirements.

- *Do the full-time professors have skills that complement one another, or are they working from the same knowledge base?* For example, I have known programs in which all of the teachers had law degrees and most of the curriculum was devoted to contracts. Students justifiably complained that they were being taught the same material in classes that had different titles. When one professor comes from a more standard music background, and another comes from the business world, students benefit by comparing their opinions and insights.

- *Is the school a member of MEIEA, and do they attend its annual conferences? Is there a MEISA chapter on campus?*

Internships

Internship programs give students the opportunity to work in the real world of the music industry. Many provide job leads, or even jobs. They allow students to enter the network of people who are recommended to others in the music industry's relatively small circle of contacts.

Students attending colleges in a major music business center have a great advantage in obtaining a meaningful internship, over a student in a program in, say, upper Michigan. There are two substantial programs in the Nashville area: at Belmont University, in Nashville, and at Middle Tennessee

Drexel University's Mad Dragon Records

Professor Marcy Rauer-Wagman started Mad Dragon Records in 2003 as part of the Drexel University music business program. The label is entirely student-staffed, with Prof. Rauer-Wagman serving as the CEO. In addition to the label, the school operates a concert promotion company, a booking agency, and video production and music publishing companies. Mad Dragon also operates its own MySpace page, *http://www.myspace.com/ maddragonrecords*. This is probably the most comprehensive music business operation in any college at this time. Prof. Rauer-Wagman notes that the label pays royalties that are significantly better than

MAD Dragon Records staff with the group Hoots & Hellmouth at their CD release party at Johnny Brenda's in Philadelphia. L to r: Chrsitianna LaBuz, Biff Kennedy, Andrew "Hellmouth" Gray, Rob Berliner, Terry Tompkins, Sean Hoots, Marcy Rauer-Wagman. Photo: Doug Seymour, courtesy MAD Dragon/Drexel University.

either the majors or independents, because of its student-run status: "It's all not-for-profit, too, so we're able to give everything we make after expenses back to the artists."

The label has succeeded in landing a record deal with independent label Rykodisc for Matt Duke, one of the Mad Dragon artists. In 2006, they signed prominent singer/songwriter Jules Shear, who had previously recorded for major labels without achieving much success. Shear had written hits for a variety of artists, notably Cyndi Lauper ("All Through the Night"). Shear's deal gave him a 50 percent royalty, an unheard of amount by industry standards, plus the backing of an enthusiastic group of college students. As he told a reporter from the *New York Times*, "When a room full of 20-year-olds tells me my record is relevant, that beats a room full of 50-year-olds at a major record label telling me my record isn't relevant."

Extending the Record Label Model

Because college music departments tend to be set up as separate entities, each teaching specific subjects, sometimes the student graduates without developing an overall sense of how the business works. Imagine a situation in which a song-writing class writes songs, which are then recorded by students in the audio program. The performance department provides vocalists or additional musicians when they are needed. Students in arranging and composition can add horn or string parts if they are needed, to be played by performance majors. Finally, business students have the job of selling the product to record or publishing companies and can also assist in promoting the product. When a student-run label exists, the "sale" can be executed to the student label.

The major difficulty involved is scheduling, because in order for this to come off, the various professors and students must cooperate with one another. In a large music program, this can be a challenge. The up-side is that the student will have literally experienced life in the real world of the music business.

State University, in nearby Murfreesboro. Students at these colleges who wish to work in the country music industry have a huge advantage.

College Record Labels

A number of colleges, including the University of Miami, Drexel University, and the University of Colorado at Denver, have their own record labels. If these labels function in a serious way, they provide a superb training opportunity to teach students how records get airplay, how recordings are distributed, and how digital media offer new outlets, as well as other label functions. Many of today's students are more likely to be working for independent labels or running their own companies than working for a transnational company.

Students should also be encouraged to pursue all of the commercial opportunities available for the college labels' productions, just as major labels do today. That means contacting music supervisors to try to get songs into films, working with local filmmakers to place songs in independent films, and contacting advertising agencies to place students' songs in commercials. At the administrative level, chairs of these programs need to treat faculty members who are administering the label as though they were teaching a class. This means providing load relief or making the role of running the label the equivalent of teaching a class. What could be a more useful class for music industry students than the hands-on operation of a record label, from signing talent, reaching a contractual agreement, A&R involvement in record production, seeking distribution, to promoting the finished product to radio stations and to record stores?

MUSIC BUSINESS EDUCATION IN THE TWENTY-FIRST CENTURY

Disaster struck the music industry at the dawn of the twenty-first century. CD sales declined as people began downloading music without paying record companies. They in turn could not pay artists or songwriters. Many record company employees with distinguished résumés were laid off, and it became increasingly difficult to obtain jobs. Some of these ex-record company employees took refuge in academia and joined college music business or audio engineering programs. The number of audio engineering jobs also declined, as it became possible to make quality recordings with relatively cheap home studio equipment. Some of the really large recording studios went out of business and record companies reduced their recording budgets. Meanwhile, independent record stores closed in droves, as the public lost its taste for compact discs. The number of independent music instrument stores also declined. Some were replaced by giant chains, especially Guitar Center, and others simply went out of business.

In many respects, it has been difficult for college music programs to adjust to the changes in the music industry. The music industry programs are suffering anxieties similar to the ones that afflicted music education programs some twenty years ago. There is a huge amount of activity in today's music industry, but much of it is coming from start-up, Internet-based businesses that are highly speculative and cannot offer the security that employment at the large record companies used to give.

Where Do We Go From Here?

The biggest problem in music business education is how to teach students to develop the sort of entrepreneurial skills that will enable them to survive in today's unpredictable music business. Teaching a four-semester music business sequence that concentrates on contracts and major label deals is no longer a useful exercise. Of course, students must learn how to navigate the world of contracts, but there are many other skills that today's student needs to develop, including:

General Educational Skills: Learning to read, write, and spell. These skills are essential tools for to writing a press release or constructing a good résumé.

Languages: More and more Americans are bilingual, yet there is a huge shortage of Americans who can speak Chinese, Japanese, or Hindi.

Better General Education: Would a student in 2010 be better served taking psychology and cultural anthropology than advanced harmony? Perhaps it is time to reconsider the way that so many programs subordinate music business and general education to traditional music classes.

Breaking Down Barriers: Owning and operating a home studio is a great tool for musicians who want to record their own work. They can even make some money renting the studio to others. College programs should include audio engineering and music business as part of the curriculum. Many of them already do so, but students are often not taught that both might be equally useful in their careers. In addition, students should be comfortable with analog recording equipment as well as ProTools and other digital packages.

Developing Versatility: Most students will *not* keep the same job for their entire music career. They need to keep an eye on the future and be prepared to roll with the punches. Music business programs that are simply sending their students to classes in general business programs need to think more deeply about whether the material the business professors are teaching is actually applicable to the music industry.

DEVELOPING ENTREPRENEURIAL SKILLS

Teaching students to understand contracts and copyright is mostly a matter of following the rules in music industry textbooks. However, teaching students to develop entrepreneurial skills is one of the real challenges for music business educators. How can students learn to develop the sort of skills that enable them to start a new business or to develop a new idea?

Getting Rich on Guitar Pins

One of my favorite stories of individual entrepreneurship involves Billy Rich, of Tulsa, Oklahoma. Billy went to the University of Texas and studied business, secure in the knowledge that he could get a good job after graduation with his father's real estate firm. In college he enjoyed playing guitar at fraternity parties and other affairs, but he knew that he didn't have the skill to become a successful professional guitarist. Billy graduated from college and went to work for his father's firm, but he soon discovered that he hated working in real estate.

In 1979, Billy attended the Oklahoma State Fair, and noticed two people wearing pins that showed ears of corn. A bell rang in his mind. If he couldn't be a guitar player, maybe he could sell guitar pins. After doing some research, he found a manufacturer in Taiwan, and placed an order for pins. The pins were images of well-known vintage guitars. Now all he had to do was to sell the pins.

Billy wandered over to a local vintage guitar store. He looked in one of the glass cases, and noticed a check written to the store by Z.Z. Top's guitarist Billy Gibbons. Like many checks, it had Gibbons's home address and phone number written on it. Billy copied down the address, and sent a few guitar pins to Gibbons. A few days later his phone rang, and Gibbons ordered a thousand dollars' worth of guitar pins.

This was the beginning of a flourishing business. Since then, Rich has sold vintage guitar calendars, created a limited edition of Batman Guitars, and he sells guitar tools of various kinds, such as truss rods.

There are dozens of businesses that have had modest beginnings. Some are accidental, while others are the culmination of a well-planned scheme that involves research and experimentation. College programs can't teach students to develop ingenuity, but they can show them how to capitalize on their creative ideas. The entrepreneur must sense some sort of opening in the market for her invention and then her college training in business needs to step in to show her how to make the idea feasible. In the next section, we'll cover the basics of this process.

ESTABLISHING A BUSINESS: AN INTRODUCTION

This section deals with setting up a business. This is a necessary step if you are planning to sell or market a product, but it is equally important for anyone setting up a full-time performing group. Here we will introduce various business models that are currently available for the beginning entrepreneur.

Sole Proprietorships

When an artist or group goes on the road and begins to make a reasonable amount of money, their business manager will offer various ways to simplify dealing with the business aspects of a career. The simplest form of business is a **sole proprietorship**. This is a business that is owned and operated by a single individual. All profits or losses belong to the owner of the business. The advantage of this form of business is that the owner has complete control over everything that happens. The artist can take four weeks off to write songs by simply notifying the manager or booking agent. No other steps are necessary. Taxes, accounting fees, and business licenses are simple and relatively straightforward. The business should be registered with the state, county, or city, and the fees to do this are relatively modest.

The disadvantages of this business setup are similar to those in establishing home-grown record labels. In most instances, there will probably be a lack of financing and an inability to raise funds. All expenses—such as the need for a new sound system or a fancy publicity brochure—come out of the artist's pocket. Any claims made against the business are claims made directly against the artist.

Partnerships

Many bands form **partnerships**, in which two or more people jointly operate a business and share any liabilities that result from that business. Income goes to the partners but is taxed at individual tax rates. Each partner files a separate tax return, and there is no restriction on the number of permissible partners.

GENERAL AND LIMITED PARTNERSHIPS   In a **limited partnership**, the owners are only investors and do not manage the partnership. Limited partnerships are created when money is needed to operate a business, but the original group or the new investors do not want to share in management duties. Limited partners only risk the amount of money that they invest, regardless of other losses that the business may experience. In **general partnerships** both partners operate the business and share liabilities or profits.

Under either of these models, a formal partnership agreement is created and signed by all partners. Office supply stores have generic partnership forms available. These forms include the name of the business, its principal location, the amount of investment by each partner, and so forth.

BANDS AND PARTNERSHIP AGREEMENTS   It is important that bands create a partnership agreement in the early part of their careers. This agreement should specify who owns the equipment, the music publishing rights on the songs, who is authorized to spend money, and what procedures will be followed if a band member leaves or is fired.

When bands do not have this sort of agreement, different members often have differing memories. For example, if one member bought a guitar amplifier for $800 but the band contributed $300 of band money to help purchase it, who owns the amplifier if the group breaks up? Such arguments are aggravated when a group's breakup is acrimonious or if one member is fired.

In the early part of a career, some band members are overly generous in giving away shares of the band's income. For example, if the band writes on a napkin that the road manager is entitled to 20 percent of the band's income, this is the equivalent of a legal document. Believe it or not, it doesn't matter if the band was under the influence of alcohol at the time. This *actually* occurred, and in this case a road manager won a legal judgment awarding him a percentage of the band's earnings.

Songwriting and publishing credits need to be clearly established in the partnership agreement. Imagine a situation in which a drummer shares in the publishing rights of a band's songs. The band breaks up, and the lead singer and guitarist form another band, record the songs that the drummer partially owns, and the new group's album sells three million copies. The drummer is going to be very happy, but it is doubtful if the other two musicians will be pleased with the result.

Corporations

In **corporations**, investors are shielded from individual liability and are issued shares of stock. Corporations are run by corporate officers, who make management decisions. Some states require a board of directors and secretary, and often corporations are formed with the help of lawyers. The corporation adopts bylaws that set forth the governance of the company, including such details as when meetings take place.

Subchapter **S corporations** divide the expenses and income among shareholders, and the S corporation does not pay a corporate tax. Therefore, earnings are taxed at the individual shareholder's rate. In *Navigating the Music Industry: Current Issues & Business Models*, Professor Frank Jermance notes that many individuals in service-based professions choose the S Corporation model. Extra workers—such as publicists or road managers— are hired as "independent contractors," so that the S corporation avoids paying withholding taxes, Social Security, and unemployment taxes.

TAXES, INVESTMENTS, AND SAVINGS

Very few artists in popular music are able to sustain strong long-term careers, as the Rolling Stones, Madonna, and Bruce Springsteen have done. Of course, these superstars have business managers, who take care of their taxes, investments, and retirement accounts. Artists who have careers that last from five to ten years or even less must be particularly careful to invest their money carefully and to develop retirement accounts that will take care of them in later years. Unfortunately, the industry is rife with stories of artists who made a single hit record and then disappeared from the industry. Often their money has been mismanaged under the incorrect assumption that this was simply going to be the start of a successful career. The industry refers to artists who have made a single giant hit record as "**one hit wonders**."

Accurate recordkeeping is key to dealing long term with taxes and other government regulations. Many musicians hate to keep detailed records of income and expenses and do their best to ignore these matters. The expenses that musicians should track include the purchase and maintenance of musical instruments or equipment, airfares, car rentals, cab fares, fees to managers, agents, business managers, publicists and entertainment lawyers, accountants, rental of rehearsal spaces, and money paid to road managers and recording studio rentals. Equipment should be depreciated. If part of a house is used exclusively for musical endeavors, a musician can deduct the expenses of renting or owning that particular space. In other words, if the musician owns a five-room house, and one room is used for a recording studio and the other for a practice room, two-fifths of the expenses of the house can be deducted from the musician's taxes. Other deductions include music lessons, fees paid to music arrangers, union work dues, expenses for photos or media kits, Web sites, and business cards. If the band tours, out-of-town motels and meals are deductible and some insurance costs may qualify as well. If the band tours in a van, gasoline expenses can be deducted whenever the band tours, and a percentage of the maintenance of the vehicle can be deducted, depending on the mileage used for playing gigs, as opposed to personal use.

The IRS will not allow a taxpayer to define something as a business if it continually loses money. Under those conditions, they will rule that the business is really a hobby. If the artist has a bad year or two where the business loses money, the IRS permits the taxpayer to take a loss for that particular year. If the band receives income without taxes being withheld, their accountant will undoubtedly wish to get the band to pay quarterly taxes so that they do not get stung by a huge tax bill at the end of the year. If the band tours abroad, many governments withhold taxes from their income. If the amount is relatively small, it is often possible to file for a refund. This is something that the band's accountant should do.

The Musician's Union requires that a band pay **work dues** whenever it performs. The work dues are based on the union minimums, so a superstar can come into a town, play a $100,000 gig with a trio, and end up paying 3 percent of the union scale, or $3000. Let's say that the scale wages for the performance total $600. At a 3 percent union work tax, the bill would be all of $18.

If a group employs a regular staff, such as a road manager and sound engineers, they can deduct their income as tax-deductible expenses. If the employees are independent contractors, no withholding of taxes is necessary. The IRS has a list of twenty categories that determine whether employees qualify as full-time employees or are independent contractors. They relate to such matters as instructions from the employer, personal contact with the employer, and whether work is done on the employer's premises.

Employers may favor independent contractor status, but there are some disadvantages for employees. They cannot be represented by unions, they do not receive unemployment compensation or health insurance, and they are not covered by a pension plan. They must also pay all of their own Social Security taxes, whereas a regular employees' share of that tax is 50 percent.

Tax Audits

A tax **audit** occurs when the IRS feels that an individual's return has been incorrectly completed, whether accidentally or purposefully. Self-employed musicians are more apt to be audited then, say, employees of the Ford Motor Company. The IRS may feel that their deductions or expenses are excessive, or they may be suspicious that their income has not been properly reported.

If a musician is audited, she or he absolutely needs to have an accountant present, and to be as courteous as possible in a reasonably stressful situation. Any obvious mistakes that a musician makes in calculating income or expenses may cause someone to be audited. Simple mathematical errors constitute a red flag to the IRS, as does a very high amount of deductions. If an employer sends a 1099 to the IRS that reports paying a musician income but the musician does not report this income, an audit is likely to follow.

LONG-TERM CAREERS

Musicians and singers who work in various aspects of the business—writing songs, arranging music, producing records, doing commercials or studio work—have to be extremely good at what they do or develop multiple skills.

Singer/songwriter Deborah Holland (see Chapter 7) says that musicians "either must be the absolute best at what they do, or change their focus three or four times" during their career. She lists examples of an artist who wanted to be a star but became an engineer, a songwriter/producer, and then a film composer and jingle writer. She pointed out to me that these people followed leads in the industry that didn't necessarily fulfill their initial dreams, but these leads enabled them to make a living over a protracted period of time.

Even "big names" in the business often have to seek out new opportunities to extend and maintain their careers. Early in his career, Quincy Jones was the leader of an innovative jazz band. His band got marooned in Europe, and he stayed there, studying composition with the famous French teacher Nadia Boulanger. He supported himself by writing string parts for French rock and roll records. He then came back to the United States, where he became a vice president for Mercury Records, producing pop records. He went on to become a massively successful record producer, producing Michael Jackson's *Thriller* album. Along the way, Jones wrote numerous film scores, produced occasional instrumental records, had his own label imprint with Warner Brothers Records, and started his own music publishing company.

Many record producers started their musical career as musicians or songwriters. The key ingredient is to figure what to do after you have followed your muse. Musical styles change and those in the pop music business, must acknowledge these changes. Mitch Miller, the 1950s' pop music guru, was convinced that rock and roll was a temporary phenomenon, and so were many other record producers of the 1940s and 1950s. He was unable to adjust to the changes in the pop world, and eventually lost his job as a major label executive. The trick is to find some area of musical expression that intrigues you, even if the styles or genres that originally drew you to the music industry no longer are in vogue. Another approach is to be a contrarian and to bring back a style that succeeded and then disappeared. An example of a rediscovered music genre was the brief swing revival in the 1990s.

Terms to Know

AES (Audio Engineering Society) *186*
Audit *196*
Corporation *194*
General partnership *194*
Internship *189*
Limited partnership *193*
MEIEA (Music & Entertainment Industry Educators Association) *186*

MEISA (Music & Entertainment Industry Student Association) *186*
NAMBI (NAMM Affiliated Music Business Institutions) *186*
NAMM (National Association of Music Merchandisers) *186*

One hit wonder *195*
S corporation *194*
Sole proprietorship *193*
SPARS (Society of Professional Audio-Recording Services) *186*
Work dues *196*

For Class Discussion

1. How did you decide to attend your current school?
2. Do you know students in similar programs in other schools? How would you compare their course of study with yours?
3. Have you ever done an internship? If so, what were your experiences like?
4. What does each class member think they will be doing five years from now? How will they get to that place from their current role as students?
5. What examples can the students or instructor cite of local entrepreneurs who have come up with innovative ways of pursuing their careers?
6. Do you know anyone who has started their own music-related business?
7. When would it be desirable to enter business as a sole proprietor? When would a partnership be preferable?
8. Have you ever signed a band agreement?
9. Have you ever been in a band that broke up, or do you know someone who has had that experience? How did the band dispose of its assets?
10. What are the advantages of incorporating?
11. Why is it critical for musicians to keep accurate records of their expenses?
12. How do you plan to establish a long-term music career?

CHAPTER **12**

Songwriting and Composing

In previous chapters, the reader learned about various aspects of song-writing. There are songwriters who never perform, some who perform only on a limited basis, and some whose energies are equally split between songwriting and performing. In Chapter 7, the reader learned about the royalties that can accrue from songwriting. This chapter focuses on the many issues involved in establishing and maintaining a career in song-writing. These include some common pitfalls, such as falling for so-called Song Sharks, making a demo, working with a music publisher, and getting songs recorded by major artists.

SONG SHARKS

Song Sharks are people or companies who rely on an amateur songwriter's gullibility and lack of business sophistication. They advertise in magazines like *Popular Mechanics*, or in other non-music publications, claiming that they're looking for promising new songwriting talent for new recording opportunities. The other way that they reach out to songwriters is by contacting writers whenever their works are registered at the Library of Congress, because this information is available to anyone.

Song Sharks maintain that they will make professional demos of your songs and place them on a compilation album that goes to hundreds of radio stations. In return, they require the writer to pay a fee for these services. Seven years ago, a story appeared in a local newspaper in Oregon about a nurse who was an amateur songwriter, and who had been bilked out of thousands of dollars by a Song Shark operating out of Nashville. She had answered one of his ads and he told her that she had great talent, and he would like to record her song. This "publisher" then in fact recorded her song, in a mediocre if professional performance by Nashville musicians and singers who do this kind of work on a mass production basis. The publisher then told the writer that he liked her song so much that if only she could give him more money he would enhance the song by adding a string section. The gullible writer came up with the money and, sure enough, he added the string section. Initially, the publisher had been very supportive and positive, but soon the writer found it increasingly difficult to reach him. Calls were not returned. Soon his telephone was disconnected and she never heard from him again.

It is difficult to take legal action against Song Sharks, because the smarter ones do exactly what they say they will do. They will place a song on a compilation album along with the work of a dozen other gullible song-writers. They will then send the CD to several hundred radio stations, just as they have promised. The radio stations understand the game, and the CD goes right into their wastebaskets.

A variation on this theme is ads looking for lyrics that can be set to music. These are called **song poems** by the companies running the ads, although no such thing actually exists ("lyrics" might be more accurate). In any case, once the poem is submitted, the Shark will write back to a victim praising its possibilities, and then recommending that the poet pay a variety of fees to have the song set to music and a demo recording created. Usually

Taxi

Taxi is a company in Los Angeles that solicits membership from songwriters and artists. Applicants pay a fee, currently $300, which earns them the right to submit songs for critique. A small fee is also charged for each song submitted. The submissions are reviewed by a variety of people with experience in the business as songwriters, A&R personnel, and so on. If the listener decides that a song or an artist is good enough, they will submit the material or the artist to decision makers in Los Angeles who have the ability to place songs into films.

Taxi's ads single out people often in remote locations who have achieved success through Taxi's submissions. However, Taxi provides no data on what percentage of submissions they pass along and what percentage actually are picked up for films or records. Certainly, if the songwriter or artist is in a city far away from a music business center, or has no contacts in the business, Taxi may be a useful service.

Nevertheless, I must confess to a certain wariness to the notion of having to pay people to listen to material. It might be wiser to contact representatives of ASCAP, BMI, or SESAC, utilize the annual *Songwriter's Market*, or even to establish contacts or move to a music business center before joining Taxi. If none of these alternatives work for you, then it can be a useful resource.

Taxi also sponsors an annual conclave in Los Angeles that they call Road Rally, at which songwriters get together to network. There are also many panels consisting of songwriters, music publishers, and performing rights representatives, that offer information to aspiring songwriters. There is a fee for attendance.

the services are performed, although the quality of the setting and recording will be very poor. The victim is left with a sheet music arrangement and demo recording that have little use in the real world.

ASCAP, BMI, and SESAC do their best to keep songwriters from dealing with Song Sharks, but the trouble is that most writers know little or nothing about these performing rights organizations. *Songwriter's Market* also attempts to keep Song Sharks out of their listings. However, they continue to lure in the unsuspecting or naïve writer. Sharks target amateurs who have a dream, not professionals who know what they are doing.

CONTESTS

A number of organizations or corporations hold annual songwriting contests. Various prizes are offered to the winners, which may include a cash award, recording time in a professional studio, or even a record release. Most of these contests assert that it does not matter how the entrant produces a demo for the contest, because the judges are professionals. This assertion is questionable. Imagine yourself as a judge, listening to two hundred song demos. If a song's performances, arrangements, and recording quality are all mediocre, it will probably influence the judge's evaluation of the song— especially if it happened that this was the 137th song that was heard over a two-day period. If the singing, arrangement, and recording quality are highly professional, the song will certainly have an edge.

Anyone considering entering a contest should also take a close look at the prizes awarded. If the winner gets studio time or a record release, is the studio located near where the writer lives? If not, who will pay for the writer to go there? If there is going to be a record release, even if it is on a major label, how much effort will the company put into promoting the product? If the record simply becomes part of the company's monthly release, and the product is not promoted, there is very little chance it will achieve any success.

Pay attention to the fees required for entering the contest, compared to the prizes. National songwriting contests draw thousands of entries. If there is a $20 fee for each song entered and thousands of entries, simple math will tell you that the contest is more of a money-making enterprise for the people running it than for the songwriters who win the prizes.

HOW SONGWRITERS GET SONGS RECORDED

On Your Own

There are several ways for a songwriter who is not working with a publisher to get a song recorded by an artist. This assumes, of course, that the artist isn't like Paul Simon, who writes all of the songs that he records. The writer should find the last album that the artist made, and look for the name of the producer of the album and, if it appears, the name of the artist's manager. It is not a certainty that the artist will use the same producer on their next

Tom May: Singer-Songwriter

Tom May grew up in Omaha, moving to Toronto, Canada, when he was nineteen years old, after the famous Canadian singer-songwriter Gordon Lightfoot promised to help him. Tom began to get work through an agent in various towns in Ontario. A nonexistent gig in North Bay led to severing his ties to the agent. Tom made his first album for Capitol of Canada; he then returned to the United States. After a brief sojourn in St. Louis, Tom moved back to Omaha, working nine months a year, and doing quite a bit of touring. He never again signed an exclusive deal with an agent, though from time to time he has gotten gigs through them.

Singer/songwriter Tom May. Photo courtesy the artist.

These days Tom lives in Washington state, across the river from Portland. Tom May is an example of a performing singer-songwriter who has a quietly successful career. He combines working in the Portland area with touring and festival work, mostly booking himself. His work falls into a number of areas:

- Tom tours extensively, doing everything from large concerts to house concerts. He has toured in Ireland, and in other European countries
- He has about a dozen CDs out, most of them on his own label, although his latest is on Waterbug Records
- Tom has a syndicated radio show called River City Folk. It runs on 150 radio stations and on XM satellite radio. The show originated in Omaha over twenty years ago, and at that time was a paid gig, but eventually the funding dried up. Tom has continued it nonetheless, and it is a real service to the folk community, affording many performers the opportunity to get broad exposure.
- Tom books and MCs the annual Winterfolk Show. This show is a benefit for Sisters of the Road, an organization that helps to feed the homeless and poverty-stricken citizens of Portland.
- In 2007, he was the primary author of a book about singer-songwriters, titled *Promoting Your Music: the Loving of the Game* (Routledge). Each of his activities helps build his over-all career as a singer-songwriter.

album, nor does it necessarily follow that the artist and the producer remain friendly after the completion of that particular album. However, at least it is clear that the producer has recently had access to the artist.

Most likely, the producer and the manager both have offices, and by using Google or a similar search engine, you should be able to find them. It is always best to ask permission to send songs, because some people will simply not accept unsolicited material, fearing that this may later lead to charges of plagiarism and consequent lawsuits. If the writer is sending a song to an artist, it is best to send only a single song. If a songwriter sends more than one song, the chances of the material getting listened to become more remote and the person listening may feel that the writer hasn't really tailored the song to the artist. If the writer is unable to contact the producer or the manager of the artist, the next best bet is to target a publisher (see later in this chapter).

Another strategy to get songs recorded is to find a local band that is looking for new material. This enables the writer to get some reactions to the songs from band members and the public. It is a good idea to get the band to do a demo of the song. The demo might prove useful in helping the writer get a music publishing deal, and if the song is a good one, it may help the band get a record deal. Many local bands produce their own recordings. If the band records a songwriter's song, it is a good idea for the writer to retain the publishing rights, to parlay the recording of the song into a music publishing deal.

Contacting Music Publishers

The single best resource for contacting music publishers is the annual *Songwriter's Market*. This book lists music publishers, with names, addresses, descriptions of what musical genres they prefer, and tells whether they accept unsolicited material. If, for example, you are attempting to get a song to Emmylou Harris, who writes some material but also records many songs by outside writers, you should look on a recent album, and see what publishers have songs on that album. Obviously, if they have a song on a recent album by Emmylou, they have some relationship with her and can reach her. If you expect them to promote your song to her, then you need to be willing to give them the publishing rights to the song.

Songwriter's Market also lists record producers, agents, and managers, songwriting retreats, and contests. It also includes helpful articles on various aspects of songwriting. As good as the book is, a writer needs to exercise common sense in using it. For example, if you are a hip-hop writer and you see a publisher in Fargo, North Dakota, that claims to specialize in hip-hop music, investigate the company very closely. Is it logical that a hip-hop publisher would be located in Fargo? When examining the list of the recordings that a publisher claims to have obtained, if they are almost all on a record label with an unfamiliar name, the chances are that the record label is owned by the publisher. To put it another way, the chances that they will promote a new writer's music to artists in the major music industry towns are small.

Demos

When a songwriter or a publisher wants to get a song recorded, they usually make a **demonstration recording**, or **demo**, of the song. The purpose of the demo is to influence an artist or record producer to record the song. Usually demos are not made with much orchestral support, because they are designed to present the song in a simple and direct way. However, the question of whether demos should be extremely basic, with a vocal and a piano or guitar background, or more extensively produced is a controversial one. A produced demo means that it is virtually the equivalent of a finished record. The production might include a band, backup vocals, and even strings and horns.

The decision partly depends on who is going to listen to the demo. If the listener is an experienced record producer, they may prefer the demo to be simple. This is because they will have their own ideas of how the final recording should sound and these ideas may be radically different from those of the songwriter or music publisher. If the person listening judges music by "feel" rather than through their musical background and experience, the demo needs to be more elaborate. For example, there are people in the industry who know next to nothing about music but can have a good fix on popular taste. This sort of listener might hear the songwriter playing an acoustic guitar powerfully and rhythmically, but not recognize that the song in question is a rock song, because there are no drums on the demo. As foolish as this sounds, it can be true.

Another problem in making a demo is whether the person who sings it should tailor it specifically for the artist. For example, if a writer is doing a song demo because they hope that Trisha Yearwood will record the song, should the writer hire a female singer who can at least roughly copy her style of singing? This scenario presents two problems. Some singers will find this irritating, which may lead them to turn down the song. And, if the demo does not result in Yearwood recording the song, the writer has a demo that is so clearly aimed at a specific singer that it might put other artists off. A compromise solution is to use the same instrumental track but to record different vocal versions of the song, which are given to different artists.

Bob Dylan and the Basement Tapes

While recovering from his motorcycle accident in 1966–1967, Bob Dylan holed up with a group of musicians in Woodstock to cut some demo recordings of new songs that he was working on. Some of these recordings were actually used as demos to pitch Dylan's songs to other performers, such as "The Mighty Quinn," which was covered by the British pop-rock group Manfred Mann, and "You Ain't Going Nowhere," which was recorded by The Byrds. Others were just for Dylan's own amusement or to test out an arrangement that he might use on one of his own studio recordings.

Because Dylan was not releasing official recordings or performing during this period, these tapes became almost mythical to his legions of fans. A portion was released on one of the first and most infamous of the "bootleg" albums of the 1960s, known as *The Great White Wonder*. The bootleg was so successful that eventually Dylan allowed an authorized version of the sessions, called *The Basement Tapes*, to be issued by his label, Columbia, in 1975.

If the writer uses a musician on the demo who comes up with inventive musical figures, that in itself may attract a producer or singer. Often these figures will be used in the actual recording of the song. These figures are usually brief, but memorable musical phrases. By contrast, it is a mistake to include long instrumental solos on a demo recording. A simple and brief intro will suffice. The producer, artist, or even a prospective publisher are interested in the song, not the band or the arranger. If you decide to use a number of musicians and singers on the demo, it may also be an expensive proposition. You will have to pay the musicians and singers and use more time in the studio.

When a songwriter presents a demo to a music publisher, or if the songwriter is also an artist and makes a demo for a record company, it is a good idea to never present more than three songs at a time. Usually the strongest song should be presented as the first song on the demo, because the person listening may never listen to the second song if they dislike the first one. If the decision maker likes the material, they will ask to hear more. All demos should have contact information written on the demo and on the package. There have been instances in which a publisher liked a song but had no way to contact the writer, because that information wasn't included, or the CD was separated from the package, which had been thrown away. Lyric sheets should always be submitted with demos. They should be legible and accurate.

TRADING SERVICES   One way of reducing demo costs is by trading services. For example, if Susan the Songwriter is a fine guitarist but not much of a singer, she may trade playing guitar on a friend's session in exchange for her friend singing on her demo. It is also possible to reduce recording costs by trading services with a recording studio. In this scenario, the songwriter-guitarist agrees to do some demo session work for the studio in return for getting free studio time. Sometimes the trade doesn't involve musical services. If the songwriter is, for example, a carpenter, installing new shelves or other woodwork might be traded with the studio for recording time.

Holds and Recordings

If an artist or producer hears a song that they like, they will often ask the songwriter or the music publisher to place a **hold** on the song. This is a gentleman's agreement that is not a contract but an informal deal where the publisher or songwriter agrees not to show the song to other artists while the person who requested the hold decides whether to record it. A hold should never be confused with an agreement that the song is going to be recorded and released by the label.

Unfortunately, this situation can create some bad consequences for the songwriter:

- *The artist or producer holds the song for months without actually recording the song.*

Only It *Wasn't* A Hit!

In the late 1960s, I wrote an R&B song called "Only A Woman." A successful New York arranger named Bert deCoteaux heard the song through the efforts of my music publisher. Bert loved the song, and placed it on hold. The publisher and I were both really looking forward to this recording, because Bert had an excellent track record of taking R&B songs and transforming them into crossover pop hits.

A short time later he went into the studio with a new artist. Unfortunately the singer became extremely nervous in the studio, and Bert was not satisfied with any of her performances.

The recording was never released, and Bert released his hold on the song. All of this occurred during a period of two to three months, during which time the publisher did not play the song for anyone else. The song was not recorded until I did a recording of it thirty years later, using a different singer.

- *The song gets recorded, but the artist has recorded twenty-four songs for a twelve-song album, and it turns out to be one of the twelve songs that doesn't make the cut.*
- *The artist has every intention of cutting the song, but in the time between the period when the hold was initiated and the actual recording session, the artist changes the album concept, and your song no longer fits.*
- *The producer has a hold on the song, but the producer is fired from the project.*
- *The artist loses his or her contract with the record company before the song can get recorded.*

There is no way to defend against any of these possibilities. It is the responsibility of the publisher to stay in contact with the producer, the artist, and the record company. If an artist or producer holds a song for an excessively long period of time, the publisher may warn them that it is going to shop the song elsewhere. If the publisher makes this choice, it may antagonize the artist or producer, who may retaliate by returning the song or refusing to listen to other songs controlled by the publisher.

Publishing Deals and Reversion Clauses, and First Recordings of a Song

It is possible to sign deals with a publisher for a single song, for several songs, or to have an exclusive contract with a publisher. Exclusive deals generally provide for the writer being on staff and receiving a weekly "draw" or advance (see Chapter 7).

From a writer's point of view, songwriting agreements should always contain a **reversion clause**. This clause gives the publisher a certain amount of time to obtain a recording of the song or the rights revert back to the songwriter. The amount of time can range from six months to two years. The

"How Do I Live"—If I Don't Have a Hit!

In 1977, pop songwriter Diane Warren was asked to write a theme song for the film *Con Air*. The country singer LeAnn Rimes was hired to record the song, titled "How Do I Live." However, the movie's producer decided he didn't like Rimes's version, and so he hired another country singer, Trisha Yearwood, to rerecord it for the film. Rimes liked the song so much that she decided to release it anyway and it became a major country hit, outselling Yearwood's version (also released as a single). Ironically, both were nominated for a Grammy award for the song in 1998. Rimes was invited to sing the song on the broadcast, but Yearwood took home the award—which was announced just as Rimes was finishing her performance!

publisher may argue against granting a reversion clause, because of the time and money invested in promoting the song. Sometimes a compromise can be reached, where the writer refunds the cost of the publisher's demo in return for getting the publishing rights back.

The songwriter and publisher control the first recording of a song. If someone is a singer-songwriter and has written a song, and another artist wants to record that song, the writer can make that artist wait until her or his own version is issued. Once that occurs, the song must be licensed to anyone who wishes to record it. This was more important years ago when it was not unusual for three or four versions of the same song to be released at about the same time. Today this seldom happens, but occasionally a song is used in a movie and two versions come out almost simultaneously.

Promotional Possibilities for the Songwriter

Even if a music publisher does a good job for the songwriter, it is wise for songwriters to exploit whatever industry contacts they may have. Songwriters may know producers, members of a band, or even friends of artists. When pitching songs to any of these people, the songwriter should make sure that the publisher knows about it, so they do not pitch the same song to the same people. If a publisher is not aware that the song had already been pitched to a potential user, it may make the buyer question the publisher's professionalism or business relationship with the songwriter.

Songwriters may also find themselves in casual social situations with an artist or a producer. This can create a more favorable listening environment for the song. It is also possible that a publisher has unsuccessfully pitched a song to a producer, but the songwriter gets it directly to the artist, who decides to do it.

When two songwriters collaborate, they should pool all of their contacts. One writer may know the perfect person to record a particular song, or one may mention someone that would be a good bet and find out that the other writer used to be a member of that artist's back-up band. If two songwriters under contract to different music publishers collaborate on a song, there are four sets of possible contacts that can come into play. These are the contacts of each of the songwriters plus the contacts of each publisher.

COLLABORATIONS

In Chapter 6, I discussed collaboration agreements. However, there are other aspects of collaboration that deserve attention.

Traditionally, song collaboration was fairly straightforward. One person wrote the lyrics, the other wrote the melody. This sort of collaboration still occurs, principally on the music for Broadway musicals. However, collaboration in contemporary music tends to place the songwriters in less specific roles. Two people may get together with two guitars or a guitar and keyboard. One person may have the germ of a song idea, and both parties contribute to both the words and the music of the song. In many cases, one of the writers finds writing lyrics easier, the other one is better at coming up with melodies. Nevertheless, both writers contribute in both areas, albeit not necessarily equally.

There are many reasons that writers seek collaborators. A young writer may be looking for a cowriter who has more contacts, skills, and experience. An older writer may feel somewhat jaded and is looking to find a cowriter who can bring new energy and enthusiasm to the process. Some people enjoy the pressure of being in a room with someone else, and the stimulus that someone else's input can provide. A writer may usually write alone, but feel the need for some fresh input.

For a collaboration to work, the writers need to share something of a common work ethic. Some people work best in the morning; others like to work all night. Some people like to work at home; others prefer an office. Some people work very quickly; others work very slowly. Some writers like to collaborate with many different partners; others prefer to work intensively with one or two people. Over time, a songwriter ought to develop enough self-awareness to know the sort of person who will make a good collaborator. The songwriter should also recognize that some songwriters work much better alone. Not everyone needs to collaborate.

Collaboration Agreement

When writers work together on a project, they often sign a **collaboration agreement** that specifies that each one will get an equal share of a song. Without such an agreement, disagreements may emerge in the future, when one writer feels they wrote, for example, closer to two-thirds of a song than half of it. Obviously, if a cowriter ends up feeling that they have done most of the work on a continuing basis, the agreement should be revised, or the writers should part company. Collaboration agreements assume particular importance when two writers have never worked together before.

Collaboration: Happy Accident

Sometimes finding a collaborator is an accidental process. A close friend, the late Artie Traum, told me a story about a talented singer-songwriter named Pat Alger. The two had performed together in the New York area until Pat moved to Nashville to seek success as a country songwriter. Pat was running an open mike at a small club there, when a young man walked in with a cowboy hat, and performed a few songs. Pat struck up a conversation with him, and realized that he had just arrived in Nashville. Pat invited him to stay over at his house. The two hit it off, and started to write some songs together. The young stranger was Garth Brooks. Among their hits were "The Thunder Rolls," a dramatic story that

Songwriter Pat Alger.
Photo courtesy the artist.

addresses spouse abuse, an unusual topic for country music. Songs cowritten by Alger and Brooks have gone on to sell over fifty million copies!

RESOURCES

Songwriters' Guides and Trade Papers

There are dozens of books in print that discuss every facet of songwriting and music publishing. Many of them are listed in the appendix to this book.

American Songwriter are two monthly publications that are designed for songwriters. Both contain useful tips from established writers and music publishers, but the latter publication is increasingly oriented to songwriters who also perform.

Tip Sheets

Tip sheets are short publications that tell songwriters and music publishers what sorts of songs certain artists are looking for and how to contact them. The appropriate contact might be the artist's producer or manager. A tip sheet might indicate that Edna Jones is looking for Latin ballads. Many publishers subscribe to tip sheets and pass along the information to the songwriters that they have under contract. The cost of subscribing to these services is high, which is why songwriters usually rely on their publishers to collect this information for them.

Local and National Songwriting Organizations

The **Nashville Songwriters Association International (NSAI)** is the leading songwriters' organization. It specializes in country music and has many members who are distinguished publishers or songwriters. It holds large-scale annual workshops and seminars, and owns a building where songwriters can work, have meetings, or meet with the staff. NSAI also has branch organizations in many cities, and it brings some of its prized Nashville writers and publishers to these cities to hold workshops.

The **Songwriters Guild of America (SGA)** is an organization whose mission is to protect songwriters by offering contracts that favor songwriters as opposed to publishers and to assist songwriters in collecting royalties. It is not unusual for songwriters' royalties to get lost in the shuffle when music publishing companies get sold. When this occurs, the documentation of writer splits or contact information often disappears. SGA also offers to go after publishers who simply do not pay royalties. They charge the writer a small percentage of whatever monies they are able to recover.

Most cities of any size have local songwriters' associations. They meet on a regular basis, and provide opportunities for songwriters to meet collaborators. They also bring in writers and publishers to conduct seminars. Some of these organizations have regular contests, with prizes such as free recording time, performance opportunities at local events, or a free consultation with a music business attorney. Perhaps the main value of these organizations is the community they provide for songwriters. They offer supportive environments where songwriters can work together and give each other constructive critiques.

The Singer-Songwriter Genre

In the late 1960s, a group of folk music artists emerged who were performers as well as songwriters. Some of the artists included Joni Mitchell, Carly Simon, and James Taylor. These artists were referred to as **singer-songwriters**. When this movement's popularity diminished, the genre found its way into the folksong community. Today, the North American Folk Music & Dance Alliance probably has more members who are singer-songwriters than artists in any other genre of folk music. The annual national meeting is held in Memphis, and the various regional conferences of the organization provide opportunities for songwriters to network, and to receive basic music business education. ASCAP has a particularly strong profile at these events.

Similarly, the folk festivals, usually held in the summer, often have songwriting schools associated with them, which frequently include contests. Examples are the Lyons and Telluride Folk Festivals in Colorado, the annual Sisters Folk Festival in Sisters, Oregon, and the famous Kerrville Festival in Texas.

CAN A SONGWRITER SUCCEED OUTSIDE THE MAJOR MUSIC MARKETS?

Remember the story of Deborah Holland (see Chapter 7)? Many of the film or video placements that Deborah received would probably never have occurred if she had lived outside of the Los Angeles area. While it is possible to be successful living outside the major music business centers, for songwriters who do not perform, or for whom performing is a secondary option, it is more difficult to live in an isolated area. It is also much more difficult to keep up with the day-to-day developments in the business. For example:

- What new publisher is hot?
- Which publisher has sold his business?
- What publisher has a reputation for not paying royalties on a timely basis?
- What music supervisor has moved to another company?

Decisions about what song will be used in a film or a new TV pilot or a national advertising campaign are sometimes made very quickly. Even though modern technology has changed the nature of communication, you simply are not going to run into music supervisors on the streets of Boise, Idaho.

Some songwriters live outside the three music business towns but live in a music business center on a part-time basis. Hit country writer Steve Seskin lives in the San Francisco area and essentially commutes to Nashville. Because so many members of the Nashville songwriting community collaborate with other writers, it is even more difficult to have a strong presence in the Nashville music community and not either live in town or spend a great deal of time there.

COMPOSING

It is virtually impossible to make a full-time living composing music. Except for a few major film composers such as Bill Conti or John Williams, there are relatively few full-time film composers. There never were more than a small number of successful film composers, but opportunities have become much more difficult today. Typically, films used to feature sixty to ninety minutes of instrumental music. However, today, a film is more likely to feature fifteen pop songs (either preexisting, created for the film, or a mix of the two), with five minutes of incidental music that is used to connect various transitions. The songwriter has assumed many of the roles that used to be performed by the composer.

In the world of pop and jazz music, composers make a living because they record their own songs or instrumental pieces. If they are successful as artists, then they earn additional income from their original music.

In classical music very few individuals make a living writing chamber music, symphonic music, or operas. Composers survive either through grants or more typically by teaching composition, music theory, and music history at universities.

Composer's Agents and Breaking into Film and Television

Most Hollywood composers use agents to obtain work. There are a small number of agents who represent different composers. Just as in most professions, agents tend to be interested in representing composers who are already working on projects, so it's hard for a new composer to break in.

There are several ways for a composer to break into Hollywood. Sometimes on a television show or in a film, something has to be written very quickly. The composer who is working on the project may also have other responsibilities that make it difficult for him to quickly produce more music. He will therefore hire a "ghostwriter," who will write the necessary new music. This is a very delicate process, because the composer of record may or may not acknowledge the contributions of the ghost. The worst case scenario for the ghost occurs when the composer conducts the score written by the ghost, under the pretense that he wrote the music. However, Edward Faulkner's *Music On Demand,* the classic work on the business of film scoring, also cites some instances in which composers freely acknowledged the contributions of their ghosts and went out of their way to recommend them to the producer for additional work. It takes a secure individual to behave in this way. Many composers would become paranoid if the director and producer liked the ghost's music too much, because they might fear that they might be endangering their own future prospects if they credited the ghost's work.

Another way to break into film composing is to work with a film student on a project that will be entered in film festivals. There is little or no money available in student films for music. A composer must be careful to restrict the use of the music to contests. If the film goes into commercial distribution or on to television, the composer should be compensated. Failure to include this clause in the contract may result in the film making money without the composer ever earning a cent.

On a local level, film editors can also be a source of work for the composer. This applies not only to feature films, but also to documentaries or industrial films. Sometimes the film's producers have not made any arrangements for music, because they are too busy dealing with the script, the actors, and the location where the film is being shot. They may ask the film's editor for a recommendation.

In Hollywood films, the composer gets a script and a complete and timed breakdown of the action, but on a local level the composer may have to do all of this work.

Other Composing Opportunities

JINGLES   Many songwriters also utilize their skills in writing **jingles**, short songs used to promote a product. Besides the obvious and visible market for commercials that run on radio and television networks, there are hundreds of commercials written for local and regional products. Many banks, for example, operate in a particular region or even a specific city. Some commercial producers rely on music libraries (see later in this chapter) to provide a generic instrumental melody that can be repurposed for different markets. For example, a commercial for a car dealer in Dubuque may be used by another dealer in San Diego, with different copy and singing inserted into the same instrumental tracks. These commercials are known as **drop-ins**. Jingle work can be found by dealing with local advertising agencies. Unlike songs that appear on recordings, the composer is paid a flat fee for this work, although the performing rights organizations do pay performance money to the composer. Because commercials usually run for only fifteen to thirty seconds, these are relatively low fees. However, if a commercial runs repeatedly or for an extended period of time, the payments may add up.

RINGTONES AND RINGBACKS   **Ringtones** are those ever-popular (and sometimes annoying) brief melodies that are used on cellphones. A single cellphone user may download hundreds of ringtones to identify different callers or to suit an individual mood. Some of these ringtones are snippets of popular songs, but others have been specifically composed to be memorable, catchy, and easily heard in a noisy, crowded environment. *Billboard* has created a Hot Ringtones Chart, attesting to the popularity—and financial importance—of pop songs used as ringtones.

The income made from ringtones breaks down as follows:

Consumer price $2.50

Record label share $1.00

Artist share 0.24

Publisher share 0.25

Performing rights share 0.09

Remember that the publisher splits its share with the songwriter 50/50, and that the performing rights society pays both the publisher and the songwriter.

Ringtones are the sound you hear when someone is calling you; **ringbacks** are the tones that callers hear when they phone you. Again, these can be personalized so that Caller A might hear a snippet of "Flight of the Bumblebee," while Caller B might hear the *Star Wars* theme. Ringbacks can be newly composed or drawn from the same sources—pop songs, movie themes, classical snippets—that are used for ringtones.

And The Winner of the Ringie Award Is . . .

In June 2006, the *New York Times* reported that the RIAA was extending its gold and platinum sales status to ringtones. The new Master Ringtone Sales Award was being launched "to recognize the growing popularity of enjoying music through cellular phones." In the words of the *Times*, "The association defines an eligible ringtone as an original recording, rather than a synthesized instrumental version, of a hit song. Tracks will be certified gold (500,000 downloads), platinum (one million downloads), and multiplatinum (starting at two million and following in increments of one million). The first awards, plaques decorated with a cellphone motif, consisted of 84 gold, 40 platinum and 4 multiplatinum certifications. The multiplatinum winners were T-Pain's 'I'm N Luv (Wit a Stripper)' (Jive), D4L's 'Laffy Taffy' (Atlantic), Black Eyed Peas' 'My Humps' (A&M) and Chamillionaire's 'Ridin' (Universal)."

Pop artists have been quick to exploit the growing ringtone/ringback market. Led Zeppelin signed an exclusive deal for its catalog to be mined for ringtones by Verizon Wireless in fall 2007. Verizon also began offering a service called College Ringbacks, in which special college songs would be heard by alumni phoning into their alma maters. Artists including Britney Spears offered "exclusive" ringtones for their fans for download on their Web site, or in return for purchasing VIP concert tickets and the like.

VIDEOGAMES   Although ringtones and ringbacks pay royalties to composers, **videogames** and music libraries are another story. Video gaming has become a major industry, with 2007 revenues of over $18.8 billion, and 2008 revenues on track to exceed $21 billion. Compare these revenues to the RIAA's reported CD sales of under $11 billion for 2007. The bad news is that videogame companies try to avoid paying royalties to composers, preferring to pay a single buyout fee.

Videogame composing is challenging for the composer, because many of the games are interactive, and the composer must provide musical options that match the story options in the game. When a videogame uses an existing song, the producers will have to license that song. It is a negotiable matter as to whether the songwriter and publisher will be paid royalties or whether the producers can obtain the song for a flat fee. Obviously the better known a song is, the less likely a publisher is to accept a buyout.

MUSIC LIBRARIES AND OTHER OUTLETS   **Music libraries** are collections of music that a production company assembles in order to meet requests for music for film, television, and commercials. The compositions are often used by multiple buyers. Music libraries do not pay royalties, and because the music tends to be generic, the fees for using the music are low compared to the cost of commissioning and recording original music.

There is also a market for music to be used in non-musical television shows, such as sports events. At a music business seminar, a speaker from Fox TV reported that he had used over a million musical fragments in a single year.

Other opportunities for composers include writing music for industrial films, dance companies and slide shows, and writing special material for night club acts for performers. **Industrial films** are short documentary films that are essentially extended commercials for a particular product.

MUSIC ARRANGERS

A **music arranger** is someone who takes a basic melody and fleshes it out for all the various instruments that will perform it on a recording. Arrangers do not get paid royalties but are paid on a per-song or project basis. Because many film composers never studied orchestration, there is a continuing need for arrangers who can actually take a basic melody and arrange it for musical instruments. Arrangers must know the range and function of all the instruments in the orchestra, and be familiar with electronic and world music instruments and with numerous musical styles.

Arrangers are also employed by Broadway shows, where often they have to be capable of doing lightning-fast work. When a Broadway show is in its tryout phase—something that often takes place outside of New York—it is common for the lyricist and composer to write many songs that are briefly thrown into the show. If the director doesn't feel the song is working with the show's plot lines, the song is thrown out. All of this music gets orchestrated by the arranger, who often works very long hours in order to get the music into the show as quickly as possible.

Another role for arrangers is to work for a music print publisher. These companies are constantly producing band and choral arrangements, and they also use arrangers to transcribe songs or solos that come from successful records. In order to be successful at this job, the arranger must have good musical training and an excellent ear. It is a real plus to be proficient at the guitar and the keyboard. Because print arrangers often deal with current hit songs, the arranger must be able to work quickly under considerable time pressure. Once a hit goes off the charts, demand for printed versions of it quickly diminishes.

Terms to Know

Collaboration agreement *208*	Music arranger *214*	Ringtone *213*
Demonstration record-ing (demo) *203*	Music library *214*	SGA (Songwriters Guild of America) *210*
Drop-in *212*	NSAI (Nashville Songwriters Association International) *209*	Singer-songwriter *210*
Hold *205*		Song poems *200*
Industrial film *214*	Reversion clause *206*	Taxi *200*
Jingle *212*	Ringback *213*	Tip sheet *209*
		Videogame *214*

For Class Discussion

1. Does your local church use any original music?
2. Do you know anyone who has entered a songwriting contest? If so, what happened?
3. Is it possible for a songwriter who does not perform to make a living?
4. Can a songwriter living in a town with little or no musical activity succeed?
5. Have you ever submitted an original song to someone? What happened?
6. Where would you look for a songwriting collaborator?
7. Do you know anyone who has been solicited by a Song Shark?
8. How would you compare the effectiveness of a mostly instrumental film score with one that uses fifteen songs and a few minutes of instrumental music? Which one serves the film better? Why?

CHAPTER **13**

Careers in
Music Teaching

M any musicians make a part-time or full-time living teaching music.
There are a number of opportunities for musicians who wish to
teach. These include:

- *Private lessons (individual or group)*
- *Teaching in the public or private school system (choral or band director)*
- *College professor or instructor (full time or adjunct)*
- *Teaching at summer music camps*
- *Teaching workshops or master classes for instrument manufacturers or music publishers.*

TEACHING INDIVIDUAL AND GROUP LESSONS

There are no formal requirements that qualify a musician for private teaching. For better or worse, anyone can declare themselves to be a private music teacher. Teachers get students through word-of-mouth references and referrals from music stores who do not offer lessons or offer a limited amount of instruction.

The manager of a music store's teaching facility will usually want to hear a prospective teacher play, look at their resume, and spend enough time talking with the teacher to become convinced that he or she has the skills to teach. There are some teachers who are too disorganized to show up on a regular basis or in a timely fashion, or who will cancel a lesson any time that they get any sort of performing gig. These teachers never last long at a music store teaching facility. Some facilities also ask the prospective teacher to give a sample lesson, in which they can observe the teacher's abilities on a first-hand basis.

Some studio operations handle all of the scheduling and the financial matters, and pay the teacher by the lesson. Lessons are usually a half-hour or an hour long. Other stores simply rent the teacher space, and it is her or his responsibility to schedule students. Teaching programs at the better-organized stores have brochures that describe teachers and their specialties. An example would be: "Ann Jones studied flamenco guitar for three years in Granada, Spain, with Paco de Lucia, and has performed with the Glory Street Flamenco Music Troop. She has a bachelor's of music in guitar from Peabody Conservatory and has recorded two solo albums."

Hourly rates for music lessons vary from one city to another, based on the interest in music lessons, the supply of teachers, and the condition of the economy. Rates of $35 to $50 an hour seem to be typical in many cities. When the teacher works for a music store, they will either charge the teacher by the hour, or take a percentage of the teacher's take. This percentage varies from 20 to 33.3 percent. The percentage or hourly rate will vary according to the value that the store places on its lesson program, and the amount of services that the store itself provides in terms of scheduling, cancellations, and so on.

Teachers who give lessons in their homes, or those who set up their own schedules at music stores, need to establish a few ground rules in order to safeguard their livelihood. The teacher needs to establish a cancellation policy, and set up rules about payment. Many private teachers require students to pay for lessons a month in advance. They also should set up a cancellation policy that requires advance notice before the actual lesson. Some teachers offer to make up lessons for cancellations, and some do not. An alternative to paying by the month is for the student to pay one lesson in advance. Failure to do so takes the student off the teacher's regular schedule. If the teacher does not enforce payment and cancellation policies, students (or their parents) may cancel lessons at the last minute, using casual excuses.

Many local community centers offer group lessons, especially in guitar. Music stores with a large room devoted to lessons may also offer group lessons. Group lessons are usually offered on a six- to eight-week basis, paid in advance. The students pay less, but the teacher makes more. Students taking group lessons tend to be less devoted to their studies, and teachers who have an emotional stake in their student's progress may find group lessons less satisfying than teaching one-on-one.

In the larger cities, symphony members often give private lessons and are able to command higher fees, sometimes as high as $100 an hour.

Attributes of a Good Teacher

Good teachers must be patient, and their lessons should reflect a balance of what the student is eager to learn with technical studies and exercises that will enable the student to accomplish these goals. There is a certain amount of give and take involved, where the student has to realize that it is necessary to practice, and the teacher has to have some grasp of what the student's goals are.

Tales from the Trenches

I haven't taught guitar lessons in a number of years, but two stories stand out from the days when I taught guitar. I was teaching guitar to a student at a college and noticed that she had very long fingernails. I casually mentioned to her at our first lesson that she would have to cut the fingernails of her left hand in order to be able to play chords. By the third lesson she had still not cut her nails, and she was finding her occasional attempts to play the guitar painful. I told her that she had a choice to make; either cut her nails or drop guitar. Mindful of that admonition, she immediately dropped guitar.

Sometimes even seemingly obvious things will escape students' attention. When I was teaching a guitar class to a half dozen people at a community center, I noticed one student who seemed alert and intelligent. Whatever I asked him to do, he picked up quickly, even as the others struggled. However, by the fourth lesson, he was still unable to play what he had learned in the very first session. I asked him how often he practiced the guitar. He replied that he thought that simply by taking lessons he would learn how to play. It hadn't occurred to him that he needed to practice at home. Like my nail-heavy college student, he dropped out soon thereafter.

Many fine musicians lack the patience to be good teachers. They often do not remember their early struggles to master an instrument, and they expect students to catch on more quickly than the students are able to do. There are also some musicians whose talent is so great that they never had to struggle to learn to play. For such a musician, a student's struggles may be literally impossible to comprehend.

TEACHING IN THE SCHOOL SYSTEM

Teaching in the schools requires that the instructor have a music education degree. Usually, the instructor will either teach chorus or band. In both cases the teacher must have the ability to conduct an ensemble. It is not expected or required that the teacher be able to actually play *all* of the instruments of the orchestra, although many band directors can play a bit on an amazing number of instruments. As school music budgets have tightened, some schools may even require a teacher to conduct the orchestra and the chorus. Teachers who can play guitar are a plus, because of the widespread interest in that instrument. As many public school programs have cut full-time music teachers, some schools have begun to employ music teachers part-time during after-school hours. These are not full-time jobs, and they don't pay benefits or offer the teacher any security.

If a teacher commutes to several schools each week, this puts a great deal of pressure on the teacher. Besides the class activities, music teachers are usually expected to lead the band at football games and other events, and participate in the Christmas show and other performances. Add this to the time spent commuting between jobs, and the teacher is left without much time to devote to developing lessons or working with individual students. It is difficult for teachers to build a program when they barely know the names of their students. It also makes it next to impossible to give students the individual attention or mentoring that is a significant part of education.

Most states have organizations of public school music teachers. One of their primary tasks has been to lobby school districts and state legislatures to fight for better funding for school music programs. They also hold annual meetings where teachers are introduced to new developments in music technology, and discussions are held on the improvement of teaching. The Music Educators National Convention (MENC) is one of the leading advocates for music programs at all levels of education. The National Association of Music Merchandisers (NAMM) is also active in attempting to preserve and expand music education programs. NAMM represents music instrument manufacturers, wholesalers, and retail music stores. All of these groups have an obvious interest in the continued health of music education programs.

COLLEGE TEACHING

Full-time college teaching offers a secure income with benefits for the professor. There are four levels of professors, each with a different pay scale. Only some teachers are eligible for **tenure**, a system that guarantees employment at the university after a professor reaches a certain level of scholarship and years of service. At the bottom of the instructional ranks are **instructors**, who are usually employed on a one- to three-year contract. They are not on a tenure track, which means that their job security is entirely related to their performance in the classroom and the music department's budget. Usually instructors are not expected to do research or publish papers.

Not all colleges follow the tenure process, but most of them do so. An **assistant professor** starts on the tenure track, and usually receives one major pretenure evaluation, which is designed to measure their strengths and weaknesses. The intent of this evaluation is to better prepare the professor for the tenure evaluation. Assistant professors are at the low end of the tenure track pay scale, and they have the least departmental input in terms of their class schedule. **Associate professors** have usually attained tenure, and are asked to serve on higher level college committees, and to be involved in job searches. After a number of years as an associate, a professor can apply to be a **full professor**. This is a process similar to the tenure process, but failure to get a full professorship does not lead to losing the job. Full professors are at the high end of the departmental pay scale.

Getting A College Teaching Job

College jobs are advertised in the *Chronicle of Higher Education,* and listed by the **College Music Society (CMS)** for members. Other organizations, such as the **Music Educators National Conference (MENC)**, also offer listings.

Music business teaching jobs are sometimes advertised in *Billboard,* as are audio engineering jobs in *Mix Magazine.*

There may be many applicants for one position, and a hiring committee usually makes a short list of five to ten candidates that it is seriously considering. At the point where the list is pared down to three to five applicants, the committee begins checking the applicants' references. Generally, three candidates are invited to the campus for a grueling regimen where the candidate gives a sample class and is interviewed by departmental faculty, by the tenure committee, and by the dean.

Full-time college professors almost always are required to have a terminal degree in their field, which is sometimes a doctorate, sometimes a Master's degree. Music theory, education, history, and ethnomusicology are areas in which a doctorate is usually necessary. In music therapy, audio engineering, and music business, a Master's degree will often suffice. College hiring committees look at the candidate's teaching and research credentials and evaluate a sample lecture. There is also a process whereby they determine whether the candidate is a good fit for the department's current program and its future direction.

For students aspiring to pursue careers in musical composition, theory, and history, teaching is an ideal profession. For others, the academic world can provide support for research and a platform to pursue creative work at relatively little risk or expense. Students should consider whether they enjoy teaching and relating to students before pursuing an academic career. Part of the job includes many time-consuming committee meetings and other service responsibilities to the college. Many programs require each professor to have a specific number of office hours where students can meet with them.

There is considerable variation in salaries from one school to another and from private to public colleges. Instructors are apt to earn an annual salary in the $25,000 to $30,000 range, assistant professors receive $35,000 to $40,000 a year, associates are paid $45,000 to $55,000, and full professors earn $50,000 or more. In addition, teachers are evaluated annually, and receive salary increases based on their performance and on the school's budget.

Part-Time College Teaching

Music and art professors usually are at the low end of college salary scales. There is considerable variation from one school to another and from private to public colleges. Part-time teachers are usually called adjunct faculty. Part-time college jobs fall into two categories. Classes are paid on a per class basis. The prevailing wage for a three-credit class will go from around $1,500 to $4,000. Instructors who teach individual music lessons at a college are paid on an hourly basis and the current wage scale ranges from $20 for a half hour lesson and up. Each college music department sets its own budget for lessons. It is easy to see that a part-time position at a college or university will not supply enough money to support a teacher.

Most colleges prefer that adjunct professors teaching a particular instrument have a master's degree in performance on the instrument that they are teaching. They may accept a Bachelor's degree if the player has a unique specialty, or an extensive series of high-level professional credits.

The same requirement applies to teaching individual college classes, such as music theory. There are occasional exceptions. For example, Cecil Effinger taught composition at the University of Colorado for many years. He had a single degree, a Bachelor's in mathematics. However, his compositions were performed all over the world and he invented numerous musical tools, such as the Tempo Watch. Obviously, the university felt that the level of his professional work was more important than mere resume credits. He became a full professor in the department. This was an unusual phenomenon, however.

Some part-time college teachers put together a schedule at three or four different colleges, and create the equivalent of a full-time job for themselves. However, they do not receive health or pension benefits, and they have no real job security, so their schedule of classes may vary from one year to the next.

The Tenure Process

Most colleges offer professors the opportunity to become tenured. Professors apply for tenure after six years of full-time teaching. The professor submits a dossier that includes a lengthy resume, teaching evaluations, credentials in the area of teaching, and service and research and/or creative work. Research is defined as writing articles and books and delivering papers at academic conferences. Colleges prefer publications that were juried by other academics, rather than popular books acquired by book editors. Research also includes creative work, such as composing or performing music. Service involves serving on academic committees or other demonstrated ways that the candidate has served the university community. Teaching is gauged by student evaluations and also by evaluations from other professors who visit the applicant's classes and sometimes also talk informally with students. The candidate is also evaluated by colleagues from other schools, who receive copies of the applicant's materials. These evaluators are chosen by department colleagues, although the candidate is allowed to suggest one of the evaluators.

The music department sets up an evaluation committee, which includes several members of the music department, plus one or two members from other subject areas. They make a recommendation to the music department, which then holds a formal vote on the candidate. The decision then goes up the food chain and ultimately the dean of the college must sign off on the applicant.

Although the individual department's recommendation is usually followed, if the vote includes some "no" votes or if the professor or application are regarded as controversial, the decision may be reversed at the committee level, or even by the dean. The president of the school must also sign off on the candidate, and on occasion the reversal of a decision comes at that level.

If candidates are denied tenure, they receive a one-year terminal contract. They can use that year to try to get another job, but, regardless, at the end of that year they must leave the school. Candidates who earn tenure are generally promoted from Assistant to Associate Professors. Tenured professors have excellent job security, and are usually fired only because a college has a critical financial exigency, or because the professor has been accused of plagiarism or outrageous behavior. When professors receive tenure, they usually are given a substantial pay raise, and given a year's sabbatical leave at half pay. Professors are eligible for a sabbatical every seven years. It is also possible for a sabbatical to be given as a one semester leave at full pay, but this is not always available.

TENURE DISPUTES   Anyone who has ever taught for any length of time at a college has witnessed some contentious tenure decisions. These may entail disputes about the value of a professor's creative work or research, personal disputes between members of a department, or vendettas against a tough-grading professor by students. There have been other cases in which bias based on race or gender has been alleged by an unsuccessful applicant.

When someone is denied tenure, they often appeal the decision. These issues often become aired publicly through newspaper articles. Their resolution is always time consuming, and may or may not result in the reversal of a tenure decision. There have also been a number of instances in which a denial of tenure has resulted in a court determining that the decision was unjust, and that the college must make a generous financial settlement.

Inevitably, there are some subjective judgments that come into play in tenure cases, no matter how much "objective" data is accumulated by the tenure committee.

Community Colleges

Community colleges are two-year programs that offer Associate's degrees in the arts. Community college professors may teach ten to twelve classes a year and the expectations for research or creative work are low. Colleges have smaller academic loads, six to eight classes a year. Teaching is considered the primary task, but there is some expectation that the professor will do research or creative work.

Summer Sessions and Continuing Education Programs

Many colleges offer summer sessions. Professors are not required to teach during the summer, but may wish to supplement their income through summer teaching. Some professors also teach short summer workshops or classes at out of state colleges. This enables them to travel as well as bring in additional income.

Many colleges offer continuing education for students who do not wish to enroll in a degree program. Opportunities exist in these programs for teaching both individual and group lessons, and for teaching workshops or short classes in such subjects as songwriting. Because many prospective students already have a degree, or do not wish to go to school for four years, this is a good source of income for part-time teachers. Other opportunities for teachers include teaching at the many **summer music camps**. These

Strumming at Banjo Camp

Summer music camps used to be focused primarily on teenage musicians who were hoping to get into a major music school or conservatory. Today, with added leisure time and interest in home music, many camps cater to older adults who are pursuing music as a hobby. Across the country, various "camps" have developed focusing on different instruments; among the most successful are various banjo camps that are held fairly regularly through the warmer months.

Bob Carlin is a working musician who has taught at many one-day workshops and weeklong camps for beginning old-time banjo players. Bob got interested in teaching because it was a natural way to augment his income; he was already traveling to play concerts in different towns, so it made sense to add a workshop to his schedule to maximize his return on his travels.

Bob Carlin leading a banjo workshop at the 2007 Philadelphia Folk Festival. Photograph by C. Ernest Tedino, courtesy Bob Carlin.

Bob quickly learned that teaching groups of students is different than teaching an individual one-on-one. In a group situation, most people want to have a good time and enjoy themselves; they're not necessarily looking to become ace musicians over a course of just a few days. Bob recognizes that a big draw of these camps is the unstructured jam sessions that occur after hours, and he encourages his students to try to play at their own level in these sessions. "Beginners can play at an intermediate level jam," Bob notes, "as long as they play very simply rather than trying to outdo the more experienced players." Bob notes that the camps have been drawing many more novice players, who have been playing less than six months, with a contingent of beginners (six months–one year), and then a sprinkling of intermediate level players (over a year).

Bob notes that sometimes a person signs up for a class just to "show up" the teacher. He remembered one class he gave in conjunction with fellow banjo player Henry Sapoznik. Henry had recorded some solos on a record Bob produced, *Melodic Clawhammer Banjo*, that came with a set of tablature, so would-be banjoists could learn the pieces. Both Henry and Bob were shocked when a student came to their workshop, pulled out his banjo, and proceeded to play all of Henry's solos, one after another. "It's always shocking when someone spits back at you an exact replica of your own playing," Bob notes. Obviously, he came just to show off for his idols!

camps vary in length from a weekend to an entire summer. They include virtually every imaginable style of music, from bluegrass to jazz or classical music. Some camps are designed for adults, and others teach children.

INSTRUCTIONAL BOOKS, VIDEOS, AND CLINICS

Instructional Books

Another way to teach music is to author instructional materials or books about music. Music publishers are always on the lookout for people who can write good, clear instructional material, and as we have already noted (see Chapter 7), these books can sell for years (if not decades), producing regular profits. There's even one author who advertises a book on the web about how to identify Song Sharks (see Chapter 12), making money warning people about the follies of paying for help with promoting their music!

Music print publishers issue many instructional books that often include CDs or DVDs. Typically, these books pay a royalty of 10 percent of the retail selling price to the author. If the author uses copyrighted songs written by other people, the fees paid for the use of these songs are deducted from royalties, and can greatly reduce or even eliminate them. This is why so many instructional works include songs that are in the public domain, such as "Row, Row, Row Your Boat." It is also why you'll see songs titled "Typical Blues Progression"; the author is trying to avoid using an actual song to illustrate a standard chord or melodic progression found in many songs.

In order to get an instructional book published, the author should submit a sample chapter or two, along with a table of contents and a market analysis that explains why there is a niche in the print music market for the work. It is best not to submit a complete manuscript, to prevent the company from using another writer to use your concepts to write a different book. Although this is unethical and not a common occurrence, I am aware of instances in which it has happened. Another reason not to submit a complete manuscript is that the publisher may be put off by having to read a ninety-six-page book, just as music publishers do not wish to listen to a sixteen-song demo.

Royalties for the sale of printed music are paid in a different way than those that come from records. The only deduction from the author's royalty is any money advanced before the publication of the work. The different music print publishers pay royalties at different time periods, ranging from once a year to every three months. In the appendix to this book you will find the names and addresses of the leading music print publishers.

SELF-PUBLISHING   With the advent of modern computers, it is possible to self-publish material through a desktop publishing program. The author can have her books printed on a demand basis, or deliver them over the Internet.

Today's book business is so structured that about half of all books sold are bought at the Borders and Barnes and Noble chains or through

Mark Hanson: Self-Publishing Success Story

Mark Hanson provides a great example of how a musician can lead a reasonable life, combining his various interests with a relatively stable lifestyle. His primary focus is his instructional books, with private teaching and performances supplementing his musical and economic life.

Mark Hanson. Photo Copyright © 2005 Mark Hanson and Accent On Music LLC. All Rights Reserved. Used By Permission.

Mark graduated from Stanford and was living in Palo Alto, California, in the mid-1970s. He played in three different groups, working three to five nights a week, did some teaching, and began to write down some of the music that he was teaching to students. By the early 1980s, he completed his first book, an introduction in to the alternating thumb guitar–picking style of country icon Merle Travis. He sent the book out to several music publishers. Some felt that it competed with some of their existing material, others simply rejected it. This led him to start his own company, Accent On Music.

While this was going on, Mark continued to play gigs, and from 1986 to 1989 he worked at *Frets* magazine. He started writing for *Frets* as an occasional freelance writer, and two years later was hired as an assistant editor. The magazine was sold, and Mark was offered a chance to stay with the new company, but he elected to leave. He feels that the contacts that he made at *Frets* gave him entry into the music industry.

After he had self-published two books, Dave McCummiskey, the West Coast representative for Music Sales Corporation, helped Mark work out a deal where he continued to publish his own books, but they distributed the books to retail music stores. Mark sells his books by mail as well, primarily from his Web site. Twenty-five years later, Mark has built up a catalog of guitar books and DVDs. Most of them are in his company, with a few others owned by Alfred Music, which they picked up when they bought Warner Brothers Music print division. Mark also published a few small handy guides written specifically for Music Sales, which they own. The Warner Brothers material was in book form and included five videos, reaching a different market. Counting books and DVDs, Mark has written thirty different instructional guides. He and his wife Greta Pedersen operate their company out of a home office near Portland, Oregon. Operating the business includes continual updates of the company's Web site, and responding to mail order inquiries and orders.

Over time, Mark has developed a regular writing schedule. He finishes a book in September, and brings it to the January NAMM show. In addition to writing books, Mark does about a clinic a month in music stores, where he sells his books as well as teaches. At times, Collings Guitars sponsors the workshops, because Mark plays Collings instruments.

Amazon.com. Although self-publishers can get their books sold by Amazon, they rarely get their work placed in the chain bookstores. However, if your book starts to sell, it is always possible to contact the chains and if they find that the sales are occurring, they may pick up your book.

There are two independent book distributors, Baker & Taylor and Ingram. The major music publishers, notably Hal Leonard (see Chapter 7), distribute some self-published materials to music stores. It is possible that one or more of these distributors will be willing to distribute your book, but the book will probably simply sit on their warehouse shelves, awaiting orders from stores. In other words, promotion for the book will have to come from you.

There are certain key independent book stores such as The Strand in New York City, The Tattered Cover in Denver, Powells in Portland, Oregon, and Elliott Bay Books in Seattle. To do a reading at these stores, it is necessary to convince the person in charge of author bookings that the book will draw people to an author's reading. If the author lives in the town where the bookstore is located, she or he can also print flyers or posters advertising the appearance. Some radio and local television stations are willing to interview authors and this can help build the audience at the bookstore, and even to sell books at stores where the author has not appeared.

CDs and DVDs

Instructional books are fine for those people who are comfortable reading music or guitar tablature (see Chapter 8). However, many musicians learn better by ear or by watching a master musician perform. Recognizing this natural marriage, entrepreneurs began in the late 1950s to issue record and book combinations. Oak Publications was among the first, with its famous *Folk Singer's Guitar Guide,* consisting of a book and LP, which was issued just as the folk boom was occurring in the late 1950s. LPs eventually were replaced by cassettes and then CDs, but the basic idea of a narrated instructional record was established.

The advent of home video made it possible to combine music and sound. This is an obvious advantage, because it allows the student to see closeups of hand positions and other techniques that are important in learning any musical instrument. Companies such as Homespun Tapes have built big businesses out of creating instructional materials in video format.

With the advent of YouTube, many amateurs and semiprofessionals are posting their own instructional materials online. Although the quality varies greatly, this is opening yet another opportunity to spread your own personal teaching style and philosophy to players worldwide.

Clinics

Teachers and professional musicians can also be employed by manufacturers of musical instruments or music publishers to travel to music stores in different parts of the country. They are given the title of "clinicians" because they lead specialized **clinics** for players in different styles or on different instruments. The teacher presents demonstrations of instrumental styles, or, in the case of music publishers, plays from method books for band or chorale teachers. College band programs often cosponsor clinicians to come to the school to work with their students. Some clinicians supplement their income by pursuing performing opportunities in the cities where they offer clinics.

Terms to Know

Assistant
professor *219*
Associate
professor *219*
Clinics *227*
CMS (College Music
Society) *219*

Full professor *219*
Instructor *219*
MENC (Music
Educators National
Conference) *219*

Summer music
camps *223*
Tenure *219*

For Class Discussion

1. Have you ever taken private lessons from a music instructor before you attended college?
2. What do you think are the characteristics of a good private music instructor?
3. Did you take chorus or band in junior high school or high school? Describe the experience.
4. Do you think the tenure system is useful? Why?
5. In your opinion, does a good college professor have to do research and creative work?
6. How does a good professor inspire a student to learn?
7. Do you think that student evaluations are a fair measure of teaching?
8. Would you ever consider college teaching as a career? Why, or why not?
9. Is there a music professor in your college that you regard as a mentor? Why do you feel that way about him or her?

CHAPTER **14**

Recording Careers

There are thousands of recording studios all over the United States, varying from home studios in a garage or even a bedroom to massive rooms that are capable of recording film scores with 105 live musicians. Many young people have had recording equipment in their homes for years. Engineering careers often begin with musicians who want to record their own music. From these modest beginnings, they move into full-blown engineering and record production careers.

AUDIO ENGINEERING

A Brief History

Audio engineering has probably gone through more technological evolutions over the past sixty years than any other single aspect of the music industry. Until the late 1940s all music was recorded direct to disc. The singer performed live with the accompanying orchestra and any background singers, and if anyone made a mistake the process had to be repeated. Les Paul and Mitch Miller experimented during the 1940s with the process of **overdubbing**, where music was recorded, and then that recording was played to the singer or instrumentalist, and another part was recorded on top of it. This was a clumsy process, and in order to compensate for the consequent loss of sound quality, the producer had to add a considerable amount of echo.

The first post–World War II tape recorders were monaural machines, meaning that they were recorded on a single **track**. (A track is the name for a single audio stream.) By the mid-1950s, stereo recorders were in use, and now the engineer had two tracks to play with. The singer could wait until the orchestral parts were completed before recording her or his own part.

In the early 1960s three-track recorders replaced the two-track machines. The addition of this extra track changed how the producer worked, anticipating the way recording is done today, over forty-five years later. The key question for the producer becomes what to put on track number three: Should it be an instrumental solo, a string section, horns, background vocals? After the producer made that decision, she or he was now confronted with the question of how to mix the product down to stereo. To put it another way, what sounds should be most prominent, what should be in the background, and what should be barely audible?

From the three-track recorder, the industry moved to four and then eight tracks, before finally reaching a standard of twenty-four tracks. Next, engineers hooked up two twenty-four-track machines, losing two of the tracks in the process, and leaving the producer forty-six tracks to manipulate. Twenty-four track **analog** machines required the use of expensive and clumsy two-inch tape, selling for about $100 to $150 a reel. Because many artists liked to keep all or most of what they recorded, the tape costs for an analog tape album could end up being well over $1,000. The industry inevitably sought less expensive formats. Home and semiprofessional studios began to use the **A-DAT (digital audio tape)** format in 1976. These machines were inexpensive, and they too could be hooked together. Three A-DATS together offered twenty-four-track recording. The machine recorded to compact digital cassettes, which were inexpensive.

Multitrack digital recorders soon became available, in twenty-four, then thirty-six, and finally forty-eight-track formats. By the 1990s, hard disk computer recording systems were available, albeit at high cost. Long and bitter arguments transpired among audio engineers, producers, and artists about the sound quality of hard disk systems. By the mid-1990s, the **ProTools** hard disk system was available at a relatively low cost, and even small studios began to record on these hard disk systems.

The undeniable advantage of hard disk recording is the ease of editing. Time-consuming edits that used to be done using razors wielded by a very nervous engineer are now done in fractions of a second. The arguments about sound quality continue and some artists record to analog and mix to digital. Their argument is that analog sound is "warmer" and more "human." Not everyone agrees with this sentiment and certainly the quality of digital is improving rapidly. This controversy is quite similar to the arguments between proponents of vinyl records and compact discs.

LEARNING AUDIO ENGINEERING

On-the-Job Training

There are three general possibilities for those wishing to pursue audio engineering as a career: on-the-job training, college audio programs, and vocational and two-year programs.

In on-the-job training, the prospective audio engineer apprentices himself to a recording studio. Initially, they may not even be given any responsibilities that relate to the recording process, but they can serve as valets, drivers, clean-up personnel, or what the British refer to as "tea boys," making coffee or tea for the clients. Gradually, the apprentice is allowed to work with the equipment, setting up microphones and assisting the engineer in various ways, such as helping to keep a written record of what instruments are recorded on which track. The next step is that the engineer starts to record demos. Demos are relatively low-pressure recording sessions. Making a mistake will not endanger the reputation of the studio. If all goes well, the apprentice will then start to do actual sessions.

The advantage of breaking into the audio world this way is that— unlike a college internship—there is no time limit on how many hours the apprentice is in the studio. It is also true that some studio owners would rather train prospective engineers than get them out of a college or vocational program, where the teacher's philosophy may not match up with the recording practices of a particular studio.

The downside of this sort of on-the-job training is that often the apprentice is expected to work long hours, and often receives no compensation. Furthermore, there is no guarantee that the studio will ultimately hire the apprentice and a "tea boy" credit is not exactly something that brightens up a résumé.

College Programs

An increasing number of colleges have their own recording studios and they offer two-year AA degree programs or four-year degrees in audio engineering. A much smaller group of colleges even offer a Master's degree in audio.

College programs offer a basic program in audio, starting with the theoretical aspects, and moving into actually working in the studio. Some programs also require some classes in the acoustics of sound and many demand that the student take the basic two-year theory and harmony package required of all music students. An engineer recording a large orchestral piece will often be handed a score to follow, so this basic knowledge of music is more useful to the audio engineer than to the music business major. College audio programs may also require that the student take private lessons in a particular instrument or in voice for two years, and pass some sort of proficiency exam. As is the case with music business majors, most colleges require that a student do an internship, usually in the junior or senior year.

How can a student determine whether a college program is a good one? Some things to look for include:

- *Have the instructors actually worked as recording engineers?*
- *Do the instructors continue to work in the field?* If the instructor's training occurred thirty years ago, and he or she hasn't done an actual recording session in twenty years, there is a good chance that she or he is not up to date on technological developments.

- *How much hands-on time does the student get in the studio?* It may sound good to the prospective student that the school has five different rooms in operation, but if there are six hundred audio majors, how much time does each student get to operate the equipment?
- *Are there any work-study jobs available at the school's recording facility?* If students are able to get some work-study hours, not only will they be paid for their work, but they will have access to the studio schedule, and therefore be able to fit their own projects into the general time scheme. For example, a work-study student may discover that many others in the program want to work at night, and few wish to work on weekend mornings. Using this information, she or he can then get more recording time for personal work, without compromising the needs of other students.
- *Are the internship programs in quality studios and are there opportunities to work in studios that are out of town?* The prospective student may want to look into the quality of the studios where the college has placed interns. If the student wants to do postproduction work on movies, she or he may want to know whether students have ever interned in Hollywood or at George Lucas' facility in the Bay Area.
- *Are graduates of the program currently working in the industry, and will the school allow you to talk to them?* When outstanding students come out of a particular program, the word gets around in the studio world, and they are more apt to hire other graduates from that program. If a school does not allow you to contact their graduates, common sense tells you that there may be problems in the program.
- *Are the instructors experienced in both analog and digital mediums? Is there both analog and digital equipment available for students to work on?*
- *Is the studio equipped to do post-production work, adding music to video?* This is a critical factor, because the market for video games nowadays is stronger than the market for albums.
- *Is the program accredited by the Accreditation Board for Engineering and Technology (ABET)?* They accredit both two- and four-year programs.

Vocational Programs

Many professional recording studios offer classes in order to supplement their income during times when the studio is not booked. There are also a number of vocational schools that have programs that last anywhere from one to a full four years. Some of these programs, like the one at Full Sail, offer a B.A., and others offer certificates of Associate Arts degrees. Private vocational programs are quite expensive, and the prospective student should consider many of the same factors listed earlier before enrolling in one. The advantage of vocational programs is that there are few if any general classes; all of the student's time is devoted to audio. This is also the disadvantage of these programs, because they do not provide the student with a general education. Sometimes engineers need psychological and communication skills that are more likely to be gained in a college's liberal arts program than in the studio.

OPERATING A STUDIO

There are many ways to approach operating a recording studio. Many studios are essentially home studios that are an outlet for the work of the owner. Somewhere along the line the studio owner needs some money, and tries to rent the studio, or the owner has friends who are impressed with her or his engineering skills, and they ask if they can rent the studio.

Because of the nature of ProTools recording, home studios can now survive comfortably in a basement or a garage, so they do not immediately require a huge expenditure of money. Small home studios can be used for demo projects for CDs that don't require large groups of musicians playing together or for jingles (see later in this chapter).

In order to open a medium-sized or large recording studio in a town, the first step is to do a market survey of what studios there are in the immediate area, and what part of the business they service. For example, there may be a studio specializing in jingles or one that deals mostly in recordings of local bands. Another facility may deal in postproduction work: the insertion of music into industrial or feature films and television commercials. This is not to say that a single studio can't do all or a combination of these things, but generally the studio will develop a specific client base that it services. Each of these categories of work has somewhat different requirements.

There are a variety of ways to finance a recording studio. Small home studios are often built simply by using the gear that an owner has already accumulated. Sometimes record companies will finance a medium-sized studio for an artist of some renown, because they may end up spending less money in a studio that is owned by the artist than they would have to spend renting a facility. It is also possible, although not necessarily likely, to get a business loan from a bank. Obtaining a loan involves creating a business plan, with the help of a lawyer and/or accountant, which has a reasonable projection of the income that the studio will earn. However, getting bank approval for such a loan is not likely unless the studio owner has a successful track record in the business.

If someone is planning to open a studio in a major city, the location of the studio may add greatly to the costs involved. Renting, leasing, or buying space in New York or Los Angeles can add a tremendous amount to the expense of starting the business. If the studio moves to a nearby location outside the city, costs may be reduced, but other problems will come into play. Studio musicians and artists may find it difficult to brave traffic conditions if the studio is twenty miles north or west of New York, or located not in Hollywood or nearby communities but in the San Fernando Valley. If the studio is designed to attract self-contained groups who rarely need additional musicians or singers, this is less of a problem.

Studios prize vintage gear, especially microphones. The studio will usually have a brochure that lists what sort of microphones they use, or the sort of recording equipment and outboard gear they have. Many even include a number of musical instruments that the studio may stock for use by clients. Larger studios usually lease, rather than purchase, equipment. Leases allow the studio to use equipment without owning it. The advantage to the studio is that it is not committed to owning equipment that may quickly become obsolete. The disadvantage is that the studio must pay a monthly fee for the lease, and if the studio has some slow months, coming up with the money is difficult. Many lease deals include a purchasing option.

Some of the large studios are now doing two levels of work: complete projects and another sort of work where they provide a service that a smaller studio cannot fulfill. For example, someone might record an album in a home studio, but mix it in a large studio. Another example would be that an artist wants a huge orchestra on one or two songs of an album, so he brings the basic track for those songs that were recorded in a small studio into the larger facility to do the additional recording.

Larger studios also may provide clients with special services, such as renting obscure vintage gear from other sources, when the client insists that obtaining such gear is essential. When a studio does this, they will generally mark up the price, so that they receive additional income for their trouble.

Once a studio is operating at or near capacity, it often will add another room to the facility. If the space leased is large enough, this represents a good source of additional revenue, because the increase in studio overhead is relatively small compared to the cost of opening a new facility.

Studio Rental

Studio rental rates can be influenced by a number of factors:

- *What is the competition charging in your geographic area?* If there is an abundance of studios that have roughly the same equipment that you offer, and they are charging very low rates, for example, $25 to $35 an hour, you may need to either relocate or expand the services that you offer
- *What special services does your competition provide?* If your studio was designed by an industry giant, like Tom Hidley, and you have a collection of rare and wonderful microphones, you may be able to charge more than your competitor is charging.
- *Card rate versus off-hours.* Most studios have an hourly rate that they will quote over the phone or even in brochures. However, it may also prove prudent for the studio to lower its rates if the client is willing to rent during off hours, or to book a large number of hours for a single project. If the studio allows this, they may insist on a deposit to protect themselves against frivolous cancellations.
- *Lock-outs.* In a **lock-out**, the studio guarantees that a particular artist has access to a studio for as many hours as they choose to work

without additional charges. For the studio this is a guarantee of a specific income for what may be a lengthy period of time, such as a month or more. For the client, it means that whenever she or he wishes to record, whether it be a finished track, a demo, or a sketch of a new song, an engineer will be available.

- *Track record.* If a studio is able to cite a number of recent successful records that they recorded, they can raise their rates above those charged by other competitive studios that cannot flash such credentials. Any studio that has been involved in recording gold and platinum records will have copies of these recordings on the wall in a very visible place.

Jingle Studio

A studio that specializes in commercials must have engineers that are extremely quick and professional. Most jingle sessions include an hour to cut instrumental tracks, and an hour or two to add the singers. This is not the world of contemporary record-making, where a producer might take three hours or more to get a good drum sound. One reason an engineer needs to work fast is that sometimes the air date for a commercial may be a few days after the completion of the recording project. Under these circumstances the advertising agency has already arranged what shows they want the commercial used on, and how many times the commercial will be aired. Another concern is that union musicians are paid a one hour minimum fee for playing on commercials. The current fee is $110, and after the first hour the payments increase by a third for each twenty-minute increment.

In addition to these factors, the engineer must have the ability to keep everyone happy. The singers may want a particular headphone mix, while the advertising agency might have someone in charge of the sessions who likes a disproportionate amount of bass. In New York, there are music houses that do nothing but create music for jingles. These companies employ people who are usually excellent musicians. They write the music for projects, and often write or co-write the lyrics with someone on the creative team of the advertising agency. In most cities, there are no music houses, so it is the ad agency people who are, in effect, in charge of the music.

Recording Project Studio and Post-Production Facilities

Studios that specialize in record projects tend to be booked at night, sometimes all night. Although jingle studios tend to be rather neat and innocuous, recording project studios are the ones that may have guest house facilities, spas, or even food available on a twenty-four-hour basis. These are high-end facilities. More typical urban studios have coffee and tea available, a recording room, and a control room.

The rates at recording studios vary widely. In recent years, the number of large and expensive rooms has diminished. The largest cities still require a few rooms with enough space for a large orchestra. Large studios often have three

Zen and the Art of Producing Jingles

Sometimes working with an ad agency person who isn't very knowledgeable about music can lead to some unusual difficulties. However, it always pays to keep your cool and go with the flow, as these two stories illustrate.

A vocalist-friend of mine was singing a solo on a national network commercial for a major product. Nothing was going right. The advertising agency producer kept asking for retakes and nothing the singer or the engineer did seemed to make him happy. The engineer was a person who had recorded literally thousands of jingles in his New York recording studio. Everything in the studio was designed for efficiency, so, for example, the drum set was already in place and the microphones were set up before the musicians got to the studio.

The engineer was scratching his head trying to figure out what was going wrong. Suddenly, he had a flash of insight. The singer was dancing along with his vocal performances. The engineer observed that the dancing was making the agency producer acutely uncomfortable. The engineer went into the recording room and said to the singer, "I'm going to say some pretty weird things. Just go along with what I say." The singer, hoping a solution was in sight, agreed.

The engineer then told the agency producer that he was going to try for a "special sound." He told the client that he was going to move the singer to the opposite end of the studio, literally out of sight of the producer. With a straight face, he informed the producer that a special sound would result from setting up a baffle around the singer, and that he knew the client would love the sound of the vocal bouncing off the baffle into the microphone.

Another take of the jingle was completed, one in which the agency producer did not witness the singer going through his gyrations. The producer raced into the studio, hugged the singer and said "That's the sound, the sound I've been looking for." The singer and engineer exchanged only the slightest of smiles.

Another story that illustrates the travails of working with ad agency producers is one that I experienced myself. I was playing banjo on a commercial for a major national product. The musical style of the jingle was intended to be bluegrass. The agency producer seemed to be happy with what I was playing, and he walked over to me and said, quite seriously, "Can you get a bluegrass-Latin-rock-Eddie Peabody feel on the next take?" Of course, these four styles are totally different: Eddie Peabody was a famous tenor banjo player of the 1920s–1930s who played tunes such as "Lady of Spain" and had nothing in common with bluegrass, Latin, or rock music! I immediately grasped that the agency rep had little if any knowledge of music, but I gave him a big smile, and said "No problem." Although I had no idea of what he actually wanted to hear, I was able to play something that satisfied him.

or four different rooms, set up for different sorts of projects. There may be a large recording room, a medium-size recording room for combos, a mixing room, and a small room suitable for voiceovers for commercials or for soloists.

Post-production rooms must have video playback equipment, so that sound can be recorded to picture. In many cities, there is not enough work to justify having a post-production facility.

Resort Studios

Another approach is to deliberately go well outside the metropolitan area, and to build a studio in a location like Woodstock, New York. That is, in fact, the location of Bearsville, a studio that goes back to the days of Bob Dylan's tenure in Woodstock in the late 1960s. Caribou Ranch, which the reader encountered in our discussion of the Denver scene (see Chapter 8), was located an hour and a half away from Denver in the mountains. It had quite a run in the 1970s, when such artists as Elton John, Chicago, and the Beach Boys recorded albums there. James Guercio, the owner of the studio, was the producer and manager of the band Chicago at that time, so he had a built-in client base for the studio.

Other studios followed this sort of resort concept, including one in Montreux, Switzerland. Chris Blackwell, founder of Island Records, built a studio in the Bahamas. Resort studios offer artists accommodations, food, and a relaxing atmosphere where clients can avoid the pressures of everyday life.

One problem with the resort environment is that the owner is obligated to find a reliable and competent audio repair technician, because of the studio's isolation from any urban center. This may prove to be difficult, because these technicians do not tend to be available in remote locations. This adds to the expense of running the studio.

Mixing and Mastering Studios

Certain engineers and studios have a reputation as being specialists in mixing or remixing records. George Massenberg is known as a remix specialist, to the point where he now rarely records basic tracks.

Mixing board at a modern recording studio. Photo: Andy Crawford, courtesy Dorling Kindersley Media Library.

Mastering is the process that occurs at the end of recording an album, where a stereo master is made to send off to the CD duplicator. Some studios do mastering, but in the major recording centers there are certain studios that specialize in mastering to the exclusion of other recording services. Mastering is a delicate process, because the engineer is now taking a final **mix**, and tweaking it. If the bass recorded on the left channel is boosted, for example, all of the bass frequencies on that channel will also be louder. This could include a bass trombone, the bass register of the guitar, and so on. Certain mastering engineers specialize in giving records more "punch," accentuating the rhythm of a song to make it sound brighter and more dynamic on the radio. In the mastering process, the engineer will also make sure that there are no glaring volume differences when the listener goes from one cut of the album to the next tune.

Mastering engineers do not usually mix records or record basic tracks. Because mastering studios generally do not do recording, they can be located in a relatively small space. Some mastering studios are located way outside the mainstream of the music industry. Air Show is a mastering studio that has two facilities, one in Springfield, Virginia, and the other in Boulder, Colorado. Gateway is another mastering studio with an outstanding reputation, and it is located in Portland, Maine. Because mastering does not involve the use of musicians or arrangers, it is quite feasible to do this work in these locations. Air Show has mastered a number of reissue projects, which may involve many challenges if the original recording was done years ago. Mastering studios may charge hourly rates, or set a rate for an album. An album may cost as such as $3,000 to master at the top mastering studios.

ENGINEERING AS A CAREER

No one begins a career as a chief engineer at a major studio. Instead, after graduating from being a "tea boy" or intern, usually the next step up the ladder is to serve as a second engineer. The larger studios employ second engineers to assist the engineer during the recording process. There are

Library Music

Library music is used for commercials, radio station IDs, and low-budget movies. Some studios or engineers develop sound libraries that they in effect rent to producers in these mediums. The income per use is small, but sometimes the same piece of music used as a bank commercial in Dallas is running for a car dealer in Raleigh, North Carolina. The local user or the studio simply inserts different copy that describes the service offered in the jingle or the name of the local radio station. Often these sound libraries have CDs of their offerings, broken down by moods, tempos and musical styles. Some recording studios carry a number of sound libraries, and insert the appropriate piece according to the desire of the client.

many instances in which second engineers got their big break when an engineer became ill, or was simply too busy to do a particular project. If the recording goes well, the second engineer not only has found a client, but word will get around at the studio and even at competing facilities. Most engineers are paid by the hour. Some of the larger facilities employ engineers as full-time employees, but others use them on a freelance basis, employing them as independent contractors.

The advantage of being on staff is that the engineer will have the security of earning a weekly wage and probably enjoy benefits such as health insurance. The disadvantage of being on staff is that the engineer cannot pick and choose projects, but must accept any assignment. This could include jingles, bands that have difficulty tuning their instruments, singers who don't sing in tune, or simply music that is boring.

For the most part, engineers work for flat fees and do not receive any royalties. Some of the biggest names in engineering *do* receive a point or more on records that they work on. The best-known remix engineers may also receive a small royalty on the sales of a record. When an engineer owns part or all of the studio, she or he enjoys the profits of the business, or shares its losses, as the proprietor of any business does.

Engineers can expect to work long and unpredictable hours, and they have to have or cultivate enormous patience to deal with the egos and insecurities of recording artists, producers, and record company executive producers.

Engineers who work on films experience a varied musical palette because part of the film may be recorded with a massive orchestra, another section might be an oboe solo, and there may be recordings or re-recordings of hit songs that have to be inserted into the film. It is a complex task, because the engineer must balance not only the musical score, but the dialogue, and sound effects. The final mix is very time-consuming and difficult, and in this instance the engineer must balance the varied wishes of the composer, the film's music supervisor, the director, and even the producer of the film.

Engineers and Record Production

Although engineers play a vital role in the recording process, by and large it is the record producer and/or the artist who makes the final decisions about what is going to go on the recording. Some engineers become frustrated at their limited role in the decision-making process, and others become disenchanted because they receive no royalties or only a small royalty for their endless hours of work. Because of both of these factors, many engineers have opted to move into record production

Other Engineering Careers

Audio engineers can pursue a number of other career opportunities. Celeste Baine's book *The Musical Engineer: A Music Enthusiast's Guide to Careers*

Making a Living as an Engineer

For an engineer working in a mid-sized city, it takes a lot of different jobs—and some creative juggling—to make a good living—but it can be done. Dean Baskerville is an audio engineer with a degree in music. Dean lives in Portland, Oregon, and has a home studio in his basement. The studio is well-suited for working with singer-songwriters who record all or most of their own musical parts. There is enough space for overdubbing one or two other musicians or singers, but not much more than that.

Dean Baskerville. Photo courtesy Dean Baskerville.

Dean is also a freelance engineer who works at two of the better-equipped studios in town. One of these studios is Kung Fu Bakery, owned by a producer and guitarist named Tim Ellis. The other is Dead Aunt Thelma's. Thelma's is a studio tucked into a residential district that is owned by the Catholic church. The name comes from its earlier owners, who were basically hippie songwriters. Thelma's does many church choral projects, and also worship music for churches, although Kung Fu does quite a few alternative rock records. Both of these studios employ full-time engineers, and Dean is used to doing projects that they are unable or unwilling to do. He also uses their rooms when he is doing a project that is too big to fit into his own facility.

Recently, Dean has begun to supplement his income by teaching audio part-time at Mount Hood Community College. He enjoys teaching, and finds it a good complement to his everyday work.

By building a client base for his own studio and mixing in other engineering work and teaching, Dean has been able to make a good living doing something he loves.

in Engineering and Technology lists careers in recording audio games, post-production work for film and television, corporate audio work, live sound, and designing sound equipment among the other career paths for audio engineers.

SESSION MUSICIANS

Session musicians and singers play or sing on recordings issued under other people's names. They also sing on commercials, and do back-up work on movies. The highest level session people earn lucrative incomes, especially those who sing on national commercials recorded under union contracts.

In the major music business centers, session players and singers are hired by contractors. Jingles in these cities are usually produced by independent jingle houses who keep lists of singers and musicians that they prefer to use.

Because so many country music stars record songs written by songwriters, rather than by artists, session singers in Nashville often break into this field by recording demos of songs.

In medium-sized cities outside the major music markets, there are usually a small number of core musicians who play or sing on recording sessions. Very few musicians or singers can make a full-time living doing session work outside the major music business centers. Session musicians in these cities generally fill out their schedules through live performances, operating recording studios, or teaching music.

Session musicians and singers must be flexible and willing to modify their music to meet the needs of a particular project. They must be reliable and focused, and the more instruments and musical styles that they have mastered, the broader are their work opportunities. Woodwind players, for example, are expected to play clarinet, saxophone, and flute. If a musician only plays one of these instruments, she may still be able to do some session work, but she will not be hired for sessions that require the musician to play multiple instruments. The most in-demand musicians are comfortable either reading music at sight, or improvising parts on demand of a producer.

During the 1960s and through the 1980s there were a significant number of musicians doing session work in the major music business centers. This number has been substantially reduced because samplers, synthesizers and drum machines have replaced many of the musicians who did this work. New York has an active theater business, and many of the theaters have union agreements that require the use of an orchestra. Consequently some of the New York session players are apt to be found working in Broadway shows.

Session work is often accessed by recommendations from people who are actively doing session work. Sometimes a buzz will develop around a particular musician who is actively working in clubs, and that can result in a musician getting some calls to do recording sessions. Even in the largest cities word of mouth plays a significant role in breaking into studio work. There are many stories of musicians who broke into session work because someone became ill or simply did not show up on a recording session.

RECORD PRODUCTION

The word **producer** does not really define what a record producer does. In the movie industry, a producer is responsible for arranging the financing of a film, and generally has limited creative input. It is the film's director who makes most of the creative decisions, although when a film is not going well, it is usually the producer who fires the director. In other words, the producer has some overall control of movie projects, but it is the director who quarterbacks the film, working with the actors and actresses, the cinematographer, and the composer and music supervisor.

It is best to think of the record producer as being the director of the project. And in a process parallel to the role of the director of a movie, problems may surface on a recording project. Sometimes the record producer and the artist don't see eye to eye, sometimes the artist's manager doesn't feel as though the project is going well, and sometimes the record company's A&R representative feels that the record is not going in the right direction. In this situation, it is usually the A&R person who will negotiate some sort of settlement that involves removing the record producer from the project.

Backgrounds of Record Producers

There is no single way to break into record production. Various successful record producers have come from:

- *Engineering.* Obviously, a producer-engineer is ideally equipped to deal with the recording process.
- *Music arranger.* A music arranger may be a terrific producer for an artist who is going to be backed by a large orchestra.
- *Studio musician.* A studio musician should have an excellent grasp of contemporary sounds and is apt to know many excellent players.
- *Hit songwriter.* If the artist does not write songs or only writes lyrics or music, a superb songwriter may be just the ticket to put the artist over the top. Producers often co-write songs with artists.
- *Former or current artist.* An artist who has had a successful career and logged many hours in recording studios may be an ideal candidate for producing a particular artist.
- *Knowledgeable music fan.* Some producers have no formal background in music or in engineering, yet they seem to have a great feel for what the public wants to hear.
- *Master psychologist.* Some artists need encouragement, some require patience, and others may work best when they are placed under pressure. The psychologist is a producer who has figured out how to work with a particular artist.
- *Something Undefinable.* There are some producers that have the magic touch, even though no one can figure out exactly what that touch is. Such a producer picks the right songs and the right musicians and engineer, finds an arranger perfectly suited for a project, and always makes the correct decisions. One book about record producers refers to this type of producer as Merlin the Magician.

BREAKING IN

Anyone who has a home studio has the potential of breaking into record production. As the cost of recording equipment has come way down, learning how to produce recordings is more of a function of a producer's willingness to devote time to a project, as opposed to raising the money to do so.

For those who don't have a home studio, or access to one, college recording studios are an ideal training ground to start a career in production. Often local artists love the idea of getting free studio time, in the hopes of getting a quality demo that they can use to get club bookings, a manager, or a record deal. The only common problem that comes up working in a college studio is that, because the needs of many students have to be met, the producer will not be allowed to use an unlimited amount of studio time. Some of this time pressure can be alleviated, as discussed earlier, by using the studio during hours that students are less eager to work. Typically, this time would be early morning sessions. Unfortunately, if you are recording a working band, they may not be willing or able to work in the morning.

WHAT PRODUCERS DO

Now the reader knows where record producers come from. But what do they actually do? The first thing they do is to work with artists in pre-production. The producer and the artist get together and the artist runs through his repertoire. The producer makes suggestions about arranging the songs, about lyrics, melodies, or "**hooks.**" Hooks are recurring musical and lyrical figures that hook the listener into the song. The producer talks to each musician and singer about what he or she is playing or singing. The producer looks at such matters as the structure of the song, its length, whether or not it highlights the sound of the band, whether the song was written in the best key for the singer, and so on.

In the process of pre-production, it usually becomes apparent whether the artist and the producer are going to be able to work together. Of course, all parties are on their best behavior, so that an amiable initial meeting is not a guarantee that everything will go well, but if there is immediate conflict between the parties, it is indicative of what lies ahead.

Assuming that their initial meeting was fruitful, the producer and act will discuss a number of issues:

- *When will the recording occur?* The factors involved in this decision include the availability of the producer, who may have other projects, the question of whether the artist has enough songs for a complete album, and the schedule of the band. If the band is about to go on a six-month foreign tour, then obviously this will delay the project. Another factor is the record company's scheduling process. They may have a specific goal in mind, in terms of when the last album came out, when the band is touring, and other artists' albums on the label that are already on the release schedule.
- *In what city will the album be recorded? At what studio and with what engineer?* The choice of where the recording will take place is influenced by internal band decisions. Does the band want to record in their hometown? Is there a competent studio there? Or would the band prefer to leave town to record, so as to avoid any distractions during the recording? How willing is the producer to disrupt his life in order to meet the wishes of the band? If the band elects to record out of town, will the record company support this decision, and will it pay for accommodations for the band with a per-diem allowance for food?

These issues involve the relative power positions of the various parties. If the producer is a superstar, with many projects waiting in the wings, then the band will have to accommodate to her or his schedule. By contrast, if it is the artist who is a superstar and the producer has a lesser stature, the producer is the one who must accede to the artist's wishes.

In the Studio

Once the recording starts, the producer has blocked out a certain amount of time for the act to record the basic tracks and vocals. This is particularly important if the band has to go on the road. Estimating how long it will take to record an album is a voyage into the unknown, particularly if the producer and the act have never worked together before. If the producer or members of the band are perfectionists, the only certainty is that the album will take longer than anyone anticipated. (Guns N' Roses' 2008 album, *Chinese Democracy*, is the poster child for perfectionism: It took fourteen years to complete.)

The producer's first step in making the recording is usually to record the basic rhythm tracks, and then have the lead singer do a "dummy vocal," which the band can follow while they add parts. A dummy vocal is simply a rough vocal performance that is meant to keep the band mindful of the song's lyrics and how the singer will eventually perform the song. There have been many instances where a dummy vocal has proved so good, that it is used in the final version of the song.

STUDIO PSYCHOLOGY   As the recording evolves, many stressful situations will occupy the producer. They can involve musical disputes within the band, personal situations affecting the mood of the artists, and/or negative input from the lead singer's girlfriend or boyfriend, the record company representative, or hangers-on at the studio, and so forth. If various members of the band write songs, musical disputes often evolve around the question of which songs are going to be recorded. The producer must be careful not to appear to favor one band member over another, but it is a delicate issue, because the truth is that some band members are likely to be better at writing songs than other members are.

It is the role of the producer to keep things positive and enthusiastic, but just as is the case with a football coach, there is more than one way to motivate a band. Some artists relate to praise, some to creative suggestions, and some even do well when the coach gets angry. This is where the psychological aspect of production comes to the fore. The producer needs to know and understand the act, and to work accordingly.

Some of the issues that are apt to come up in the studio include limiting the number of visitors and hangers-on allowed to come to the sessions and the availability of drugs and alcohol. Some artists bring unfinished songs into the studio, and this can waste a substantial amount of time and energy, while the song is being completed and the studio logs up more billable hours.

LOCKOUTS When a producer anticipates the need for a long recording schedule, he or she may choose to rent a studio on a lockout basis, where for a certain number of weeks or months the band can do whatever they wish in the studio, but no other clients may use it. There are producers who own their own studio, such as Sylvia Massy Shivy, who has a facility in northern California that also offers accommodations for visiting artists. This can be a good deal for the record company and the artist, by minimizing expenses, and it also brings cash flow into the studio.

The Mix

When the album is completed in rough form, the multitrack master must be mixed down to two tracks. Artists' attitudes about the mix vary:

- *Some artists want to be present at every mix session.* This sort of artist simply wants total creative control over the recording process.
- *Some bands will appoint one or two members to be present at the mix.* In this example, the band realizes that these particular people have a better fix on the overall sound of the band than other band members do. Sometimes it is simply a matter of one band member having the patience and ability to concentrate. Frequently everyone in the band knows that a particular individual is capable of long hours of sustained concentration and listening.
- *The producer mixes alone, but gives one or more members of the band a CD to approve or modify.* When a band goes on the road, this is the only practical solution. The band can then instruct the engineer about a specific passage of a song, or the sound of a particular instrument that does not work for them.

When reissue projects are undertaken, often the band and even the original producer has no input into the remix. There is also an audiophile's vogue for remixing CDs in surround sound. In such cases, the sound is mixed for home theater setups that utilize five speakers. Certain engineers have made a specialty of doing surround sound, but so far the market has not proved to be large for this format.

COMPOSITE VOCALS AND PITCH CORRECTION One of the most time-consuming aspects of the mix is the combining of multiple vocal tracks to produce a single performance. This is called creating a **composite vocal**, because different bits of many performances are put together to form the finished product. I have witnessed a session where the producer, the engineer, and the artist each came to the mix with a complete lyric marked, noting which vocal track had the best first line of a verse, the best last line of a chorus, and so on. This becomes an extremely time-consuming task, while the various parties argue about which track has the most convincing performance of a particular phrase or line. It is easy to go for perfection rather than the sort

Strawberry Fields Forever

John Lennon recorded "Strawberry Fields Forever" in two different versions. When he heard the performances, he liked aspects of both vocals, and couldn't decide which one was better. He discussed the problem with producer George Martin, who suggested that they combine the two performances. The only problem was that one version was in a different key than the other! Martin ingeniously sped up the lower-pitched version to make it "match" the second take. The combined vocal had the surreal quality that Lennon was seeking.

of gripping performance that will capture the attention of the non-musician listener.

One of the many modern studio tools is **pitch correction**, a piece of gear that will correct the pitch of an out-of tune singer. Like composite vocals, pitch correction can correct a mildly flawed performance, or it can create endless drudgery for the engineer and producer, attempting to make a poor singer into an acceptable one.

PRODUCTION STYLES

The career of an average record producer is not a lengthy one. Many producers become locked into using a particular sound and after a certain period of time that sound becomes dated. Some producers' records always have identifiable sounds that over a long period of time may become boring to the public.

The choice of a producer may depend on whether the artist buys into that producer's consistent sound, or whether the artist prefers to work with a producer who builds the sound around the project, as opposed to forcing the artist into the producer's sound.

The Wall of Sound

Among the most famous producers of early rock was boy genius Phil Spector, who created the so-called Wall of Sound. Rather than using a simple accompaniment of guitar-bass-and drums, Spector would employ armies of musicians and vocalists, to give his recordings a thick, almost symphonic texture. The "artists" were secondary to the production, so that Spector's records all had a consistent sound and style. This worked well for the nearly interchangeable girl groups of the early 1960s, but became a problem as Spector branched out into other styles. This became most apparent when Spector worked with the Canadian poet-songwriter Leonard Cohen on Cohen's 1977 album *Death of a Lady's Man*. Spector's grandiose style did not fit well with Cohen's understated vocals and deeply personal songs.

Musical Issues

Producers utilize very different musical methods in producing an act. Some have a very definite and identifiable sound that they apply to all artists. Phil Spector, one of the pioneering rock-and-roll producers, used tremendous doses of echo and gangs of rhythm instruments doubling parts in unison to create his famous Wall of Sound. The feeling of déjà-vu that you sometimes get from listening to a record is not only the result of the producer's style but also his choice of musicians.

During the 1960s and 1970s, it seemed as though the so-called wrecking crew played on all of the Los Angeles rock sessions. The wrecking crew was a stable of studio musicians who worked on virtually every pop session of the day. For example, The Mamas and The Papas' records used almost the exact same musicians who played on the records made by the Fifth Dimension. Hal Blaine's ubiquitous tomtom sound, where he would sweep across a whole series of tomtoms became *the sound* of West Coast drumming, no matter who produced the record.

Other producers pride themselves on *not* having an identifiable sound. Instead, they try to use a sound they feel will complement the artist, rather than one that is identified with them as producers. Other producers take a middle position. The consumer cannot always identify their work, but they may expect to hear a particular instrumental sound, like a slide guitar, on many of their records.

When an artist feels that they have been subordinated to the producer's sound, they may go along with this for a time, but eventually they will rebel and turn to a different producer. Some producers become embittered when this occurs, feeling that they were responsible for the artist's success. There are also instances in which the artist may try a new producer and end up returning to the original one.

There have also been instances in which an artist chooses a particular producer because of the work that he or she made with a famous artist on a very successful record. The artist subsequently may discover that the sound of that record came mostly from the work of an engineer, coupled with the artist having some production skills. There are also occasions where producers accept a job working with an artist strictly because they need the paycheck, not because they believe in the artist. This may become apparent when the producer spends little time on pre-production, constantly ignores the artist's wishes, and makes disparaging remarks about some members of the artist's band. Often producers would rather work with studio musicians that they have worked with before, than to deal with an artist's band. The artist will have to make the decision as to whether the chances of increased success are worth the risk of alienating his band.

Even successful artists can face this dilemma. If they choose to work with a new producer, she or he may pressure them to use a different set of musicians, using the argument that "you hired me because you said you wanted a different sound." Experienced studio musicians can quickly come up with catchy instrumental hooks, and they rarely make musical mistakes. The artist's band members may find themselves in the embarrassing position of having to learn the licks that the studio musicians created, because that is what the consumer who has bought the record expects to hear.

Artists Producing Themselves

It is quite common for actors to want to move into the directing role. Similarly, recording artists often develop the desire to produce their own records. This gives them more control over their own project, saves the additional expense of paying a producer, and can also be something of an ego trip, giving the artist another credit on the album. It also simplifies any possible scheduling conflicts with the producer. All the artist needs to do is to find a studio and an engineer that are available during the time that the artist chooses to record.

The downside of artists producing their own work is that it is often difficult for them to make objective decisions. For example, the artist may have written a truly heartfelt tune about a broken romance, which also happens to be a mediocre song. Although an outsider might be able to say that the song is not good, the artist is less likely to be able to step back and evaluate the song apart from the situation itself. Another problem in self-production is that the artist is singing a song and at the same time trying to judge whether that particular performance is coming off. Of course, that decision can be deferred to the playback of the song, but this may result in the artist spending undue amounts of time in the studio. Artist-producers may not be good at working with musicians or at sensing the right time to take a break or the right time to go for one more take before the break. These are subtle decisions that cannot be planned or anticipated.

When self-production occurs, the artist often relies heavily on the engineer for such matters as stopping a take where the instruments are out of tune. The engineer in turn may be unhappy, because he feels as though he was not hired to produce the album, but to operate the recording console. Some artists deal with this situation by giving the engineer co-production credits, and thereby getting a share of the royalties on the album, if it sells well.

There are other reasons for co-production situations as well. Imagine that an experienced country artist wants to record a Mexican-flavored album but feels that he doesn't know enough about Mexican music. He or she may hire a producer to co-produce in order to get that level of input and involvement from someone who is more knowledgeable about that musical style. There are also production teams, such as Jimmy Jam and Terry Lewis, who split the responsibilities of producing a project. As long as the team understands their separate roles and the situation does not degenerate into control or ego problems, a production team can work well together.

Taking Flyte: Jimmy Jam and Terry Lewis

Jimmy Jam and Terry Lewis are perhaps the most successful R&B producers of the last twenty-five years, responsible for "over 100 albums that have exceeded gold, platinum, and multi-platinum status, an incredible 15 No. 1 pop hits and 25 No. 1 R&B chart toppers, [and] multiple Grammy Awards," according to their Web site.

The duo got their start playing in Prince's backup band, The Time. Ironically, they were fired by Prince when they took a break from an early 1980s tour to produce a record for Atlanta's S.O.S. Band. The duo was snowed in and unable to rejoin the tour on time, so Prince dismissed them. In 1986, the producers had their first major success collaborating with Janet Jackson, an artist whom they have continued to work with over the following decades. They founded their own Flyte Tyme studio, record label, and music publishing businesses to capitalize on their success.

Lewis notes that—unlike other R&B and hip-hop producers—they've been able to adjust as musical styles change. He attributes this to their roots as working musicians: "When we first started out, we had to play everything just to get work. To market yourself as a musician and get paid, you had to have flexibility. You can't do the same thing with everyone. I think, if anything, that has been the mainstay of our longevity, the fact we can adjust as music has evolved and changed . . ."

Producers Functioning as Engineers

Some producers like to do the engineering on their sessions as well. Others opt to have someone else operate the board, because they want to concentrate on the performances, rather than on the technical aspects of the recording. Producers who have an engineering background will certainly want to be involved in some of the technical aspects of the recording, such as the mix or microphone placement, but in many situations they may defer to the engineer. Similarly, producers who are excellent arrangers will want some input into the musical arrangements on an album, even if they are not the one writing the charts.

HIP-HOP PRODUCERS

Hip-hop producers often combine the functions of producer, engineer, and arranger. They are especially aware of the beats on a particular tune. This is one of the crucial aspects of hip-hop. The producer may also perform on the recording. A talented rapper/producer will often appear alongside the featured artist, particularly when that artist is first starting out. In this way, the producer introduces the new artist to his or her already established fan base.

In hip-hop, artists seem to move seamlessly between roles as producers, songwriters, beat specialists, and engineers. Kanye West might be a producer on one album, the artist on another. Although at times artists have turned to production roles, hip-hop is different in that a number of the producers continue to have careers as artists while they produce other artists, run their own labels, and so on. There is no real precedent for this, although in the past certain individuals, such as Quincy Jones and the late Curtis Mayfield, have performed multiple roles simultaneously. Mayfield was a singer, songwriter, producer, guitarist, arranger, and composed movie scores. Jones has been a band leader, arranger, A&R executive, record label owner, producer, composer of multiple movie and television scores, and an artist.

A&R (ARTIST AND REPERTOIRE)

From the inception of the record business through the mid-1950s, record producers were record company employees. Known as **A&R (artist and repertoire)** men, they were expected to find and sign talent and to produce their records. Most of the pop recording sessions of the pre-rock area used written musical arrangements. The producer's role was to find songs for artists, hire an engineer, and go into the company's recording studio to record the songs. Remember, most artists did not write their own songs in the era before rock and roll.

Some labels have continued to hire producers for their A&R staff. For example, David Foster, who is a musician, arranger and producer, has been a staff producer for Warner Brothers for years. Foster's credits include producing Barbra Streisand, Toni Braxton, Celine Dion, and Chicago, as well as numerous other artists. Rob Cavallo has also worked as a staff producer at Warner Brothers. In addition to producing Green Day, his credits include the Goo Goo Dolls, Chris Isaak, and Jewel. When producers are on staff for a label, they also get some sort of royalty participation for their productions, sometimes as royalty percentages, and other times as bonuses for successful

The Rise of the Independent Producer

During the early 1950s, Jerry Leiber and Mike Stoller began to achieve success as songwriters. The two Los Angeles writers were barely out of their teens. By the mid-1950s, they moved to New York and were producing records for Atlantic. This was a unique arrangement, because they were not employees of Atlantic but freelance producers who received royalties for the records that they produced. They were also permitted to produce recordings for other labels.

Leiber and Stoller were enormously successful, producing The Coasters, The Drifters, and many other acts. Their deal with Atlantic changed the financial arrangements between record companies and producers. Soon dozens of independent producers hung out their shingles, and because the older record company producers had little experience with rock and roll, staff A&R functions became more oriented towards discovering artists, and helping the artists find appropriate producers. As more of the new artists began to write songs, the job of finding songs became much less important to the role of an A&R person.

sales years. Nonetheless, most music produced today is done by independent producers, not staff producers. As you will recall from our discussions
about the Nashville scene (see Chapter 8), this is somewhat less true in country music, where a number of record executives like Tony Brown, Tim
Dubois, and Paul Worley are perfectly capable of producing artists as well
as of signing them.

Other Production Duties

Producers are responsible for reporting recording sessions to the musician's
union, and ensuring that all checks are paid within several weeks of the
actual recording date. Failure to report sessions causes the record label to be
subject to financial penalties.

Producers are supposed to work within specific recording budgets. If
they become aware that the money budgeted is not sufficient to complete the
project, they must go to the label to ask for more money. The record company
may elect to spend the money, or it may choose to shelve the project or
replace the producer. It is also the duty of the A&R person to supervise the
recording fund. The two should be working closely together to make sure
that the project is coming in under the amount budgeted.

Some producers own their own recording facilities. There is nothing
wrong with this arrangement, unless the producer is over-billing the hours
spent, or if the act would really prefer to record elsewhere, but the producer
refuses to do so.

PRODUCER COMPENSATION

Producer's royalties are typically 2 to 3 percent of the retail selling price of
records, although superstar producers may get as much as 5 percent.
Producers also get advances for their work. Because albums take months or
even years to produce, a producer will insist on these advances.

Producer royalties differ from artist royalties in an odd way. The artist
only gets royalties on records sold *after* a record has finally recouped its
costs. However, producers get royalties from the first record sold, minus
whatever sum they got as an advance. Consequently producers can make
enormous amounts of money from multi-platinum selling records. For
example, imagine a record that sells two million copies. If the producer gets
a 3 percent royalty, and for simplicity's sake, we determine that this amounts
to 50 cents an album, and he got an advance of $50,000, his royalty is one mil-
lion dollars, minus the advance, or $950,000 ($1,000,000 – $50,000)

Other Monetary Issues

If the label produces an artist's greatest hits album and a producer is represented on it by six of twelve songs, he or she will be paid a proportional
royalty for those six songs. If his royalty was 3 percent of the retail price, the
royalty will now be half of that, or 1.5 percent.

Quite a few contemporary records are produced by a number of producers working independently. There might be, for example, six producers, each doing two songs, or even more producers than that on a single project. Under these circumstances, producers might seek a most favored nation clause, to make sure they are not being paid less money than the others working on the project (see Chapter 5). There are a handful of producers, such as The Neptunes, who reportedly receive $100,000 for producing a single track of an album. Obviously, this situation can only prevail while these producers continue to produce multiple hits.

The average career of a record producer is about five years. Musical styles change, new producers come in with new sounds, the technology changes, and soon the young guns turn into the old guard. When this occurs, some producers move into other industry roles such as music supervisors for film or executives of record companies.

PRODUCERS AND GENDER AND RACE DISCRIMINATION

For years, virtually no women functioned as record producers. Ethel Gabriel worked in A&R at RCA from the mid-1940s until 1984, after a career as a trombone player and bandleader. She produced Perry Como, the Living Strings, and Living Guitars, and also produced artists in Nashville, during a forty-year career at RCA, resulting in fifteen gold records. Ethel also produced the first disco record. However, Ethel was virtually a solo act as a woman producer for years. Helen Keane, Bill Evans's manager, did produce his records. It is currently more common for women to produce records. Some of these producers include Linda Perry, Tina Clark, Missy Elliott, and Sylvia Massy Shivy. Missy is a multitalented writer, artist, and producer, and Sylvia is one of the few women who have successfully produced hard rock acts.

Producers are in a position of control and power in the recording studio environment, and men do not always respond positively to having women in charge. Similarly, there is a shortage of top female executives in music publishing and record labels. Despite this, women such as Sylvia Rhone, Julie Greenwald, Florence Greenberg, Estelle Axton, Sylvia Robinson, and Judy Gerson have been able to forge distinguished careers as record company and music publishing executives.

Some female artists have demonstrated their production abilities by producing their own records. Among this group are Sheryl Crow, Lauryn Hill, and Joni Mitchell. However, because these producer-artists do not work with other artists, it is difficult to classify them, strictly speaking, as record producers.

For years, very few black record executives worked with white artists. Quincy Jones was one of the first black producers who multitasked, working on white rock and roll records as well as R&B and jazz records. King Records executive Henry Glover was another pioneer, working with both country and R&B artists in the 1950s. Tom Wilson produced Bob Dylan and Simon and Garfunkel records in the 1960s, but black producers almost invariably were consigned to producing black music. The industry has had no such compunctions about white producers producing black musical artists. As world music styles proliferate, hopefully this practice will evaporate.

PRODUCER MANAGERS

There are a handful of personal managers who represent record producers; they are called **producer managers**. They pitch producers for projects and negotiate fees and royalty percentages. They may work with the producer to get lower-cost studio time. On the positive side, a producer manager may obtain work for a client from a record company when another client is unable or unwilling to do a project. On the negative side, the producer may lose a project because the record company becomes enchanted with a higher profile producer that the manager also represents.

A producer manager is not apt to be interested in a young producer who has no track record of success. A manager may prove useful to a producer at the midpoint of a career, or for a high profile producer who simply doesn't enjoy negotiating deal points with a record company.

SIGNING A RECORD DEAL WITH A PRODUCER

Some producers try to sign an act directly. They will then attempt to negotiate a deal with a record label. The act is then under contract not to the label, but to the producer. If the act is comparatively unknown, and the producer is a prestigious one, this is not necessarily a bad idea. The act must understand, however, that it is not under contract to a label. If the label likes the act but not the producer, the band may never know that this has occurred. If they do know, they can't do anything about it, unless they are willing to buy off the producer. Recall the story of Bruce Springsteen and his travails with manager-producer Mike Appel (see Chapter 4).

If the producer also wants to publish the band's music and to manage the band, the act should be very careful. How strongly will a manager represent an act in negotiating with a producer, if the producer is also its manager? And remember, publishing is an important source of a band's income. If the act needs money and is able to retain its publishing, it can sell off half or all of its publishing rights to a music publishing company (see Chapter 7).

Historically, a few record companies, especially Motown and more recently Sanctuary, have tried to tie up all of the artist's revenue sources, including music publishing, management, and production. This is clearly more advantageous for the record company's interests than for the artist's. The so-called 360 deals offered by record labels recently are reviving this practice (see Chapter 3).

Terms to Know

A&R (artist and
  repertoire) *249*
A-DAT (digital audio
  tape) *229*
Analog *229*
Composite vocal *244*

Hook *242*
Library music *237*
Lock-out *233*
Mastering *237*
Mix *237*
Overdubbing *228*

Pitch correction *245*
ProTools *229*
Producer *240*
Producer manager *252*
Session musician *239*
Track *228*

For Class Discussion

1. What recording studios exist in your hometown? How many are home studios, how many are professional operations?
2. Have you ever recorded in a studio outside your home or college? If so, how did that process differ from your previous recording experiences?
3. Can you cite an example of music that you heard on a commercial that you think was library music, rather than original music? Why do you think so?
4. Is anyone that you know making a living as a freelance record producer?
5. Have any locally produced records enjoyed national exposure and sales?
6. If there are major acts in your hometown, do they record locally?
7. What do you think is the primary role of a record producer?
8. Of the various styles of record producers discussed in this chapter, what would you look for if you were an artist seeking a producer?

CHAPTER 15

Concert Promotion

THE CONCERT PROMOTION BUSINESS

There was a time when most large cities had a concert promoter who presented concerts by touring acts. Some cities even had several concert promoters. When there were multiple promoters, they specialized in different musical genres. Over the years, however, national companies took over the local promoters or put them out of business by grabbing the top acts. Today, the two leading promoters are **Live Nation**, formerly a division of Clear Channel (a large radio network), and **AEG (Anschutz Entertainment Group)**. Not only do these companies promote concerts, they also own venues. According to *This Business of Promotion and Touring,* in 2006, Live Nation owned, operated, or had booking rights to 153 venues throughout the world and produced over 28,000 events a year. The December 20, 2008, issue of *Billboard* reported that Live Nation produced 9,237 shows in 2008, producing nearly $2 billion in ticket sales. AEG reported 2,324 shows, with over $1 billion in grosses. The smaller groups, including C3 Presents, Nederlander, and Beaver generated $53, $39, and $30 million, respectively.

It is difficult to compete with the two giants for the top acts, because they can offer an artist a multiple-city tour in major venues. It is clearly easier for a manager or a booking agent to make a single deal that will essentially secure an entire tour. Another advantage of dealing with one entity is that the promotion company can allocate their promotional dollars to any city or cities where ticket sales are slow, while reducing advertising in markets where sales are going well. A local promoter may lack the advertising budget to stimulate ticket sales for a concert that is in financial trouble.

One of the reasons that promoting concerts has become such a centralized business is that there are more and more large arena venues in existence. This development has occurred for a number of reasons. Sound systems have become infinitely more powerful, and can now handle virtually any size locale. There are a handful of superstar acts that gross huge amounts of money, year after year. Acts like the Rolling Stones, U2, Bruce Springsteen, Madonna, and The Eagles seem capable of selling out every large venue throughout the world, even at very high ticket prices. These acts don't tour on a regular basis, but in effect tour enough to keep their fans willing to pay high ticket fees. Many of the groups mentioned above are getting on in years. Of the major touring acts, only the Dave Matthews Band is a relatively young group. Perhaps only older wealthy professionals are able and willing to spend $100 and up for concert tickets. The younger acts draw younger people who don't have that kind of discretionary income.

Most local promoters have been relegated to working in niche music areas that don't interest the two major promoters because there simply isn't enough income that can be generated from the promotion of niche acts. By contrast, a local promoter knows what musical styles are popular in the area, knows what bands are apt to draw a decent audience, and is often willing to promote a show without the possibility of a blockbuster return on investment.

In several cities, local promoters have sued Live Nation, alleging that they used illegal practices to stifle competition. A number of these suits seem to have been settled before they came to trial, and the aggrieved party is not allowed to discuss the case as part of the settlement.

THE ROLE OF THE PROMOTER

Promoters can present an entire tour or work with a booking agent to bring an act to their particular town. Superstar deals offer relatively little profit for the presenter. In many cases, the act receives 90 percent of the net income, after approved expenses. These expenses can include:

- Renting the venue
- Hiring security to protect the act and to prevent any sort of trouble at the event
- Advertising in local media: newspapers, radio and television
- Hiring additional local personnel, such as stage hands
- Purchasing insurance to protect the venue from vandalism, or the audience itself against any sort of violence or accidents, or inclement weather conditions that might cause the concert to be cancelled
- Honoring the group's demands (contract riders). A **rider** is a clause or series of clauses attached to a contract with the artist's demands, such as catered vegetarian food, specific beverages, and transportation requests
- Paying the ticketing agency that sells tickets for the concert, such as Ticketron, applicable taxes, and box office and credit card fees

The promoter also gives away a certain number of **complimentary (comp) tickets**, sometimes specified in the contract, to local media, charities, critics, and others. The act itself usually will have a guest list that specifies that some attendees will be admitted without charge. Accounting for these tickets can be controversial. There have been situations where promoters have been accused of actually selling certain tickets that are supposed to be given away, and not giving the act their percentage of income on these sales.

Although the bulk of arena shows take place during the spring and summer when the weather is almost universally warm in the United States, certain acts may deliberately tour at other times of the year. For example, Christmas is generally regarded as a dead time for touring, but Mannheim Steamroller has done a holiday show for many years that draws very well. The fact that it has sold millions of Christmas recordings has helped solidify its hold on that season. The Trans-Siberian Orchestra has enjoyed similar success with Christmas tours.

Because superstars generally play giant venues, other acts have staked their claim on secondary markets, medium-sized cities that don't often see major concert artists. In different ways, Jimmy Buffett and the Grateful Dead are examples of this sort of act. A Buffett performance is a sort of communal ritual with his Parrothead fans glorying in drinking and dancing. Dead shows gathered tie-dyed fans who associated the band with peace, love, flowers, and drugs, and who loved the group's trancelike extended jams.

Promoting A Show

There are a number of tried and true methods that a promoter can implement in promoting a show. Promoters have to do a market analysis of a particular city in order to determine whether an act can play successfully in that town. This includes:

- Does the band get radio play?
- Will the band be in town before the day of the show? If any band members arrive early, it may be possible to get record company assistance to have them do radio appearances, newspaper, and television interviews. Will the act do radio interviews from wherever they are on the road?
- Are the band's recordings in the local record stores?
- Will the record company provide support in the way of posters, flyers, T-shirts, or a possible in-store performance at a key record shop?
- What age group does the act appeal to? This will directly affect the sort of media buys that the promoter will decide to do. If Hannah Montana is coming to town, her teen and preteen fans don't interact with the sort of media that Metallica would attract. If the act appeals to the college audience and large colleges are nearby, it may be worthwhile to advertise in college newspapers and to put posters and flyers up at the student unions and other campus hangouts.
- What other acts that may draw people away from the promoter's show are appearing on the same night? Again, this may affect the form of advertising that the promoter needs to do.

- Are there key TV personalities, disc jockeys, or newspapers in this particular market that need to be cultivated? Perhaps a local TV or radio personality has a daughter who loves the act and would be thrilled to have dinner with them.
- How much business is the act doing on its current tour? Reading such industry papers as Pollstar or Variety may indicate whether the show is headed for trouble. By contrast, consistent sell-outs would seem to forecast smooth sailing.
- Has the band done well in this area in the past? Past success should indicate that the band has a local following. However, if the band has appeared too much in an area, or too recently, it may be difficult to promote a major event.
- Does the band promote heavily on the internet? If the band has a strong MySpace or YouTube presence, their own Web site, or a fan club, the promoter needs to make sure that this particular date appears in all of these places.
- Is the band an endorser of some musical product? If this is the case, a promoter should be able to get posters and flyers into the local music store, alongside displays that feature the band playing a particular guitar or sitting behind a brand-name drum set.

At some point, the research needs to end and the promoter has to determine how much money will be spent on various sorts of media buys. A time line is then established to list everything that must be done before the concert, including:

- Contacting the record company, especially if they have a local promotion representative in or near the promoter's town.
- Sending out press releases, hopefully colorful ones that tell an interesting story. Maybe the band is known for visiting hospitals or attending local baseball games. The promoter must look for anything that will get attention from the press.
- Making sure that the band is listed in the calendar or coming events section of the local newspaper. These listings are free, but the promoter must keep up with the person who is currently handling the calendar section, and know how much advance each outlet requires.
- Placing articles into neighborhood papers in large cities. These papers are given away without charge. It helps if the performance is going to occur in the part of town that the newspaper serves, but it is a mistake for the promoter to assume that they will never publicize a show taking place in another part of town.
- Utilizing a street team to publicize the show, posting flyers all over town, just as the pay-to-play clubs do.
- Monitoring ticket sales. If sales are lagging, the promoter can increase media buys, try to get a radio station to come aboard as a cosponsor, or it may be necessary to cancel the show.

Payment Formats

There are a number of ways that a promoter and an act may work a deal, including:

- A flat fee. In a **flat-fee deal**, the act receives a specific amount of money. Whether the show does well or not, the promoter guarantees to pay the act the fee agreed upon. When a show is offered free to the public, as part of a state fair, or other event that does not charge admission, obviously the performers will be paid a flat fee, because there is no income from ticket sales.
- Guarantee + percentage. The promoter guarantees the act a certain fee, but the payment increases if the promoter makes money on the show. One example would be an offer of $2,000 against 50 percent of the net, whichever is greater. Let's say that the venue holds a thousand people and tickets are priced at $10. If the event sells out, the total gross, is $10,000. From that, the promoter deducts advertising, any applicable taxes, payment for a sound crew, and possibly rental fees for the venue. Let's say that the total of all of these expenses is $4,000. The promoter's net is $6,000 and the act gets $3,000 or $1,000 above the initial guarantee.
- Flat fee plus bonus. A combination of the first two options; under this scenario, the act receives a guarantee, and an additional bonus if a certain number of tickets are sold. This arrangement may work for an act that isn't yet a blockbuster, but is showing signs of breaking through.
- Straight percentage deal. A superstar contract might have the performer getting 90 percent of the gross, minus specified expenses. It is almost as though the performer is sponsoring the event and paying the promoter as though he were a booking agent. If a star has a guaranteed draw, as Bruce Springsteen and The Rolling Stones do, this is not as bad a deal for the promoter as it seems. Remember these are arena shows that can draw fifty to one hundred thousand people, with high-priced tickets. Sometimes superstars use a single promoter to sponsor a series of concerts. This is a matter of convenience. The act knows the promoter and can deal with a single person for the entire tour, rather than with thirty promoters in thirty cities.
- If possible and necessary, have the act do live or call-in radio interviews, and even a short and free performance at a record store.
- Give away a few tickets to a popular local radio station. The giveaways should attract fans to the concert.

PAYBACKS   If a show is a financial bomb for the promoter, it is always possible to ask the act to give back part of what has turned out to be an excessive guarantee. I am aware of situations in which an act has given back $500 in such a situation, which represented a substantial portion of their guarantee. This will only happen if the act is convinced that the promoter adequately promoted the show or if the booking agency has a long-term relationship with the promoter and convinces the act that the poor attendance wasn't the promoter's fault.

An act may be motivated to return some money if weather conditions were awful, or if a traffic situation made access to the facility next to
impossible. It will be obvious to the act that the promoter is not to blame
for these events.

LOYALTY   It is not uncommon for a promoter to spend a couple of years
promoting an act in a market, bringing up attendance and income for that
performer's show, only to lose the act to another promoter. The agent may
take the position that the promoter is great at building an act up, but doesn't
have the muscle or financial resources to take the risk of moving the next
show to a much larger facility. In some cases, the agent may offer the promoter
that opportunity, in other cases the agent will simply assume that the act has
gotten too big for the promoter's pocketbook or promotional abilities. There
isn't much that the local promoter can do about this.

GEOGRAPHIC LIMITATIONS   Promoters often seek a clause stating that for a
specified period of time an act may not play within a certain geographic
area. For example, Denver and Boulder are only about twenty-five miles
apart. If the University of Colorado in Boulder is sponsoring a stadium concert, they do not want that act to play a similar venue in Denver, because
each show will draw people who could just as easily go to the other performance, thereby cutting the gross of both shows.

REPLAYS   If a club books an act early in its career, it often attempts to place a
clause in the contract that says that the club has the right of first refusal to book
the act again, within a specified time period. The club will take the position
that it helped break an act in its territory. Therefore, should the act become successful, the club would like to be rewarded by having the right to have the act
perform a return engagement. If the act is represented by a booking agent, the
agent will attempt to insert a clause that says if the act returns to the club, its
fee will increase. Even with such a clause, if the act achieves overnight success,
it will either have to play the club again at a relatively modest fee or it will
have to buy the club out of the contract, so that the act can play larger venues
and make more money.

Ticketing

Ticketing for arena concerts is usually handled through a computerized ticketing firm. The widespread availability of computers has greatly affected the
sale of concert tickets. According to *This Business of Concert Promotion and
Touring*, 70 percent of Ticketmaster's domestic tickets were sold online by the
end of 2006. These tickets can be delivered via e-mail, or even text messaged
to cellphones. Before the advent of computers, the announcement of large
concerts by blockbuster acts was a sort of urban ceremony, with people waiting in line all night to get the seats that they wanted.

The four companies extensively involved in concert ticketing are New
Era/Paciolan, Tickets.com, **Ticketmaster**, and Vertical Alliance. Each has its
own particular system for selling tickets, and they bid for the right to sell

tickets at arenas. Some of these companies service other entertainment functions, such as sporting events.

Tickets are usually purchased with credit cards and the ticketing company tacks on a service charge for the ticket. The service fee is based on the ticket price so that the higher the ticket price, the higher the fee. The venue gets a percentage of this fee as a royalty for using this particular provider.

When a concert is an immediate sellout, some of the buyers will resell their tickets on the internet at inflated prices. This is particularly common for the best seats in the house. There are even ticket brokers who have established businesses that re-sell tickets at a profit. Some acts have even offered a percentage of their tickets to these brokers, using the code name **dynamic pricing**. The motivation for an act to do this is to increase their revenue, although it may have the negative effect of irritating their fans. In *This Business of Concert Promotion,* David Goldberg, a Ticketmaster vice president, claims that 15 to 20 percent of ticket sales in a large concert end up traded on the various secondary markets for tickets. To avoid the re-selling of tickets, the Fall 2009 Miley Cyrus tour is going to utilize paperless tickets.

Another common strategy used by promoters is **pre-sales**, where a certain number of tickets are reserved for fan clubs or holders of particular credit cards. Some promoters use pre-sales as an indicator of the strength of a show. The promoter can adjust the advertising budget in either direction, based on these numbers.

Anyone who has attended a large concert has also seen private parties attempting to sell tickets to the show, often at inflated prices. These are usually individuals who are simply out to make some money by re-selling tickets that they bought at the regular selling price. There are also instances where they are simply trying to get rid of tickets that they bought but couldn't use.

Ticket Wars

As promoters have realized the amount of money to be made in ticketing fees, they've tried to cut out the middleman and take over this part of the business. Notably, Live Nation, the concert promotion firm, has made an exclusive deal with the Philadelphia-based venue SMG to take its business away from Ticketmaster. Shortly thereafter, Ticketmaster announced it was ending its long-term relationship with Live Nation, in a disagreement over fees and control of customer data. As of 2009, Live Nation has its own ticketing firm, Live Nation Ticketing.

Meanwhile, the ticketing agencies have been hungrily viewing the concert promotion business. Ticketmaster bought a controlling interest in talent manager Irving Azoff's Front Line Management. Presumably Ticketmaster hopes to expand its reach into 360 or 360-like deals, and to encourage such Front Line superstars as Christina Aguilera, Jimmy Buffettt, and The Eagles to utilize their services.

As of early 2009, Live Nation and Ticketmaster agreed to merge their operations. However, antitrust concerns were raised by others in the music industry and the government, and as of this writing it is not clear whether such a merger will be approved.

Music T shirts and other memorabilia on sale at a New Orleans' music store. Photo: Greg Ward, courtesy Rough Guides, Dorling Kindersley.

Merchandising

Because merchandising has become such a lucrative part of the touring business, it is essential that the promoter, the venue, and the artist's representative have a clear understanding of who will sell the merchandise, and where it will be sold. The promoter does not share in this income, but many venues demand a percentage of the sales. State or city sales taxes must be paid in whatever location the merchandise is sold.

In many instances, acts make more income from merchandise sales than they do from the performance itself. This is because other than paying a percentage to the venue, there is little overhead involved in merchandise, except for shipping the goods and paying someone to sell them. If the venue is receiving a percentage of the sales, often they will provide people to sell the merchandise. The public seems to have an unlimited appetite for tour jackets, T-shirts, and baseball caps. Other groups have come up with such additional merchandise as bumper stickers and snow scrapers. Sometimes the artists bring a person whose job is to sell merchandise, and sometimes the venue provides someone who sells the band's product. If a band is popular enough, retail stores also carry this merchandise. A number of rap stars and entrepreneurs have developed their own clothing lines into lucrative businesses.

Insurance

It is absolutely essential for the promoter to have insurance. Insurance should cover the following possibilities:

- Any sort of injury. This can be injuries to the performers, an audience member falling down the stairs, and any sort of violence or vandalism that might harm people or damage property. The insurance must cover injury or even death due to negligence on the part of the performer or the venue. There have been several instances in the last few years where a smoke machine misfired and caused fatal injuries.
- Cancellation insurance. Cancellations could involve weather conditions, traffic, or an artist's illness.

Performing Rights

Any public performance requires that the promoter or the venue be licensed by ASCAP, BMI, and SESAC. It is never the responsibility of the artist to obtain such a license, unless the artist is also the promoter of the event. In past years, promoters tended to ignore SESAC, because it is a much smaller organization than its peers and had comparatively few important writers in its roster. However, because Bob Dylan and Neil Diamond are now SESAC writers, it is a good idea to get a SESAC license.

Contractual Matters

Contracts with superstars can be exceedingly complicated, because the technical demands of the act can be considerable, and so can their requests for special services, such as food, drink, and hotels. Contracts between an act and a promoter, generally negotiated by an agent, will include such matters as:

- Time, date, and length of the performance
- Details about the sound check
- Billing on the show
- The form of payment (cash or certified check, or cashier's check.) Usually the payment must be made at the completion of the show
- If payment is made by check, there must be language in the contract that indicates the person or company to whom the check must be made out
- If the show is booked on a percentage basis, there will be some provision for an act's representative to view the gross and the expenses involved
- A 50 percent deposit before the contract is signed
- The cancellation policy
- If the artists are union members, a contract must be filed at the local union and work dues must be paid to the applicable local of the union
- If the show is taking place in a foreign country, the promoter must specify in what currency the act will be paid

SPECIAL PROVISIONS   The artist may include a variety of special provisions that the promoter must fulfill. The late jazz pianist Oscar Peterson specified in writing that he would not perform if the piano was not properly tuned, and on several occasions he refused to play a show, citing that reason. Other acts may demand or request specific rented instruments or amplifiers, vegetarian food, and so on.

CANCELLATIONS   Cancellation policies are set forth in the contract between the promoter and the act. Some contracts give the act the right to cancel a concert because of weather conditions. The contract may state that the act is paid despite weather problems, or it may specify that a make-up date is to be arranged by mutual agreement. Artists may also wish to cancel if they obtain last minute bookings on network television shows. If this clause is in the contract, there is usually a specified time frame within which the artist may cancel. This can be a hardship for promoters if they have already begun to advertise the show and to sell tickets. Refunds must be issued for tickets sold before the cancellation was made.

When ticket sales lag, sometimes it is in an act's best interest to cancel a show. The promoter and the act's representative must reach an agreement on the appropriate fee. Because touring acts have to go from one town to another, partial payment of the fee may not take care of the expenses of the road personnel, or the travel from the previous city to the next one. Nevertheless, a cancellation may be advisable, because no act wants the show to go on for half a house. This may result in the news circulating in

---

Drive, He Said!

There are instances where an act takes it on itself to halt a show in midstream. A few years ago, I had a student who was interning for a record label. One of the label's biggest acts was scheduled to do a show at Red Rocks, a natural amphitheater located west of Denver. The lead singer in this act was considered a notoriously difficult person. Barry Fey, the promoter of the event, was prepared for anything to happen. The band did their first number, and the singer was dissatisfied with the sound. He took his microphone and threw it into the audience, left the stage, and boarded the limo, telling the driver to return him to the hotel.

As the limo drove away, the promoter got on the phone and called the limo driver. He had the Denver policeman who was heading security for the show talk to the artist. The policeman told the singer and the driver that they needed to immediately return to the venue to do the rest of the show or he would have the singer arrested for inciting the crowd to riot. Barry added that the band would never work again in Denver if he refused to do this, and that he would call many other promoters nationwide to tell them what had happened. He also told the limo driver that *he* must immediately turn the vehicle around or he would "never drive another limo in this town," so to speak.

The singer meekly returned to the venue and did the rest of the show without incident. Had he not returned, there might have been a full-scale riot.

trade papers or the mass media that in Peoria, they only drew two thousand people in a venue that holds five thousand. This could seriously impact the act's reputation with other promoters, and result in a loss of income much more serious than one bad payday. Whenever a show is cancelled without any specific explanation, there is a good chance that the act simply isn't doing good business. In such instances, the band's publicist or the promoter comes up with damage control: a vague but authoritative-sounding explanation for the cancellation.

In the same vein, certain performers have become notorious for missing shows because of personal problems, and promoters become reluctant to hire them. Rumors of drug use, illness, or other problems can seriously derail a band's career. Although superstars may be able to recover from a string of no-shows, a beginning band will probably be doomed.

When a promoter doesn't come up with the proper payment upon completion of a show, the act's lawyer may sue for breach of contract. When there is a great deal of money involved, this makes sense, but for a beginning act, the sums involved may not justify the legal expense.

PROMOTING NON-TRADITIONAL CONCERTS

Promoters don't only work booking major arenas. The next biggest area is clubs and bars. In many major cities, these clubs often have a dedicated clientele and can help establish an act on its way up the ladder to mainstream success. There are many other types of events that are put on, sometimes by professional promoters and sometimes by amateurs.

Clubs

Nightclubs used to be a fixture of major cities across the country, featuring live music and dancing. Most of these clubs have disappeared with the advent of movies and other less-expensive forms of entertainment. However, there remain a network of clubs that cater to different musical styles or specific audiences that are much smaller than the shows promoted by Live Nation and other major outfits. Although some club owners may own more than one venue, it is more usual for each owner—who usually serves as the promoter as well—to book for a single club. It is up to the artist's management to string together enough of these bookings to make it worthwhile. For certain styles of music—jazz and cabaret music, for example—the performer may be able to play a series of nights at a single club, appearing every few months on a regular rotation.

At one time, the musician's union controlled a large percentage of the work in night clubs in the United States. Those days are long gone, as a result of the increasing presence of self-contained bands, and court rulings that musicians employed in clubs are independent contractors and not regular employees who have the right to bargain through a union.

PAY TO PLAY   For years, the clubs in New York and Los Angeles have been placing musicians in a position where they actually have to **pay to play**. Here is how pay to play works: A club "hires" a band to play on a Saturday night. The band asks what it will be paid. The club manager says that they band will be on a bill with two other acts. Each act will be responsible for selling 50 tickets to the show. (What he means is that the band will actually have to purchase tickets to the show.) The tickets cost $10, but the band can buy them for $6. If the band sells all of their tickets, it will have earned $200 (the difference between the $10 price and the $6 that they paid for them). The capacity of the club is two hundred people, and if the show sells out the club owner will split the remaining $500 between the three bands. However, the promoter will deduct $100 from this amount for the sound person, so the band will actually split $400.

The best case scenario has the band making $200 on ticket sales and $133 for the sell-out performance. They will then earn $333 for the night's work. However, if the band only sells twenty tickets and the show does not sell out, the band will earn 20 × 4, or $80, but they will have purchased twenty tickets for $120. In this situation, it will have cost the band $40 to play the gig! This does not include the price of gas, whatever the band is paying a roadie, or any other expenses.

Why would anyone agree to work under these conditions? When a group works in Los Angeles or New York, they will do their best to invite industry people: A&R representatives from record companies, music publishers, and media critics. In the band's view, it is their only chance, as the industry cliché puts it, to "build a buzz."

Let's assume that the band has accepted these terms. Note that the club will only minimally promote the event, if at all. How is the band going to get fifty people to come to the show? They will probably try any or all of the following techniques:

- Create posters, flyers, and stickers and post them around the club and in places where fans of their musical style might hang out, including record stores, music stores, and supermarkets. Note that the band must create the materials and post them, because the club will not take responsibility or spend their time and money to do it. Posting flyers without permission is illegal in many cities and if band members are caught doing this, they may be fined.
- Post information about the show on their Web site or their MySpace page.
- Attempt to persuade friends, boyfriends, or girlfriends or family members to sell tickets.
- Worst case scenario: The band actually offers friends $2 for every ticket that they sell. This of course reduces the band profit from $4 a ticket to $2 a ticket and the friends will probably expect to get in free and to bring a friend with them, which will cost the band an additional $12.

How do club owners justify pay to play? Their rationale is that they are doing the musicians a favor by allowing them to play, and that the band can use the fact that they played at the club to get other gigs by adding it to their press kit. Obviously, the club business is very competitive and the owner will cite the high costs of renting the facility, maintaining the club, and so on, as a rationale for instituting a pay to play policy.

There are other, more benevolent versions of gigs that do not offer guarantees to musicians. In a typical example, the club may guarantee the band nothing, but give them either a percentage of the money that comes in at the door or of all the door receipts. The club manager may also want to pay the sound person or the person collecting the door charge out of the receipts from the door. The band, in turn, will argue that these people work regularly for the club, and should be paid by the club, not out of the band's pocketbook. In this situation the band can't *lose* money on the gig, if we don't count the expense of getting to the gig, but it is unlikely to see a huge return for the investment of time. At least the band will be rewarded if it builds up a fan base and is able to draw an ever-increasing number of people to its shows. When this occurs, the club may very well give the band one night a month, or even a regular weekly gig, which can act as a sort of meeting place for the band's fans.

Performers are always better off if they are given a guaranteed sum of money, plus a percentage of the profits. The club owner will argue that presenting music is a great risk, and that if the performers are good, they will either do well or at least build an audience that will ultimately bring in enough people to pay them a decent wage.

OPEN MIKES AND CLUB JAM SESSIONS   When a musician moves to a new town, he will look for ways of introducing his music to people that have probably never heard of him. **Open mikes** are situations where clubs allow people to come in and play for a short period of time. Usually the club provides the sound, and an MC who introduces the acts, and sometimes plays a set of his own. These sets are usually fifteen or twenty minutes long, or even shorter. Some artists use open mikes to determine whether audiences like new material. Usually the MC is paid something, although not much, for introducing the acts and for creating a positive atmosphere for the musicians and the audience.

Another version of the open mike is the club session, in which a small group of musicians constitute a house band or a rhythm section, and other musicians "sit in." The house band is usually paid, but the people who sit in are not compensated. Sometimes a musician may serve as a promoter, approaching a bar or club to "host" a session. In return for bringing in a certain number of regular musicians, the promoter will get a small fee or a percentage of the food and drink that is consumed during the session!

Open mikes and jam sessions have their place, but musicians need to be careful not to offer free services on a regular basis. Unless you live in a very large city, there is a limit to how many times people will come out to see an act and it's certainly a better idea to have those visits be ones where the artist gets a paycheck.

College Gigs and Block Booking

There are two organizations whose mission is to bring artists to college campuses: **NACA (the National Association of Campus Activities)** and the **APCA (Association for the Promotion of Campus Activities)**. Both groups hold conventions where acts showcase for the college buyers. When an act does well, a group of the colleges will get together and offer to book them at a reduced price for a number of gigs within a short period of time. This can be a good deal for all parties, depending on the fee and the amount of travel involved.

Dealing with the college market can be difficult, because many of the promoters are students who have little experience putting on shows, and they don't always approach that task in a professional manner. From an agent's point of view, there is the additional frustration that the students may graduate or lose interest in booking after a year, and the agent has to cultivate contacts all over again. It is not unusual for booking agents and managers to begin their careers booking college shows on "someone else's dime." Sometimes these college promoters simply don't have the skill or motivation to do sufficient advertising, and even when the act is getting a flat fee they won't enjoy playing to an empty house. Some colleges, especially larger ones, hire professional presenters to present their concerts to ensure the quality and success of their events.

Art Centers and Arts Organizations

There are local, state, and regional arts councils all over the United States. The regional arts organizations hold conferences that are use a format similar to the NACA meetings. They have juried showcases and artists are selected to appear and to play for the attendees. There are also exhibit tables, where artists can solicit gigs whether or not they have officially showcased. **Block bookings**—in which a group of shows is booked all at once—can result from these conferences and some organizations publish program books where acts who do not attend can advertise their services.

Although some agents do participate in these events, in many instances this is more of a do-it-yourself situation. The artist who attends these events often negotiates directly with the buyer/promoter. Making it more difficult for the artist, many arts organizations work by committee, and there isn't one person with the authority to make booking decisions. Arts councils book quite a bit of family entertainment, so all of the people attending or who get booked are not musicians. They may include comedians, jugglers, storytellers, dancers, and actors.

Jazz musicians playing at a street fair. Photo: Laimute Druskis, courtesy Z. Legacy, Corporate Digital Archive.

Festivals and Fairs

Festivals and fairs often include a number of acts. They are usually contracted by promoters with little input from the acts, because there may be dozens of performers involved. The promoters rent the space (sometimes an open field), provide or contract out basic facilities (such as food and water), and provide some type of stage and (depending on the size of the event) a sound system and lighting. Sometimes these events are rather loosely organized, with no one ensuring that acts keep to their allotted time slots, or no single person in charge of lighting or sound. In these cases, the act may show up to perform at noon only to find that they have to hang around several hours and then find themselves playing instead after most of the audience is gone! Sound and lighting is virtually guaranteed to be primitive, at best, except at major festivals.

Promoters may also seek corporate sponsors to help underwrite a festival. Bands need to be aware in advance of who these sponsors are, in case they have an objection to performing in front of a large banner promoting Miller Beer, for example. Sometimes a band may have its own sponsors who would object to them helping to promote a competitor's goods.

Corporate Events and Conventions

Often corporations promote appearances by artists at corporate events. These gigs usually are booked by the company without the use of a promoter. The corporation may feel that the act has the proper image for their product, or simply is tremendously popular with their employees. The company will contact the act through their agent or manager. These bookings do not usually involve a promoter, because there is no advertising involved, and the venue is generally wherever the company is holding its meeting or convention. The event will not be publicized to the general public, partly because the nature of the gig is to provide a special treat for corporate employees that is deliberately not available to anyone else. These events often pay thousands of dollars, and may involve first class air travel or the use of private jets. The act is paid a flat fee, because the house is predetermined by the number of convention attendees.

Nonmainstream Music

There are a variety of musical styles that are not necessarily in the mainstream of American music, but have loyal followers who have built an organization whose objective is to promote their particular sort of music. For example, bluegrass music has the **International Bluegrass Music Association (IBMA)**; folk music aficionados banded together in the **North American Folk Music and Dance Alliance**. Each of these groups has a national convention and the Folk Alliance sponsors regional conventions in various parts of the United States and Canada. These conventions feature performer showcases, workshops, and presentations devoted to the history of the music (see Chapter 12).

At these national meetings, agents are also in attendance, although they are generally more interested in promoting people already on their roster rather in acquiring new talent. At the regional folk alliance meetings, a few people in attendance book folk festivals, together with some folk music non-profit organizations, and there are a number of people who present house concerts. Because these are specialized events, an agent who understands the nature of the meeting and the sort of music that the clients want can find a good market for appropriate clients.

Part of what happens at these organizational meetings is that musicians provide a network for one another, informing each other about new venues and places to avoid because of problems with the owner or manager. Many of the musicians are quite generous with contacts, and for the self-managed act quite a bit of work can be garnered through these connections.

In addition to these organizations, many cities have folklore or folksong societies, or blues or bluegrass associations that book a regular concert series or occasional shows or festivals. Usually the booking agents for these clubs work part-time out of their love of the music. The responsibility also rotates among club members, so from year to year a different person may be in charge of bookings. All of this makes it difficult for the artist or manager to keep track of who's in charge. Also, because these events are organized by non-professionals, sometimes basic functions such as promoting the concert, securing the hall, or obtaining proper sound equipment and lights can be poorly handled, so that the artist may have to rely on taking on some if not all of these responsibilities.

Benefits

Musicians are often called on to play **benefit concerts** for everything from feeding the homeless to health emergencies for friends or other musicians. It is wise for musicians to restrict the number of benefits that they play, because if an artist becomes readily available without charge, people may think twice about actually compensating the artist for other gigs.

Typically, local benefits are promoted by people who have some sort of administrative role in the organization but have little or no experience at promoting shows. Consequently, it is quite common for benefits to end up making very little money, or even losing money. This can result in bad feelings between the act and the organization. The latter feel that the artist didn't draw, and the artists feel that the show was not professionally promoted. Of course, either or both of these conclusions may be correct.

Some benefits are run by a non-profit group but MC'd by a musician or local media personality who chooses the talent. Some of these benefits have run for many years, such as the Winter Folk concert in Portland, Oregon. This event is a benefit for a non-profit organization that provides inexpensive meals for people who have limited financial resources. The show has been going on for over twenty years, and always sells out a theater with six hundred seats. Tom May has been the singing host of the event during the entire run of Winter Folk. He generally contacts the performers directly, but he sometimes deals with the artist's manager in choosing a headline act.

Some benefits are exactly that. All of the artists donate their time and sometimes the venue is offered without charge as well. Another sort of benefit occurs when a musician offers a reduced fee to the sponsor. Under this sort of arrangement the organization or cause receives some benefit from the event, but the musician gets paid something for his or her time. In some instances, a soloist will donate services, but require the sponsor to pay the backup band. The rationale here is that the soloist will get some positive publicity for doing the show, but for the band, basically it's just another gig.

House Concerts

House concerts are concerts presented by music fans in their own homes. The presenters develop a mailing list, but rarely advertise openly. The size of the venue dictates how many people are able to attend. These are unique events, in the sense that they are basically a labor of love. A modest cover charge may be taken at the door, and is usually shared in some way with the performer, or a hat may be passed.

The best thing about house concerts is that they are generally attended by extremely attentive audiences who are prepared to listen closely to performers in a nonsmoking, (usually) alcohol-free environment. They are also likely to buy a large number of CDs, because the event represents as much of a social evening as a performance. The audience is almost able to physically touch the performer. A CD in effect serves as a souvenir postcard of the event.

Often the presenter provides refreshments, and some house concerts even include dinner as part of the festivities. Because the performer gets all of the money taken in, and usually sells a healthy number of CDs, house concerts often pay surprisingly well. Many of the presenters offer hospitality to the performers, feeding and housing them during their visit.

Although it is possible to find house concerts on the Web, they rarely advertise anywhere because they are not really commercial events, and most of the presenters prefer to have some control over who comes into their home.

Sometimes musicians present house concerts for musicians who are passing through their area, because no one else wants to present their friends. The artist who regularly does house concerts will build up a network of contacts and presenters. Sometimes people who have no experience as presenters do house concerts, but because they have not built up a mailing list, the attendance is small. The only other downside to house concerts is that the presenters may expect more socialization out of the visiting performer than that person is willing to offer, if the show is coming in the midst of or at the end of an exhausting road trip. Similarly, the audience for these shows is more demanding than it might be for other performances, in the sense that they expect to talk informally with the performer. Most hosts and audiences are polite and respectful, and seem genuinely honored to deal with performers on an informal basis in a one-on-one situation.

Terms to Know

AEG (Anschutz Entertainment Group) 254

APCA (Association for the Promotion of Campus Activities) 267

Benefit concert 270

Block booking 267

Complimentary (comp) tickets 255

Dynamic pricing 260

Flat-fee deal 258

House concert 270

IBMA (International Bluegrass Music Association) 269

Live Nation 254

NACA (National Association of Campus Activities) 267

North American Folk Music & Dance Alliance 269

Open mike 266

Pay to play 265

Pre-sale 260

Rider 255

Ticketmaster 259

For Class Discussion

1. Do you know of any local concert promoters?
2. Are there people who present concerts at your school? What failures or successes have they experienced?
3. How many venues exist in your town that hold over five hundred people? What acts do they seem to book?
4. Name three acts that you feel will be superstar concert acts five years from now.
5. What styles of music seem able to generate large audiences in your home town and which musical niches don't seem to generate fans?
6. Does your college book touring acts?
7. Where would you advertise an act that is going to play at your school?
8. What was the last concert that you attended? Describe your experience.
9. Do you know any band that played a job in your home town but was not paid by the club owner or promoter?
10. Have you ever attended a house concert?

CHAPTER 16

Music Merchandising

M usic merchandising involves the sales of records as well as the music products industry, which manufactures and sells musical instruments all over the world.

RECORD STORES

The decline in CD sales resulted not only in the closing of independent record stores, but also has brought about the demise of large record chains. Tower Records, in particular, was a large chain noted for its deep stock in many genres of music. Its bankruptcy in 2007 was a huge loss to independent record labels because often Tower was the only shop in town that carried an extensive stock of their music.

There are still a number of independent record stores in most major cities, but the number of smaller stores is on a steady decline. Terry Currier, independent record store owner and one of the founders of the Coalition of Independent Music Stores (CIMS; see later in this chapter), estimates the number of record stores at thirty-five hundred, down from about seven thousand in 2001. Many of the record stores that remain have survived by carrying used CDs, DVDs, posters, toys, clothing, and other "lifestyle" consumer items in addition to recordings. Independent stores such as Deadly Dragon in New York City or Down Home Music in the San Francisco Bay area, have survived by serving niche markets. A few other stores, such as the Amoeba Music stores in California, are successful because their enormous stock makes them a destination stop for music fans.

Used CDs

Whether or not you like the CD as a medium of sound, it is virtually inde-structible, and the sound of a used CD is typically just as good as the sound of a new one. Also, instead of having to buy a CD for $11 or $12 from the distributor and sell it at a discount from the $18 or $19 list price, record stores can buy used CDs for relatively low prices from their customers, and sell them for $8 or $9. Some stores will pay as little as a dollar or even less per CD and therefore make a significant profit. According to Terry Currier, stores on the East Coast tend to pay less for used product than those on the West Coast. The store can also pick and choose what they wish to buy, because they are buying directly from consumers. These used CDs also come with an artist's track record as part of their history. A used CD by a popular artist is an easy sell; a new CD by an unknown artist may take much longer to sell.

Record stores take a risk in buying a used CD, because they may not be able to sell it, and they can't return it to the original owner. New product comes with a 100 percent return privilege. To be successful at selling used CDs or used vinyl records, the buyer has to have a real knowledge of the customer base, what they want, and what they are willing to pay for it. It's also useful to know what albums are collectibles or out-of-print items that can be sold on eBay or at record shows for huge markups.

There is no hard data on the sales of used CDs. They are not scanned by the SoundScan process. SoundScan is an electronic system that registers the sales of albums when they occur in retail stores. The bar code on the CD is scanned at the cash register at the time that album is bought by the consumer. *Billboard* began to use the system in 1991. Before that time, the *Billboard* charts were based on a combination of record sales and radio station charts. Many people questioned the accuracy of the *Billboard* charts, and one of the first things that emerged from the use of SoundScan was that country music record sales were greater than anyone had previously imagined.

Today Soundscan is used in fourteen thousand outlets, including record stores, mass merchandise record retailers, and digital sales. Some of the smaller record outlets still do not use SoundScan on their sales, so the system is never completely accurate.

Whenever data is reported on the declining sales of CDs, the numbers do not include the sales of used product. They also omit most of the sales that occur when artists sell product from the stage, although a few artists actually use SoundScan and report their sales, in an effort to get on the charts and garner radio play.

Used Product and the Birth of Independent Record Coalitions

When record stores first started selling used CDs, the major record distributors, record labels, and some artists became outraged. Record companies did not get a piece of the action, and they also felt that the sale of used product

The Dance: Garth Brooks versus Used CDs

Used CD sales annoyed the record labels and artists, both of whom felt they lost income to this—entirely legal—trade. By the mid-1990s, the record labels and a few artists were so annoyed by the sales of used CDs that they decided to take action. The companies struck at independent stores that sold CDs by threatening to remove them from their co-op programs. Record companies do co-op advertising, in which they and the record stores share the cost of placing ads in local publications to promote new releases. A loss of these co-op dollars could be very damaging to the store.

Terry Currier. Courtesy Music Millennium.

Representing the aggrieved artists, country superstar Garth Brooks then took it upon himself to pressure Capitol Records not to ship his new album, *In Pieces*, to any store that sold used CDs. Brooks' product was very valuable to the stores, because he was at the height of his popularity and demand was great for any new release.

Terry Currier owns the major independent record retailer Music Millennium, with two outlets in Portland, Oregon, and is noted for his support of all music forms and his independent spirit. Reacting to Brooks's threat to withdraw valuable product from stores that sold used CDs, Currier decided to hold a Garth Brooks CD barbecue. The barbecue became a media circus. Not only did the Portland media pick up on the event, but Terry took the show on a West Coast road show, from Bellingham, Washington, to San Diego, California. The tour received publicity on national TV and in magazines, and T-shirts were made celebrating the event. MTV even followed the tour. The bad publicity led Brooks to back down. The labels also removed their threat to cut co-op advertising dollars to the independents.

sometimes cut into the sales of the same album as a new CD. Artists did not receive any royalties on these sales either.

Record Store Coalitions

Garth Brooks's threat to remove his product from independent retailers became the impetus to form a new organization, the **Coalition of Independent Music Stores (CIMS)**. It functions as a support group for independents. Stores operating in different cities consult with one another about mutual problems, such as pay scales and benefits for employees, marketing, and what is selling. Until the organization formed, stores only knew their competition in their own town, and naturally they did not generally compare trade secrets with them.

Currently, there are fifty-eight stores in the organization, down from a peak of seventy-two. The organization is actually owned by twenty-seven of the stores, down from the original thirty-seven partners. The coalition's tenth anniversary convention was held in Seattle on April 28, 2008. The typical CIMS store, if there is such a thing, is a multigenre music store. Members of the board visit before stores are admitted into membership.

The birth of CIMS has inspired others to form independent record store coalitions. The **Association of Independent Music Stores (AIMS)** tends to have more members that specialize in specific genres of music. Another group called **The Music Monitor Network**, was founded in 1997, and consists of small chain stores, with anything from two to thirty locations. These organizations fulfill some of the same functions as CIMS, and are in effect friendly competitors of each other. The membership of all three organizations share many similarities, so the decision to join one or another often comes down to personal relationships among store owners or individual choice.

NATIONAL ASSOCIATION OF RECORD MERCHANDISERS (NARM) The **National Association of Record Merchandisers (NARM)** was founded in 1958 and includes retailers of all sizes, wholesalers, and individual educators and music industry professionals. NARM holds annual conventions, and works with the record labels on combating piracy and on educational programs that involve the music industry. It is a much larger organization than any of the independent coalitions, and many of the stores in these groups are also members of NARM.

Independent record distributors and the smaller labels used to have their own organization, NAIRD (the National Association of Independent Record Distributors). The organization later changed its name to AFIM, the American Federation of Independent Music, but it no longer exists.

Retail Record Stores Today

For many years, record companies marketed their product to a narrow age range from pre-teens to young adults. Nowadays, anyone going to a record store sees a much older demographic. In an article in the July 18, 2008, *New York Times*, Alex Williams referred to today's record stores as a "temple of nostalgia." Between legal and illegal downloading, a lack of young superstars who have been able to sustain long-term careers, the ever-increasing popularity of such new media as videogames, ringtones, and ringbacks, the long-term prognosis for record stores does not appear to be very positive. The same article cites the percentage of fifteen- to nineteen-year-olds buying recorded music as 12 percent in 2005, down from 17 percent in 1996. The twenty- to twenty-four-year-old age group was less than 13 percent, down from 15 percent. During the same years, the amount of music bought by adults over the age of forty-five had risen to 25.5 percent from 15 percent. To make matters worse, these numbers include legally downloaded songs, as well as record sales. It doesn't require much imagination to extrapolate that for the most part it is the younger buyers who are doing the downloading.

In the past, new recording formats have benefited both the labels and retail stores. When LPs replaced 78's, consumers embraced the advantages of the new format. It became easier to build a record collection because the physical recording was lighter, less prone to breakage, and easier to store. Plus, consumers were inspired to "repurchase" earlier recordings from the 78 era in the new format. This cycle repeated itself with the introduction of cassettes, and eventually CDs. In fact, the sales boom of the mid-1980s can be in many ways attributed to the labels' savvy reissuing of back catalog material in the new CD format.

However, today's newest format—digital downloads—poses a new set of challenges to the labels and stores. Stores have been hurt by digital music because people who used to shop at retail stores now do a large percentage of their shopping on the internet. "Big box" stores such as Best Buy can make up some of the lost CD revenue in sales of the players—notably iPods—and also some retailers have introduced artist-specific iPod download cards, a way of selling a download through a physical retail space. Nonetheless, traditional record stores are hurting.

Of course, there are always new wrinkles in retail. To survive, some stores have added other product lines, including posters and other rock memorabilia, toys, instruction books, and even musical instruments. Other stores have invested heavily in used records, which constitutes a large percentage of their business, and, as discussed earlier, an excellent profit center. Nonetheless, stores have to be able to offer something special, that cannot be acquired through file sharing, to maintain their profitability and attract customers.

The future of music stores is dependent on a number of factors that are difficult to predict. One way that the industry has embraced is to fight digital downloading or at least minimally control the downside of illegal file sharing and duplication. Will the **RIAA (Record Industry Association of America)** succeed in ultimately finding some form of **digital rights management** that will curtail file sharing? At this writing, the RIAA is not only going after individuals, but also going after colleges who are essentially providing access to file sharers on their computer networks. The very latest news from the RIAA (as of June 2009) is that they are going to focus on getting Internet service providers (ISPs) to report the names of customers who are illegally downloading music. Supposedly, RIAA is currently negotiating such a solution, and is going to file fewer suits against individuals. The projected plan is that the ISP will send the customer a letter of warning. If the customer does not comply with the warning, the ISP will report the customer to the RIAA, and will cease offering Internet service to him. The RIAA

The Format That Wasn't

The music industry has tried to introduce various formats over the years that have not caught on or were popular for a brief period of time. Who remembers eight-track tapes today, a briefly popular format of the mid-1960s?

During the late 1990s, I attended a convention in Boston of MEIEA, the organization of music educators who teach in college music business programs. A gentleman from BASF, the German tape manufacturer, delivered an impassioned speech about how compact cassettes were going to be the next big thing. Phillips Electronics had invested a considerable amount of money in researching a better quality cassette player that played high quality digital compact cassettes. The idea was that Phillips would make a double cassette player. One player would handle the old analog cassettes, and the other would play the digital product.

The gentleman proudly held up mock-ups of covers of the new digital cassettes, and he asserted that without question this would be the dominant format in a couple of years, if not sooner.

I have no idea where these digital cassette albums came from, but I do know that they never appeared on the marketplace.

would then go after consumers who were committing multiple illegal downloads. This loss of Internet privileges has just now been legislated in France.

Another possibility is the invention of some new and unknown format that will be available at the retail store. Certainly, the retail store needs to function as a general entertainment center to draw people away from their homes and their various home entertainment devices, whether they are flat-screen TVs, videogames, or movies.

In the meantime, we are seeing the partial resurrection of vinyl. This medium has long been buried, but a surprising number of consumers are returning to it. Vinyl records require turntables and speakers, cannot be heard on iPods, but they contain space for more interesting cover art, and the liner notes are easy to read. Stores have promoted vinyl as having a "warmer sound" than CDs, and many older consumers have fallen for the nostalgia of the format of their youth. There are only a handful of vinyl pressing plants left and for them this renewed interest in vinyl is a blessing.

HOME COMPUTERS AND THE GROWTH OF DIGITAL MEDIA

The digital revolution has come about thanks to the advent of inexpensive and powerful home computers, the growth of the Internet, and high-speed connections to the Web. Combined, these three revolutions enabled consumers to directly purchase—or share—digital media files with each other, without involving a record company or record store.

Initially, home computers provided opportunities for music fans to post messages on message boards about their favorite music. One of the first music-related Web sites was the Internet Underground Music Archive (IUMA). Artists could advertise their work, and, if they chose, offer music for downloading. Initially, accessing these files was time consuming. By 1991, the **MP3** format was developed. In this format, files were greatly compressed, so that the material could be played back through the Web in minutes. The Winamp record player performed like a phonograph, only it was inside the computer itself.

In 1998, Michael Robertson founded the Web site mp3.com. Initially he focused on unknown artists, who were happy to post their music on the site, even though the music was distributed without charge. In *Playback: From the Victrola To MP3: 100 years of Music, Machines And Money*, Mark Coleman notes that Robertson's site went from drawing 150,000 visitors a day in 1998 to nearly a million regular users by 2001.

In 2000, Robertson introduced a new feature that allowed users to put their record collection online. Record companies and music publishers responded with lawsuits. The courts ruled against mp3.com, and the company was forced to settle with the major labels, as well as the performing rights organizations. The settlement cost mp3.com $130 million and then the company was bought by Vivendi (at the time the corporation that owned Universal Records, the largest record conglomerate) for $372 million.

Meanwhile, a young college student named Shawn Fanning had developed a hobby of trading music with his college friends. Shawn created a program that he named **Napster**. It enabled computers to become virtual servers, so that users who had the software could view, share, and download the mp3 files stored on each other's hard drives. Napster simply facilitated the trading, but did not itself house any of the music files. As more and more users signed on, an increasing amount of content became available.

Record labels were unhappy, but record sales continued to increase in 2000. Napster became cool, particularly in the eyes of college students. Those artists who took a position against it, such as the heavy metal group Metallica, experienced a backlash from some of their fans. After all, why would someone pay money for a product that was available free?

As if things weren't bad enough, computer manufacturers started to include CD drives in their machines. Blank CDs were available at many chain stores, and now the consumer could burn their mp3 files onto CDs in any order they chose. Apple Computer even used the slogan "Rip, Mix, Burn" in their advertising. In effect the consumer had become a personal CD manufacturer. There was also little degradation of sound on the newly burned CD. The only thing the CDs lacked was packaging or album notes.

The price of blank CDs dropped as they became increasingly popular. By the end of 2001, sales of blank CDs exceeded those of prerecorded ones. Copying them could be done quickly, cheaply, and efficiently.

When record sales started to decline in 2001, the labels felt that they had to strike back. When CDs were ripped, the record companies lost income. The "hip" consumer was not bothered by stealing from the big guy, but it also didn't seem to bother them that neither artists nor songwriters derived any income from the digital copies. In fact, the artists could still utilize the exposure to raise their performing profiles, and to sell merchandise. Songwriters, however, who derived all of their income from CD sales, radio play, and the sale of printed music, were heavily affected by the new technologies.

iTunes and the iPod

With the labels opposing digital downloads while consumers embraced the new technology, it seemed as if no one could break the logjam. Along came Steven Jobs, the visionary founder of Apple Computers. In the early 2000s, Apple was developing new hand-held digital music players that it would market as the **iPod**. Jobs knew that the machine's success hinged on Apple's ability to offer popular music to play on the device. Jobs contacted all of the major labels, and brokered the first digital downloading agreement that was universally embraced by all parties. It called for a set price of .99 per download through Apple's iTunes store, of which the labels kept .79 cents. The new iTunes store opened online in 2003.

In order to assure the labels that songs sold would not be pirated, Apple created a system that compelled the consumer to listen to the iPod, because the material could not be played on any other player. Naturally, Apple was as much motivated by creating a unique platform that forced the consumer to buy their player as they were concerned about protecting the record companies' product. By 2008, iTunes was the largest seller of music in the United States. Sales on iTunes even exceeded those at Wal-Mart, the largest brick and mortar retailer. From a record company standpoint, this was a mixed blessing, because Wal-Mart was selling CDs, while iTunes was usually downloading individual songs. Although Wal-Mart and Best Buy utilized other companies in their attempts to compete with iTunes, none of these systems have come close to capturing the consumer as well as iTunes.

The labels, unhappy with the fixed price of .99 per tune no matter whether the song was a major hit or a dead track from the back catalog, formed their own coalition in association with the popular social networking site **MySpace** to introduce a new online service in 2008, which offers free streaming music along with the opportunity to download tracks through Amazon.com. It is too soon to predict the popularity of this approach. In any case, it has become a moot point, because iTunes itself has now adopted a variable pricing system.

As rapidly as the digital music domain has grown, it would probably move even more quickly if not for the lack of standardization of digital download formats. The industry has been down this road before, with 33 1/3 versus 45 rpm formats, and in the video world with VHS versus Betamax. Nevertheless, the downloads sold through iTunes and Microsoft's

Raising a Ruckus

As the major labels became more aggressive in their targeting of illegal file sharing in the late 1990s and early 2000s, they began to use their trade organization, the RIAA, to sue colleges and universities whose internal computer networks were being used by their students as a means to illegally share music files. One business was initially developed to address this situation. Ruckus software and its associated Web site was marketed to colleges as a safe way to offer their students free music. Ruckus would license the music from the major and independent labels for streaming listening, and support itself through fees to the college itself, advertising, and selling its software. Some colleges quickly signed up for the service, feeling it would protect them from potential lawsuits.

By 2007, Ruckus had slightly changed its business model. No longer relying on universities to "sign up" or pay a fee to join the network, Ruckus was offered to anyone who had an email extension of .edu (presumably students or college employees). Advertising and software sales revenue supported the service, which was still designed as a free way to listen to music online, while also offering the ability to purchase downloads. Nonetheless, Ruckus's reliability and service has had mixed reviews from students.

less successful Zune player use different codes, and therefore they are both not uniformly compatible with digital players.

Digital Retailing

Professor Storm Gloor of the University of Colorado at Denver points out in a written study sent to the author, and utilized in this section of the book, that the digital stores parrot the methodology of the normal retail record store by displaying their best-selling items. Just as Amazon creates recommended choices for consumers by analyzing their book-buying history, the digital sites recommend new music to the customer. They may also indicate recommendations by their own staff.

Two other advantages enjoyed by the digital platforms are:

- *24/7 service* Digital services never close
- *Perpetual stock* Sales of digital media don't require the server to order more copies

Two disadvantages are:

- *Different download sites may have the same recording in different format, or the product may have a different bit rate, which affects the audio quality*
- *The consumer is often aware that they may be able to access the same digital information without charge, albeit illegally*

SUBSCRIPTION MODELS   In a subscription model, the customer pays a monthly fee, entitling him to download a certain number of tracks. This model is used by the company emusic. Anything bought from this supplier can be burned to a CD or transferred to a portable player without any restrictions. Napster uses a different model, with the consumer permitted an unlimited number of downloads per months. However, Napster tracks cannot be burned to CDs. This is not too surprising when one considers that Napster is now owned by a record label (Universal). In both of these systems, when a subscription lapses, the consumer loses access to the files.

The iTunes music store is an a la carte model, where the consumer pays for each track. There is never a subscription fee, or any commitment on the part of either the consumer or the company. This music can also be burned to a CD. Amazon.com offers a competing service to iTunes.

A compromise between subscription services and a la carte purchase is offered by Real Networks' Rhapsody, Yahoo Music, and MySpace Music. They allow subscribers to stream music, in other words to listen, but the purchase of tracks is on an individual basis.

OTHER DIGITAL MODELS   Amiestreet.com prices their digital downloads based on popularity. The more popular the song, the higher the download fee. Record labels think that this is a logical model, but they would prefer to see all new product sold at a higher rate, and catalog product made available at a lower price.

Spiral Frog does not charge for downloads but the consumer is compelled to view advertising. To download more tunes the consumer must return to the site and view more advertisements.

Burnlounge.com is an a la carte digital service that requires a basic startup fee, and then allows the consumer to establish their own retail digital store where they sell downloads and generate commission income for themselves.

Illegal Downloading and Legal Alternatives

Despite the RIAA's continual attempts to prevent illegal downloading, it is still a common phenomenon. Snocap and Playlouder are two companies that are attempting to establish the legal sale of peer-to-peer retailing. In these models, the content owner is compensated each time their music is transferred to any site.

The success of these legal alternatives to illegal file sharing will depend upon the RIAA's ability to shut down the illegal sites, or the organization's ability to convince the consumer to "do the right thing." There is a bit of a conflict here, because the RIAA's lawsuits have resulted in some negative public relations. For example, when a teenager uses her or his grandmother's computer to rip music, the grandmother has the legal responsibility to settle the RIAA's lawsuit. These legal actions cast the organization's image in a negative light to consumers.

It would appear that either the RIAA has to develop a foolproof mechanism that will enable it to identify *all* file sharers, or it has to prosecute only the most egregious cases, and focus on developing an image of itself as the friend of the songwriter and artist.

At the present time, there are so many young people willing to spend time hacking into supposedly foolproof and protected computer systems, that it appears the RIAA might be better off spending its energies on how songwriters and artists are negatively affected by file sharing. Digital rights management (DRM) prevents or controls the number of copies that a consumer can make from a single digital file. iTunes tracks can be burned to a CD five times, for example. Major labels have even made attempts to limit the downloading of their CDs, but this proved both futile and damaging. Once again hackers figured out how to defeat these programs. Ultimately, the subscription solution may be the best one, but it also requires some sort of DRM, because simply informing a user that they can't access tracks that have already been downloaded is not a practical alternative.

Watermarks are digital markings that can identify data from the downloader. The performing rights societies are experimenting with the use of watermarks to identify songs played on the radio. However, inventive hackers are finding ways to strip identifying information from digital music files.

Digital Distributors

There are a number of digital distributors. Some of them, notably **CD Baby**, distribute CDs as well. CD Baby charges the record label (often the artist himself) a flat fee of $4 per CD, and the label sets whatever it wishes as the retail price. The label or artist prepares a description of the product that is comparable to a shorter version of the classic "one sheet," that distributors send out with new record releases. CD Baby then farms out their CDs to several dozen digital distributors, and takes a small commission for instituting the transaction. When the label (or artist) is owed $20, CD Baby sends out a check. CD Baby charges a one-time fee of $35 to place each CD on its Web site.

The company also provides clients with various tips on how to promote their records, and for a small fee it offers them the use of a credit card machine that is essentially on loan to the artist for as long as she maintains her business relationship with CD Baby. This is useful when the performer is doing gigs, and enables the artist to avoid the complexities of dealing with a bank.

The beauty of digital distribution is that it avoids various parts of the chain of brick and mortar distribution. For the record label, it offers:

- *No continuing manufacturing costs.* Distribution consists of digital files sent electronically to the digital retailer.
- *No shipping or postage costs.*
- *Instant delivery to radio, television, dance deejays, and jukebox services.*

- *A promotional tool, giving the labels the opportunity to offer free or discounted downloads of specific tracks.*

For the record retailer, advantages include:

- *No need for a storefront or the thousands of square feet of retail space to make room for thousands on thousands of different recordings in hundreds of musical genres.*

For the artist, digital distribution allows full artistic freedom, including:

- *No need to deal with traditional record labels.*
- *An artist can release one, two, three, or four songs, rather than producing an album's worth of new material.*

Finally, there are many benefits to the consumer, including:

- *The ability to store entire music libraries in a single handheld device. Consumers can include whatever songs they wish, rather than having a home library of CDs that includes many songs that they are not interested in hearing again.*
- *No need to leave home to get the latest releases.*
- *Easy-to-create playlists to fit moods or themes, without having to go through their entire record collection.*
- *Recommend tracks to one another, audition tracks through MySpace or YouTube, and then instantly purchase tracks or albums.*
- *Share critiques of specific artists or songs with each other.*

The disadvantages of digital delivery include:

- *The availability of thousands of albums and songs make promoting product more difficult. How will a particular new release stand out?*
- *The ease of friends sending tracks to one another without payment of any kind will decrease the earnings of artists and even more of songwriters*
- *Digital distribution has caused a large number of record stores and chains to go out of business. This has led to the loss of thousands of jobs in the music industry. This trend will likely accelerate as digital distribution diminishes the sale of CDs.*
- *The quality of digital audio files is inferior to that delivered by CDs.* This is a very serious problem that will affect artists in a number of ways. Most artists spend countless hours recording their albums, whether in a commercial recording studio or a home facility. There is the actual recording, the mixing process, and the mastering process. The artist wants the music to sound as good as the technology permits. Between the necessary compression of data for mp3 files, and low-quality output of the portable players, consumers are hearing an inferior sound.

- *A hard drive crash or a computer virus could result in a consumer losing an entire music collection. So could the theft of a home computer, laptop, or external hard drive.*
- *The artist may have recorded an entire CD, but the consumer is quite likely to only buy one or two tracks.* This is a critical artistic problem for musicians. In many cases the artist has agonized over the order of tracks on a CD, has spent many hours in the studio determining whether the songs recorded fit into a single project, and in some cases has even organized an entire album around a concept or group of concepts. For the consumer to entirely bypass the artist's wishes, and simply rip a song or two, is an upsetting notion to the artist who is serious about how an album is presented. It is quite likely that artists will rethink the entire notion of making concept albums, a genre that began in the mid-1960s with the Beach Boy's *Pet Sound,* and the Beatles' *Sergeant Pepper* albums.
- *Jupiter Research has projected that in the next five years digital sales will rise from their current 18 percent of the sales of recorded product to 41 percent. Of course, this is a prediction, not a fact.*

THE MUSIC PRODUCTS INDUSTRY

The music products industry encompasses the manufacturing, wholesaling, and retailing of musical instruments as well as musical accessories, printed music, and instructional music audio and video products.

Manufacturers

According to the April 2008 issue of *Music Trades,* the top ten music and audio suppliers, in order of revenue, are: Yamaha, Harman Professional, Fender Musical Instruments, Shure, Inc., Steinway Musical Instruments, Gibson Guitars, Kaman Music Corp., Digidesign, Jam Industries, and Loud Technologies. Yamaha's estimated revenue for 2007 was $704 million. It is interesting to observe that of these ten companies, five are involved in the manufacturing of sound equipment and microphones. Hal Leonard is the largest of the music print publishers, with estimated revenues of over $145 million, more than double the revenues of second place Alfred, whose income was $ 71.5 million.

The total sales of music products' top suppliers for 2007 were $8,174,489,036, an increase of 4.4 percent over the previous year, with total employees at 33,339, an increase of 3.8 percent. From 1999 to 2007, each year has brought an annual increase in the gross income, except for the years 2001, 2002, and 2006. In a longer projection, the number of employees, however, has actually fallen from 35,121 in 1999 to 33,339 in 2007. The top ten companies account for 46 percent of the revenues generated by all 125 companies in the survey. The figures quoted represent global sales for these companies. Finally, the same Music Industry Census reports the *retail value* of all

U.S. music products and audio sales at $7.5 billion, which is about two-thirds of the sales generated by record companies in the United States.

American manufacturers are moving many of their formerly domestic operations to Asia, because of cheaper labor costs. This has been a sort of gradual progression, with instruments initially being made in Japan, then in Taiwan and Korea, and then in China. Because Chinese labor costs have begun to rise, more instruments are currently being built in Indonesia and Vietnam. Often American manufacturers send their product designers to these countries to help them design instruments that will be saleable in the American marketplaces in terms of design and quality.

Some American instrument makers have secondary product lines that are manufactured in Asia, such as Martin Guitars did until 2007 with their Sigma Guitar line and Gibson has done with their Epiphone product line. There are also some American companies, such as Saga and Johnson, that are strictly importers of musical instruments, usually from China. They create product names that have characteristically American names, such as Shenandoah or Blue Ridge, but the instruments are made in Asia. Some of these importers actually use the same factories, which simply place different product names on the same instruments. A large number of guitars sold in the United States are made in Canada, because the Canadian dollar is generally worth about 20–25 percent less than the U.S. currency.

Some companies have the components made in Asia but then assemble and set up the instruments here, as a means of ensuring better quality and meeting the needs of the American markets. Gold Tone has been a pioneer in this hybrid manufacturing model.

Breaking down the sales numbers by categories, the top ten categories reported in the same issue of *Music Trades* are, in order:

- *Fretted instruments*
- *Sound reinforcement*
- *School music*
- *Printed music*
- *Percussion*
- *Acoustic pianos*
- *Microphones*
- *General accessories*
- *Computer music*
- *Instrument amplifiers*

Between sales of acoustic guitars and such related instruments as banjos, mandolins, and electric guitars, the market for fretted instruments in 2007 was 2.868 million instruments sold, with a retail value of $1.176 billion. Sound reinforcement represented $903 million in sales, school musical instruments $598 million dollars, and printed music $590 million.

Wholesalers

Wholesalers carry extensive lines of music product lines, including printed music. These companies serve the same function as one-stops do in the world of record distribution. A small music store can make a single phone call, and order all or most of the musical merchandise that they need. For a small store this is a tremendous convenience. Many of the high-end music products makers do all of their own selling, and their products are not available through wholesalers. Other instrument makers simply prefer to make their products available only to their franchised dealers.

MUSIC RETAILERS

The 2008 *Musical Merchandise Review* annual guide to music stores listed over eight thousand musical instrument dealers in the United States, classified in various categories. These categories include piano and keyboard instruments, band and orchestra, drums and percussion, fretted instruments, print music, sound reinforcement and recording equipment, DJ equipment, and karaoke products.

Full-line stores carry all or most of these products. Combo stores are rock-and-roll–oriented stores that specialize in guitar, bass, drum, and electronic keyboard instruments. Fretted instrument dealers carry guitars and other instruments in the guitar family, like banjos and mandolins. In most medium-size or large cities, there is at least one store that is the local outlet for sheet music. These stores carry a few musical accessories, but generally do not sell musical instruments.

The stores listed in the MMR directory are almost entirely brick-and-mortar operations that have retail storefronts. In addition to these stores, a number of mail order operations specialize in specific musical instruments. Vintage guitars, for example, are sold in dozens of locations throughout the country by entrepreneurs who do their business by mail or phone, on the Internet, or through catalog sales. Retail guitar magazines have dozens of ads by these enterprises, and many of them sell only expensive instruments. Similar businesses exist for other instruments, but the vintage guitar market for both electric and acoustic guitars and affiliated instruments is the largest.

Sales Trends

Guitar sales are clearly the most dominant single product in the musical instrument world, with almost 3 million acoustic and electric guitars sold in 2007, as opposed to just under 1.65 million in 1999. Consumer demand for fretted instrument strings and instrument amplifiers continues to be high. Other retail trends reflect a blend of growth and decline. Piano sales have diminished by 40 percent from 1999 to 2007, including grand pianos, vertical pianos, and digital pianos. Printed music sales have gone up steadily since 1999, with the exception of 2001, with an average increase of just over 3 percent a year.

Chain Stores

The largest of the musical instrument chain stores is Guitar Center, which currently has 313 locations. The following table lists some other multiple-location stores:

Chain Name	Number of Stores
Sam Ash Music	46
Music Go Round	36
Fletcher Music Co.	23
Daddy's Junky Music	20
Schmitt Music Co.	16
J.W. Pepper & Son	15
Piano & Organ Distributors	14
Jordan Kitt's Music	12
George's Music Stores	11
Mills Music, Inc.	11
Sherman, Clay & Co.	10
Kennelly Keys Music	9

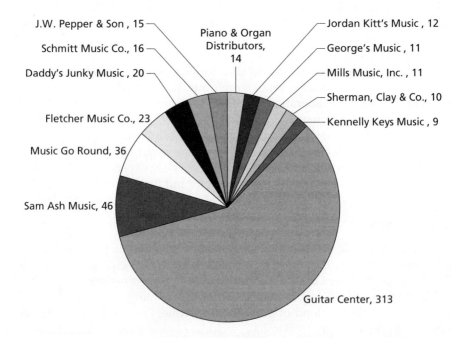

Another thirty-five stores have between four and eight locations, and an additional twenty-three stores have three locations.

The Guitar Center

The massive Guitar Center chain has done much to bring high-quality instruments to the malls of America. Like many chains, it began as a single store in Los Angeles, a spinoff of the popular Organ Center on Sunset Strip, opening its doors in 1964 just as Beatlemania was about to spawn a thousand would-be rock stars. The store became legendary for the celebrity members of the Los Angeles music scene who shopped there. The store quickly expanded to take up an old movie theater and warehouse on the block, eventually occupying forty thousand square feet, and offering everything a guitarist might need, from instruments to amplifiers to accessories.

Guitar Center's superstore model became the basis for the chain's quick growth in the 1980s and 1990s. The store is broken further down into specialized rooms, so high-end acoustic guitars are kept separate from electric outfits. Part of the Guitar Center's expansion has included the absorption of the mail order music company Musician's Friend, and the band instrument chain Music Arts.

The publicly traded company was purchased by Bain Associates, a private equity group, in June 2007. Bain also owns the Home Depot chain. It is unclear if the quality of service and knowledge of employees will be continued under the new ownership.

In order to combat the power of the chain stores, independent music stores have formed their own organization, the **Independent Music Store Owners (IMSO)**. The group shares information gleaned from consumer surveys, and it is in the process of exploring coordinated marketing and the development of products that would be exclusive to independent stores.

Music Stores and School Music Budgets

Full-line music stores often do a considerable business in conjunction with school music programs, renting instruments to students, repairing the school's instruments, and in many cases providing private lessons on various instruments. School band directors do not usually teach individual lessons, and even when they do, they obviously can't teach all the instruments in the orchestra.

Usually, schools in a particular district or town allow music stores to bid on the annual contract as their supplier for the school year. Many of the music stores bid on contracts that are many miles away from the stores themselves, so they deliver instruments and repairs to outlying school districts.

School band programs perform many functions in a community. Bands perform at athletic events and school assemblies, and the band members often compete in state band and choral contests. In general, school administrators are aware of the positive benefits for students and the community that accompany these programs. However, with the ever-increasing emphasis on science and mathematics, plus the tightening of municipal budgets, school music and art programs have suffered cuts in many communities. Entire categories of schools, such as middle schools, have eliminated music programs in many districts. Other programs, especially string programs, have been curtailed or eliminated at various grade levels.

When school music budgets are cut, this also affects the music stores that service these programs. Some stores have instituted their own band programs, but in many cases the stores do not have the physical facilities to make this work. One innovative program was begun by Denny Senseney in his Senseney Music store in Wichita, Kansas. Senseney perceived an opening in servicing the needs of home-schooled students. He set up two band programs for home-schooled students. This was a very successful program, because a parent could drop the student off in a safe and positive environment, run errands, and come back later to pick the student up.

In other districts, parents have mobilized to lobby for school music programs. **NAMM**, the **National Association of Music Merchandisers**, has also provided resources and support for the retention of school music education programs.

There is a trade organization that focuses on the selling of instruments and music to schools. It is called the **National Association of School Music Dealers (NASMD)**, and it holds annual meetings that move to different cities every year.

Chains versus Local Music Stores

The chain stores have a number of built-in advantages over individual stores, or stores that have two or three locations. They carry a wider variety of instruments and get better discounts because they sell more instruments across the entire country than a local store can do. Plus, they are not shut out of business by exclusive arrangements that limit their competition. Because they often have multiple locations in a specific geographic region, they can afford to advertise on cable television stations that are received in a large metropolitan area.

Most musical instrument manufacturers allocate territories to specific dealers. For example, let's say that a particular guitar manufacturer (that we'll refer to as X Guitars) has a dealer in Dubuque, Iowa (we'll call the dealer Max's Music). Dubuque is a city that has four musical instrument dealers, and the other three shops will not be able to carry guitars made by that company. Max's has an exclusive for X Guitars in Dubuque.

However, if Guitar Center were to open a store in Dubuque, they probably already carry X Guitars in their stores. Unlike any other new store that wanted to open a music shop in Dubuque, Guitar Center has immediate access to this maker's goods. It is quite likely that the older store in Dubuque that carries X Guitars has been selling them for a long period of time. Now a unique product line that Max's promoted and sold is readily available at the new Guitar Center, a store that is probably doing heavy advertising and offering attractive special deals to their customers.

Aggravating the situation, Guitar Center may be ordering five hundred X guitars a week for the many stores, while Max's Music is lucky to sell

Starting a Music Store

In March 2008, I spent several hours talking to the late Don Johnson, the editor of *Musical Merchandise Review*. We discussed the future of retail music stores.

Don Johnson (left) being interviewed at a NAMM meeting. Courtesy Symphony Publishing.

Don pointed out that opening a retail music store was something that was still feasible with a relatively small investment. He cited several stores where the business began with the owner offering lessons, some strings and picks, and a few surplus instruments. This sort of operation starts in a modest section of a city or a low-cost strip mall. Often, the owner is also the sole employee.

There is a logical progression of events, where the store picks up a product line. Over a period of time, the music store picks up other lines, the owner eventually stops giving lessons and takes on other teachers, and then part-time and later full-time employees. Usually, the store will start by carrying lesser-known brands that sell for relatively low prices. A number of stores are family businesses with the husband selling the instruments and the wife doing the books and assisting with sales when necessary.

Another scenario starts with the shop owner starting a repair business, and then moving into instrument sales. In this case, there is often an intermediate step where the owner initially sells instruments on consignment. When that proves to be successful, the owner goes into the retail business in a more serious way.

When either of these models succeeds, the owner expands the original space or moves to a larger one. At this point, the store arranges financing. Several companies assist music stores in financing the purchase of musical instruments. The store also must accept credit cards.

Shops that specialize in guitars are particularly suited to this sort of boot-strapping approach, because they don't require the amount of space that a band instrument shop needs. Traditional piano or organ stores aren't suitable for this sort of operation, because they need even more space. There are, however, piano tuners who restore and sell pianos as part of their business.

In Don's opinion, chain stores will never be competitive to either of these two operations because of the service component offered by a small store. When someone runs a one-person shop, they are extremely attentive to customer needs. Retail stores that are conversant with the latest consumer trends have a leg up on other stores. For example, currently drum circles and ukuleles are the rage in many markets.

twenty guitars a year. Because of the volume of orders that X gets from Guitar Center, they are probably offering a larger discount than Max's receives. So not only has Max's lost its exclusivity in Dubuque, but it has to sell the X brand at a higher price than Guitar Center does, because the guitars cost Max more.

Advantages of Smaller Music Stores: Service, Repairs, and Lessons

On the face of it, the situation might appear hopeless for the local music store. In fact, this is not necessarily the case. Guitar Center and the other large chains do not offer music lessons, nor do they repair instruments. (The exception to this rule is the Best Buy electronics chain, which in 2009 began to open large retail music outlets in many of their hundreds of stores. The chain has announced that it will also offer music lessons.) When someone buys an instrument at a chain store and a problem arises with it, such as a warped neck on a new guitar, the salesperson will simply tell the customer to call the manufacturer's 800 number. In the smaller shops, the problem can often be addressed by the repair person that is employed at the store. Small stores that don't have a service department often subcontract the work to an independent contractor who has a service agreement with the store, which includes picking up and servicing instruments at a separate facility. This is an enormously valuable service for the consumer, although it is probably one that isn't understood by the consumer until a problem develops.

Similarly, the large chains often sell instruments that haven't been tested before they are put on the store's shelves. Guitars, for example, may come from the factory with the action set too high for the student. At a store that services what they sell, they will have "road tested" the product before it gets to the shelf.

A store that develops a reputation for employing good repair people will reap two benefits from that association. Repair work itself can be a possible profit center for the store, bringing in store traffic. A satisfied customer often will return to purchase new instruments, trade-in old ones, and to purchase accessories or instructional books or videos. The culmination of the relationship comes when customers recommend the store to other family members and friends. Smaller stores tend to have less employee turnover and customers develop personal relationships with store personnel. Chain stores are notorious for employing younger personnel who have no plans to stay on the job for a long period of time. Consequently, personal relationships with the customer tend not to develop.

Local music stores usually offer lessons, which are offered on a weekly basis. Usually the store manager and the teachers discuss what sort of instructional materials and accessories the store should carry. Because some full-time music teachers have as many as 50 students a week, the sale of instructional material can result in solid additional income for the store. When a student reaches the level of needing a better instrument, the store manager and the teacher will likely discuss what brand of instrument can be sold at a reasonable price. The store will thus have a ready customer base, as well as a source for good used instruments to sell to the next generation of beginners.

EMPLOYEE VERSUS INDEPENDENT CONTRACTOR STATUS   Most music stores treat their repair people and teachers as independent contractors. The store rents the space to the teacher for an hourly fee. Independent contractors do

The Music Store as a Community Center

I have been the Western correspondent for *Musical Merchandise Review* for over twenty years. In 2007, I was doing a story on Larry's Music in Medford, Oregon, a small town not far from the California border. A local musician came in and talked to a salesperson for about a half-hour. It turned out that this particular musician would come in about once a week, to check out new equipment, and to talk to the musicians who operate the store. For him this wasn't shopping, it was about being part of a community. When Guitar Center came to the area, the Larry's store manager visited the new superstore, and established a respectful relationship between the two stores. Larry's manager realized that the strength of his store was that it provided a sense of community and continuity that a forty-five-year-old musician is not apt to find at Guitar Center.

A community does not need to be limited by geography. Specialized instrument dealers like the Button Box in Massachusetts have built a virtual community of people interested in concertinas, accordions, and other squeezeboxes. The store sponsors an annual "Squeeze In" that draws players from around the world. Besides repairing and selling vintage instruments, the store's owners have branched out into instrument manufacture as well, making their own line of Morse concertinas. The store has become a Mecca to concertina players, who will often plan a vacation trip to include a stop there. This kind of intense relationship is difficult to replicate in a chain-store setting.

Other music stores specialize in such relatively limited sales vehicles as oboes or tubas. Such stores are apt to do a large mail order or Internet business, because they provide the customer with a choice of specialized instruments that even large stores in major cities may not be able to match.

not have taxes deducted from their salaries, and they also do not receive health insurance or any other benefits.

Some music stores arrange all the lessons, and the teacher simply calls in and gets his or her schedule. Other stores only rent the space, and it is up to the teacher to schedule the lessons. Virtually all music stores, whether they give lessons or not, have lists of local musicians who are proficient at various styles in any number of instruments. A very large percentage of parents want to know where their children can get lessons before they purchase an instrument.

Discounting, Map Pricing, Catalog Sales, the Internet, and Offshore Instruments

Some of the largest cities have stores that pride themselves on doing a volume business with large discounts. This is particularly true of the music stores in Los Angeles and New York City, but to some extent this condition prevails in any of the larger American cities. Like the chain stores, the big discount stores often do not service what they sell.

Over time, instrument manufacturers began to realize that the heavy discounters were degrading the quality of product lines, and forced some excellent smaller dealers out of business. To combat these trends, the manufacturers introduced the **Minimum Advertised Price** or **MAP**. The concept of the MAP is not to allow anyone to advertise a price that is lower than this somewhat discounted number. There is some controversy in the music products industry about whether the MAP is set at a reasonable percentage. Some stores also object to the idea that the manufacturer can control the price of items. The Supreme Court has validated MAP, but some stores are lobbying Congress to prohibit it. The basic question is whether the price is high enough to enable the store to make a reasonable profit.

A number of other problems have plagued the local music dealer. One parallels the problem of the proliferation of chain stores, and that is the proliferation of mail-order catalog discounters. Musician's Friend is a mail-order company that originally operated out of Oregon, and has been acquired by Guitar Center. They send out thousands of mail-order catalogs, offering discounts on strings, accessories, and combo-oriented musical instruments. The customer can order on line or by phone with a toll-free 800 number. Many local stores have been hurt by catalog sales of accessories. Guitar strings, for example, are sold to dealers at low prices, which enables the dealer to enjoy sizeable retail markups and excellent profit margins. Losing these sales is particularly painful for local stores. Some customers also order instruments on the Net, often again at sizeable discounts. As is the case with chain stores, the catalog discounters do not service the instruments they sell, but the prices can really tempt the consumer.

Many stores are now utilizing their own Web sites to fight back against catalog and discount sales. Different stores use various strategies for their Web sites. Some of these methods of selling on the net are:

- *Only use the Web site for informational purposes and to draw customers to the store*
- *Use the Web site for high-end vintage or rare items*
- *Use the Web site to sell more specialized items that can draw a better price in other geographic areas*
- *Put everything in the store on the Web*

Each of these strategies has its virtues, but it is the job of the store owner to analyze the most practical alternatives for the local market. If the store expects to draw high traffic on the Web, someone must update the Web site on a regular basis, otherwise people will not return to it. The store must decide whether the amount of revenue that the Web site generates is worth the time spent establishing and maintaining it. Some stores include an 800 number on the site to provide the customers with personal service. Other stores have an 800 number but don't bother with a Web site.

For the last few years, a number of chain stores, including Wal-Mart and Target, have begun importing inexpensive instruments that are made offshore, usually in Asia. Although these stores do not specialize in the sale of musical instruments, their instruments are the newest competitive headache for independent music stores.

Because these stores don't provide any sort of instrument adjustment or repair, a store that has repair personnel needs to decide what to do when a parent shows up with an inferior instrument in need of repair. There are several different strategies that I have observed stores adopting when this occurs:

- *We don't repair instruments that were bought elsewhere.*
- *We can repair your instrument, but because you didn't buy it here, the repair is going to cost you more than it would if we were servicing something that we sold.*
- *We can repair your instrument, but it is going to be at the end of our repair line, because our first obligation is to repair what we sell.*
- *We will repair the instrument.*

This last strategy is usually accompanied by an explanation that the reason that mass merchandisers can sell the instrument so cheaply is because it was made outside the United States, by poorly paid shop workers, whose level of workmanship is not up to the standards that this particular store uses in its choice of product lines. Mass marketers, of course, would argue that this is a matter of opinion.

Yet another approach is to try to encourage school music teachers to explain that the price differences between instruments often reflect differences in the quality of the workers and materials used in making the instruments. A parent may well trust a teacher's opinion more than that of a store owner, because the parents are aware that store owners may be biased in favor of their own product lines.

Quotas

Some manufacturers require stores to order a specific number of musical instruments annually, or in some instances they demand that stores carry a large number of the company's various models or instruments. Some companies then attempt to raise these numbers, in order to increase sales. This is a sore point for small retailers, who feel that they are doing their best to promote a company's products, with relatively little financial support. Even some medium-sized stores have dropped product lines when the companies started to make what dealers regarded as excessive demands in their quotas.

STORE LOCATIONS Many of the most successful music stores have had the wisdom to purchase their own building. Those who did not do so but who rented or leased their property faced steeply increasing rental costs if they chose a location in an area of the city where real estate was appreciating at a rapid clip. This often happens, because music stores are often on the frontlines of changing neighborhoods; soon fancy boutiques and restaurants move in to cater to the new population, and the music store is left to compete in a suddenly hot rental market. I have known several music store owners who passed up opportunities to buy their buildings, and lived to regret this when real estate

Sometimes Price Trumps Service

Sandy Monro, until recently the proprietor of The Great Divide Music Store in Aspen, Colorado, told me a sobering story about how—even when a store provides great service—customers sometimes will choose a relatively small savings over what might in the long run be a better overall deal. And it's not just those who watch their dollars; after all, Aspen is not known as a poverty-stricken city, in fact the *lowest* priced home in the town sold for over a million dollars last year. Aspen is also a town where many Hollywood personalities live. Some live there year round, others have second homes that they use when they come to town to ski.

Sandy had a longtime customer who is a prominent Hollywood personality, and whose son had taken lessons on guitar at the store for several years. The boy was close to his guitar teacher, and was thoroughly involved in his guitar lessons. One day the actress brought her son to the store for his weekly guitar lesson. He was sporting a brand new Martin D28 guitar, an item priced well above $3,000. Sandy inquired where the guitar had been purchased, a bit miffed because his store was a Martin Guitar dealer. The actress explained to Sandy that she had bought the guitar for her son in Los Angeles, because it was "$200 cheaper there." To say the least, Sandy was annoyed.

Many people who seek discounts in music stores seem to do it more as a matter of principle than out of necessity. Clearly the actress could easily have afforded the extra $200, and she had a long relationship with Sandy and his store, so you would think she would have preferred to give him the business. She also hadn't thought through what would happen when the guitar would need servicing or repair. Of course, many others appreciate the service component and don't look solely at the price to determine their purchases. This underscores that what one consumer might regard as service beyond the call of duty may have little meaning to another customer.

prices skyrocketed, and their rentals followed the same path. Of course, it is also possible for a music store owner to buy a building in a neighborhood that deteriorates. Should this occur, the owner begins to lose customers, especially parents, and also takes a loss on the value of the building itself. A less serious problem occurs if a store does not have its own dedicated parking spaces, and a city decides to put in parking meters in an area that formerly had free parking. Some of the key elements in store locations include:

- *Parking.* When parking is difficult to come by, customers who live in the suburbs will avoid the store. If the store is in a major city, it is best to make some sort of deal with a neighborhood parking lot that offers customers free two-hour parking.

  The advantage of mall stores is that they almost always have free parking.
- *Access to public transportation.* If the store offers lessons, many of its students will be younger than driving age, and their parents may not

wish to drive them. College-age and urban dwellers in general don't own cars and rely on public transportation to get them around town.

• *Proximity to compatible businesses.* This might include record stores, book stores or coffee shops, and restaurants. This is particularly important if a parent brings a student to weekly lessons, and is looking for something to do while the child is taking lessons.

Some mall stores work just fine, whereas in other mall locations, traffic to or even in the mall is such a problem that people find the store inconvenient. Suburban locations are often good for stores that feature lessons as a large part of their operation. Specialty shops in vintage instruments don't attract the sort of people that generally enjoy being around large shopping malls.

Of course, individual stores need to adapt to the local scene. A music store in the Pioneer Square section of Seattle is located in an extremely high traffic area. Street parking is available but is difficult to procure. Seattle is notorious for having horrendous traffic problems, especially in rush hour. One customer actually phoned the store repeatedly on the day that he was picking up his amplifier. He wanted to make sure that he would be able to find a parking spot, so that he could pick up his heavy amplifier without having to carry it for many blocks. The reason that the store doesn't move is that the area has tremendous tourist traffic, and is located in the downtown area.

Another problem for stores in malls has recently surfaced; malls themselves have experienced declining traffic and the closing of some major stores. This can turn what used to be a high-traffic area into a comparative ghost town. If the music store has a long-term lease, moving is not a good option.

Knowing the Community

It is important for stores to understand the various ethnic groups in a community, so that they can deal with a variety of customer needs. I once interviewed employees at a store in Tucson, Arizona, and found that four out of five of them spoke Spanish. Not only could these employees relate to the local Mexican American community, but they also put on musical instrument shows in Mexico and sold quite a few instruments at these shows.

A music store in Corvallis, Oregon, sold a considerable number of guitars to a Mexican-American church in a nearby town. One of the store's two owners is teaching herself to speak Spanish and has a chart of the guitar with all of the parts marked in Spanish. Her husband does the repairs for the store, and this chart helps him to deal with his Spanish-language customers in diagnosing problems with guitars.

Adapting to the local community and its needs can take many other forms. A piano store in Los Angeles advertises in the Chinese Yellow Pages and has an employee who speaks Chinese. Obviously, its owner understands that the large Asian community there forms a key customer base for piano sales and lessons.

Financing, Advertising, and Special Events

Like other businesses, most music stores accept credit cards. For large ticket items, such as high-priced pianos or other instruments, many stores have arrangements with banks or lenders that allow the consumer to buy instruments on time. NAMM can help stores to make such arrangements.

For many years, the Yellow Pages dominated the advertising budgets of most music stores. As the influence of the Yellow Pages has waned, many stores have reallocated their advertising budget in the following ways:

- *Building a database of customers, including any major purchases that they have made in the store.*
- *Special sales events, advertised to good customers only, once or twice a year.*
- *Advertising in local newspapers.* Sometimes these ads are in the classified section, sometimes they are display ads. The newspapers may be daily or weekly papers.
- *Holding workshops for music teachers.* This is a particularly valuable form of advertising for school band and choral teachers.
- *Radio ads.*
- *Cable TV ads.* Stores that have branch operations can often advertise on a cable station because one commercial reaches all of their customers. This is cost-effective.

Another effective form of advertising is to hold clinics with well-known musicians. Often the expense is shared with the manufacturer of the instrument that the musician endorses. Musicians that give clinics generally choose between two approaches. One method is to carefully explain whatever techniques the teacher demonstrates. The other technique is to impress the audience with the teacher's technical prowess. As long as a store presents both sorts of clinicians at various times, almost all customers will be satisfied. Stores that are not large enough to accommodate a large group rent space elsewhere for these events.

When a musician does a workshop, the store displays a large number of instruments made by whatever company has brought the musician. Often he will demonstrate each instrument. If the event is successful, the store will sell some of the instruments at the event itself, and several more during the next week. In addition to selling instruments, these events give the store a high profile in the community and create goodwill among musicians and music fans. Uptown Music, in Keizer, Oregon, reinforces this notion of community service by asking workshop attendees to bring some canned food to their workshops. The store then donates the food to the local food bank.

EXPORTING MUSICAL PRODUCTS

Exporting instruments made in the United States involves a variety of problems. Exporters must watch the value of the dollar in relation to the value of currency of each country where they are exporting goods. The value of currency fluctuates on a daily basis, and in some countries there are profound differences from one day to the next.

Different countries require differing levels of import tax levies. Sometimes these levies can be quite eccentric. For example, guitar makers may be required to pay a 10 percent import tax, but amplifiers may be taxed at 20 percent. Obviously, the consumer who purchases an electric guitar is quite likely to wish to purchase a new amplifier at the same time. If the price of an amplifier needs to be greatly marked up to account for the import duties, then that sale may be lost.

TRADE SHOWS

NAMM (National Association of Music Merchants)

NAMM is the trade organization that solicits membership from music stores and musical instrument manufacturers and wholesalers. Although the exhibitors are mostly American, quite a few foreign manufacturers also display their products. Each year the organization holds its enormous winter trade show in Anaheim, California. This four-day show is a musical extravaganza featuring exhibits by all major and numerous minor makers of musical instruments, as well as by print music publishers, and recording and sound equipment manufacturers. Throughout the show, NAMM holds educational seminars for music retailers that consist of panels of experts discussing everything from financing a music store, to choosing a location, insuring a business, and establishing intelligent pricing policies.

The manufacturers present their new products, and take orders. Some of these companies do a huge percentage of their annual business at the NAMM show. Often they feature special discounts or extended credit terms for stores that buy at or just after the completion of the show. Some of the exhibitors sell their products at a steep discount on the last day of the show, in order to avoid having to ship all of their merchandise back to their headquarters. There are also numerous product demos by famous musicians.

The event is not open to the general public, only to people in the industry. However, some consumers manage to attend the show, usually through tickets given by music stores to their best customers, or because they have some acquaintance or family member that works in the industry. NAMM is an amazing event and music manufacturers such as the piano makers Steinway, Bosendorfer, Baldwin, Yamaha, and Kawai are exhibitors. Attending NAMM is a bit like registering for the Olympic Games as a race walker, because there are thousands of feet of floor space taken up by the event, and any attendee will be utilizing lots of shoe leather.

NAMM has a summer show, which has been held in different cities. Recently, the organization has moved the show back to Nashville. In recent years, NAMM had moved the show from Nashville to Indianapolis and Austin, and the other two locations didn't seem to satisfy attendees. Retail stores like coming to Nashville, but the town lacks a convention center large enough for the needs of the show. What Nashville does possess is an atmosphere that attendees enjoy. Nashville is within driving distance of many major eastern and midwestern cities, and the summer show is generally a bit more slower-paced than the massive winter event.

From the point of view of store owners, wholesalers, and manufacturers, NAMM is a valuable resource. Store owners get to see new products and to establish or re-establish relationships with the various manufacturers. Retailers can also use the show as a vehicle for establishing credit with suppliers. Those who attend the show get the special discounts, see new products demonstrated, and meet with their peers to exchange sales techniques and hash over mutual problems. Small stores or those located in remote areas may seldom see sales representatives, so the show provides them with an opportunity to develop relationships with people with whom they have only had telephone contact.

For the manufacturer or wholesaler, the show is an opportunity to meet new store owners or managers, and to develop the kind of relationships that can lead to long-term sales growth. The manufacturers can also get feedback from the retailers, the people in the trenches, as to what sort of product designs or displays are working, and which ones they would be better off discarding. Some manufacturers even bring prototypes, pilot models of new products to the show, in order to determine whether the products will work for retailers. Foreign manufacturers often come to NAMM seeking to find wholesale distributors for their products, or to make contacts with large retail stores. Because so many dealers attend the Anaheim show, this is a good outlet for an initial foray into the American music products market.

The annual show is not the only reason for a retailer to join NAMM. The organization helps to promote school music programs, and to assist in passing public legislation supporting its members. It has also joined with organizations and corporations in order to provide funding for research on the importance of music to children, and to promote music in a variety of ways. NAMM has supported research designed to prove that music "makes you smarter." These studies have achieved some mainstream recognition through media responses in such outlets as the *Today* show and the newspaper *USA Today*. This has helped maintain school music budgets and parents have been stimulated to help raise money independently for these programs.

The organization offers discount service providers for such financial services as insurance and financing. NAMM also commissions and publishes materials that assist the store owner. Currently, NAMM's membership includes nine thousand retailers and manufacturers of music products from eighty-five countries.

NAMBI

NAMBI is the acronym for **NAMM-affiliated Music Business Institutions**. In 1978, NAMM realized the value of having a student and college-affiliated educational wing to help support college programs in the music products industry. According to the NAMBI Web site, courses in institutions that give music products degrees should include:

- *Marketing*
- *Sales*
- *Computer skills*
- *Finance*
- *Business communications*
- *Economics*
- *International marketing*
- *Music publishing*
- *Advertising*
- *Retail management and sales*

NAMBI students are required to complete an internship; NAMM offers internships, as do many of the major players in the music world. The organization gives scholarships to its college-affiliated programs. It is expected that students who receive these scholarships will attend either the winter, summer, or both shows. Stipends are also given to faculty who teach in NAMBI-affiliated programs, which assist them in attending the shows. Because travel funds for faculty have been declining in recent years, this stipend has become a valuable resource for music products college faculty members.

When students attend the show, they can see first hand the many opportunities in the music products field and gain a better sense of where they can develop their careers. A number of retail music stores conduct interviews and hire students on the spot.

It is interesting that NAMBI offers strong support for music product educational programs in a way that the record industry has never done for music industry programs. Although record company personnel speak or appear on panels at MEIEA conventions, there has been almost no financial support from the record industry for the organization. ASCAP and SESAC have consistently offered such assistance and BMI has done so in the past.

THE VALUE OF MUSIC PRODUCTS EDUCATION   The music products student has a big advantage over the music business major, because of the organizational support offered by NAMM. The industry itself has basically created opportunities for students to network with their employers. Many students also get the equivalent of music products internships by working in a music store while they attend school. Nevertheless, the sort of business training that colleges offer, coupled with the opportunities that NAMM has available, makes for a powerful combination.

International Shows

The Frankfurt Music Fair (Musikmesse) is an international music show that attracts many European musical instrument manufacturers and retailers. Most days of the show are closed to the public, but on one day toward the end of the show consumers are welcome. Any U.S. company that wishes to do extensive business in Europe attends Frankfurt. Virtually all German music stores attend Frankfurt. Don Johnson reported that there is more interest in traditional acoustic instruments at the Frankfurt show than there is at NAMM, especially on the day that is open to the public.

Recently, China has instituted a similar show in Shanghai, run by the same people who run the Frankfurt Music Fair. At the Shanghai show, attendees can visit factories, and manufacturers can make deals to have instruments designed or built in China. Don Johnson told me that attendees at the most recent Shanghai show outnumbered those at the Frankfurt Music Show. Undoubtedly in future years, companies that wish to do business in Asia will need to attend this show. Smaller and more specialized shows take place in other countries as well.

Terms to Know

AIMS (Association of Independent Music Stores) *276*
CD Baby *283*
CIMS (Coalition of Independent Music Stores) *275*
Digital rights management *277*
iPod *280*
Independent Music Store Owners (IMSO) *289*

MAP (Minimum Advertised Price) *294*
MP3 *279*
Music Monitor Network *276*
MySpace *280*
NAMBI (NAMM-affiliated Music Business Institutions) *300*
NAMM (National Association of Music Merchants) *290*

National Association of School Music Dealers (NASMD) *290*
Napster *279*
NARM (National Association of Record Merchandisers) *276*
RIAA (Record Industry Association of America) *277*

For Class Discussion

1. Is there a future in record store retailing?
2. Do you buy CDs? If so, where do you buy them?
3. Do you shop at iTunes?
4. From your point of view, what are the advantages and disadvantages of shopping at a retail music store or on the Internet?
5. Where do you buy musical instruments?
6. What retail music stores are located in your hometown? Do they give lessons or do repairs?
7. Have you ever attended a clinic or masterclass at a music store?
8. Do you pay attention to what country a musical instrument was made in? Does this matter to you?

CHAPTER **17**

■ ■ ■ ■ ■

Individual Entrepreneurship

lmost all of the books about the music industry have emphasized the opportunities available in working through the established system: record labels, music publishers, and so on. The most recent books about the industry have focused on the importance of the Internet and have recognized the so-called **long-tail theory** espoused by Chris Anderson, the editor of *Wired* magazine. The long-tail theory maintains that the spread of new media outlets opens up opportunities for artists or businesses to promote their wares in new ways at minimal expense and therefore to find a marketing niche for their work. Anderson contrasts this with the old-line theories of mass merchandising, where a product that could not enter the mass marketplace had no ability to find its place in the market.

This chapter will primarily deal with the realities of pursuing a career in music in the twenty-first century. As everyone is aware, the number of musicians and outlets for their music has been steadily growing, while the mass marketing of recordings is declining. Although there will always be stars and superstars, the reality of careers in today's music world is a great deal of flexibility and creativity is necessary to make a living in the music field. My intention is to profile a number of people who are currently working and making a reasonable living in today's music market.

Despite the many challenges, and more than any other art form, music does have a relatively large number of practitioners who are members of the middle class. Studio musicians, symphony orchestra musicians, songwriters, and busy freelancers are among this group. Contrast this with the position of visual artists, writers, theater people, and dancers. In a town such as Portland, Oregon, for example, there are probably more members of the symphony alone than there are people making a full-time living in the theater community. One of the challenges that any beginning musician faces is that there's no one path that ensures success; the personal stories in this chapter will illustrate just a few of the many possibilities that musicians have successfully pursued.

This chapter will focus on two basic questions:

1. What are possible career paths for people who wish to pursue long-term careers in music?
2. How a music career can be realized at a time when so many careers in music are dependent upon a musician's ability to develop a variety of skills over a period of years?

I will return to these questions at the end of this chapter, but first let's look at some case studies of how several musicians have handled their careers over time.

RANDALL WILLIAMS: MUSICIAN/EXPLORER

I wracked my brain to come up with a phrase to describe what Randall Williams does. I refer to him as an "explorer" because I don't really know anyone else who does exactly what he does.

Randall has a music degree in voice, and studied and lived in Europe. Along the way he picked up seven languages. He returned to the United States, and attended a concert featuring Bill Nash in Dallas, where Bill was playing guitar using partial capos. A capo is a mechanical device that enables guitarists to change keys while still working in their favorite keys. A partial capo covers some of the strings of the guitar, but not others, resulting in some unusual chords.

Using his music training, Randall developed a system for using partial capos. He was able to parlay this method into a number of workshops for Kyser, one of the main companies manufacturing partial capos. They paid him to go to conferences, festivals, and trade fairs, where he taught workshops and sold the capos. Kyser then funded a DVD about partial capos, and Randall has gone on to write two instruction books for Hal Leonard, explaining his technique. As further proof of his entrepreneurial skills, he is currently working part-time doing public relations work for a songwriter. Through this work, he intends to test some of his theories about "viral audience building in a Web 2.0 age."

The other side of Randall's career is a love of travel. Most recently, he has traveled to Haiti, the Dominican Republic, and Puerto Rico, where he played with local musicians, and recorded and filmed the jam sessions. His intent is to do more international travel, and to make video and audio recordings of the trips, and some writing as well.

In addition to all of this, Randall is a songwriter who has recorded a number of CDs, and continues to perform and record his music. Currently he lives in Columbus, Ohio. By combining performing and songwriting, teaching, workshops, and writing instructional materials, he has built a

Randall Williams. Photo by Russ Haire, courtesy the artist.

viable career. Randall Williams is living proof of the value of languages—both linguistic and technological—in the twenty-first century.

MARY KADDERLY: VOCALIST, JAZZ SINGER, AND ACTRESS

One way to make a living in the music world is to juggle a number of roles simultaneously. Mary Kadderly's career combines work as an actress, a singer, a songwriter, and a teacher.

Mary Kadderly has a BA in Theater Arts with a minor in music. She can be found working regularly as a jazz vocalist in clubs in Portland, Oregon. She teaches voice at Portland Community College and privately, and teaches piano privately as well. Mary has also given jazz vocal workshops with Nancy King, a critically acclaimed jazz vocalist. She has recorded several CDs on her own label, and her most recent album *I Go Zoom*, consists of her own original music. The style is a blend of jazz and blues. Mary has just completed a children's multimedia project, which will consist of a book and a companion CD.

Mary has an entirely different career as an actress. She has also acted in films for HBO and Warner Brothers, including a role as a jazz singer in the Robert DeNiro film *Men of Honor*. She has also acted in a number of productions in Oregon.

NOAH PETERSON: JAZZ WITH AN OPEN MIND

Noah Peterson is a saxophone player originally from Billings, Montana. He served in the Marine Corps as a saxophonist in the early 1990s, attending the Armed Forces School of Music. He moved to Portland, Oregon in 1994, and studied music at Merylhurst University.

Making a living as a jazz musician is not the easiest of tasks. Noah is succeeding through a combination of versatility, and a willingness to be open to integrating his music with a variety of musical genres. A typical year for him might include 250 live gigs. To give an idea of his versatility, the bands that Noah currently performs with include:

- His own jazz ensembles, which range from a duo to a quintet
- An electric-acoustic blues band
- A zydeco band (Noah plays rub-board in this group, not saxophone!)
- A band led by an acoustic singer-songwriter
- A Praise Team for the Hope Christian fellowship
- The Northwest Community Gospel Choir

Noah has made six CDs under his own name, two as a band leader, and others as a member of various bands. He has also performed on a number of other people's CDs. He also has recently become active in video production for musicians and bands. Noah is also an elected member of the Executive Board of Local 99, the Portland local of the American Federation of Musicians.

MICHAEL KEARSEY: MULTITALENTED BASS PLAYER

For a versatile musician, the number of possible gigs is limited only by the amount of energy and time that any one musician has at his disposal. Michael Kearsey is a Portland electric bass player, an example of someone who is rarely without a weekend work night, a tribute to his versatility and contacts. Michael regularly plays with:

- A jump blues band
- A zydeco group
- A Jimmy Smith–style organ trio
- A jazz quartet of college friends
- An Arabic music band called The Brothers of the Baladi, co-led by Michael and his friend Michael Beach

Michael's musical history goes back to playing in a band that Ric Ocasek had in Boston before he started The Cars. Originally a guitar player,

J. Michael Kearsey (on bass, second from left) with Brothers of the Baladi. Photo: Julie Keefe, courtesy the artist.

Michael began to play electric bass in college so that he could play with a jazz quartet. Since moving to Portland, Michael has been a jingle writer, done voiceovers, written five soundtracks for Oregon Public Broadcasting, and recorded videos and two CDs that are sold as portraits of Oregon in tourist shops throughout the state. One of the CDs has sold over twenty thousand copies.

The Brothers of the Baladi go back some thirty years to when Michael Beach was living in California and became entranced with Arabic music. Michael Kearsey joined the band in 1989, and they have recorded eleven albums. The band has had several would-be agents or managers, but has essentially accomplished everything on its own with a revolving cast of musicians anchored by Beach and Kearsey. After 9/11, the Brothers found that interest in Arabic music greatly declined, even though the band members were not Arabs. Gradually, they have worked their way back, building a West Coast fan base.

CHRIS DANIELS: BAND LEADER, PRODUCER, AND COLLEGE PROFESSOR

Like Michael Kearsey, Chris Daniels has succeeded through versatility. He is a college professor, arts administrator, songwriter, and he uses his considerable organizational skills as a band leader. Chris' story is also one that shows the role of good timing and luck in any musician's career. Although it never was his goal, Chris has become a well-known musician in Holland, much better known there than in his hometown of Denver, Colorado.

In 1989, Chris Daniels recorded a CD produced by legendary piano player Al Kooper, called *That's What I Like About the South*. After six months, Al was unable to make a deal for the album, so Chris signed with an independent Denver label called Redstone. The album was picked up by Armed Forces radio, and from there got to a Dutch record company. They offered Chris $20,000 and guaranteed a minimum of two European tours. Although there was supposed to be a 10 percent retail record royalty, most of the profits that Chris realized came from bandstand sales. There were four European tours and a second CD. Chris's band functioned as a sort of Dutch Blood, Sweat, and Tears, Because there were only three Dutch national radio stations, saturation play on one station made the record skyrocket. The record's success also got page one coverage in the Dutch rock journal *Orr*. Currently, Chris is doing his sixteenth Dutch tour. Later, the band signed to Sky Ranch/Virgin Records and starting in the early 1990s began to tour in Italy, France, Denmark, and Switzerland.

Chris's band (Chris Daniels and the Kings) has made records for Harmony Records in Los Angeles, their own label Sky Ranch, Flying Fish/Rounder, Flat Canyon, and K-Tel, the TV marketing company. Currently, their records are distributed by Burnside (BDC) in Portland who are "doing a great job." Chris has dealt with various managers and agents and has set up his deals so that any business that he creates after a gross of $150,000 is not commissionable.

In looking back at his career, Chris feels that in today's music market performers must be multifaceted, doing their own booking, running a Web site, teaching lessons, and also writing charts. He also feels they must know enough about business to set up limited liability corporations, draw up band agreements, and even road managing. Chris has also been the director of a nonprofit arts organization, and currently is an Assistant Professor in the music and entertainment program at the University of Colorado at Denver.

MARY FLOWER: TEACHER/PERFORMER

Mary Flower was one semester short of a theater degree at the University of Indiana when she turned to music as a profession. Moving to Denver in the 1970s, she went through a variety of musical careers. She was in a duo with country-folk singer-songwriter Katy Moffatt, and was the ringmaster for an ever-changing group of woman musicians called The Motherfolkers. Because she was raising two children, she preferred not to travel much. When her children grew up, she found her niche as an instrumentalist-blues singer-songwriter-composer. Mary is equally adept at guitar and Dobro, and began to perform widely as a soloist and accompanist in the Denver area. Mary also won a Colorado Council on The Arts & Humanities individual arts fellowship during her time in Denver.

Mary Flower. Photo by Sidney Smith/Absolute Images.

After attending a summer workshop at the Augusta Heritage Center, she was invited back to teach there in 1993, and has been back almost every summer since then. She moved to Portland in 2005, and now tours in Europe as well as all over the United States. After several self-released albums, she now records for New Orleans' Yellow Dog Records. She also teaches guitar when not on tour, and has recorded some instructional DVDs.

Mary balances traditional and original music. Like many of the artists discussed in this book, she books herself, except for getting some work from an agent in England. She is also in demand as both a vocalist and an instrumentalist, working on other people's records in addition to her own. Mary has twice finished third in the fingerpicking guitar concert at the Winfield, Kansas festival. "Just me and about thirty guys," she told me.

Most of her workshop teaching takes place in the summer, as do many music festivals, so she balances out the summer with weekend concerts during the rest of the year, private teaching, and gigs in the Portland area. Mary Flower's balancing act works out for her, because between singing, playing, performing, writing, and teaching, there is always something going on in her career.

OTIS TAYLOR: BLUESMAN

Otis Taylor moved to Denver as a teenager in that early 1960s. He began to hang out at the Denver Folklore Center, where he studied guitar, banjo, and harmonica. At a very young age, he went to London, and nearly landed a record deal there.

When he came back to Denver, he didn't pursue music as a hobby, but opened a successful antique business. Otis began to start playing music again in the mid-1990s, performing in Denver and Boulder, and eventually landing a recording contract with Canadian company Northern Blues. Currently, he records for Telarc, and recently he produced an album of black musicians playing the banjo.

Although Otis has gone through several management deals that didn't work out, he is very entrepreneurial, and after attending a film scoring workshop at the famous Sundance Festival, he has placed several of his songs on TV (*Crossing Jordan* and *Surface*) and has scored several films, including *Purvis of Overtown*. Otis has won several *Downbeat Magazine* awards and a prestigious W. C. Handy Award. He has toured Europe on numerous occasions and has played most of the major blues festivals.

Because Otis writes blues about such social issues as lynchings and racial injustice and because he plays banjo as well as guitar, his work lies

Otis Taylor. Photo courtesy the artist.

somewhere between folk, protest music, blues, and electric blues. The very thing that makes his music interesting is what makes finding a precise career niche difficult at times. Lately, he has designed a guitar for Santa Cruz Guitars and a banjo for Ome Banjos. Juggling his work as a recording artist, record producer, songwriter and designer of musical instruments is a complex dance but a stimulating one.

MISTY RIVER: THE POWER OF FOUR

Misty River is a quartet of women musicians who play accordion, banjo, fiddle, and acoustic bass. Their music has elements of bluegrass, country music, folk, and Irish influences, and they also write some of their own songs. The band started at a casual open mike performance at an Irish pub in Portland in 1997. The owner insisted that the four of them were a band, and he was equally persuasive about hiring a band that didn't exist and had no professional aspirations. This accidental beginning has led to a ten-year career, six CDs, and hundreds of acclaimed performances. Laura Quigley, the bass player, is the daughter of Carol Harley, who plays banjo and guitar in the group. Chris Kokesh plays fiddle, and Dana Abel plays accordion. All four band members sing, and they are particularly noted for their vocal harmonies.

Misty River. L to r: Laura Quigley, Chris Kokesh, Carol Harley, and Dana Abel. Photo by Owen Carey, courtesy Carol Harley.

This book has not dealt in any detail with the way that family responsibilities impinge upon being in a band, a situation that is not unique to women, but is particularly applicable to them. Dana has a three-year-old and a five-year-old, and she lives in Eugene, 105 miles south of Portland. Another intervening life event occurred when Carol was diagnosed with leukemia in 2004. She is part of an experimental medical program, and has been able to keep working on her music, despite this.

Much of the band's success has come from the way that the various members share responsibilities. Dana, who has a Master's degree in environmental engineering, does all of the financial recordkeeping. Carol does the booking and promotion, Laura drives the bus and handles the sound equipment, and Chris does the most songwriting and does graphics for the band's albums and promotional materials. It is worth noting that the band's promotional material is outstanding, in terms of design and creating interest for the buyer and the consumer. This division of labor between the four members is quite unusual for a band. Each one has been able to use her specific skills in the band, and yet each one has also maintained an individual musical identity and ambitions outside the band itself.

The band has utilized its assets to great advantage. They have secured many bookings through the regional arts organization Arts Northwest, a group that focuses on family entertainment. A showcase in Memphis resulted in their being accepted to a community concert series, in 2007–2008, through an organization called Nashville Live On Stage. The band set their own price and toured for three days at a time.

After ten years of touring, the band is taking a one-year break. In the meantime, Chris is pursuing her singer-songwriter ambitions, and playing with a bluegrass musician and in another band. Carol has a side project called Misty Mamas. Dana expects to spend time with her children, and Laura is working at a horse barn. Carol is also looking forward to studying some new instruments and "getting some rest."

CONCLUSION

In presenting the case studies in this chapter, I have elected to choose people who have been in the business for a while. This is to give the reader a grasp of how a long-term music industry career evolves. Every single person profiled here has had career disappointments, frustrations, and triumphs. What they have in common is an ability to relate their careers to an ever-changing music business landscape. In many cases, they have sustained their careers either by making conscious artistic choices or by taking advantage of available opportunities. Mary Flower, for example, has moved from performing traditional folk music, playing in a duo that was somewhere between folk, rock, and country music, working as a guitar teacher, developing a focused concert program on women in the blues, teaching summer workshops, and touring nationally and even internationally. Although her basic identity is as a soloist, she supplements her income and challenges herself by singing and playing on a variety of recording projects, and has also recorded audio and video instructional materials that are in wide distribution.

The only similarity among all of these various musicians is that none of them does one thing on a full-time basis. Their activities range from performing, recording, film scoring, international touring, booking festivals, teaching, and hosting radio shows. It is up to readers to scope out how they are going to combine their skills, talents, and training into workable career goals. Technology changes constantly as new forms evolve and are superseded by new developments. Someone seeking a music industry career needs to be able to anticipate change and re-tooling when necessary. Survival requires an open mind and a capacity for objective analysis. This has never been an easy industry to deal with, but it increasingly presents interesting challenges for the intelligent musician or entrepreneur. More than ever before, this is frequently the same person.

Terms to Know

Long-tail theory *303*

For Class Discussion

1. What musicians or music entrepreneurs exist in your community?
2. What sort of training enabled them to do what they do?
3. Do you know any people who are pursuing a variety of careers in music simultaneously?
4. Of the people profiled, who comes closest to your own career aspirations?
5. Do you know anyone like Tom May, who is able to use community service in such a way that it also benefits his career?
6. If you had an Arabic band, what strategies would you have pursued after 9/11 in order to continue to work?
7. Which of the musicians profiled here comes closest to your own career goals?
8. Do you have a five-year plan for how you intend to pursue your musical career?
9. What sort of city would be best suited for pursuing a multifaceted music career?

CHAPTER **18**

The Future

BRAVE NEW WORLD

We have discussed many career possibilities that exist for the student who desires to work in the music business as a musician or in the industry itself. Today, we have moved from a world of major labels and an industry that was largely in the hands of major corporations to an era where technology is leading us in many new, unexplored directions.

Some artists have been able to use the internet to promote their careers, whether through their own Web sites or social network spaces such as YouTube or MySpace. For example, jazz composer-band leader Maria Schneider won a Grammy in 2004 for an album that was only available through the Internet. The bad news is that, as with so many other aspects of life, when it comes to new technology, timing is everything. The social networks—MySpace and YouTube—are a perfect example of the musician's dilemma. If a musician or entrepreneur jumps in on a new development too soon, there isn't enough of a consumer audience for it to be useful. If the user waits too long, then the same situation prevails as has always been the case with major labels. If there are over a hundred million friends on MySpace, why would any one new subscriber obtain any real value from the platform? Jumping in somewhere in the middle, before the space is flooded, but after it has some audience, is obviously the right move, but how is it possible to know when the timing is right?

Perhaps the role of the record label will become more promotional than product-oriented. Many artists are capable of making their own recordings, but their problem is driving traffic to their network or Web site. This is always going to take promotional muscle, and, of course, dollars. The whole shape of that process is changing, through the use of the social networking

Illegal File Sharing as Market Research

The big labels are of course uniformly against unpaid file sharing, but even they recognize that the songs that are most actively shared are likely to have the potential to be major hits. A company called **Big Champagne** tracks illegal downloads. It doesn't reveal who is doing the downloading, but can tell purchasers how many plays of a specific song have been ripped by consumers. This is valuable information to record labels, so the very same people who oppose illegal file sharing are paying close attention to which of their products are being shared "off the books." Labels and artists could also trace the growing popularity of a song or performance as sharing either grows or wanes.

groups and through **affinity groups** such as last.fm and imeem. These services make recommendations to consumers that tell a subscriber if they like a particular recording, they are apt to also like the work of another artist.

For composers, it really is a new world out there. Traditional outlets, such as film scoring, may be suffering, but there is a market in composing for videogames, ringtones, and ringbacks. Additional opportunities exist in writing music for PowerPoint presentations, and for Web sites. Composing for video games may represent the challenge of the future for composers, because they have an interactive component, with the consumer controlling the music cues as well as the actions of the various superheroes.

In the meantime, many issues remain to be resolved. There are adherents of giving music away or at least restricting the length of copyright protection. Stanford professor Lawrence Lessig has advocated a fourteen-year term, with a fourteen-year renewal. If the owner of the copyright fails to renew the copyright, it goes into the public domain. Lessig points out there are many copyrights that are still valid, but which the publisher is not promoting. Possibly one solution to the problem would be that if the publisher fails to renew the copyright, it reverts back to the writer. This would protect the songwriter from the dissolution of publishing companies that have often been brokered back and forth, to the point where the writer doesn't even know who the publisher is.

To put it another way, if music is really free for the asking, how can a songwriter dream of having a career? Artists can make up the loss of revenue through performances and merchandise sales, but pure songwriters do not have this option.

OTHER CAREER OPPORTUNITIES

Because of space limitations, this book has not covered a number of possible careers in music in any depth. Music therapy is a relatively young field, and as our economy improves, it may represent an interesting career in the future. A relatively recent branch of music therapy is music **thanatology**. In thanatology, musical performances are designed to assist a dying patient. As studies continue to analyze the psychological importance of music as a therapeutic tool, music therapy promises to be a viable career in the future. In addition to its being offered in an institutional setting, it holds promise in terms of individual therapy. Colleges offer Bachelor's and Master's degrees in music therapy, and there are even degree programs in thanatology.

Performing careers are available playing with various Armed Services bands. These bands play at patriotic ceremonies, such as the president's inauguration. Music librarians work not only in large libraries and college libraries, but also for symphony orchestras.

Other sorts of careers involve working for such music trade organizations as NAMM, NARAS, NARM, NSAI, and the three performing rights organizations. The national offices of unions employ people in various capacities, such as monitoring recording agreements, and dealing with such specific areas as the symphony orchestras. In medium-sized and large cities, local offices of the unions have full-time staff members, as well as paid elected officials. Some of these positions are full-time jobs, but the AFM also has many elected part-time paid positions, serving on the locals' Executive Boards.

Music critics write for local newspapers, and there has been a proliferation of music magazines. Some of these jobs are full-time and others are freelance jobs where the writer is paid for particular articles. Other jobs exist in music-related fields, such as radio, television, and advertising.

GRANTS

Another source of income for musicians is grant programs. Grants are offered by the federal government, through the **National Endowment for the Arts (NEA)** and the **National Endowment for the Humanities (NEH)**. States also have such grant programs. The difference between them is that arts grants are given for creative projects, whereas humanities programs involve critical studies about music. However, humanities programs may fund performances when they are mixed with a scholarly lecture component.

Other grants are available through cities, and from private foundations. Some of these grants are extremely specific, for example, a scholarship for Armenian-Americans from a specific county in Louisiana.

Many grant programs favor grants that involve underserved populations, whether they are neglected because of poverty, ethnicity, or geographic isolation. Grant programs can provide a musician with occasional additional income, and the ability to do projects that are not necessarily commercially viable. Many colleges offer grants to college professors to pursue areas related to their teaching or creative work.

Although some grant programs offer funding to individual artists, a good deal of the funding is given to organizations, or funneled through them, as in the grant described below. Often the organization will have to produce some **matching funds** to qualify for the grant. Consequently, often the artist

Squeezing Out Funding from the Government

In 1975, a young English concertina player in New Jersey applied for a grant through the National Endowment for the Humanities. He hoped to raise a small amount of money to travel to England and record concertina players. At the time, the NEH had a special program called Youthgrant in the Humanities, which was aimed at young scholars. The NEH however did not give funding directly to scholars, so he had to find a local arts organization that would sponsor his application. Through a high school teacher, he was put in touch with the town's arts council, which sponsored local art exhibits. The actual application was somewhat daunting, with a good deal of paperwork involved (there were no PCs at the time) that all had to be filled out meticulously to qualify for the award.

To his surprise, the full grant was approved, but there was a catch. Although he had applied to visit England for the purpose of recording concertina players there, the granting agency's guidelines stipulated that the money could not be used for foreign travel or to purchase goods like recording tape (not to mention recording equipment). It seemed odd to him that the grant was approved, given these limitations. When he enquired of an officer at the NEH, he was told he could go ahead with the plan, but he would have to account for these items in a way that would be acceptable.

The fact that the NEH was willing to sponsor a high-school student to study an instrument as little known as the English concertina showed that—at least at that time—it is possible for a musician with a creative idea to find funding, if he or she does the legwork and completes the paperwork involved.

must find a non-profit arts organization to receive the grant. An example of the way this process works would be a grant given to the Detroit Symphony for a composer to write a new symphonic work for the orchestra.

An organization called The Foundation Center offers many resources that relate to grants. For a modest fee, they will send you a printout that specifies grants that have been funded in a specific subject area. State arts councils are funded by the taxpayer, and offer a great resource in terms of providing information about grant programs available in your state. Their offices are usually in the capital city of the state.

It is important for musicians to be aware of grants, because they can provide opportunities for artistic growth that are often unavailable in the world of commerce. Many musicians shy away from completing the necessary paperwork, but it is not really that difficult to pursue these opportunities. Anyone applying for state grants can meet with the grant-giving organization, because as a taxpayer you are actually a partial funder of the program. Federal grant officers are often accessible by telephone. State arts and humanities councils sometimes hold meetings designed to assist grant applicants in understanding the grant process. Meetings with private foundations are more difficult to arrange, although many of them publish annual reports. Reading these reports will give the applicant a good idea of what sort of programs the foundations fund, and how much money they typically offer.

Many grant applications fail for the simple reason that the applicant does not follow the guidelines set forth in the grant application. Once an applicant is funded for a grant, they have something of an edge in future grant proposals, because clearly they have satisfied the criteria of at least one grant-giving application.

During the course of my musical career, I have received several grants, including a one-year grant from the National Endowment for the Humanities. The purpose of the grant was to write a biography of a gospel music composer named Wesley Westbrooks. The grant paid for a year of research, and there was a considerable amount of additional money that paid for travel to the various places where Wesley had lived, worked, and studied.

In my opinion, I would never have received this grant if a friend of mine hadn't reviewed the original proposal and pointed out a number of places where it was vague and unfocused. It is a good idea to find an intelligent friend who is not involved in your project to read over your proposal. If they find it is unclear, there is a good chance that the funding agency will have similar feelings about it.

PUTTING A CAREER TOGETHER

Many people start out with a focus in one area and, by developing other skills, they adjust to changes in popular taste and the industry itself. It is incumbent on the student to keep up with the industry, read the trade papers, network with other students, join appropriate music business organizations, attend trade conferences, and explore this ever-changing terrain.

Terms to Know

Affinity group *315*	Matching funds *316*	NEH *316*
Big Champagne *315*	NEA *316*	Thanatology *315*

For Class Discussion

1. Do you know anyone who has successfully used the Internet to promote their career in music?
2. What will generate revenue for the music business in the year 2020?
3. What is the long-term perspective for copyright in the United States?
4. Is the restriction of illegal file sharing even possible?
5. How do you keep up with trends in the industry?
6. How do you think recordings, digital or CD, will be promoted in the future?
7. Do any bands that you know sell merchandise?
8. Do you know anyone who has ever applied for a grant?
9. Do you know anyone who has ever received a grant?
10. Have you ever considered applying for a grant?

Additional Resources

Note: Virtually every medium-sized or large city has a free weekly newspaper that lists clubs and gigs. Examples are *Westword* in Denver and the *Village Voice* in New York.

ARTS ORGANIZATIONS

Canada Council www.canadacouncil.ca
National Endowment for the Arts www.nea.gov
National Endowment for the Humanities www.neh.gov

Note: Each state or Canadian province has its own state arts and humanities council.

Regional Arts Organizations

Arts Midwest www.artsmidwest.org
Arts Northwest www.artsnw.org

Consortium For Pacific Arts & Cultures (no Web site) 2141-C Atherton Rd., Honolulu, HI 96822 808-946-7381
Mid-America Arts Alliance www.maaa.org
Mid-Atlantic Arts Foundation www.midatlanticarts.org
New England Foundation for the Arts www.nefa.org
Southern Arts Federation www.southarts.org
Western States Arts Foundation www.westaf.org
Young Audiences www.youngaudiences.org

Note: Young Audiences sponsors concerts in the schools. There are branches in most major cities.

Arts Advocacy
www.artsusa.org

LOW COST LEGAL ASSISTANCE FOR MUSICIANS

A group called Volunteer Lawyers for the Arts offers low-cost legal assistance to artists. The national headquarters are in New York, and their Web address is www.vlany.org
They have offices in many American cities.

MAGAZINES (MUSIC TRADE PAPERS)

Billboard www.billboard.com
Broadcasting www.broadcastingcable.com
Hollywood Reporter www.hollywoodreporter.com
Musical America www.musicalamerica.com

Music Row www.musicrow.com

Pollstar www.pollstar.com

The Music Connection www.musicocnnection.com

Note: The Music Connection prints regularly updated lists of record companies, personal managers, and music supervisors throughout the year

DIGITAL TRADEPAPERS

Two excellent digital newsletters about the music industry are the weekly *Encore* and the weekday *Dean's List*. They are both available through free subscriptions at www.encore@ celebrityaccess.com and deankay1@deankay.com

MAGAZINES DEALING WITH MUSIC PRODUCTS

MMR (Musical Merchandise Review) www.mmrmagazine.com

Music & Sound Retailer www.msretailer.com

Music Inc. www.musicinc.org

Music Trades www.musictrades.com

Note: There are dozens and dozens of magazines dealing with specific genres of music.

MUSIC EDUCATION

College Music Society (CMS) www.music.org

Music & Entertainment Industry Educators Association) (MEIEA) www.meiea.org

Music Educators National Conference (MENC) www.menc.org

Society of Audio Professionals (SPARS) www.spars.com

MUSIC PRINT PUBLISHERS

Alfred Music www.alfred.com

Mel Bay Publications www.melbay.com

Cherry Lane Music www.cherrylane.com

Carl Fischer Publishing www.carlfischer.com

International Music Publishing Co. www.bournemusic.com

Neil Kjos www.kjos.com

Hal Leonard Publishing Corp. www.halleonard.com

Music Sales Corp. www.musicsales.com

SONGWRITING AND PUBLISHING ORGANIZATIONS

ASCAP (American Society of Composers, Authors and Publishers) www.ascap.com

BMI (Broadcast Music, Inc.) www.bmi.com

Harry Fox Office www.harryfox.com/

SESAC, Inc. (Society of European Stage Authors and Composers) www.sesac.com

SGA (Songwriters Guild of America) www.songwritersguild.com

SOCAN (Society of Composers, Authors & Music Publishers of Canada) www.socan.ca

Note: There are many songwriters' organizations in different American states and in Canada. Further information can be found in the annual Songwriter's Market. The most influential of these groups, which has satellite organizations in various cities, is NSAI (the Nashville Songwriters Association International www.nashvillesongwriters.com

UNIONS

AFM (American Federation of Musicians) www.afm.org

Note: There are also over two hundred locals of the AFM in many cities in the United States and Canada.

AFTRA (American Federation of Radio and Television Artists) www.aftra.org
SAG (Screen Actors Guild) www.sag.org

WEB SITES TO SUBMIT MATERIAL TO MUSIC SUPERVISORS, ADVERTISERS, RECORD COMPANIES, OR DIGITAL SALES SITES

Audio Sparx www.audiosparx.com
CD Baby www.cdbaby.com
Evolution Music Partners www.evolutionmusicpartners.com
Feature Sounds www.featuresounds.com
Indie911 www.indie911.com
Latin Music Artists www.latinmusicartists.com
Pump Audio www.pumpaudio.com
Shelly Bay Music www.shellybay.com
Song Catalog www.songcatalog.com
Song U. www.songu.com
The Orchard www.theorchard.com

MUSIC LIBRARIES

Archive of Contemporary Music www.arcmusic.org
Associated Production Music www.apmmusic.com
De Wolfe/Corelli/Jacobs Music Library www.dewolfemusic.com
Extreme Music www.extrememusic.com
Fresh Music www.freshmusic.com
Killer Tracks www.killertrack.com
Metro Music Productions www.metromusic.com
Music Bakery www.musicbakery.com
Opus1 Music Library www.opus1musiclibrary.com
Rip Tide Music www.riptidemusic.com
Studio Cutz www.studiocutz.com

OTHER INDUSTRY ORGANIZATIONS

Canadian Academy of Recording Arts & Sciences (CARAS) www.carasonline.ca
Country Music Association (CMA) www.cmaworld.com
Gospel Music Association www.gospelmusic.org
National Academy of Recording Arts & Sciences (NARAS) www.grammy.com

Note: NARAS also has local/regional chapters in Atlanta, Austin, Chicago, Los Angeles, Memphis, Miami, Nashville, New York, Philadelphia, San Francisco, Seattle, and Washington, DC.

National Association of Campus Activities (NACA) www.naca.com
National Association of Music Industry Professionals (NARIP) www.narip.org
National Association of Music Merchants (NAMM) www.namm.org
National Association of Record Merchandisers (NARM) www.narm.org

National Music Publishers Association www.nmpa.org
Recording Industry Association of America (RIAA) www.riaa.com
Women in Music National Network www.womeninmusic.com

BOOKS

Many of these books overlap into multiple aspects of the music industry, but I have listed books under the categories that seem most applicable.

GENERAL GUIDES OR TEXTBOOKS ABOUT THE MUSIC INDUSTRY

Baskerville, David. *The Music Business Handbook and Career Guide: eighth edition*. Thousand Oaks, CA: Sage Publications, 2006.

Borg, Bobby. *The Musician's Handbook: A Practical Guide to Understanding the Music Business, revised edition*. New York: Billboard Books, 2008.

Brabec, Jeffrey, and Todd Brabec. *The Insider's Guide to Making Money in the Music Business, sixth edition*, New York: Schirmer Trade Books, 2008.

Dean, Michael W. *The $30 Music School*. Boston: Muska & Lipman, 2004.

Goldberg, Justin. *The Ultimate Survival Guide to the New Music Industry: Handbook for Hell*. Hollywood: Lone Eagle, 2004.

Halloran, Mark, Esq, Editor and Compiler. *The Musician's Business and Legal Guide, fourth edition*. Upper Saddle River, NJ: Pearson, 2008.

Krasilovsky, M. William and Sydney Shemel, with contributions by John M. Gross and Jonathan Feinstein. *This Business of Music, tenth edition*. New York: Billboard Books, 2007.

Krasilovsky, M. William and Sydney Shemel. *More about This Business of Music, fifth edition*. New York: Billboard Books, 1994.

Moore, Steve. *The Truth about the Music Business: A Grassroots Business & Legal Guide*. Boston: Thomson Course Technology, 2005.

Nagger, David and Jeffrey D. Brandstetter. *The Music Business Explained in Plain English, revised edition*. San Francisco: Daje Publishing, 2003.

Passman, Donald. *All You Need To Know about the Music Business, sixth edition*. New York: Free Press, 2006.

Note: The three books listed here are a unique history of the American music industry from its very inception. They constitute an invaluable resource, although they are long out of print. The late Russell Sanjek was a long-term executive at BMI.

Sanjek, Russell. *American Popular Music and its Business: the First Four Hundred Years. Volume I, The Beginning to 1790, Volume II, From 1790 to 1909*. New York: Oxford University Press, 1988.

Sanjek, Russell and David Sanjek. *American Popular Music in the 20th Century*. New York: Oxford University Press, 1991.

Thall, Peter M. *What They'll Never Tell You About The Music Business: The Myths, the Secrets, the Lies (& a Few Truths.)* New York: Watson-Guptill Publications, 2002.

Weissman, Dick and Frank Jermance, Editors. *Navigating the Music Industry: Current Issues and Business Models*. Milwaukee: Hal Leonard Books, 2003.

Weissman, Dick. *The Music Business: Career Opportunities & Self Defense, third revised edition*. New York: Three Rivers Press, 2003.

Wilofsky Gruen Associates. *Global Entertainment and Media Outlook, 2005–2009*. New York: PriceWaterhouseCoopers, Sixth Annual Edition, 2005.

AGENTS AND MANAGERS

Davison, Marc. *All Area Access: Personal Management for Unsigned Musicians*. Milwaukee: Hal Leonard, 1997.

Eliot, Marc. *Down Thunder Road: the Making of Bruce Springsteen*. New York: Simon & Schuster, 1992.

Frascogna, Xavier M. Jur. And H. Lee Hetherington. *Successful Artist Management, fourth revised edition*. New York: Billboard Publications, 2004.

Goldstein, Jeri. *How to Be Your Own Booking Agent: The Musician's and Performing Artist's Guide to Successful Touring, revised second edition*. Charlottesville, VA: The New Music Times Inc., 2004.

The IMF Handbook 2000 (no author listed). *A Guide to Professional Band Management*. London: Sanctuary Publishing, 2000.

Kragen, Ken with Graham Jefferson. *Life Is a Contact Sport: Ten Great Career Strategies That Work.* New York: William Morrow & Co., 1994.

Marcone, Dr. Stephen. *Managing Your Band: Artist Management: The Ultimate Responsibility, fourth edition.* New York: High Marks Publishing, 2007.

Weiss, Mitch and Perri Gaffney. *Managing Artists In Pop Music: What Every Artist and Manager Must Know to Succeed.* New York: Allworth Press, 2003.

ARTS ADMINISTRATION AND GRANTS

Note: Also see resources section.

Frohnmeyer, John. *Leaving Town Alive: Confessions of an Arts Warrior.* Boston: Houghton Mifflin, 1993.

Hall, Mary and Susan Howlett. *Getting Funded: The Complete Guide to writing Grant Proposals, fourth edition.* Portland, ME: Portland State University, 2003.

Wolf, Michael. *The Entertainment Economy: How Mega-Media Forces Are Transforming Our Lives.* New York: Times Books, 1999.

AUDIO ENGINEERING

Note: There are numerous textbooks and histories of audio. This list includes books about the business of audio.

Baine, Celeste. *The Musical Engineer: A Music Enthusiast's Guide to Careers in Engineering and Technology.* Springfield, OR: Engineering Education Service Center, 2007.

Fisher, Jeffrey. *Profiting from Your Music and Sound Project Studio.* New York: Allworth Press, 2001.

Stone, Chris. *Audio Recording For Profit: The Sound of Money.* Boston: Focal Press, 2000.

CENSORSHIP OF MUSIC

Korpe, Marie, Editor. *Shoot the Singer! Music Censorship Today.* London: Zed Books, 2004.

Negativland. *Fair Use: The Story of the letter U and the Numeral 2.* Concord, CA: Sealand, 1995.

Nuzum, Eric. *Parental Advisory! Musical Censorship in America.* New York: Harper Collins, 2001.

DIRECTORIES

Billboard, Musical America, and Pollstar all publish annual guides that variously list agents, managers, venues, and all kinds of information about a variety of music industry matters. The Musical America directory is the essential tool for classical musicians and vocalists. The Musician's Atlas is an annual guide that lists booking agents, clubs, managers, entertainment lawyers, and so on. The Music Business registry, www.musicregistry.com, publishes an annual guide to film and television music, an A&R guide that is updated every eight weeks, a directory of music publishers, and other publications that deal with everything from music supervision to starting an independent record label. The publications can be ordered as books, or delivered online.

INTERNATIONAL MUSIC BUSINESS

Barfe, Louis. *Where Have All The Good Times Gone? The Rise and Fall of the Record Industry.* London: Atlantic Books, 2004.

Bernstein, Arthur, Naoki Sekine, and Dick Weissman. *The Global Music Industry: Three Perspectives.* New York: Routledge, 2007.

Burnett, Robert. *The Global Jukebox: the International Music Industry.* London: Routledge, 1996.

Davis, Sarah and Dave Laing. *Guerrilla Guide to the Music Business, second edition.* New York: Continuum Press, 2006.

Condry, Ian. *Hip-Hop Japan: Rap and the Paths of Cultural Globalization.* Durham, NC: Duke University Press, 2006.

Ewbank, Allison J. and Fouli T. Papageorgieu. *Whose Master's Voice? The Development of Popular Music in Thirteen Cultures.* Westport, CT: Greenwood Press, 1997.

Lathrop, Tad. *This Business of Global Music Marketing.* New York: Billboard Books, 2007.

Little, Jonathan and Katie Chatburn, Editors. *Musicians' & Songwriters' Yearbook, 2008.* London: A&C Black, 2008.

Makoway, Mark. *The Indie Band Bible: The Ultimate Guide To Breaking A Band, second printing, Canadian edition.* Vancouver: Madrigal Press, 2001.

Mitchell, Tony, Ed. *Global Noise: Rap and Hip-Hop Music Outside the U.S.A.* Middletown, CT: Wesleyan University Press, 2001.

No author listed. *Music in Europe; Sound or Silence?* Utrecht: Buma-Stemra, 2004.

Norris-Whitney Communications. *Music Canada, ninth edition.* Toronto. Ontario: Norris-Whitney Communications, 2007.

Neate, Patrick. *Where You're At: Notes From The Frontlines Of A Hip-Hop Planet.* New York: Riverhead Books, 2004.

Selwood, Clive. *All the Moves (and None of the Noks): Secrets of the Record Business.* London: Peter Owen, 2003.

Simpson, Shane. *Music Business: A Musician's Guide to the Australian Music Industry.* London: Omnibus Press, 2002.

Stim, Richard. *Getting Permission: How to License & Clear Copyrighted Materials Online & Off, third edition.* Berkeley: Nolo Press, 2007.

Taylor, Timothy D. *Global Pop: World Music World Markets.* New York: Routledge, 1997.

Wallis, Roger and Krister, Malm. *Big Sounds from Small Peoples: The Music Industry in the Third World.* New York: Pendragon Press, 1984.

LEGAL ISSUES

Note: The Brabec brothers' book, the books by Halloran, Krasilovsky and Shemel and Passman book, all of which are referenced earlier, also discuss many contractual matters.

Moore, Steve. *The Truth about The Music Business: A Grassroots Business and Legal Guide.* Boston: Thomson Course Technology, 2005.

Schulenberg, Richard. *Legal Aspects of the Music Industry: An Insider's View.* New York: Billboard Books, 2005.

MUSICAL CAREERS, AND JOBS IN THE MUSIC INDUSTRY

Atkins, Martin. *Tour: Smart And Break the Band.* Chicago: Smart Books, 2007.

Belleville, Nyree. *The Complete Guide to House Concerts and Other Satisfying Alternative Venues.* Vallejo, CA: Pro Music Press, 2003.

Bunt, Ruth. *Music Therapy: An Art beyond Words.* London: Routledge, 1994.

Cann, Simon. *Building A Successful 21st Century Music Career.* Boston: Thomson Course Technology, 2007.

Chertow, Randy and Jason Feehan. *The Indie Band Survival Guide: The Complete Manual For the Do-It–Yourself Musician.* New York: St Martin's Griffin, 2008.

Davis, Rick. *Get Media Airplay: A Guide to Getting Song Exposure, Music/Product Tie-Ins, Brand Integration Discoveries and Radio-Play Spins.* Milwaukee: Hal Leonard, 2006.

Field, Shelly. *Career Opportunities in the Music Industry, fifth Edition.* New York: Facts On File Publications, 2004.

Grierson, Don and Dan Kimpel. *It All Begins with the Music.* Boston: Thomson Course Technology, 2009.

Hanser, Susanne B. *The New Music Therapist's Handbook, second edition.* Boston: Berklee Press, 1999.

Haring, Bruce. *How Not To Destroy Your Career in Music: Avoiding the Common Mistakes Most Musicians Make.* Los Angeles; Lone Eagle Publishing Co., 2005.

Hatschek, Keith, *How To Get a Job in the Music Industry, second edition.* Boston: Berklee Press, 2007.

Heflick, David. *Make Money Performing In Schools: Definitive Guide to Developing, Marketing & Presenting School Assembly Programs.* Orient, WA: Silcox Productions, 1996.

King, Sahpreem A. *Gotta Get Signed: How To Become A Hip-Hop Producer.* New York: Schirmer Trade Group, 2004.

Kirkpatrick, Carol. *Aria Ready: The Business of Singing.* New York: Leyerle Publications, 2003.

Makoway, Mark. *The Indie Band Bible: The Ultimate Guide to Breaking A Band.* Vancouver: Madrigal Press, 2001.

May, Tom and Dick Weissman. *Promoting Your Music: The Loving of the Game.* New York: Routledge, 2007.

McLeod, Douglas and Kimberli Ranson. *House Concerts: A Guide for Musicians and Hosts.* Austin: Woodworks Publications, 1999.

Musician's Atlas, '08. (an annual publication.)

Pollock, Bruce. *Working Musicians: Defining Moments from the Road, the Studio and the Stage.* New York: Harper Entertainment, 2000.

Popyk, Bob. *The Business of Getting More Gigs as a Professional Musician*. Milwaukee: Hal Leonard, 2003.

Ridgway, Julian. *Bandalism: Do Not Destroy Your Group*. London: SAF Publishing, 2007.

Shih, Patricia. *Gigging: A Practical Guide for Musicians*. New York: Allworth Press, 2003.

Spellman, Peter. *The Self-Promoting Musician: Strategies for Independent Music Success*. Boston: Berklee Press, 2000.

Stiernberg, John. *Succeeding in Music: A Business Handbook for Performers, Songwriters, Agents, Managers & Promoters*. San Francisco: Backbeat Books, 2003.

Volez, Susan. *The Musician's Guide to The Road: A Survival Guide & All Access Pass to Touring*. New York: Billboard Books, 2007.

Weissman, Dick. *Making a Living in Your Local Music Market: Realizing Your Marketing Potential, third edition*. Milwaukee: Hal Leonard, 2007.

Wumble, David. *The Indie Bible: The All-In-One Resource for Recording Artists, sixth edition*. New York: Schirmer Trade Books, 2004.

MUSICAL GENRES (BUSINESS ASPECTS)

Christian Music

Alfonso, Barry. *The Billboard Guide to Contemporary Christian Music*. New York: Billboard Books, 2002.

Arrin, Reed, Editor *The Inside Track to Getting Started in Christian Music*. Eugene, OR: Harmony House Publishing, 2000.

Beaujon, Andrew. *Body Piercing Saved My Life: Inside the Phenomenon of Christian Rock*. Cambridge, MA: Perseus Press, 2006.

Howard, Jay R. and John M. Strock. *Apostles of Rock: The Splintered Worlds of Contemporary Christian Music*. Lexington: University Press of Kentucky, 1999.

Peacock, Charlie. *At The Crossroads: An Insider's Look at the Past, Present and Future of Contemporary Christian Music*. Nashville: Broadman and Holman Publishers, 1996.

Classical Music

Beeching, Angel Myles. *Beyond Talent: Creating a Successful Career in Music*. New York: Oxford University Press, 2005.

Badal, James. *Recording the Classics; Maestros, Music & Technology*. Kent, OH: Kent State University Press, 1996.

Highstein, Ellen. *Making Music in Local Glass Land: A Guide to Survival and Business Skills for the Classical Musician, Expanded & updated fourth edition*. New York: Concert Artists Guild, 2003.

Kirkpatrick, Carol. *"Aria Ready": The Business of Singing*. New York: Leyerle Publications, 2003.

Tindall, Blair. *Mozart in the Jungle: Sex, Drugs and Classical Music*. New York: Atlantic Monthly Press, 2005.

Country Music

There are dozens of books about country music, but these books provide a good foundation for understanding the country music business.

Bond, Sherry. *The Songwriter's and Musician's Guide to Nashville*. New York: Allworth Press, 2000.

Foehr, Stephen. *Waking Up In Nashville: Music and Voices from the Capital of Country*. London: Sanctuary, 2002.

Kosser, Michael. *How Nashville became Music City: 50 years of Music Row*. Milwaukee: Hal Leonard, 2006.

Folk Music

Darling, Erik. *"I'd Give my Life!" From Washington Square to Carnegie Hall: A Journey by Folk Music*. Palo Alto, CA: Science and Behavior Books, Inc., 2006.

Scully, Michael F. *The Never-Ending Revival: Rounder Records and the Folk Alliance*. Champaign: University of Illinois Press, 2008.

Weissman, Dick. *Which Side Are You On? An Inside History of the Folk Music Revival in America*. New York; Continuum Press, 2006.

Hip-Hop

Dupri, Jermaine, with Samantha Marshall. *Young, Rich and Dangerous: The Making of a Music Mogul*. New York: Atria Books, 2007.

Liles, Kevin. *From Intern to President: Make It Happen, the Hip-Hop Generation Guide to Success*. New York: Atria Books, 2005.

Walker, James l. Jr., Esq. *This Business of Urban Music: A Practical Guide to Achieving Success in the Industry, from Gospel to Funk to R&B to Hip-Hop*. New York: Billboard Books, 2008.

Jazz

Note: Although hundreds of books have been written about jazz, very few discuss specific details about the business aspects of jazz. The Spellman book details the difficulties of experimental jazz musicians attempting to make a living.

Gray, Herman. *Producing Jazz; the Experience of an Independent Record Company*. Philadelphia: Temple University Press, 1988.

Kelley, Norman, Editor. *R&B Rhythm & Business*. New York: Akashic Books, 2002.

Kofsky, Frank. *Balck Music, White Business: Illuminating the Political Economy of Black Music*. New York; Akashic Books, 2002.

Spellman, A. B. *Black Music; Four Lives*. New York: Schoken Books, 1970.

MUSIC FOR FILM AND TELEVISION

Adams, Ramsey, David Hnatiuk, and David Weiss. *Music Supervision: The Complete Guide to Selecting Music for Movies, TV, Games and New Media*. New York: Schirmer Trade Books, 2005.

Blumenthal, Howard J. and Oliver R. Goodenough. *This Business of Television: The Standard Guide to the Television Industry, third edition*. New York: Billboard Books, 2006.

Davis, Rick. *Get Media Airplay: A Guide To Getting Song Exposure, Music/Product Tie-Ins, Brand Integration Discoveries, And Radio-Play Spins!* Milwaukee: Hal Leonard Corporation, 2006.

Faulkner, Edward. *Music On Demand: Composers and Careers in the Hollywood Film Industry*. New Brunswick, NJ: Transaction Books, 1983.

Jay, Richard. *How to Get Your Music in Film & TV*. New York: Schirmer Trade Books, 2005.

Wentz, Brooke. *Hey, That's My Music! Music Supervision, Licensing and Content Acquisition*. Milwaukee: Hal Leonard, 2007.

MUSIC PRODUCTS

Note: There are four monthly magazines that deal with music merchandising. Their contact information is referenced in the resources section of this Appendix.

MMR. *Directory of Musical Instrument Dealers, 2008*. Needham, MA: Musical Merchandise Review, 2007.

The Music Trades. *The Purchaser's Guide to the Music Industries: The Definitive Source For Music & Audio*. Englewood Cliffs, NJ: The Music Trades, 2007.

MUSIC PUBLISHING, SONGWRITING, AND COPYRIGHT

Note: There are dozens of books about songwriting, and this list includes only a few of the most important books on that subject.

Beall, Eric. *Making Music: Make Money: An Insider's Guide to Becoming Your Own Music Publisher*. Boston: Berklee Press, 2004.

Braheny, John. *The Craft and Business of Songwriting, third edition*. Cincinnati, Writer's Digest Books, 2007.

Blume, Jason. *This Business of Songwriting: A Practical Guide to Doing Business as a Songwriter*. New York: Billboard Books, 2006.

Citron, Stephen. *Songwriting: A Complete Guide to the Craft, revised and updated edition*. New York: Limelight Editions, 2008.

Emerson, Ken. *Always Magic In the Air: The Bomp and Brilliance of the Brill Building Era*. New York: Penguin Books, 2005.

Flanagan, Bill. *Written In My Soul: Conversations with Rock's Greatest Songwriters*. Chicago: Contemporary Books, 1987.

Frith, Simon and Lee Marshall, Editors. *Music and Copyright, second edition*. New York: Routledge, 2004.

Gillette, Steve. *Songwriting and the Creative Process: Suggestions and Starting Points for Songwriters*. Bethlehem, PA: Sing Out, 1995.

Hirschhorn, Joel. *The Complete Idiot's Guide to Songwriting, second edition*. New York: Alpha, 2006.

Kohn, Al and Bob John. *The Art of Music Licensing, second edition*. New York: Prentice Hall Law and Business, 1996.

Lydon, Michael. *Songwriting Success: How to Write Songs for Fun and (Maybe) Profit.* New York: Routledge, 2004.

Moser, David. *Music Copyright for the New Millennium.* Vallejo, CA: Pro Music Press, 2002.

Poe, Randy. *The New Songwriter's Guide to Music Publishing, third edition.* Cincinnati: Writer's Digest Books, 2005.

Samuels, Edward. *The Illustrated Story of Copyright.* New York: St. Martin's Press, 2001.

Songwriter's Market 2008 (This is an annual reference work, published by Writer's Digest Books, in Cincinnati, Ohio.)

Warner, Jay. *How to Have Your Hit Song Published, Revised and updated.* Milwaukee: Hal Leonard, 2006.

Webb, Jimmy. *Tunesmith: Inside the Art of Songwriting.* New York: Hyperion, 1998.

Weissman, Dick. *Songwriting: The Words, the Music & the Money, Revised.* Milwaukee: Hal Leonard, 2010.

Whitsett, Tim. *Music Publishing: The Real Road to Music Business Success, fifth edition.* Vallejo, CA: Mix Books, 2000.

Wixen, Randall. D. *The Plain and Simple Guide to Music Publishing.* Milwaukee: Hal Leonard, 2005.

Zollo, Paul, editor. *Songwriters on Songwriting: Expanded fourth edition.* Cambridge, MA: Da Capo Press, 2003.

NEW MEDIA AND THE FUTURE OF THE MUSIC BUSINESS

Alderman, John. *Sonic Boom: Napster, MP3, and the New Pioneers of Music.* Cambridge, MA: Perseus Publishing, 2001.

Demers, Joanna. *Steal This Music: How Intellectual Property Law Affects Musical Creativity.* Athens: University of Georgia Press, 2006.

Gordon, Steve. *The Future of the Music Business: How to Succeed with the New Digital Technologies, A Guide for Artists and Entrepreneurs.* San Francisco: Backbeat Books, 2005.

Hoffert, Paul. *Music for New Media; Composing for Videogames, Web Sites, Presentations and other Interactive Media.* Edited by Jonathan Feist. Boston: Berklee Press, 2007.

Jennings, David. *Nets, Blogs and Rock'n'Roll; How Digital Discovery Works and What It Means for Consumers, Creators and Culture.* London: Nicholas Brealey Publishing, 2007.

Knepper, Steve. *Appetite for Self-Destruction: The Spectacular Crash of the Record Industry in the Digital Age.* New York: Free Press, 2009.

Kot, Greg. Ripped. *How The Wired Generation Revolutionized Music.* New York: Scribner, 2009.

Kusik, Dave and Gerd Leonhard. *The Future of Music: Manifesto for the Digital Music Revolution.* Boston: Berklee Press, 2005.

Lessig, Lawrence. *Free Culture: The Nature and Future of Creativity.* New York: Penguin Books, 2004.

Spellman, Peter. *The Musician's Internet: Online Strategies for Success in the Music Industry.* Boston: Berklee Press, 2002.

Vincent, Francis. *MySpace for Musicians: The Comprehensive Guide to Marketing Your Music Online.* Boston: Thomson Course Technology, 2007.

RACE AND THE MUSIC BUSINESS

Abdul, Raoul. *Blacks in Classical Music.* New York: Dodd, Mead, 1977.

Cashmore, Ellis. *The Black Culture Industry.* New York: Routledge, 1997.

Mahon, Mauren. *Right to Rock; The Black Rock Coalition and the Cultural Politics Of Race.* Durham, NC: Duke University Press, 2004.

Souvignier, Todd and Gary Hustwit. *The Musician's Guide to the Internet, second edition.* Milwaukee: Hal Leonard, 2002.

RECORD LABELS AND THE RECORD BUSINESS

Avalon, Moses. *Million Dollar Mistakes: Steering Your Music Career Clear of Lies, Cons, Catastrophes and Landmines.* San Francisco: Backbeat Books, 2005.

Bordowitz, Hank. *Dirty Little Secrets of the Record Business: Why So Much Music you Hear Sucks.* Chicago: Chicago Review Press, 2007.

Bowman, Rob. *Soulsville U.S.A.: The Story of Stax Records.* New York: Schirmer, Books, 1997

Cook, Richard. *Blue Note Records: The Biography.* Boston: Justin, Charles and Co., 2003.

Cornyn, Stan and Paul Scanlan. *Exploding: The Highs, Hits, Hypes and Hustles of the Warner Music Group.* New York: Harper Collins, 2002.

Grunow, Peter and Ilpo, Saunio. *An International History of the Recording Industry.* Translated by Christopher Mosely. London: Cassell, 1999.

Hall, Charles and Frederick J. Taylor. *Marketing in the Music Industry, second edition.* New York: Simon & Schuster Custom Publishing, 1998.

Holzman, Jac and Gavan Daws. *Follow The Music: The Life and High Times of Elektra Records.* Newnan, GA: Jawbone Press, 2000.

Hutchison, Tom, Amy Macy, and Paul Allen. *Record Label Marketing.* Burlington, MA: Focal Press, 2006.

Kennedy, Dan. *Rock On: An Office Power Ballad.* Chapel Hill, NC: Algonquin Books, 2008.

Lathrop, Tad. *This Business of Music: Marketing & Promotion, revised and updated edition.* New York: Billboard Books, 2003.

Marmorstein, Guy. *The Label: The Story of Columbia Records.* New York: Thunder's Mouth Press, 2007.

Schwartz, Dayelle Deanna. *I Don't Need A Record Deal! Your Survival Guide for the Indie Music Revolution.* New York: Billboard Books, 2005.

Summers, Jodi. *Making and Marketing Music: The Musician's Guide to Financing, Distributing and Promoting Albums, second Edition.* New York: Allworth Press, 2004.

Wade, Dorothy and Justine Picardie. *Music Man: Ahmet Ertegun, Atlantic Records, and the Triumph of Rock 'n' Roll.* New York: W.W. Norton, 1990.

RECORD PRODUCTION

Note: There are also a number of books that cover the history of the recording process, the ones mentioned here are more recent works.

Avalon, Moses. *Confessions of a Record Producer: How to Survive the Scams and Shams of the Music Business.* San Francisco: Miller Freeman Books, 1998.

Coleman, Mark. *Playback: From the Victrola to MP3, 100 Years of Music, Machines and Money.* Cambridge, MA: Da Capo Press, 2005.

Burgess, Richard James. *The Art of Record Production.* London: Omnibus Press, 1997.

Cunningham, Mark. *Good Vibrations: A History of Record Production.* Surrey, UK: Sanctuary Publishing, 1996.

King, Sahpreem A. *Gotta Get Signed: How To Become A Hip-Hop Producer.* New York: Schirmer Trade Books, 2005.

Massey, Howard. *Behind the Glass: The Record Producers and How They Craft the Hits.* San Francisco: Miller Freeman Books, 2000.

Perry, Megan. *How to Be a Record Producer in the Digital Era.* New York: Billboard Books, 2008.

Ramone, Phil, with Charles L. Granata. *Making Records: The Scenes Behind the Music.* New York: Hyperion, 2007.

Rapaport, Diane Sward. *How to Make and Sell Your Own Recording, revised fifth edition.* Upper Saddle River, NJ: Prentice-Hall Inc., 1999.

Summers, Jodi. *Making and Marketing Music: The Musician's Guide to Financing, Distributing and Promoting Albums.* New York: Allworth Press, 2004.

Wexler, Jerry and David Ritz. *Rhythm and the Blues: A Life in American Music.* New York: Albert Knopf, 1993.

REGIONAL MUSIC

Azerad, Michael. *Screaming Life: A Chronicle of the Seattle Music Scene.* San Francisco: HarperCollins West, 1995.

Berry, Jason, Jonathan Foose, and Tad Jones. *Up from the Cradle of Jazz: New Orleans Music Since World War II.* Athens: University of Georgia Press, 1986.

Morrell, Brad. *Nirvana and the Sound of Seattle.* New York: Omnibus Press, 1996.

Reid, Jan. *The Improbable Rise of Redneck Rock, new edition.* Austin: University of Texas Press, 2004.

Weissman, Dick. *Making a Living in Your Local Music Market: Realizing Your Career Potential, revised thirty-fourth edition.* Milwaukee: Hal Leonard, 2010.

VARIOUS SUBJECTS, INCLUDING CONCERT PROMOTION, PUBLICITY, RADIO, AND SO ON.

Burlingame, Jon. *For The Record.* Hollywood: Recording Musicians Association, 1987.

Davis, Rick. *Get Media Airplay: A Guide to Getting Song Exposure, Music Product Tie-Ins, Brand Integration Discoveries And Radio Play Spins!* New York: Hal Leonard, 2006.

Farr, Joey. *Moguls and Madmen: The Pursuit of Power in Popular Music.* New York: Simon & Schuster, 1994.

Fisher, Marc. *Singing in the Air: Radio, Rock, and the Revolution That Shaped a Generation.* New York: Random House, 2007.

Faulkner, Edward. *Hollywood Studio Musicians.* Chicago: Aldine Atherton, 1971.

Heylin, Clinton. *Bootleg: The Secret History of the Other Recording Industry.* New York: St Martin's Griffin, 1997.

Hutchison, Tom, Amy Macy and Paul Allen. *Record Label Marketing.* Amsterdam: Elsevier, Focal Press, 2006.

Jackson, Randy. *"What's Up Dawg?" How to Become a Superstar in the Music Business.* New York: Hyperion, 2004.

Karmen, Steve. *Through the Jingle Jungle; the Art and Business of Making Music for Commercials.* New York: Billboard Books, 1989.

Kaylor, Mark. *Confessions of a Session Singer: Scandalous Secrets Of Success Behind The Mic.* New York: Backbeat Books, 2007.

Kimpel, Dan. *How They Made It: True Stories of How Music's Biggest Stars Went from Start to Stardom.* Milwaukee: Hal Leonard, 2006.

Ladd, Jim. *Radio Waves: Life and Revolution on the FM Dial.* New York: St. Martin's Press, 1991.

Leach, Joel. *A Concise Guide to Music Industry Terms.* Pacific, MO: Mel Bay Publications, 2005.

Levine, Michael. *Guerrilla P.R.: How You Can Wage An Effective Publicity Campaign Without Going Broke.* New York: Harper Business, 1993.

Little, Jonathan and Katie Charborn. *Musicians' Songwriters' Yearbook: 2008.* London: A&C Black, 2007. (Note: This is an annual guide.)

Negus, Keith. *Music Genres and Corporate Cultures.* New York: Routledge, 1999.

Oseary, Guy. *On The Record: Over 100 of the Most Talented People in Music Share the Secrets of Their Success.* New York: Penguin Books, 2004.

Park, David J. *Conglomerate Rock: The Music Industry's Quest to Divide Music and Conquer Wealth.* Lanham, MD: Rowan and Littlefield, 2007.

Pettigrew, Jim, Jr. *The Billboard Guide to Music Publicity, revised edition.* New York: Billboard Books, 1997.

Pinskey,Raleigh. *The Zen of Hype: An Insider's Guide to the Publicity Game.* New York: Carol Publishing, 1991.

Taylor, Livingston. *Stage Performance.* New York: Pocket Books, 2000.

Vogel, Harold L. *Entertainment Industry Economics: A Guide for Financial Analysis: Fourth Edition.* Cambridge: Cambridge University Press, 1998.

Waddell, Ray D., Rich Barnet, and Jake Berry. *This Business of Concert Promotion and Touring.* New York: Billboard Books, 2007.

WOMEN AND THE MUSIC INDUSTRY

Carson, Mina, Tisa Lewis, and Susan M. Shaw. *Girls Rock! Fifty Years of Women Making Music.* Lexington: University of Kentucky Press, 2004.

Dickerson, James. *Women on Top: The Quiet Revolution That's Rocking the American Music Industry.* New York: Billboard Books, 1998.

Marcic, Dorothy. *Respect: Women and Popular Music.* New York: Texere, 2002.

O'Brien, Karen. *Hymn to Her: Women Musicians Talk.* London: Virago Press, 1995.

Post, Laura. *Backstage Pass Interviews with Women in Music.* Norwich, VT: New Victoria Publishers, 1997.

GLOSSARY

A&R. See Artists & Repertoire (A&R)

A-DAT (digital audio tape). A form of digital recording that was introduced in the mid-1970s enabling home recorders to create 24-track *masters.*

Administrative Rights. The *music publisher* or publishers designated to have final approval to represent the author in all rights negotiations.

Advance. A sum of money paid up front to a creator for a song, record, or publication. This money is recouped from any *royalties* earned through sales of the item.

Affinity group. An affinity group consists of different musical performances that share certain qualities, such as theme, subject matter, instrumentation, and so on. Web services such as lastfm use affinity group models to suggest artists who you might enjoy hearing, based on those you have listened to in the past.

American Society of Composers, Artists and Performers (ASCAP). One of three American *performing rights organizations (PROs)* that control royalties for songwriters and music publishers on radio, television, and in live performances. ASCAP is the oldest of the three, founded in 1909, and traditionally represented composers of popular song and classical music.

Analog recording. A recording device that converts soundwaves into mechanical or electric patterns (such as the grooves on a record). On playback, the original sound is recreated. Analog recordings are continuous, as compared to *digital recordings* that convert sounds into individual numbers.

Anti-trust law. Legal rules that restrict mergers of companies either in the same business (and thus control too large a portion of the market) or across several parts of the same business (for example, a record company also owning management, music publishing, and related music businesses). Enforcement varies from country to country.

Artists & Repertoire (A&R). Record executives who scout for and sign talent.

Arts administration. The business side of running an arts organization.

Audit. An official accounting performed usually by a CPA to determine if a record company (or other business) has fairly paid what is owed to an artist.

Back end deal. A songwriter may agree to allow the use of his/her material in a successful TV show or other medium without any advance payment, because the show is so popular that royalties from its broadcast rights are certain to be high.

Benefit concert. A concert that is staged to benefit a particular charity or cause.

Block booking. The process of hiring talent for multiple events, often various colleges and arts centers, in order to obtain a lower fee per show and to ensure a certain amount of work for an act.

Booking agent. Agents who find jobs for musical artists with individual venues.

Bootleg. An illegally produced copy of a sound recording. *See also* Piracy

Broadcast Music, Inc. (BMI). A *performing rights organization (PRO)* founded by the radio industry in 1940 after ASCAP attempted to impose greater fees for radio play of its copyrighted material.

Bundle of rights. A group of rights held by a music publisher as specified by contract with the creator.

Business Manager. A business manager handles an artist's financial arrangements, including investments and taxes.

Canadian Content Laws (CANCON). Canadian law mandating that 35 percent of radio play must come from recordings that contain two of four Canadian components: artist, producer, and on the songwriting end, composer and lyricist. *See also* Foundation to Assist Canadian Artists on Record (FACTOR)

Catalog product. Older releases owned by the major labels that can be reissued with minimum expense. Also called *back catalog*

Censorship. Government or individual actions to restrict the recording or performance of certain songs that may be found to be offensive or in some way disturbing to authorities. The level of censorship varies from country to country.

Chat board. An Internet site where fans can discuss their favorite groups or songs.

Children's music. Music created specifically for young listeners but that will also appeal to their parents.

Clinic. A masterclass run by a professional musician, usually lasting a day, held at a school or music store. Clinics are often sponsored by musical instrument manufacturers as a means of promoting their product.

College Music Society (CMS). Organization of college music faculty. CMS holds an annual national conference, as well as regional meetings, and provides various support services to its members, including workshops, training, and job referral services.

Commission. A fee collected by a manager, agent, or other person working for an artist, usually drawn as a percentage of the amount received.

Community orchestra. An amateur orchestra formed by local musicians who enjoy playing classical music together.

Compact disc (CD). CDs were first introduced in the mid-1980s as a sonically better and less fragile way of storing music than the earlier *LP*. Music is stored in *digital* files on a CD, unlike the *analog* method used for LPs, which some feel gives better overall sound quality to the record.

Complimentary (comp) tickets. Free tickets given to critics, friends of the performers, or other insiders.

Composite vocal. A vocal *track* that is assembled from various different performances, either by one singer or a group of singers.

Compulsory license. A license required by copyright law; for example, after its first recording, any performer can record a song. The publisher or songwriter cannot block it.

Conflict of interest. A situation in which two parties have conflicting goals and financial interests or where a single individual represents two conflicting parts of a business arrangement. For example, a manager who also owns nightclubs would have a conflict of interest in representing artists, because he or she might not negotiate the best rates for performances at their clubs.

Conservatory. A specialized school for the training of classical musicians.

Controlled composition clause. A situation in which a record company limits songwriting and publishing royalties from the sales of recordings. Usually, they reduce the current fee by 75 percent; the current 9.1 cents fee per song is reduced therefore to 6.825 per song. The *music publisher* cannot be compelled to accept this rate, but on the other hand the record company can elect not to record songs unless the publisher agrees.

Co-publishing. Two or more entities that own a share of the publishing rights to a song or catalog of songs are said to be its co-publisher.

Copyright. Ownership of a song or recording, verified by filing with the Copyright Office at the Library of Congress in Washington, DC. The specific rights granted through copyright have changed over the years.

Copyright infringement. When a song is recorded by artist without compensating its creator, this is a case of copyright infringement. There are two types of infringement: accidental or intentional. Punishment is greater for the latter type, for obvious reasons.

Corporation. A corporation is a legal entity designed to shield individual investors from liability for its actions. Corporations usually have a board of directors who hire management to oversee their activities.

Cover record. A hit record for one artist that is copied (often in an identical arrangement) by another. This was particularly prevalent in the 1950s, when R&B singles were often copied by white pop artists, because the originals could not be played on popular radio.

Cross-collateralization. A contract that calls for any unearned royalty advances or other expenses incurred under earlier agreements to be recouped against the new project. Thus, if an artist owes the record company for unearned costs of his first album, these may be charged against any royalties due on his next one.

Crossover artist. An artist who has hits in one genre (such as country or R&B) who "crosses over" to success on the pop charts. Michael Jackson was considered a major crossover success when his Thriller album sold in the millions to the pop audience.

Cut-out. A recording cut out of the current catalog, usually discounted.

Cylinder. Early recording format before the existence of records.

Deal memo. A simple memo that sets forth the general terms of a contract that are later formalized in more detail

Demo. A demonstration recording of a song or album that is not considered to be a finished product.

Development deal. An agreement between a record company and an artist wherein the company offers financial support and works with the artist in the studio and on tour, reserving the right to make an actual record if and when the company feels the artist is ready.

Digital recording. A means of converting soundwaves into digital information (or numbers). *Compare to* analog recording

Digital rights management (DRM). Software designed to make it impossible for consumers to illegally copy music files.

Double contract. A double contract is a means for an agent to increase his/her income by representing both an artist and the club/venue who is booking the acts. For example, an agent might have a contract with a performer that specifies payment of $500 for a *gig*, and another contract that charges the buyer $1,000 (and thus pocket both a commission on the $500 and the difference between the fee promised the artist and the fee actually charged).

Double dipping. An agent who collects both a percentage of profits and a commission from an enterprise. For example, an agent might jointly own a band's publishing company, and thus collects 50 percent of its gross income On the other 50 percent (the songwriters' share), she then charges the band an additional commission for representing them.

Drop-in. A standard commercial that can be customized for local use; for example, the same backing track might be used for different purposes by individual retailers who could add their own product information.

Dynamic pricing. Selling tickets in advance of a concert to a specialized ticket broker who then marks them up above their face value. This technique is used by some acts to increase their take on concerts that are likely to sell out.

End caps. Retail display at the end of a bin of albums, offering visibility and access to the consumer.

Engineer. The person who oversees the recording equipment in a studio, setting up and operating it to obtain the best possible sound.

Ethnomusicology. The study of musics of other cultures. *See also* World Music

Federal Communications Commission (FCC). Federal commission that regulates radio and television.

File sharing. The illegal sharing of digital music files.

Flat-fee deal. The performer is paid a fixed amount, no matter what is collected in ticket sales or other revenues for an event.

Folio. A group of individual songs published together as a collection of songs. Often, the songs on a single album will be included in a related folio for those who want to learn to perform them on their own.

Folk music. Music "of the people," although more generally an acoustic form of music, usually performed on guitars or banjos, expressing social issues.

For-hire agreement. *See* Work-for-hire agreement

Foundation To assist Canadian Artists on Record (FACTOR) A Canadian government grant program to assist in the costs of making recordings. *See also* Canadian Content Laws (CANCON)

Free goods. Record company giveaways to music critics or radio stations given for promotional purposes.

General partnership. A business arrangement in which the partners share costs and profits, and also any liability for the actions of the firm. *Compare* Limited partnership

Gig. A common term used for a job played by a musical act.

Grand rights. Rights that govern performances in theatrical productions.

Hold. An informal arrangement in which an artist puts a "hold" on a new song that he or she is considering recording so that it cannot be offered to another performer.

Hook. A catchy, short melodic phrase that grabs the listener's attention.

House concert. A concert put on by individuals in their own homes. House concerts are common for folk musicians and singer-songwriters.

Import tax. A tax levied by some countries on any imported merchandise. Import taxes are designed to protect and encourage local businesses.

Independent record label. Smaller record label not affiliated with the four trans-national record labels. *See also* Major label

Individually and severally. Legal term indicating that members of a group may be liable both as individuals and as a group to perform terms of a contract.

Industrial film. A commercial film, such as a film used for training workers or to promote a company's mission.

Industry showcase. A showcase designed to expose artists to music industry decision-makers, prominent reviewers, radio DJs, and other influential insiders.

Internship. An introductory position at a company, often given to college students. Usually this position is unpaid.

iPod. A popular portable device introduced by Apple for the playback of digital music files, which may be purchased at the company's *iTunes* store.

iTunes. Apple's online store for selling downloads of songs for its *iPod* player.

Jingles. Short, catchy melodies written to promote a commercial product.

Key man clause. A contractual clause that stipulates if a "key" person leaves the record company, the artist may be free to follow him or her, or the contract may be terminated.

Kill fee. A fee paid if a contract is terminated by a company before the artist has a chance to complete the work.

Latin Academy of Recording Arts & Sciences (LARAS). *See* National Academy of Recording Arts & Sciences (NARAS)

Library music. Music organized as a library of tunes and sold for multiple use in television, radio, movies or audio-video presentations.

Limited Liability Corporation (LLC). A simple corporate organization that limits the liability of its individual owners, while not requiring the extensive paperwork of a corporation

Limited partnership. A business arrangement in which the partners share the cost of establishing the company, but do not manage it. Their liability is limited to the amount they invest. *Compare* General partnership

Listening station. A place where CDs can be previewed in a record store.

Lock-out. A situation in which the recording studio is available on a twenty-four-hour basis only to the act that rents the studio. Others are literally "locked out."

Long-tail theory. Developed by Chris Anderson, the long-tail theory says that the spread of new media outlets opens up opportunities for artists or businesses to promote their wares in new ways at minimal expense and therefore to find a marketing niche for their work.

LP (long playing record). Developed in 1948, the LP was a twelve-inch record that was played back at 33 1/3 *rpm*, allowing about twenty to twenty-five minutes of music to be held on each side of the record. This was a considerable improvement over the earlier *78s*, which had a maximum playing time of three (10-inch) or five (12-inch) minutes per side.

Major label. One of the four transnational record labels: Sony (Columbia/BMG), Universal, Warner, and EMI.

Master. Originally, the metal stamping part used to create disc records. Now used to describe the original or source material (tape, digital files, etc.) used to reproduce CDs or other sound media.

Matching funds. Nonprofit organizations that receive grants from foundations or the government are often required to produce matching funds in order to qualify for the grant. For example, if the government gives a group $5,000, the group has to match that $5,000 by either raising that amount privately or in salaries or by other means.

Mechanicals royalties. Royalties paid to songwriters and publishers from sales of recordings.

Middle of the road (MOR). Conventional, easy to listen to popular music.

Mix. The final assembly of a *master* recording, adjusting all component *tracks* in a way to create the best overall sound for a performance.

Most favored nations clause. A contractual clause that specifies that no one will receive a higher advance or royalty rate than any other in a collection or compilation featuring copyrights owned by several different parties.

MP3. A file format that is commonly used for music files. These files are compressed in order to take up less space on a computer hard drive and to be easier to send over the Web.

Music arranger. Orchestrates music for various instruments.

Music camps. Specialized camps, usually held in the summer, to train promising young musicians.

Music Educators National Conference (MENC). An organization representing music teachers, from elementary to college level. MENC hosts an annual convention, publishes a magazine, and lobbies for music as a key part of educational curricula.

Music Performance Fund (MPF). A fund deriving from record sales that funds live music performances.

Music print publishers. Lease print rights from a music publisher.

Music publisher. Owner of copyrights in individual songs.

Music supervisor. Supervises music for film or television shows.

MySpace. A social network Web site that has developed a large following among fans of contemporary music. A separate MySpaceMusic site has been established, where bands and individuals post information, songs, and other materials for their fans.

Napster. A website that enabled individual listeners to share music files with each other. Napster was most popular in the mid- to late 1990s, until the music industry was able to effectively shut it down. A revival of Napster now serves as a "legitimate" music downloading site.

National Academy of Recording Arts & Sciences (NARAS). Music trade organization that is in charge of the annual Grammy show. NARAS also sponsors several educational initiatives and provides support for the recording industry. In the 1990s, NARAS established LARAS (Latin Academy of Recording Arts & Sciences) to promote Latin music.

Niche market. Specialized market, for example, bluegrass music

Oklahoma (poor man's) copyright. A method of copyrighting a song in which the author sends a registered copy of the work to him/herself, in the belief this will establish copyright. However, this method is not recognized by U.S. courts as a legitimate registration.

One sheet. A single page promotional piece issued by a publisher or record company to promote a song, album, or performer.

One stop. A record distributor that carries recordings from all record labels and sells to independent record stores.

Open mike. Usually held at a club, open mike events allow individuals to sign up to perform a song or two without auditioning first. It is a good way for unknown performers to possibly win over an audience, and to land a paying *gig* at the club.

Option. A provision in a contract that allows a record or publishing company to renew an agreement. Many of these contracts have three to five options. The options are not mutual but are held only by the company.

Overdubbing. Literally, the dubbing of one sound on top of another on a recording. In current usage, the "overdubbing" actually occurs on separate tracks of a tape.

Pay to play. An arrangement by which a performer actually pays to buy tickets from a venue in order to perform there. They then resell the tickets to their fans. Only if the act covers the cost of the tickets will they break even. This is a common custom in New York and Los Angeles, and has spread to other cities as well.

Payola. Illegal payments made to radio people in order to obtain airplay for a recording. The famous "payola scandal" of the late 1950s brought down the career of DJ Alan Freed, one of the first great promoters of rock 'n' roll.

Performance rights. Performance rights give radio and television stations, as well as live venues the right to play music. *ASCAP, BMI,* and

SESAC administer these rights and pay royalties to songwriters and music publishers.

Performing rights organizations (PROs). Organizations that deal with performing rights. *See also* ASCAP, BMI, and SESAC

Personal manager. A personal manager is an overall career guide for an artist, dealing with all facets of the artist's career.

Phonograph. The name generally given to machines originally developed in the late nineteenth century that played back sound recordings, whether they were cylinders or *discs*.

Piracy. Illegal copying of copyright works. *See also* bootleg

Playlists. A list of favorite songs maintained by an individual listener, either on iTunes or another Web-based service. Sharing playlists is one way that fans have of letting others know about their favorite songs.

Power of attorney. Powers granted (usually on a limited basis) to one party to act on the behalf of another; specifically, a personal or business manager may have power of attorney to sign contracts for an artist.

Pre-sales. A pre-sale occurs when a ticket broker reserves a certain number of tickets for an event for members of fan clubs or holders of particular credit cards.

Producer. Broadly speaking, the person who oversees a recording session, working with the artist, accompanying musicians, arrangers, and recording *engineers* to produce the final product.

Promotion and distribution deal (P&D). A record deal where a major label takes a percentage of the income of an independent label in return for manufacturing, promoting, and distributing ts recorded product.

Public domain. A work that has fallen out of copyright that may be freely performed without compensating its creator.

Rack jobber. Rack jobbers distribute recorded product to chain stores.

Record distributors. Distributors place albums in record stores.

Recording Industry Association of America (RIAA). Record company trade organization. The RIAA has been particularly active in prosecuting cases of illegal *file sharing*, as well as lobbying government in areas of interest to the *major labels*.

Recoupment. If an *advance* is paid on a contract, the amount is recouped against the *royalties* owed.

Re-play. When an act plays a repeat job at the same venue.

Reserves. Royalties held back by a record company in case some of the records shipped are returned by distributors or stores

Residuals. Repayments for commercials recorded under union contracts. Residuals are received by both singers and musicians. Also, special payments for union members based on the number of sessions that they've played on and the total number of recordings sold.

Retail. The price charged to the consumer. *See also* Wholesale

Reversion clause. This clause stipulates that if a publisher does not obtain a recording of a song within a specified time, the publishing rights to the song revert back to the songwriter.

Rider. A provision in a contract that contains additional requirements for the agreement, For example, a well-known rock band might require M&Ms in all their dressing rooms at every concert.

Right to work state. A state where workers cannot be required to join a union.

Ringback. A brief melody heard that identifies a cellphone caller to the person he/she is phoning. When Caller A phones Caller B, B hears A's ringback.

Ringtone. A brief melody that indicates to you that someone is calling you on your cellphone.

Rome Convention. Seventy-eight countries are signatory to this agreement, which stipulates that performers as well as songwriters should receive income from performing rights. The United States has not signed this agreement, because it does not recognize performing rights for artists.

Royalty escalation clause. An increase in royalties paid after a certain quantity of records are sold.

Royalty. A fixed amount—usually a percentage of retail or wholesale price—paid to the creator for every record (or piece of sheet music, or other publication) sold.

RPM (revolutions per minute). The measurement for the speed at which a *turntable* rotates. LPs rotated at 33 1/3 rpm, while singles were known as "45s" because they spun at 45 rpm.

S corporation. A special form of *corporation* that divides all costs and earnings among its shareholders, who are taxed as individuals on any profits.

Sales tax. A tax levied on the price of goods when they are purchased by local, state, or federal governments.

Session musician. A musician who makes a living by playing on recording sessions.

Seventy-eights (78s). The format for disc recordings from the early 1900s through 1948, 78 records rotated at 78 rpm, and could hold three minutes of music per side (on the standard 10-inch record). The format was replaced by the *LP (long playing)* record.

Signing bonus. An additional amount paid to an artist to sign a contract with a record company or music publisher as an incentive.

Singer-songwriter. A performer who writes her or his own material.

Single. After World War II, recordings issued on 45 rpm discs were given this name because each side featured a single song. Compare with *LPs*

Society of European Stage Authors & Composers (SESAC). The smallest of the *performing rights organizations.*

Sole proprietorship. A business owned and operated by an individual, who assumes all liability for it.

Song shark. Unscrupulous music publishers who solicit writers and charge them to promote their songs, with the promise that they can make them hits.

Songpluggers. Independent promoters who solicit recordings of songs for a percentage of the song's earnings.

SoundScan. By using bar codes, SoundScan tabulates the sales of albums. SoundScan's information is based on a select group of retailers (mostly the major chains), so its numbers do not reflect the entire sales of any given recording.

Special Payments Fund. A bonus fund for musicians based on the number of union recording sessions they perform on and the total number of records sold on which union members perform.

Street team A promotional team paid by a record company to put up flyers and distribute recorded product to create "grassroots" buzz for a new act.

Sub-publisher. A foreign publisher who is licensed to handle a U.S. publisher's copyright in its market.

Suggested retail list price (SRLP). The *retail* price that a record company or music publisher recommends for each item. Individual stores are free, however, to charge what they want.

Sunset agreement. The negotiation that occurs between an artist and a manager when a management contract comes to an end and is not renewed by the artist. This may or may not be part of the management agreement.

SXSW (South by Southwest). A major annual festival held in Austin, Texas, which since the mid-1990s has become one means for new bands to gain the attention of critics and record companies.

Synchronization rights. The rights to synchronize music with a film or video. Commonly referred to as *synch rights.*

Tablature. A system of writing music for guitar (or other instruments) without using standard music notation.

Tenure. Job security for teachers in the public school system or in colleges. Tenure gives teachers seniority, and makes it very difficult to fire them.

Thanatology. Music for people in a hospice situation who are near death.

Three-sixty (360) deal. A deal in which a record company has the rights to a piece of an artist's income from all revenue streams, including recording, song publishing, touring, merchandise, and so on.

Ticket broker. An organization that specializes in selling concert tickets, such as LiveNation.

Tip sheet. A newsletter-like publication for publishers and songwriters, with information about artists or producers looking for songs.

Tour support. Money given by record company to aid an act in touring. The money is an *advance* against *royalties*

Track. In recordings, an individual track represents one distinct stream of information. For example, modern recording equipment may have 64, 128, or more individual tracks, each able to hold specific information, that is then mixed to create a final product. Track is also the term used to describe an individual song on an LP or CD record.

Turntable. The flat, rotating plate on a *phonograph* onto which the *78*, 45, or *LP* disc is placed. DJs continue to use turntables at discos and clubs to play recordings, and hip hop performers use them to create accompaniments for rappers.

Turntable hit. A song that gets excellent radio airplay but fares poorly in retail sales.

Union. An organization formed to protect workers rights in negotiations with business owners and management. Unions have been formed to represent workers in various industries. Individual unions have further united to form larger groups (such as the American Federation of Labor [AFL]) to represent larger issues concerning all workers.

Upstream record deal. An arrangement whereby a *major* record label distributes product from an *independent label*, with an option to place the artist on the major label if the recording is a commercial success.

Value-added tax (VAT). Tax on the "value" added to a product during the process of its manufacture, distribution, and ultimate sale. For example, plastic is transformed into a disc to make a CD; music is then encoded on the CD; the CD is packaged; it is distributed to stores; and eventually sold to a consumer. At each stage, VAT is charged. In Europe, virtually all consumer goods have a VAT.

Videogame. An interactive game originally played in arcades but not commonly played online or through using specialized gaming systems, such as Ninetendo's Wii.

Viral marketing. Spreading the word about a new band or song through an online medium such as Facebook or MySpace, as one individual passes information to another.

Water mark. A digital marking identifying product used to help prevent illegal copying.

Wholesale. The price charged for an item to a dealer or distributor, as opposed to *retail* (the price charged to individual purchasers).

Work dues. A fee charged by the union to its membership, based on a percentage of the union minimum wage that is required for a performance.

Work-for-hire agreement. An employment agreement that attempts to eliminate or limit royalties, by defining them as part of the agreement between the employer and the composer. In a work-for-hire agreement, all rights remain with the buyer (the company contracting the work).

World music. Music that comes from or uses music from other cultures

INDEX